D0408192

In Defense of Faith

In Defense of Faith

The Judeo-Christian Idea and the Stuggle for Humanity

David Brog

ENCOUNTER BOOKS
NEW YORK · LONDON

Copyright © 2010 by David Brog

All rights reserved. No part of this publication may be reproduced,
stored in a retrieval system, or transmitted, in any form or by
any means, electronic, mechanical, photocopying, recording,
or otherwise, without the prior written permission of
Encounter Books, 900 Broadway, Suite 601,
New York, New York, 10003.

First American edition published in 2010 by Encounter Books,
an activity of Encounter for Culture and Education, Inc.,
a nonprofit, tax exempt corporation.
Encounter Books website address: www.encounterbooks.com

Manufactured in the United States and printed on
acid-free paper. The paper used in this publication meets
the minimum requirements of ANSI/NISO Z39.48 1992
(R 1997) (Permanence of Paper).

FIRST AMERICAN EDITION

LIBRARY OF CONGRESS CATALOGING-IN-PUBLICATION DATA
Brog, David.
In defense of faith : the Judeo-Christian idea and the struggle for humanity
/ by David Brog.
p.   cm.
Includes bibliographical references and index.
ISBN-13: 978-1-59403-380-3 (hardcover : alk. paper)
ISBN-10: 1-59403-380-3 (hardcover : alk. paper)
1. Life and death, Power over—Religious aspects—Judaism.   2. Life—
Religious aspects—Judaism. 3. Jewish ethics—History.   4. Faith
(Judaism)   5. Humanity.   I. Title.
BJ1469.B76 2009
241—dc22
2009038323

For my brothers and best friends,
Michael and Steven Brog

What is hateful to you, do not do to your fellow man.
That is the whole Torah, and the rest is just a commentary.
Go then and learn it.
—HILLEL, CIRCA 10 CE

So in everything do to others what you would have them do
to you, for this sums up the law and the prophets.
—JESUS OF NAZARETH, CIRCA 30 CE

But know, my son, that the principle behind the whole Torah
is this: What you yourself hate, do not do it to your fellow man.
—RABBI AKIVA, CIRCA 100 CE

Table of Contents

Preface

IN RECENT YEARS, attacks on religious faith have become both more common and more vicious. In books, movies, and on television, the faiths that have nurtured our civilization are increasingly portrayed as exotic new threats to an otherwise pure America. It is as if we in the West are suffering from some cultural autoimmune disorder. We are destroying our own roots.

To the extent that they contain any discernable logic, most of these critiques share the same two-point premise. They assert, in so many words, that only an idiot could believe in God and revealed religion. They then proceed to claim that idiots who believe in God and revealed religion have been responsible for most of the hatred, war, and bloodshed here on earth. Even the more scholarly of these efforts are often angry in their tone and stunningly simplistic in their analysis. Yet over the years, surprisingly few worthy retorts have emerged. This is my effort to provide one.

I decided at the outset that I would only respond to the second of these two points. No matter how cogent or complete, rational arguments alone cannot generate religious devotion. Belief in God demands a leap beyond logic—the leap of faith. Thus nowhere in this book will readers find arguments for God's existence or exhortations to adopt any particular religious faith.

Instead, I focus entirely on rebutting the second point made by these critics: that people of faith are responsible for our greatest sorrows. This is an assertion that can be tested by reference to objective fact. And a review of the relevant history proves just how far from the truth this claim actually is.

THE STORY OF THE WEST contains chapters in which religion was too powerful. There have been times in our past when faith has ridden a wave of certainty toward a crest of intolerance. For those of us living in the West today, this is not one of those times.

We live in an era of mounting skepticism. The struggle of our time is not to seek freedom from oppressive faith. Instead, our challenge is to preserve the foundations of faith that undergird our civilization. By every measure, we in the West are rejecting religion in increasing numbers. As we turn our backs on this spiritual heritage, we are also forgetting our cultural debt—namely the Judeo-Christian source of our most cherished values. With stunning hubris, we act as if we've built the towering moral edifice in which we had the good fortune of being born.

Indeed, when it comes to our morality, too many of us are playing the role of the rebellious teenager. Our forebears sacrificed and struggled to construct, preserve, and bequeath to us a noble tradition with an elevated moral code. Yet we cannot see beyond the imperfections of this tradition to recognize the great gift at its core. And in our ingratitude and outright sabotage we slowly erode the structure that would preserve this moral heritage for our children. Yes, the sins of the fathers are sometimes visited upon the sons.

⁓

CONTRARY TO WHAT IS SO commonly assumed, we're not simply born "good." We have not evolved a greater capacity for compassion over the millennia. To the extent that human beings enter this world with any altruistic impulses, they are tragically limited.

Throughout the ages, humans have demonstrated an instinctive altruism toward their families and their tribes. As human societies grew larger and more complex, the definition of one's "tribe" has often expanded to include entire races, religions, and nation-states. Yet the one constant throughout most of human history has been that those outside this shifting zone of compassion—those not in our "ingroup"—have never been deemed worthy of empathy or concern. These outsiders can be enslaved. And they can be killed. Slavery and genocide are hardly historical anomalies. They have been the overwhelming rule.

The radical idea at the root of the Judeo-Christian tradition is that all human beings are created in the image of God. Both Judaism and Christianity therefore stress the sanctity and equality of *all* humans. Even more importantly, these faiths demand not merely that we recognize the value of our neighbors, but also that we love them and act on this love by serving them. From the Judeo-Christian perspective, the neighborhood grows to encompass the entire world, and the ingroup swells and swallows all outgroups. Hated strangers become beloved brothers.

This belief in the equality and sanctity of all humans combined with this call to actively love them is what I refer to throughout this book as the "Judeo-Christian idea." The Judeo-Christian idea was something new in the West. And it continues to inspire our highest ethics down to the present day. When you feel compassion for a Haitian earthquake victim or an African AIDS patient, you are feeling a connection and an altruism that is exceptional in human history. And you must thank the Judeo-Christian tradition for it. In our civilization, such love has no other source.

⌇

GIVEN THE IMPRESSIVE RECORD of the Judeo-Christian idea in the modern world, those who wish to discredit this tradition must resort to deception and demagoguery. Typically, their arguments rely upon the logical error of faulty generalization. These critics try to condemn all religion at all times by citing atrocities committed by the adherents of certain religions at certain times.

In particular, to prove that Christianity and Judaism are evil today, our atheists typically cite atrocities committed by radical Muslims. Quite often, they supplement their arguments by invoking medieval Christian atrocities. To the extent that they discuss modern Christian or Jewish violence at all, these critics trot out the same few examples of extremist acts that were immediately and universally condemned by the very faith communities they seek to denounce.

When it comes to religion, too many otherwise astute observers are willing to accept this logical sleight of hand. They would certainly never do so in other contexts. Suppose, for example, that our topic was not religions but nations. And suppose that a critic of the United States sought to condemn our country by arguing that the Soviet Union committed many atrocities. Alternatively, imagine that this critic tried to convince us of America's present evil by enumerating centuries-old American sins. Neither argument would be the least bit persuasive. We are quite capable of making the obvious distinctions which such generalizations seek to blur.

By the same principle, citing the evil of militant Islam is hardly an indictment of Judaism, Christianity, or any other religion. In fact, the barbarity of militant Islam does not even discredit Islam as a whole, since the militants represent a minority of Muslims. Likewise, the behavior of Christians or Jews centuries ago cannot sustain a valid critique of these faiths today. The fact that so many anti-religious books and movies make such specious arguments and yet are still taken seriously shows just how skeptical of religion we have become.

The simple premise of this book is that once the focus is narrowed in two important ways, it becomes difficult to deny that faith has been an overwhelming force for good. The first limitation is one of scope: I've restricted my analysis to the Judeo-Christian tradition in the Western world. The second limitation is one of time: I've confined my review to the modern era—the past few centuries. What emerges is a record that is surprisingly clear and singularly impressive. In the modern era, the Judeo-Christian tradition has been the West's most prolific source of compassion, humanity, and human rights.

∽

I MUST STRESS, in the clearest of terms, that this book is not a work of comparative religion. This is a book about Western civilization. Thus far, only one faith tradition—the Judeo-Christian—has had a significant role in shaping Western culture. It is certainly possible that this Judeo-Christian monopoly on our morality may erode as more Muslims, Hindus, and Buddhists immigrate to the West. Yet as of this writing, such religious newcomers have yet to shape our culture to this extent.

Thus the fact that this book does not focus on other faith traditions is in no way a critique of these traditions. It is not my intention to slight any other religion or its moral code. These other faiths are simply outside of, and therefore irrelevant to, the scope of my analysis. I am the first to admit that I simply don't know enough about non-Western religions to pass even the most rudimentary of judgments upon them.

Whenever I use a superlative in connection with the Judeo-Christian tradition, therefore, I have tried to be clear that this superlative applies not on a global scale, but simply within the Western context. When I write that the Judeo-Christian tradition has been the greatest source of compassion *in the West*, it should be clear that I am in no way commenting on any of the religions which have influenced cultures in the rest of the world. If I have at times left out such limiting language, it is to avoid repetition rather than to claim superiority.

I have no doubt that some individuals who never bother to read this preface or this book will nevertheless criticize me for denigrating non-Western faiths. There is little a writer can do to protect himself from critics with strong opinions and faulty logic. And today, the blogosphere ensures that even the most dishonest of critics gets a voice. But to the extent that facts still matter in our public discourse, I have set forth my goals and intentions here in clear English.

~

THIS IS A BOOK about religion and politics, Christians and Jews, the righteous and the wicked. Given the controversial and personal nature of these topics, I believe it is essential that I state at the outset my own faith, background, and journey. Only then can you factor into your reading any bias I might bring to my analysis.

Starting with my religion, I am a Jew. I am a Jew not only by birth, but by faith. I am not a Messianic Jew or a Jew for Jesus—I do not believe that the Messiah has ever appeared on earth. Nor am I an alienated or self-hating Jew. I embrace my Jewish faith and seek knowledge of my Creator through the paths and texts provided to me by my Jewish ancestors. While I do not observe all of the *Halacha* (Jewish law), I do recognize the Halacha as a central component of my religion. If there be fault in my failure to observe it, the fault lies with me, not with the law.

Yet my Jewish faith does not in any way prevent me from admiring Christianity and devout Christians. On the contrary, I see a deep kinship between Judaism and Christianity. Yes, our faiths do differ on important theological questions, most notably the identity of the Messiah. But when we narrow the scope from theology to morality—the focus of this book—our two faiths are practically identical.

Thus when I see Christians doing beautiful things in the name of Christianity, I do not see outsiders serving a foreign God. Quite to the contrary, I see brothers serving the God of Abraham, Isaac, and Jacob. We Jews and Christians must love and respect one another. And we should, for a change, focus on all that we share. We are brothers and sisters in faith not because we agree on everything, but because we agree on so many of the truly important things affecting our lives in this world. And these values and beliefs that we cherish are under assault both at home and abroad.

While I identify as a Jew, however, I understand well the perspective of secular critics of faith. For most of my life, this was a perspective I shared. In my younger days, I would not have written this book. I'm quite confident that I would not even have purchased it. At the time, it was my considered opinion that the Judeo-Christian tradition had about as much to do with my morality as the religious beliefs of the early Aztecs. After all, I was a considerate, thoughtful, and at times compassionate young man, yet I had never seriously studied Judaism. It therefore seemed absurd to assert that any goodness I possessed came from a Jewish faith about which I knew so little. I was wrong.

It was only when I took a step back and examined the source of my morality that I realized the profound extent to which it is Judeo-Christian. It was only when I questioned the conventional wisdom regarding faith that I realized how flawed this conventional wisdom is. This is not a book written by someone who has never doubted God or the tenets of his faith. It is a book written by someone who has also questioned the secular orthodoxy that, today, is even more dominant and demanding.

AS I NOTED EARLIER, I never intended this book to be an argument for faith in God. Yet by the time I had finished writing it, I found that the content had nevertheless touched me at this deeper level. I hope that it will have a similar effect on others. In particular, it is my prayer that this book might contribute in some small way toward bridging a gap and solving a problem. The gap is between people of faith and the skeptics who cannot believe in a loving God. The problem is that, deep down, even the skeptics want to believe.

We are not merely a lost generation. And we are not lost only here, in America. Our predicament is much deeper and of much longer duration. Centuries of skepticism, doubt, and contempt have taken their toll. Millions of us across the Western world have been rendered spiritual eunuchs. It's not that we don't long for God. The problem is that we're incapable of consummating the relationship. Faith and grace have been drained from us, leaving only those most primitive of instincts: our obsessions with self and things material. We are a race of accountants counting the grains of sand on our beaches. We are a tribe of technicians, fixing the hands of a clock that counts down the seconds of our lives.

Yet the desire, the longing for God—this remains. No thoughtful human can deny it. Our scientists tell us that this longing is a product of our evolution. Our scriptures tell us that this longing has been planted in us by God. The cause, quite frankly, is irrelevant. The desire is real, and it is breaking our hearts. Yet in our incapacity to believe we find ourselves staring, paralyzed, as the love of our lives disappears into the distance.

The Protestant theologian John Wesley wrote that in faith he discovered "that love of God, and of all mankind, which we had elsewhere sought in vain." At first, I was jealous of John Wesley. I longed for the love but lacked the faith. And then it struck me: Perhaps the converse is also true. Perhaps through the love of all mankind we can find faith and God.

For even if we don't possess faith, we still believe in love.

∾

THE PREDICAMENT OF the lonely skeptic can be summed up as follows: We call out to God but he does not answer us. We seek the face of God, but we see nothing. God hides his face from us.

One of the great consolations of reading the Bible is the reminder it constantly provides that we are hardly the first humans to suffer whatever pain is troubling our souls at any given moment. And so it is with God's hidden face. In the Psalms, King David cries out to God in despair, "Why, Lord, do you reject me and hide your face from me?" This is a theme to which David repeatedly returns in his darker moments.

David was not the first biblical figure to seek God's face in vain. In the book of Exodus, Moses asks to see the God to whom he has so often spoken. God responds by saying that he will pass before Moses and speak his—God's—name aloud. But God also tells Moses, "You will not be able to see My face, for no human can see Me and live."

In the wonderful passages that follow, God instructs Moses to seek shelter in a cleft in the rock of Mount Sinai. He explains to Moses that he is going to protect him with his hand while he passes by him. After he has passed by, God relates, he will remove his hand and allow Moses to see his back.

Then God does what he had promised. God descends to Moses in a cloud and passes before him. As he does so, God proclaims his name for Moses to hear:

> The Lord, the Lord, the compassionate and gracious God,
> slow to anger, abounding in love and faithfulness, maintaining
> love for thousands of generations, and forgiving wickedness,
> rebellion, and sin.

There is no better summary of the Judeo-Christian idea than this. In naming himself, God stresses the love, compassion, and mercy at the core of both Judaism and Christianity.

Whether or not one believes in its divine provenance, the Bible is the source of profound wisdom about the human condition. The fact is that if we seek the face of God—direct proof of his existence—we will search in vain. We must seek instead the attributes of God. Indeed, the attributes of God—his love, kindness, and mercy—are all around us.

I am too much a prisoner of my secular background and liberal education to have an easy faith. For me and so many like me, faith has always been a struggle. And it has been a struggle I have at times abandoned. But I have been privileged in recent years to work closely with men and women who love God and try their utmost to act with his love and compassion. And when I watch such wonderful people, I sometimes see in them the reflection of something very bright. When men and women of faith act on their faith to reflect the attributes of God, they are in a very concrete way bringing the divine into our world.

In the pages of this book, I share some of the most compelling examples of men and women who have lived out the love and compassion at the core of their faith and changed the world in the process. As you read these pages, I hope that you can also see in these people the reflection of a great light. I cannot prove to you that you are seeing God's back as he passes through our world. But I can promise you that this reflection—the light shining forth from those who love their fellow human beings so completely—is one of the most beautiful sights you will ever see.

The Sanctity of Life and Its Discontents

It may be worth remembering that our present absolute protection of the lives of infants is a distinctively Christian attitude rather than a universal ethical value.[1]

—PETER SINGER, PROFESSOR OF BIOETHICS, PRINCETON UNIVERSITY

THE ROMANS WERE not the first anti-Semites. But they embraced, at times enthusiastically, this most ancient of hatreds. The Romans conquered most of Europe and the Mediterranean world. They pacified peoples far more powerful, numerous, and wealthy than the Jews. But they could never fully subdue this small tribe in the far southeastern corner of their empire.

The Jewish rebellions were not merely military. The Jews also engaged in a determined cultural resistance. Unlike other conquered peoples who eagerly adopted Roman ways, the Jews clung with persistence to their ancient religion and distinctive morality. As Jews migrated to the empire's leading cities, they even began attracting Roman citizens to their synagogues.

In the year 70 CE, Roman legions crushed a major Jewish revolt and destroyed the city of Jerusalem. Not long thereafter, the Roman senator and historian Tacitus tried to quash the Jewish cultural challenge. In his major work, the *Histories,* Tacitus attacked the Jews as "wicked," "stubborn," and "lascivious." Turning his attention to the Jewish religion, he asserted:

> Among the Jews all things are profane that we hold sacred; on
> the other hand they regard as permissible what seems to us
> immoral.

Tacitus then listed a number of these Jewish moral perversions.
Among the beliefs he found particularly "sinister and revolting"
was the fact that, for Jews, "it is a deadly sin to kill an unwanted
child."[2]

The Romans were proud practitioners of infanticide. So were
the Greeks before them. Both Plato and Aristotle recommended
that the state adopt a policy of killing deformed infants. The
Roman philosopher Seneca wrote approvingly of the common
practice of drowning abnormal or weak children at birth. The
earliest known Roman legal code, written in 450 BCE, permitted
fathers to kill any "deformed or weak" male infant or any female
infant, no matter how healthy.[3] Indeed, female babies were the
primary victims of Roman infanticide.

The Roman approach to human life was highly utilitarian.
They believed that females and weak males were never going to
grow up to be effective farmers, soldiers, or leaders. They would
therefore contribute little to the families and society that sustained them. With nothing in the Roman moral code to dictate
otherwise, many parents decided that killing these babies made
more sense than raising them.

Infanticide became so common a practice in the Roman
Empire that parents could discuss it without the slightest
remorse or shame. Here, for example, is a letter from a Roman
soldier to his wife:

> Know that I am in Alexandria.... I ask and beg you to take
> good care of our baby son, and as soon as I've received pay-
> ment I shall send it up to you. If you are delivered [before I
> come home], if it is a boy keep it, if a girl, discard it.[4]

The Jews embraced a different and quite revolutionary view
of human life. They were neither utilitarian nor pragmatic. The

Jews attributed a mystical value to every single human being. And they valued all humans equally, regardless of their age, gender, health, or ability. The Romans simply could not understand this Jewish fetish for human life, and they condemned it with the disdain they reserved for the most irrational of superstitions.

∼

CULTURE FORGES MORALITY. It is our culture that defines for us what is right and what is wrong.* We did not evolve our belief in the sanctity of human life along with our opposable thumbs. Nor are we moral geniuses who reasoned our way to this insight. Most civilizations throughout most of human history never arrived at this view. The only reason we in the West recognize the sanctity and equality of all humans today is because centuries ago a small tribe on the eastern shores of the Mediterranean injected this radical idea into our cultural thought-stream.

Our culture is pervasive. It surrounds us as completely as the air we breathe. And, like the air we breathe, we often forget that it is there. From the moment we're born, we are bombarded by our culture's unique moral code. Our first stories and books impart introductory lessons on right and wrong. Our parents and teachers communicate the culture's norms in every compliment they give and every criticism they level. The culture's prevailing morality permeates our workplaces, saturates our entertainment, and pursues us to our retirement homes. The culture never rests.

It is therefore easy to forget that so many of the things we think we "just know" were actually lessons we drank in with our mother's milk. In fact, many observers seem to believe that they arrived at certain Judeo-Christian insights through their own

---

*In emphasizing the centrality of culture to the transmission of morals, I do not seek to deny that there are absolute moral truths fixed by God or inherent in nature. My point is simply that we humans tend to come to knowledge of these and any other moral codes by means of the cultures in which we live. When religious people worry about the movies their children watch or the lessons they learn in school, they are acknowledging this overwhelming cultural power.

independent moral genius. Here, for example, is a popular contemporary critic of religion describing how humans can simply reason their way to recognizing the evil of slavery:

> The moment a person recognizes that slaves are human beings like himself, enjoying the same capacity for suffering and happiness, he will understand that it is patently evil to own them and treat them like farm equipment. It is remarkably easy for a person to arrive at this epiphany.[5]

This reasoning forms a perfect circle. Yes, once people accept that slaves are human beings like themselves they may well oppose slavery.* But why on earth would people ever recognize that slaves are human beings like themselves? The author of these words seems to have forgotten how very few people on the face of the earth have ever looked into their slave's eyes and seen a brother. The Egyptians never did. The Greeks never did. The Romans never did. Most of the Enlightenment philosophers never did.

Growing up in the heart of a Judeo-Christian society, such critics begin life on a high moral summit and believe that they have scaled a mountain. Yet such moral ingratitude is hardly new or rare. No less a figure than Thomas Jefferson made this mistake. Jefferson grew up in a Judeo-Christian culture that taught the equality of all men, and he enshrined this principle in the Declaration of Independence with the words "all men are created equal." Yet he famously introduced this piercing moral insight as one which is "self-evident."**

The idea that all men are equal is anything but self-evident. And while Jefferson may have been capable of paraphrasing the

---

*Even though the Judeo-Christian tradition has always recognized the full humanity of slaves, it actually took many centuries for this idea to translate into opposition to slavery.

**Some scholars argue that the words "self-evident" were actually added by Benjamin Franklin.

idea, even he famously failed to grasp its full meaning. When he spoke of men being created equal, Jefferson meant men—not women. And he meant white men. When it came to slavery, therefore, Jefferson never fully arrived at the "remarkably easy" moral epiphany of this institution's patent evil. While he saw abolition as a worthy goal for some future generation, Jefferson never pressed the issue in his own day and he never freed his own slaves.

There are some critics of the Jewish and Christian faiths who reject their core morality. But in the modern West, the more popular critique of the Judeo-Christian tradition comes from those who fully embrace its morality but simply fail to recognize the source. These critics employ the ideas, values, and vocabulary they have inherited from the Judeo-Christian tradition to sit in judgment on that tradition and find it wanting.

Discontents at Home

Carrie Buck was an 18-year old woman who gave birth to a child out of wedlock in the wrong place at the wrong time. The year was 1924, and the Commonwealth of Virginia frowned upon such behavior. The Commonwealth concluded that Carrie was "feebleminded" and ordered her sterilized so that she could not bring any more children into the world who might inherit her deficiency. The Romans killed babies of weak mind or body. The Commonwealth of Virginia wanted to prevent such babies from being born in the first place.

In seeking to sterilize those it deemed unfit to reproduce, Virginia was hardly alone. During the 1920s and 1930s, the eugenics movement was growing in prestige and popularity throughout the United States and Europe. Proponents of this pseudo-science taught that government could help build a better society by encouraging healthy citizens to reproduce while discouraging or even preventing those deemed defective from doing so. States across America responded by passing laws establishing forced sterilization programs. Those who advocated this practice did not believe themselves to be cruel or bigoted. On the contrary, most were self-professed progressives eager to end disease and poverty by applying the latest scientific insights.

The United States Supreme Court shared the nation's enthusiasm for eugenics. When Carrie Buck challenged the Virginia legislation under which she was to be sterilized, the Supreme Court upheld the law. Writing for the lopsided majority of eight of the nine justices, the legendary justice Oliver Wendell Holmes wrote that eugenics initiatives such as Virginia's were necessary:

> in order to prevent our being swamped with incompetence. It is better for all the world, if instead of waiting to execute degenerate offspring for crime, or to let them starve for their imbecility, society can prevent those who are manifestly unfit from continuing their kind. The principle that sustains compulsory vaccination is broad enough to cover cutting the Fallopian tubes. Three generations of imbeciles are enough.[6]

The phrase "three generations of imbeciles" refers to evidence submitted at trial that both Carrie Buck's mother and daughter were, like Buck, "feebleminded." Proponents and practitioners of eugenics relied upon this horribly vague category to give them the freedom to sterilize pretty much anyone they chose. The evidence proffered to support the charge of a feeble mind often spoke more to the victim's conformity than to his or her intelligence.

Subsequent research has demonstrated that Carrie's mother was simply unconventional and, possibly, a little promiscuous. Carrie's only offense was having a child out of wedlock. The authorities ignored the fact that Carrie's pregnancy was most likely the result of a rape. The evidence that Carrie's infant daughter was feebleminded consisted of the most superficial of observations and was contradicted when she grew to be a top student.[7] What Holmes called "three generations of imbeciles" would be characterized today as a single mother and a rape victim making the difficult choice to keep and raise their babies.

Justice Holmes was not bound by law or precedent to sanction this eugenics program. Instead, he took advantage of his position on the Court to further a cause he enthusiastically supported. Holmes, like Tacitus before him, had little sympathy with or patience for the Judeo-Christian fetish for human life. Holmes was a man of reason and a man of science, and he judged humans only by reference to their utility to society.

Holmes was by all accounts quite proud of his rejection of the sanctity of human life. Here, for example, is Holmes writing to a friend:

> I think that the sacredness of human life is a purely municipal idea of no validity outside the jurisdiction. I believe that force, mitigated so far as it may be by good manners, is the ultima ratio, and between two groups that want to make inconsistent kinds of world I see no remedy except force. Every society rests on the death of men.[8]

In another letter, Holmes repeated the sentiment with even greater emphasis:

> What damned fools people are who believe things. . . . All 'isms seem to me silly—but this hyper-aethereal respect for human life seems perhaps the silliest of all.[9]

Elsewhere, Holmes opined less eloquently on this topic. In a letter to a colleague he asked: "Doesn't this squashy sentimentality of a big minority of our people about human life make you puke?"[10]

Given his rejection of the sanctity of human life, it was easy for Holmes not only to embrace eugenics but to take it to its logical conclusion. In a major address, he declared:

> I can imagine a future in which science shall have passed from the combative to the dogmatic stage, and shall have gained such catholic acceptance that it shall take control of life, and condemn at once with instant execution what now is left for nature to destroy.[11]

Far from being shocked by Virginia's sterilization statute, Justice Holmes may well have believed that it did not go far enough.

This Supreme Court ruling gave long-awaited legal sanction to the practice of eugenics in America. Eugenics proponents wasted little time capitalizing on this victory. Many additional states passed statutes similar to Virginia's, bringing the total number of states authorizing forced sterilization to twenty-nine. By 1941, over thirty-five thousand American men and women had been forcibly sterilized or castrated. Most of these were found to be "feebleminded," "morally degenerate," or exhibiting some other deficiency so vague as to apply to almost anyone out of favor in his or her community.[12]

∾

EVEN IN AMERICA, our Judeo-Christian roots are sometimes not strong enough to hold us steady when we are buffeted by new cultural winds. The Romans were not the only ones to disdain the Judeo-Christian reverence for human life. We have had plenty of dissidents right here at home.

Since the supreme value we place on human life is not self-evident but learned from culture, it can be challenged and replaced by less generous appraisals. Our values are not written on our minds or hearts with indelible ink. They have been penciled in, and they are subject to being erased. America's record of practicing eugenics is but one small example of the fragility of our moral norms.

When it comes to the mutability of moral codes, the past century has of course provided us with far more terrifying cautionary tales. In Germany, the Judeo-Christian ethic was replaced by a Nazi race-based morality which narrowed the scope of the sacred from all of humanity to "Aryans." In the Soviet Union, the Judeo-Christian ethic was supplanted by a Communist class-based morality which narrowed the scope of the sacred from humans to the working class. In the former Yugoslavia, the Judeo-Christian ethic was rejected in favor of a nationalist morality which narrowed the scope of the sacred to Serbians. The list goes on. In each case, those left outside of the newly narrowed zone of compassion were left vulnerable to the very worst that human nature can inflict.

These examples are not merely disturbing; they are obvious. We in America have heard these stories of slippery slopes before, and we are quite confident that we will not slide down them. And we very well may not, especially if we, as a nation, continue to revere our Judeo-Christian heritage to the extent we currently do. But episodes such as our embrace of eugenics should remind us that even we are not completely inured against cultural ill winds. Sometimes the house sways and the foundation is tested.

Scientific Discontents

James Watson is a scientific legend. In 1962, he won the Nobel Prize, together with his partner Francis Crick, for discovering the double-helix structure of DNA. He is the father of modern genetics.

On October 14, 2007, Dr. Watson's illustrious career came to an abrupt end. That day, London's *Sunday Times* published an interview with Dr. Watson in which he was quoted as saying that he was "inherently gloomy about the prospects of Africa." Watson then explained the reasons for his pessimism:

> All of our social policies are based on the fact that their intelligence is the same as ours—whereas all the testing says not really.[13]

Watson went on to say:

> There is no firm reason to anticipate that the intellectual capacities of peoples geographically separated in their evolution should prove to have evolved identically. Our wanting to reserve equal powers of reason as some universal heritage of humanity will not be enough to make it so.[14]

Dr. Watson had not suggested killing anyone. Nor had he called for sterilizing anyone. He may well have made his statement out of a hope that confronting this scientific "truth" would convince us to do more to help the Africans of whom he spoke. And Watson was far from the first scientist to suggest the existence of intellectual disparities among the races despite all of the evidence to the contrary.*

Yet no matter what his intentions, Dr. Watson was giving modern sanction to one of the most dangerous ideas in history. The suggestion that there are significant and immutable differences between the various branches of the human family is a profound break from the Judeo-Christian belief in the fundamental equality of all humans. Theories emphasizing these alleged differences have been excuses for slavery and rationales for genocide. Human inequality has been the mantra of modernity's greatest murderers.

Dr. Watson may have thought that he was being scientifically honest. But he was in fact being morally reckless. This much should, by now, be elementary.

∼

BEFORE HIS CONTROVERSIAL comments led to his suspension, Dr. Watson had been the director of the prestigious Cold Spring Harbor Laboratory on New York's Long Island. This laboratory has a long and proud tradition of being on the cutting edge of biological research. And, it turns out, the laboratory also has a history of controversial directors questioning the Judeo-Christian ethic of the sanctity and equality of all humans.

During the early decades of the twentieth century, the director of the Cold Spring Harbor Laboratory was a biologist named

---

*Most leading experts strongly disagree with Watson and the others who assert such racial disparities. In the weeks following Dr. Watson's remarks, authorities such as Craig Venter and Dr. Elias Zerhouni issued public statements stressing the complete absence of scientific support for the claim that there are intellectual differences between the races.

Charles Davenport. Davenport was one of America's most prominent proponents of eugenics. Early in his tenure at the lab, Davenport opened the Eugenics Records Office. This institution became the intellectual and administrative heart of the eugenics movement during the height of its influence in America.

The team at the Eugenics Records Office pursued a most ambitious agenda. They set out to identify the estimated ten percent of the American population who were believed to be too defective to reproduce.[15] At the same time, they sought to convince the states to pass legislation which would enable them to sterilize all those so identified. In 1914, the Eugenics Records Office drafted a model sterilization law to serve as a template for the states. This model law provided the foundation for the Virginia statue under which Carrie Buck was sterilized. This model later served as the basis for the German legislation, the Law for the Prevention of Defective Progeny, under which the Nazis sterilized more than 350,000 people.[16]

Beyond sterilizing alleged undesirables here at home, the Eugenics Records Office invoked the principles of eugenics in a concerted campaign to block the immigration of supposed inferiors from abroad. Embracing the racist orthodoxy of their day, most eugenicists believed that northern Europeans were genetically superior to eastern and southern Europeans. They were therefore horrified that America's immigration laws had opened the nation's doors to millions of Italians, Jews, Greeks, and other allegedly inferior breeds. They concluded that all of their other efforts to improve America's gene pool would be overwhelmed unless they stopped this massive influx of poor genetic stock.

The experts at the Eugenics Records Office worked tirelessly to reverse American immigration trends. While they accepted the existing immigration levels, they demanded that Congress shift the source of these immigrants from southern and eastern Europe to the "Nordic" countries of northern Europe. The director of the Eugenics Record Office, Harry Laughlin, championed these race-based revisions in repeated testimony before the

House Committee on Immigration and Naturalization. Laughlin so impressed committee chairman Albert Johnson that he was appointed the Committee's "Expert Eugenics Agent."

Enthusiastically accepting Laughlin's theories and recommendations, Chairman Johnson introduced and secured passage of a eugenics-based immigration bill. The National Origins Act of 1924 increased immigration quotas from northern Europe while severely restricting immigration from eastern and southern Europe. Under the new law, for example, the number of Italian immigrants permitted into America each year shrank from forty-two thousand to four thousand. Immigration from much of Asia was blocked altogether. With minor variations, these strict quotas remained in place until after World War II.[17]

It is, of course, an indirect link. But the American eugenics movement had long arms indeed. They reached past Carrie Buck and well into the heart of Europe. There they held back millions of Poles, Russians, Jews, and Italians who sought to flee an increasingly dangerous Europe with mounting urgency. For the Jews in particular, the denial of an immigration visa was typically a death sentence. One wonders how many hundreds of thousands of Jews might have escaped Hitler's grasp by immigrating to America during these years had the eugenics movement not been so successful in shutting our doors to them at this crucial juncture.

⌒

SCIENCE HAS BEEN the iron wedge by which the secular has penetrated the realm of the sacred. Science has been the sharp scalpel with which our most cherished ideas about humanity have been subjected to dissection and doubt. Those who suggest that religion is the primary source of human conflict and bloodshed are not looking closely enough. If we examine the history of violence in modern times we will often find rationales rooted in science.

The idea that all human lives are sacred and of equal value is not a product of science. The sanctity of human life cannot be proven in a laboratory. When it comes to this most profound and foundational moral insight, we in the West have only one source: the Judeo-Christian tradition. This idea was first expressed in the Bible and it has survived throughout the centuries because of the ongoing authority of the Jewish and Christian faiths. If some of the Enlightenment thinkers later embraced and reiterated this concept, they cannot be credited with an immaculate intellectual conception. It was right there in the Bibles most of them read.

The Judeo-Christian tradition has built a wall between humans and the rest of the animal kingdom. It has placed man on a pedestal and put a crown on his head. Modern science, on the other hand, has consistently sought to tear down this wall and treat man as just another species of animal. Science has sought to take that crown off our heads—and measure the size of our skulls.

We are frequently warned these days about the great danger of religion expanding into fields where it does not belong. This concern is not without justification. There are areas of expertise, especially in the realm of science, where religion can contribute little. Religion cannot help us split the atom or map out our DNA. The Bible provides no clues that can help us cure cancer. As Cardinal Baronius is said to have put it in the sixteenth century, "The Bible teaches the way to go to heaven, not the way the heavens go."

But we must also recognize that there exists an equal and possibly greater threat of science exceeding its proper boundaries. Especially when it comes to morality, science can confuse, but it rarely enlightens. Science can enable us to split the atom, but it cannot help us decide whether we are justified in using an atom bomb. Science can help us map out our DNA, but it cannot help us determine whether it is moral to clone humans. Science can help us cure cancer, but it cannot help us cope with cancer.

When science ventures beyond its core areas of competence into the realm of morality, it often leaves corpses in its wake.

Especially when scientists opine on the value or equality of human beings, they invariably chip away at a key cultural support-wall. With an air of authority to which they have no claim, scientists have called into question the key principles which protect humanity—especially the weakest among us—from annihilation. Before even grasping the danger, they could bring our whole ethical edifice crashing down. If religion does not belong in the science classroom, then it is equally true that science has no place in the ethics classroom. We need a wall of separation between science and morality every bit as much as we need one between church and state.

Philosophical Discontents

Peter Singer is a philosopher and writer who is currently the Ira W. DeCamp Professor of Bioethics at Princeton University. In 1993, Professor Singer released a book called *Practical Ethics* in which he set forth a series of controversial, and soon infamous, views.

Singer's main thesis is that we in the West have drawn our moral lines irrationally. While we cherish human life, he asserts, we do not extend similar respect to the non-human animals with which we share the planet. According to Singer, neither science nor philosophy can justify this distinction. We should not, he argues, value life according to its species. Instead, he urges us to value life on the basis of whether and to what extent it possesses certain positive attributes, such as rationality and awareness.

Singer then spells out the ramifications of his approach. He argues that we need to see beyond our Judeo-Christian obsession with human life to better value and treat many of the animals we currently kill for food or sport. From this compassionate start, however, Singer's thesis proceeds to a dark converse. Overcoming our fetish for human life, he asserts, will also enable us to more clearly see that not all human life is of equal value.

In particular, Professor Singer seeks to wean us from what he sees as an irrational attachment to newborn human babies. Using his support for abortion as a starting point, Singer proceeds to make the case for infanticide:

> I have argued that the life of a fetus . . . is of no greater value than the life of a nonhuman animal at a similar level of rationality, self-consciousness, awareness, capacity to feel, etc., and that since no fetus is a person no fetus has the same claim to life as a person. Now it must be admitted that these arguments apply to the newborn baby as much as to the fetus. A week-old baby is not a rational and self-conscious being, and there are many nonhuman animals whose rationality, self-consciousness, awareness, capacity to feel, and so on exceed that of a human baby a week or a month old. If the fetus does not have the same claim to life as a person, it appears that the newborn baby does not either, and the life of a newborn baby is of less value to it than the life of a pig, a dog, or a chimpanzee is to the nonhuman animal. Thus while my position on the status of fetal life may be acceptable to many, the implications of this position for the status of newborn life are at odds with the virtually unchallenged assumption that the life of the newborn baby is as sacrosanct as that of an adult.[18]

Given this clash between his views and the widely accepted view that infanticide is murder, Singer concludes that "these widely accepted views need to be challenged."[19] This is an assault which Singer is prepared to lead. He reminds his readers, quite accurately, that our ideas about the sanctity of human life are neither obvious nor universal, but a cultural anomaly. As Singer notes:

> Infanticide had been practiced in societies ranging geographically from Tahiti to Greenland and varying in culture from nomadic Australian aborigines to the sophisticated urban communities of ancient Greece or mandarin China. In

some of these societies, infanticide was not merely morally permitted but, in certain circumstances, deemed morally obligatory.[20]

And Singer is correct again when he identifies the source of our unusual reverence for human life:

> If these conclusions seem too shocking to take seriously, it may be worth remembering that our present absolute protection of the lives of infants is a distinctively Christian attitude rather than a universal ethical value....
>
> The change in Western attitudes to infanticide since Roman times is, like the doctrine of the sanctity of human life of which it is a part, a product of Christianity. Perhaps it is now possible to think about these issues without assuming a Christian moral framework that has, for so long, prevented any fundamental reassessment.[21]

To be fair to Professor Singer, he is not advocating that we euthanize adult humans. Nor is he suggesting that we implement the type of forced infanticide practiced by the Nazis. Singer is only suggesting that we permit parents to decide whether or not to kill their newborn babies. Furthermore, Singer has limited his actual policy advocacy to more extreme cases, such as supporting a parental right to infanticide in the case of terminally ill and severely malformed babies.

Yet, provided that parental approval is forthcoming, Singer seems quite willing to sanction a broader range of infanticide. He has argued in favor of killing babies with Down's syndrome, although he now suggests that these babies should be spared if there are people willing to adopt them. Elsewhere, Singer has suggested that even a baby with hemophilia, a perfectly treatable blood disorder, could be morally killed so long as its parents intend to have another, healthy baby in its place.[22]

When it comes to whether or not to kill a baby, the only real moral limit Singer seems to recognize is the feelings of the parents. Thus while he favors "very strict" limitations on infanticide, he acknowledges that "these restrictions might owe more to the effects of infanticide on others (i.e. the parents) than to the intrinsic wrongness of killing an infant."[23]

〜

WE IN THE WEST have benefitted enormously from secular philosophy. All of us who are fortunate enough to live in a liberal democracy owe a debt of gratitude to the classical tradition as well as to Enlightenment philosophers such as Locke, Rousseau, and Jefferson. We who benefit from the genius of the American Constitution and its system of separation of powers must thank the classical philosophers as well as the Enlightenment thinker Montesquieu. Everyone who enjoys the protection of their human and civil rights must acknowledge the role played by the Enlightenment philosophers in embracing and popularizing these concepts. The list goes on.

Yet there are limits to what philosophy can teach us. And there are certain realms where philosophers should not tread. The fact is that philosophy, like science, has been a powerful wedge by which the profane has pierced the realm of the holy. Philosophy has been another means by which our most precious ideas about the sanctity and equality of all humans have been dragged down from their commanding heights into the muck of self-interested debate. The Judeo-Christian tradition attributes to humans a mystical value beyond our particular skills and contributions. Secular philosophy has too often sought to break this spell and subject us to far less benign systems of valuation.

The idea that all human lives are sacred and of equal value is not a product of philosophy. It is not a principle that is easily deduced or even logically defended. This is a belief we must place beyond the reach of the philosopher's pen as well as the scientist's probe. The sanctity of life is one idea we are better off not deconstructing.

〜

When Professor Singer first arrived at Princeton in 1999, the university hosted a public debate between Singer and a colleague on the new professor's controversial views. Over the course of the evening, Singer repeated some of his trademark lines, including his assertion that "simply killing an infant is never equivalent to killing a person."[24]

As she was leaving the debate, a Princeton senior was asked to share her reaction to Professor Singer. "I'm not all that disturbed," she replied, "because it's just philosophy. I'd be a lot more disturbed if he were trying to implement it."[25]

Despite this student's hopes to the contrary, the barrier between philosophy and policy is a most permeable one. Ideas have a way of trickling down from the academy to the halls of power. The Spanish conquistadors invoked classical philosophy to justify massacring and enslaving the American Indians. The Enlightenment philosophers invented the concept of race and employed it to rationalize African slavery. Karl Marx was a philosophy student whose thought was heavily indebted to Hegel, Feuerbach, and other icons of his discipline. The Marxism he developed nurtured monsters as diverse as Stalin, Mao, and Pol Pot. While Hitler was no scholar, he pieced together his racist creed from the bits and pieces of German philosophy and social Darwinist dogma popular in his day.

There is good reason for that Princeton student, and all of us, to be disturbed when philosophers begin to question the sanctity and equality of all humans.

Discontents Abroad

On May 12, 2008, a terrible earthquake shook China's Sichuan province. Over the course of the next days and weeks, a familiar scene unfolded. Chinese crews worked around the clock to rescue their fellow humans from the wreckage. Some families rejoiced at finding relatives still alive in the rubble. And one could see in the terrified faces of others that their loved ones had yet to be found.

In watching scenes like these we are touched by something that seems to be truly wonderful and universal about humankind. In times of crisis, we forget our differences and rush to the aid of our fellow man. No matter what our culture, it seems, we humans will claw through rock and rubble to save our brother who is buried beneath.

Yet no matter how similar people may appear to be on the surface, important differences remain. The differences that matter are not ones of race, gender, or nationality. Our most significant differences are those of culture. The deep implications of these cultural variations are not always apparent in our day-to-day behavior toward those in our ingroup; they are often visible only at the margins. These differences are revealed in how we treat the weak, the very young, and the rather old. They are manifest in how we behave toward the strangers in our midst and beyond our borders.

The Romans treated their fellow citizens very well. It is the way they treated their slaves, their enemies, and their infants that revealed something troubling at the core of their culture. The same goes for contemporary society. Infanticide, for example, did not die out with the Romans. Nor has it only recently begun to be rehabilitated by Professor Singer and others. The fact is that this practice never went away. People continue to kill their unwanted offspring down to the present day. Which brings us back to China.

In 1990, the Nobel Prize–winning economist Amartya Sen came across some statistics that deeply disturbed him. Sen found that in China, India, and some other Asian and North African countries, men significantly outnumbered women. This is the opposite of what demographers would expect to find. In every other country across the globe, women outnumber men. While there are more male babies born on average, more female babies actually survive infancy. These females then tend to live longer lives.

Applying standard male-to-female ratios against the actual population statistics, Sen came to the shocking conclusion that there were fifty million "missing women" in China and a total of over 100 million missing women in all of Asia and North Africa.[26] In a 2003 article in the *British Medical Journal,* Sen confirmed his earlier findings and concluded that, since his 1990 study, "the total numbers of missing women have continued to grow."[27]

While the estimates vary widely, a series of subsequent studies have confirmed Sen's primary contention that massive numbers of Asian women are in fact missing. A 2000 report funded by the United Nations concluded that in South Asia "79 million women are simply 'missing.'"[28] A 2002 article in the *Journal of Assisted Reproduction and Genetics* concluded that "approximately 50 million women are 'missing' in the Indian population."[29] A 2005 United Nations Population Fund report noted that "at least 60 million girls are 'missing'" in Asia.[30] A 2007 study by Chinese researchers concluded that "the estimated number of China's missing girls was 40.9 million" at the time of the 2000 census.[31]

These "missing women" were neither overlooked nor misplaced. They didn't pack their bags and move to sunnier climes. They were killed and aborted. The overwhelming consensus is that these gender disparities are primarily the result of the gross neglect of female babies, female infanticide, and sex-selective abortion.*

The cultures of ancient China and India, just like those of Greece and Rome, were ones in which sons were typically

---

*In a 2005 article in the *Journal of Political Economy,* a Harvard graduate student named Emily Oster offered an alternative explanation for at least part of this gender disparity. She wrote that many of the countries which are missing women also have high rates of hepatitis B infection, and that women who carry this virus tend to have more male babies than healthy women. Yet a number of subsequent studies have cast

preferred and daughters were often killed. Like so many other evils, infanticide has been a universal phenomenon. In the West, the spread of Christianity effectively ended these preferences and practices. In Asia, however, they have never been fully displaced. In many parts of India and China, a preference for sons and the disposal of daughters continues down to the present day.

Asia's rapid modernization has not narrowed this gender disparity. On the contrary, it may well have exacerbated it. For centuries, parents had to wait until a child was born to determine its sex and kill the females. Today, however, there is no need to carry an undesirable baby to term. Through readily available ultrasound technology, parents can determine a child's sex much earlier and eliminate unwanted children more easily through abortion. Yet even the most zealous defender of abortion rights recoils at the use of abortion as a sex-selection tool.

In China, furthermore, the government's one-child policy has also fueled the gender gap. Much of China's son-preference is driven by the widespread belief that sons are better able to provide for their parents later in life, especially since custom dictates that daughters go to live with their husbands' families after marriage. If a couple can have only one child to support them in their old age, then there is a stronger incentive than ever to make sure that this child is a boy.

This murder of so many millions of young girls has required that a new word be added to the English language. What is taking place in China and India is a "gendercide."[32]

As the scope of this tragedy has come to light, the governments of India and China have both taken steps to address it. In 1994, the Indian government passed a law which prohibits the use of ultrasound for identifying the sex of a fetus. In 2003, this

---

serious doubt on this explanation. Oster herself came to question her thesis, and in a 2008 working paper she concluded that "hepatitis B cannot explain skewed sex ratios in China." (Oster, Chen, Yu, Lin, "Hepatitis B Does Not Explain Male-Based Sex Ratios in China," National Bureau of Economic Research Working Paper No. 13971, April 16, 2008)

law was amended to prohibit sex-selective abortion. In 2006, India launched a "cradle scheme" in which orphanages were opened throughout the country to raise unwanted baby girls.

In 1994, China outlawed both the sex identification of fetuses through ultrasound and sex-selective abortions. This law was strengthened in 2002. More recently, Chinese officials started a "Care for Girls" campaign to combat ongoing son-preference. According to China's leading government paper, the *People's Daily,* the program seeks to end sex-selective abortion as well as "the criminal activities of drowning and abandoning baby girls."[33]

Eliminating such deeply rooted practices will not be easy. When a reporter for the *New York Times* visited the Chinese city of Guiyang in early 2005, he noticed that the "Care for Girls" program was indeed being implemented. A bright red banner hung above the main street announcing that the government was going to "firmly crack down on the criminal activity of drowning and in other ways brutally killing female babies." Across the street, however, in equally large characters, was an advertisement promoting ultrasound tests at a local medical clinic.[34]

Yes, the Chinese respond to their natural disasters the same way we do. But many millions of Chinese react to the news that they are expecting a baby girl very differently than we do. No matter how much we may share as humans, our cultural differences remain. These differences are not simply quaint matters of custom or cuisine. They are very often a matter of life and death.

⟡

THIS BOOK HAS a simple premise. It is a premise which runs counter to a deeply flawed conventional wisdom. It is a premise to which history lends its most compelling testimony.

The premise is that the Judeo-Christian tradition has introduced, preserved, and promoted a key insight and a core commandment. The insight is the sanctity and equality of all humans. The commandment is to treat our sacred fellow humans with love—to love one another. These ideas—what we will collectively call "the Judeo-Christian idea"—have been neither obvious nor universal, and they are continually under assault.

The Judeo-Christian idea has been the powerful force that has enabled Western civilization to overcome many of the evils which have plagued it, evils which have been too widely accepted in too many cultures for far too long.* The Judeo-Christian idea is the reason—the only reason—why we in the West rejected the custom of infanticide and shunned the practice of eugenics. This idea is what enabled us to finally, belatedly, end the institution of slavery. This idea has empowered us to combat genocide with all of our moral force.

In asserting that the Judeo-Christian idea has enabled us to overcome these evils, we recognize that the converse is also true. Wherever we in the West have rejected the Judeo-Christian idea, we have fallen backwards. In such cases, the very moral weeds that this idea helped to extirpate have returned, taken root, and quickly choked out any moral progress that may have been made in their absence. In the twentieth century, the rejection of the Judeo-Christian idea by certain cultures enabled both slavery and genocide to return to the West, and to do so on a far greater scale than ever before.

Let us be entirely clear. In the West's moral progress, the Judeo-Christian idea has not been *an* effective force. It has been

---

*It is worth reiterating that this is a book about *Western* civilization. There may well be other faith traditions which both embrace such humanitarian ideas and have motivated men to act on these ideas. These traditions may have lifted other civilizations toward greater love and humanity. But when it comes to the West, only one such tradition—the Judeo-Christian—has had such an impact. This book does not claim to be a work of comparative religion. It is, by design, a study of one civilization and the ideas that have shaped it.

the effective force. The Judeo-Christian tradition has given the West a clear moral map. It has blazed and illuminated the path. And it has been the fire in men's souls that keeps them walking down this path, no matter how long or difficult the journey.

ONE

Our Morality:
Selfish Genes and Cultural Clout

*Be warned that if you wish, as I do, to build a society in which
individuals cooperate generously and unselfishly towards a
common good, you can expect little help from biological nature.*[1]

—RICHARD DAWKINS, EVOLUTIONARY BIOLOGIST

THE NAZI HOLOCAUST presented a tremendous
logistical challenge. It involved the assembly, registration, and transportation of millions of Jews.
The arrival of new victims at the death camps had to be synchro-
nized with the murder of prior detachments to ensure that there
was sufficient space in the gas chambers and barracks. And all of
this had to be implemented at a time when German infrastructure was under severe strain from the demands of a multi-front
war.

The Nazis placed a young SS officer named Adolf Eichmann
in charge of orchestrating the genocide's multiple moving parts.
When he joined the SS, Eichmann was a high school dropout
and unemployed traveling salesman with few prospects. But
now, for the first time in his life, Eichmann excelled at his work.
In Nazi Germany, the death trains ran on time.

After the war, Eichmann evaded arrest and eventually made
his way to Argentina. There, continuing in his bureaucratic ways,
he managed a production line at a Mercedes factory. It was in
Argentina that Eichmann was eventually captured by Israel's

Mossad and brought to Jerusalem to stand trial. An Israeli court found him guilty of crimes against humanity and sentenced him to death. Adolf Eichmann was hanged on May 31, 1962, at a prison in Ramla, Israel.

During his interrogation and trial in Israel, Eichmann never renounced his Nazi ideology and never acknowledged the immorality of his actions. Yet with uncharacteristic drama, Eichmann repeatedly renounced the Christian faith in which he had been raised. When called to the witness stand, he refused to take his courtroom oath on a Bible. The day he was to be hanged, a Protestant minister offered to read the Bible with him. Eichmann declined, noting that he had only a couple hours left to live and therefore had no "time to waste." When the Israeli hangman asked him if he had any final words, Eichmann proudly stated that he was a *gottglaubiger,* the Nazi term for those who rejected their Christianity.[2] Unlike so many of his Jewish victims who went to their deaths affirming their faith, Eichmann died renouncing his.

~

BY REPEATEDLY EMPHASIZING his rejection of Christianity in his final days, Eichmann seemed to acknowledge that this was a defining decision. And indeed it was. By severing his ties to the Judeo-Christian tradition, he was free to become a dedicated follower of moral fashion. With neither anchor nor compass, he was carried along by the racist tide that swept over Germany, never recognizing how far off course he had been blown.

After abandoning Christianity, Eichmann was first drawn to Enlightenment philosophy. While being examined by the Israeli police, Eichmann declared that he had lived much of his life according to Immanuel Kant's moral precepts. He had read Kant's *Critique of Pure Reason* as a young adult and had adopted Kant's categorical imperative as his moral guide.[3] Kant's categorical imperative is a less personal variation of the golden rule. It provides that we should perform only those acts which we would accept as general rules of action for all of society. Under this formulation, for example, we should not steal from our neighbor because we would not accept a general rule that would allow our neighbor to steal from us.

Kant's philosophy was well and good, until it became inconvenient. When Eichmann became a Nazi and was assigned to administer a genocide, even he could see that he was no longer honoring the categorical imperative. He therefore abandoned this standard as readily as he had adopted it.[4]

Having rejected the Judeo-Christian morality of his childhood and the Enlightenment morality of his early adulthood, there was nothing preventing Eichmann from embracing the new moral fashion of his day: Nazism. Indeed, Eichmann described his conversion to Nazism as "like being swallowed up by the Party against all expectations and without previous decision. It happened so quickly and so suddenly."[5] It would be difficult to find more chilling testimony to the power of culture to overwhelm and transform our morality.

Eichmann highlighted the transformative power of culture once again when discussing the notorious Wannsee Conference. On January 20, 1942, the Nazi leadership convened a meeting at a villa in the Berlin suburb of Wannsee to finalize the bureaucratic details of Hitler's "final solution to the Jewish question." Since an effort on this scale involved many different ministries and bureaucracies, it was essential that the relevant parties agree on the chain of command and the division of labor. The efficiency of the Final Solution owed much to the structure put into place in Wannsee that day.

Eichmann attended the Wannsee Conference and took the minutes. During his interrogation in Israel, he claimed that up until this meeting he still harbored some doubts about "such a bloody solution through violence." But as he heard all of the leaders of the Third Reich embrace the Final Solution, his concerns lifted. "At that moment," he told his captors, "I sensed a kind of Pontius Pilate feeling, for I felt free of all guilt."[6]

Eichmann related that throughout the Holocaust, his conscience was continually salved by the fact that he never encountered anyone who was actually opposed to exterminating the Jews.[7]

The Bible provides many moral exemplars. Pontius Pilate is not one of them. It is a tragic irony that the same Eichmann who rejected the larger moral message of the Bible reached back to the Bible to help justify his moral surrender. But Eichmann was certainly correct in identifying Pilate as his moral kin. Both men made the passions of the mob their moral north star.

~

THESE DETAILS ABOUT Adolf Eichmann's final days are taken from Hannah Arendt's famous book *Eichmann in Jerusalem*. Arendt subtitled her book "A Report on the Banality of Evil." To this day, the name Eichmann and the term "banality of evil" are inextricably linked. The book proved to be so influential that to opine on the banality of evil has itself become rather banal. Arendt lived to regret selecting a subtitle that obscured her work's deeper meaning.

Arendt's point in using the term "banality" was simple enough. Evil does not always have fangs dripping with blood. Sometimes it takes the form of an awkward and timid bureaucrat. Eichmann became a poster child for the "banality of evil" because few individuals have ever spilled so much blood from behind a desk. This executioner did not pull a trigger or flip a switch. He merely shuffled papers.

But Arendt's book and Eichmann's story provide another, more important insight into evil that has received far less attention. This story highlights the central role that culture plays in enabling our greatest atrocities. Evil people can commit individual crimes under any circumstances. But to perpetrate evil on a massive scale—to commit genocide or institute slavery—the evil of isolated individuals is not enough. When it comes to such crimes, it takes a culture.

In a healthy culture, criminals must be rebels. When a culture values human life, it condemns those who reject this value by murdering. When a culture respects private property, it punishes those who flout this norm by stealing. To be a criminal in such a society, you must step outside the moral consensus and engage in a forbidden act. Conformists in such societies, conversely, will rarely make trouble. Their drive to fit in and get ahead will keep them working hard, paying their taxes, and mowing their lawns.

When a culture goes evil, however, this dynamic is flipped. In societies which encourage the hatred and murder of certain groups, the greatest monsters are not those who rebel against the prevailing ethos, but those who most embody it. In such societies, the drive to conform turns toxic. When a culture sanctions evil, massive evil becomes simultaneously possible and banal.

We cannot stop the societal sins of genocide and slavery by locking up our sociopaths. Such atrocities cannot be blamed on deformed frontal lobes or childhood abuse. The only way to prevent such mass evil is to ensure that our cultures embrace a fundamental reverence for the sanctity and equality of all humans. Ending evil on this scale means winning the battle of ideas.

Evolution and Morality

One of the greatest barriers to recognizing the overwhelming importance of this battle of ideas is the growing belief that it is irrelevant. Despite the lessons the last century has provided in such tragic abundance, there is still widespread resistance to the notion that culture forges morality.

Some observers, as we have seen, believe that we simply reason our way to our morality, and that this task is an easy one. Others don't even think that such reasoning is necessary. The most prevalent modern myth about human morality is that we are simply born with it. With ever-increasing certainty, the conventional wisdom maintains that we humans have evolved not only our physical senses but also our moral sense. As our eyes and ears grew increasingly sophisticated over the millennia, we are told, so did our consciences. Since we are supposedly born with such deep moral insights, we have no need for religion or culture to inculcate them.

Yet while the headlines may trumpet studies showing links between evolution and morality, the fine print tells a far more nuanced story. Yes, scientists do largely agree that our genes play a role in morality by equipping us with a shared set of moral instincts. But in the less-publicized portions of their findings, these scholars likewise agree that the role of such genetic morality is a most limited one. In short, there is a broad scientific consensus that our moral instincts provide us with little more than a drive toward self-preservation and a zone of altruism largely limited to our blood relatives and close associates. When it comes to morality, we are born with the barest of bones.

Where biology ends, culture begins. The leading evolutionary biologists of our time have been quite explicit about the fact that it is culture which puts the flesh on these bare moral bones. While we may not enter this world as moral blank slates, they note, it is still our culture that does most of the writing. In reaching this conclusion, these scientists have joined a broad consensus spanning most intellectual disciplines regarding the dominant role of culture in shaping our morality.

It is important to stress that the subject of this consensus, and of this chapter, is the *transmission* of morality, not its ultimate source. Many in the faith community believe that there are absolute moral truths fixed by God. Many in the secular community maintain that there is an absolute morality inherent in nature. Yet the members of both communities largely agree that most people in most times have come to knowledge of these moral truths—to the extent they do so at all—by means of their culture. Few individuals have demonstrated an ability to stand outside their culture and assert their own independent morality without some individual or book—i.e., some cultural force—to instruct them. We have no reports of cannibals suddenly shunning human flesh, or of Romans spontaneously rescuing abandoned baby girls. These changes came only when new cultural influences, such as Christianity, were introduced in these societies.

It is also important to acknowledge that much of the evolutionary science discussed below is still controversial to many, especially those of more literal biblical faith. In addition, some of the scientists cited below hold rather controversial views on issues outside of their areas of scientific expertise. Indeed, one of the leading experts in this field, Richard Dawkins, is among the most outspoken modern critics of religion. We cite their views here only to demonstrate that even the most vehement apostles of evolution have recognized the limited role that this process has played in shaping our morality. These critics of faith have, through their study of evolution, confirmed one of the core contentions of the faithful: that religion and culture play the central role in shaping our morality. One need not agree with Dawkins or others about their politics or even their science to recognize the significance, or appreciate the irony, of their conclusions.

❦

THIS BELIEF THAT we have evolved our morality is as old as the theory of evolution. Darwin himself opened the door to such thinking. At times, Darwin wrote quite clearly about the role that positive reinforcement and other cultural influences play in determining our behavior. At other times, however, he embraced a stark biological determinism. In *The Descent of Man,* for example, Darwin wrote:

> There is not the least inherent improbability, as it seems to me, in virtuous tendencies being more or less strongly inherited.... I have heard of authentic cases in which a desire to steal and a tendency to lie appeared to run in families of the upper ranks; and as stealing is a rare crime in the wealthy

classes, we can hardly account by accidental coincidence for the tendency occurring in two or three members of the same family. If bad tendencies are transmitted, it is probable that good ones are likewise transmitted.[8]

In the course of the nineteenth and twentieth centuries, a number of Darwin's disciples adopted and developed this concept of the genetic transmission of morality. Italian psychiatrist Cesare Lombroso based a new discipline—criminal anthropology—upon the theory that criminality is primarily a hereditary phenomenon, and that certain biological types are "born criminals." The psychiatrist Hans Kurella went so far as to suggest that such born criminals could be identified by their facial features and other physical characteristics.[9]

The belief that genes determine behavior—both moral and immoral—became a prominent feature of some of the most dangerous ideologies of the twentieth century. The eugenicists sought to sterilize those they deemed "morally degenerate" to prevent such low morals from being passed on to the next generation. Modern racism stressed the idea—also introduced by Darwin—that such inequalities in moral equipment existed not only between individuals, but also between races. Thus when the Nazis condemned Jews as immoral, they traced the problem to Jewish genes, not the Jewish religion.

∽

IN RECENT DECADES, evolutionary biologists have returned their focus to the connection between evolution and behavior with increasing intensity. This field of inquiry has grown so quickly that it has developed into its own specialty, sociobiology, and has even spawned sub-specialties such as evolutionary psychology and behavioral ecology.

These new disciplines and the books written about them have come to dominate the public discourse on the source of our morality. Much of this attention is well deserved, given some of the fascinating findings coming from this field. In particular, recent studies have demonstrated quite convincingly that we humans do indeed enter this world with a shared set of moral instincts. Science, in other words, is confirming the existence of what theologians and philosophers have typically called "human nature."

Persuasive proof of these moral instincts comes from some large international studies specifically designed to test their existence. These studies have found that when faced with certain moral dilemmas, almost all people provide the same immediate responses. According to the organizers of one such study, such shared responses were observed:

> in respondents from Europe, Asia and North and South
> America; among men and women, blacks and whites,
> teenagers and octogenarians, Hindus, Muslims, Buddhists,
> Christians, Jews and atheists; people with elementary school
> educations and people with PhD's.[10]

If these reactions are seen across cultures, then they could not possibly be the product of any one culture. They would have to be inborn.

The instinctual nature of such reactions is highlighted not only by their universality, but also by their irrationality. Neither reason nor culture could generate such uniformly illogical choices. A well-publicized study involving a hypothetical situation called the "trolley problem" illustrates the point.

In this hypothetical, subjects are presented with two scenarios. In the first scenario, they are asked to imagine that they are walking down the street when they see a trolley car speeding down the track with the driver slumped over the controls. Five men working on the track will be killed if something isn't done to stop the runaway trolley. Luckily, the subjects are told, they happen to be standing near a fork in the track and can pull a lever which will divert the trolley onto a second track, thus saving the five workers. The only problem is that there is one worker on the second track who will be killed if they do so. The subjects are then asked if they would pull the lever and divert the trolley. Almost everyone says yes, they would.

The subjects are then presented with a second scenario. This time they are told that they are on a bridge overlooking the tracks when they spot the runaway trolley approaching the five workers. The only way they can stop the trolley this time is to throw a heavy weight in its path. But the only heavy weight they can reach in time is a fat man who happens to be standing next to them on the bridge. The subjects are asked if they would throw the fat man onto the tracks to stop the trolley. This time, most people say no, they would not.[11]

In each case, the subjects are presented with a situation in which they can save five lives by sacrificing one. Rationally speaking, these are identical situations. If we take the time to think it through, we should make the same choice in each case. Yet something in our wiring leads most of us to react very differently to these two scenarios. In the second scenario, people are not simply pulling a switch. The victim is closer, and they would have to see him, touch him and more directly involve themselves in his death. Most people, no matter what their nationality or religion, recoil from doing so.

Our Selfish Genes

Evolutionary scientists explain these moral instincts the same way they explain all of our other instincts, by asserting that we have evolved them over the course of millennia. They argue that the process of natural selection has equipped each of us with some limited altruistic impulses. Among these, it seems, is a disinclination to do violence to an innocent neighbor. Yet when it comes to our moral instincts, such benevolence is the exception to the rule. Indeed, evolution experts agree that the overwhelming effect of natural selection has been to implant deep within us a powerful predisposition to selfishness. When scientists say that evolution has given us moral instincts, they are by no means suggesting that evolution has made us moral.

Most scholars of evolution maintain that we are the products of millennia of vicious struggle for survival. Because our ancestors were the ones who won these bloody battles, they assert, we have likely inherited the martial and selfish instincts that enabled their success. In the words of William James:

> We, the lineal representatives of the successful enactors of one scene of slaughter after another, must, whatever more pacific virtue we also possess, still carry about with us, ready at any moment to burst into flame, the smoldering and sinister traits of character by means of which they lived through so many massacres, harming others, but themselves unharmed.[12]

Richard Dawkins, one of the leading contemporary evolutionary biologists, has given a modern twist to this idea. He suggests that the ultimate force behind this struggle to survive is not the organism, but the organism's genes. According to Dawkins, our genes are in control, and they are monomaniacal. They constantly drive us to behave in ways which will maximize how many copies of themselves are made and will endure. Dawkins coined a phrase for a gene so preoccupied with its own survival: the "selfish gene."

Dawkins is quite clear about the type of behavior that characterizes our selfish genes:

> Like successful Chicago gangsters, our genes have survived, in some cases for millions of years, in a highly competitive world. This entitles us to expect certain qualities in our genes. I shall argue that a predominant quality to be expected in a successful gene is ruthless selfishness.[13]

∼

TYPICALLY, THE INTERESTS of a selfish gene coincide with those of its host. For our genes to survive and multiply, we hosts must survive and multiply. Thus selfish genes tend to produce selfish humans. But this is not always the case. Not all of our instincts are so self-centered. Mothers have a legendary drive to care for their children. And, as we saw in the trolley problem, most of us recoil from physically harming innocent neighbors. How do we reconcile such noble drives with such selfish genes?

According to Dawkins, the answer lies in the fact that our blood relatives share our genes. If the relative survives, the genes survive. Thus from the perspective of the selfish individual, it is an act of altruism for a mother to care for her baby. From the perspective of the selfish gene, however, childcare is the most self-centered of acts. In fact, our selfish genes care so much for their copies and so little for their hosts that they will even drive us to risk our lives for our children. Thus what Dawkins and other sociobiologists have in mind when they discuss our innate altruism is more accurately seen as a genetic form of enlightened self-interest.

While such genetic altruism is largely limited to blood relatives, it can and does extend beyond the family. According to Dawkins:

> Natural selection favors genes that predispose individuals, in relationships of asymmetric need and opportunity, to give when they can, and to solicit giving when they can't.[14]

We are certainly more likely to survive if we belong to a larger network for mutual defense and support in hard times. When humans live in societies, therefore, we are exhibiting a clear tendency to enlarge the zone of evolutionary altruism from our families to our tribes and beyond. Especially in the modern world, our ingroups often expand to include our country, race, or religion. Be it the "Aryan race" or the world's working classes, Christendom or the Islamic *ummah,* modern ingroups can include millions, even billions of people.

ꞈ

SADLY, ANY SUCH expansion in the way we define our tribe does not alter certain troubling constants of our nature. First of all, the expansion is hardly irreversible. As the dean of sociobiologists, Edward O. Wilson, has observed:

The important distinction is today, as it appears to have been since the Ice Age, between the ingroup and the outgroup, but the precise location of the dividing line is shifted back and forth with ease.[15]

More importantly, any definition of an ingroup that does not extend to all humanity remains hazardous. No matter how large our ingroup, we humans retain a chilling capacity to withhold our compassion from those who remain outside of it. Students of evolution have recognized the stark limits of tribal altruism from the start. Writing about the virtues humans need to live together in societies, Charles Darwin noted that:

> they are practiced almost exclusively in relation to the men of the same tribe; and their opposites are not regarded as crimes in relation to the men of other tribes. No tribe could hold together if murder, robbery, treachery ... were common; consequently such crimes within the limits of the same tribe "are branded with everlasting infamy"; but excite no such sentiment beyond these limits.[16]

Thus while the zone of our evolutionary altruism can expand, it can just as easily contract. In both cases, it has distinct outer limits that are coterminous with our conception of self-interest. In modern times, the most troubling reminder of the dark side of our human nature has been our demonstrated capacity to dehumanize and persecute those who fall outside these limits.

The Power of the Culture

In the final analysis, the world the sociobiologists describe remains nasty and brutish. Our genes know neither love nor grace. They are strictly utilitarian. "Much as we might wish to believe otherwise," Richard Dawkins has observed, "universal love and the welfare of the species as a whole are concepts that simply do not make evolutionary sense."[17]

The leading sociobiologists harbor no illusions about the limits of our moral instincts. To a surprising extent, they frame humanity's great moral challenge the same way our religious leaders do, as one of transcending—not embracing—our biology. Indeed Richard Dawkins, a most outspoken atheist, has written of this challenge in terms which echo key insights of the Judeo-Christian tradition. According to Dawkins:

> We have the power to defy the selfish genes of our birth. . . . We can even discuss ways of deliberately cultivating and nurturing pure, disinterested altruism—something that has no place in nature, something that has never existed before in the whole history of the world. We are built as gene machines . . . but we have the power to rebel against our creators. We, alone on earth, can rebel against the tyranny of the selfish replicators.[18]

And how do we rebel? What tools enable us to transcend our biology and embrace a higher morality? Dawkins is quite clear that only culture can promote such progress. "Let us try to *teach* generosity and altruism," he urges, "because we are born selfish."[19] Elsewhere he notes that "among animals, man is uniquely dominated by culture, by influences learned and handed down."[20] Edward O. Wilson reaches an equally strong conclusion:

> Let me grant at once that the form and intensity of altruistic acts are to a large extent culturally determined. Human social evolution is obviously more cultural than genetic.[21]

⁓

PERHAPS THE BEST explanation of the relative roles of biology and culture in shaping our morality has been provided by means of an analogy to our linguistic skills. Linguists have long observed that all human languages share certain general principles, structures, and rules. Based on this insight, linguist Noam Chomsky famously hypothesized that humans must have evolved an innate language ability which predisposes us to communicate in certain similar patterns. In particular, he argued that all humans are born with a "universal grammar" that we bring to the task of developing and learning languages.

Yet despite any such universal grammar, the actual languages we humans have developed are dramatically different from one another. When it comes to the practical challenges of communication, these linguistic differences eclipse whatever shared rules may exist. English and Chinese may conform to the same general pattern, but most of us still can't speak a word of Chinese.

Many sociobiologists have argued that what is true of our linguistic equipment is likewise true of our moral equipment. Thus they describe our moral instincts as a "universal moral grammar." Yet while we may start with the same universals, different cultures branch off to develop their own specific moral grammars that are as different from one another as the languages we speak. As evolutionary biologist Marc Hauser puts it, "Once an individual acquires his specific moral grammar, other moral grammars may be as incomprehensible to him as Chinese is to a native English speaker."[22]

For morality as well as language, therefore, the shared starting point is far less significant than the specifics adopted by each individual culture. When you are lost in Santiago, knowing that English and Spanish share a similar structure doesn't help you find your hotel. And when you are being boiled in a cannibal's pot, it is of little comfort to realize that he entered this world with the same moral instincts as you. As Hauser has noted:

> To say that we are endowed with a universal moral grammar is to say that we have evolved general but abstract principles for deciding which actions are forbidden, permissible or obligatory. These principles lack specific content. There are no principles dictating whether particular sexual, altruistic, or violent acts are permissible. Nothing in our genome codes for whether infanticide, incest, euthanasia, or cooperation are permissible, and, if permissible, with which individuals.[23]

Our innate morality permits a range of behaviors, from the most altruistic to the most evil. It is our culture, not our genes, which determines where on this continuum we end up.

Thus, despite much hype to the contrary, sociobiology has actually confirmed that we learn our morality from our culture. Whatever moral instincts we share at birth, our moral codes remain largely undefined. Culture comes to fill these gaps.

～

WHEN HERNÁN CORTÉS led the Spanish conquest of Mexico in 1519, he was accompanied by a soldier named Bernal Díaz del Castillo. Years later, Díaz wrote about his experiences as a conquistador in a memoir entitled *The True History of the Conquest of New Spain.* This eye-witness account of these epic events is one of our best sources of information about the more than one hundred battles which culminated in the fall of the Aztec Empire in 1521.

During the extended battle for the Aztec capital of Tenochtitlan, Díaz had the opportunity to witness Aztec culture and religion up close, before the ultimate Spanish victory erased it forever. He was horrified by what he saw.* To cite just one example, Díaz gave the following account of the final moments of some of his fellow Spaniards who had fallen into Aztec hands:

> Our comrades whom they had captured when they defeated
> Cortés were being carried by force up the steps, and they were
> taking them to be sacrificed. When they got them up to a
> small square . . . they immediately placed them on their backs
> on some rather narrow stones which had been prepared as
> [places for] sacrifice, and with stone knives they sawed open
> their chests and drew out their palpitating hearts and offered
> them to their idols that were there, and they kicked their

---

*As we will see in Chapter Three, the Spanish conquistadors were themselves guilty of atrocities on a far larger scale.

bodies down the steps, and Indian butchers who were waiting below cut off their arms and feet and flayed [the skin off] their faces, and prepared it afterwards like glove leather with the beards on.[24]

What Díaz witnessed was no one-time atrocity. This was the fate of most Aztec prisoners of war. Nor was such ritual sacrifice reserved for enemies. At multiple celebrations during the course of the year, the Aztecs would sacrifice their own men and women in elaborate religious rituals. While the details varied depending on the particular god being appeased, these ceremonies almost always involved killing the victims by slicing open their chests and displaying their still-beating hearts to the crowd. This was invariably followed by flaying the victim's skin and wearing it in various ceremonies. By most accounts, the rest of the victim's body was eaten.

It has been estimated that when Cortés arrived the Aztecs were sacrificing as many as fifteen thousand people every year. The evidence the conquistadors found confirms such large numbers. In Tenochtitlan, they found 136,000 human skulls stacked in neat rows in the plaza. In nearby Xocotlan, they found 100,000 skulls similarly displayed.[25]

Díaz witnessed no dissidents seeking to stop these sacrifices. In fact, there is no record of any Aztec objecting to such practices. Instead, the entire society—including the victims—embraced these rituals and played their assigned roles. Believing that such sacrifices kept the sun and moon in the sky, the rains falling, and the fields fertile, no one dared object.

⌁

THE EARTH'S RICH pageant of cultures is perhaps the most eloquent testimony to the limits of our moral universals. Human nature may provide certain starting points and some distant outer limits, but it permits a vast range of behaviors in between. In this range lie both Hitler and Mother Teresa.

Far from converging upon certain universal moral truths, the world's cultures offer an exotic bazaar of moral fashions and peculiarities. Well into the twentieth century, cannibalism was an accepted practice on many islands of the South Pacific. During the same period, many African tribes practiced an animist religion that required mothers to kill twins upon their birth and a king's servants to kill themselves upon the king's death. Darwin wrote about North American Indians who "leave their feeble comrades to perish on the plains" and Fijians who, "when their parents get old, or fall ill, bury them alive."[26] The list goes on.

Such disturbing practices are hardly confined to small tribes in distant corners of the earth. In India, the custom of *sati* encouraged widows to commit suicide upon the death of their husbands by throwing themselves onto their funeral pyres. As we have seen, female infanticide was widely accepted in China and India and is still practiced in these countries, although it has largely been replaced by sex-selective abortion. In Soviet Russia, urban workers believed that the rural peasants were a hostile class. In Cambodia under the Khmer Rouge, the rural peasants believed that the city dwellers were the true enemies of the people. In America, African Americans were held as slaves until 1865, and it took another century for them to begin to win rights equal to those of white citizens. This list, too, could go on at length.

Those who would deny the role of culture in producing such moral diversity will find themselves left with some very dangerous alternative explanations. After all, many of the behaviors we find most morally objectionable today are practiced in the third world. If morality is cultural, then the persistence of such practices is simply an indication of cultural differences. If morality is biological, however, then an effort to explain these practices leads inexorably to a racist answer.

A far more satisfying explanation for this diversity is to concede that we learn our morality from our culture, and that anyone raised in a particular culture, no matter what his race or ethnicity, will likely embrace that culture's dominant ethos. We humans are not as morally objective or insightful as we would like to think. Those of us who believe that our Western morality occupies a higher plane should thank neither our genes nor our genius, but rather our good fortune at being born into our particular culture.

～

EVOLUTIONARY BIOLOGISTS HAVE thus simultaneously confirmed the existence of human nature and demonstrated its rather significant limits. They have proven that we enter this world with a set of overwhelmingly selfish inclinations. They have recognized that the only way to rise above this impoverished genetic morality is through a culture that can teach us something higher.

Any rabbi, pastor, or priest reading these conclusions might well ask, "So what took you so long?" Such observations regarding our morality are hardly revolutionary. On the contrary, the Judeo-Christian tradition has recognized these fundamentals of human nature for more than two millennia.

Genesis 8:21 relates that God observed of men that our "every inclination" is "evil from childhood." Relying on this and similar passages, Judaism teaches that we are all born with an "evil inclination." As described by the Jewish sources, this evil inclination is strikingly similar to Dawkins's selfish gene. The evil inclination is that drive inside all of us to be selfish, to place our own survival and well being above that of others, and to satisfy our base appetites without regard to the moral consequences. In the Jewish view, the great challenge of our lives is to wrestle with and overcome our evil inclination.

Christianity likewise recognizes that we enter this world with a strong selfish drive. In the Christian tradition, this belief has been elaborated at great length through the concept of "original sin." Interpretations of original sin have varied widely across different eras and denominations. Some theologians have viewed original sin as something very much akin to Judaism's evil inclination, that is, an inborn drive toward selfishness and self-gratification. Other schools of thought have seen original sin as a far more debilitating incapacity to do any good without salvation by faith. Yet all Christians would agree that we humans are born with some troubling moral limitations and that our great challenge in life is to transcend them.

Both of these faiths not only recognize our selfish nature but offer a path by which we can overcome it. Judaism teaches transcendence through law. Observant Jews believe that by striving to observe an all-encompassing set of commandments they can conquer their base impulses and more closely conform their behavior to the biblical ideal. Christianity teaches transcendence through salvation. Believing Christians recognize their fallen nature and their inability to overcome it through their own efforts, and thus seek to elevate their behavior through God's saving grace. In both cases, however, it is religion—perhaps the most powerful of cultural forces—which teaches the higher morality being sought as well as the means by which it can be attained.

ᨏ

MOST ENLIGHTENMENT PHILOSOPHERS recognized what the Judeo-Christian tradition has always maintained—and what science has so recently confirmed—concerning the centrality of culture to morality. After all, these thinkers were in the business of trying to influence and elevate the morality of their day. They would not have wasted their effort had they believed that virtue was biologically predetermined. In the age-old debate over whether it is nature or nurture that shapes our behavior, the Enlightenment philosophers were strong believers in the power of nurture.

Some Enlightenment thinkers observed that humans are born with certain moral predispositions. But they never doubted the power of culture to overcome these innate characteristics, for better or for worse. Rousseau thought that men were inherently good in the state of nature, but that the influence of culture corrupts us. Hobbes, on the other hand, believed that men were inherently brutish until society worked its civilizing influence.

Other philosophers rejected the idea that man has any such moral inclinations. They suggested that humans are, morally speaking, blank slates upon which the culture writes everything.[27] John Locke provided the classic expression of this view in his work *An Essay Concerning Human Understanding:*

> Let us then suppose the mind to be, as we say, white paper
> void of all characters, without any ideas. How comes it to be
> furnished? Whence comes it by that vast store which the busy
> and boundless fancy of man has painted on it with an almost
> endless variety? Whence has it all the materials of reason and
> knowledge? To this I answer, in one word, from experience.[28]

The offspring of the Enlightenment, the modern social sciences, have always emphasized the centrality of culture to human behavior. The founder of modern anthropology, Franz Boas, believed that the only way to understand why the peoples of the earth behave so differently from one another was to study their cultures. This is why anthropologists spend their days in the field studying cultural artifacts rather than in labs studying the genes of the people who made them.

The father of modern sociology, Emile Durkheim, also stressed the supremacy of culture. He went so far as to argue that even the most basic of human emotions, such as a father's love for his child, are learned from culture and are actually "far from being inherent in human nature."[29]

Modern psychology has likewise come down strongly on the side of culture. Sigmund Freud emphasized that human nature equips us with some very powerful drives. But he focused like a laser on the details of his patients' nurture to explain why some people develop into mentally healthy adults while others do not.

Certain schools of psychology have gone further still in stressing the supremacy of nurture. Behaviorism, a branch of psychology which came to dominate the field for much of the twentieth century, is particularly nurture-oriented. Behaviorists maintain that human behavior is the result of conditioning and responses to stimuli and thus can be understood without reference to an inherent nature. The founder of behaviorism, John Watson, set forth his faith in the power of nurture with great bravado:

> Give me a dozen healthy infants, well-formed, and my own specified world to bring them up in, and I'll guarantee to take any one at random and train him to become any type of specialist I might select—doctor, lawyer, artist, merchant-chief, and yes, even beggar-man and thief, regardless of his talents, penchants, tendencies, abilities, vocations, and race of his ancestors.[30]

The belief that culture plays the dominant role in shaping human morality is thus a rare point of consensus among science, religion, and secular philosophy.

A Sisyphean Challenge

In January 2007, an aging American veteran donated a photo album to the United States Holocaust Museum. He had found the album while stationed in Germany after World War II, and he thought that the fading photos of German soldiers might be of some historical value.[31] Thus the Holocaust Museum came into possession of what may well be some of the most shocking Nazi photos ever taken.

These photos depict no blood, no corpses, and no crematoria. What makes these photos so deeply troubling is that they capture the complete normalcy that prevailed in the Nazi ranks in the middle of a genocide. As we saw in the case of Adolf Eichmann, the most frightening monsters are the ones which take a human form.

The Holocaust Museum discovered that the album had belonged to Karl Hocker, the deputy commander of Auschwitz.

Rather than document his soldiers and staff at their death camp duties, Hocker was more interested in capturing the good times. Many of the photos show Hocker engaging in his favorite pastimes. In some he is decorating a Christmas tree. In others, he plays lovingly with a German shepherd he refers to as "my favorite dog."

The majority of the photos were taken at Solahutte, an alpine-style SS resort near the Auschwitz complex, in the summer of 1944. These photos record a visit to the resort by a contingent of SS soldiers and female auxiliaries who worked at the nearby death camp. The Solahutte photos have the look and feel of an unusually joyful corporate retreat.

A number of photos show soldiers and female auxiliaries happily relaxing in lounge chairs on a picturesque resort deck. Other photos show a group of soldiers and auxiliaries posing on a quaint bridge as a drizzle begins. After the group shots were taken, the photographer captured a few of the women running to escape the raindrops with gleeful smiles.

Other photos show a large group of soldiers participating in a sing-along on a beautiful wooded hillside. Standing in the front row are the senior officers of Auschwitz. These include the supervisor of the gas chambers, the commander of the female prisoners, and Josef Mengele, the camp doctor notorious for his sadistic experiments on human subjects. They are all smiling for the camera.

The Solahutte series also includes a number of photos under the caption, "here there are blueberries." The photos show Hocker handing out bowls of fresh blueberries to a group of female auxiliaries seated on a railing. Grinning broadly, the women eat their berries to the accompaniment of an accordion. When they are finished eating, the women hold their bowls upside down, and some feign tears for the camera.

These photos were taken during the very period that the Auschwitz gas chambers were operating at maximum capacity. At this juncture, the Soviets were advancing westward. Time was running short. Yet the Nazis were determined to complete the extermination of Hungary's large Jewish population, which had thus far survived the war. That summer the crematoria broke down from overuse and bodies had to be burned in open pits.

～

THESE PHOTOS ARE a rare, real-time documentation of the banality of evil. But like the story of Adolf Eichmann, they also illustrate a far more significant point. These photos of death camp personnel at play remind us how deeply intertwined our morality is with our culture. Most of the people in these photos were not "evil" in the traditional sense of the term. They did not stand outside their culture and challenge its norms. Instead, they embraced their culture, went with the flow, and sought to have a little fun along the way. In the process, they were cogs in a death machine that devoured six million Jews and millions of others.

Above all, these photos demonstrate just how effortless it is for humans to abandon the moral advances our civilizations have made and revert to our most primitive instincts. What culture builds, culture can destroy—and it can do so with astonishing speed.

We enter this world with a limited zone of altruism that is largely confined to our blood relatives. If we are lucky, we live in a society that teaches us to expand our zone of altruism to include ever wider circles of people. The most elevated moral systems teach us to love and serve all of our fellow human beings.

Evil cultures seek to constrict this zone of altruism back to its impoverished biological starting point. In fact, evil cultures can even override the limited altruism with which we enter the world. As we saw in the trolley problem, humans have an instinct not to harm their innocent neighbors. But what if that man standing next to us on the bridge is not innocent at all? What if he belongs to an alien tribe that is both inferior and inimical to our own? History demonstrates that when cultures teach us such lessons, most of us are capable of throwing that man over the bridge without the slightest remorse.

Most of the singing men and berry-eating women in the Nazi photos would have been shocked, even traumatized, had someone approached their party and murdered an SS man in good standing. But they could ignore the death machine operating on overdrive down the road because it killed only outsiders. Whether the victims were Jews, gypsies, homosexuals, or others, none of these victims were seen as fellow humans worthy of pity.

Not only were the Nazis in these photos ordinary people when the war started, but they were still ordinary people as it drew to a close. Operating a death camp had not changed them. They were not like our traumatized Vietnam War veterans. They did not suffer flashbacks or post-traumatic stress. They did not need to abuse drugs or alcohol to ease their pangs of anguish at what their country had asked them to do. They were told that their victims were outside the zone of compassion. With shocking ease, they narrowed their compassion accordingly.

⟿

DARWIN WAS AN optimist. As we've seen, he recognized early on that humans are inclined to confine their compassion to members of their own tribe. Yet Darwin was confident that evolution would slowly but steadily expand this zone of altruism until it included all of humanity. Darwin described a process by which mankind was growing to care "more and more" about the welfare and happiness of others. He observed that man's sympathies were becoming "more tender and widely diffused, extending to men of all races, to the imbecile, maimed, and other useless members of society."[32]

Darwin's faith in moral progress relied in large part on his mistaken belief that we inherit moral improvements along with physical ones. Thus he predicted:

> Looking to future generations, there is no cause to fear that
> the social instincts will grow weaker, and we may expect that
> virtuous habits will grow stronger, becoming perhaps fixed by

inheritance. In this case the struggle between our higher and lower impulses will be less severe, and virtue will be triumphant.[33]

When it came to moral progress, Darwin was indeed an optimist. And Darwin was wrong. Whatever moral progress man makes is fragile and precious and easily overcome. We will neither inherit nor evolve a broader zone of altruism; we must teach it. Only when our culture instructs us to love and value all humans no matter what their clan or country will our compassion extend more broadly. It is our culture, not our genes, that we must vigilantly guard from contamination.

～

IN GREEK MYTHOLOGY, the gods punished Sisyphus by condemning him to repeat the same task for all eternity. He was commanded to roll a boulder up a mountain. Every time he neared the top, however, the boulder would inevitably slip away from him and roll all the way back down. Sisyphus would have to start his labor all over again from where he had first begun.

History demonstrates that our moral progress is tragically Sisyphean. No matter how far we advance, we seem to continually revert to the impoverished genetic morality with which we entered the world. Our moral gains are not permanent. When new cultural winds begin to blow, these advances can be easily reversed. We find ourselves, morally speaking, "borne back ceaselessly into the past."

By the twentieth century German society had advanced well beyond our biological starting point and created a culture with a broad zone of altruism. But in an astonishingly short period of time the Nazis erased these gains and constricted German altruism back to a primitive level. Nazi morality, like that of a cave man, extended only to a broad category of blood relations—the so-called "Aryans." The Nazi reversion to our lowest moral common denominator was far from an aberration. Almost every age offers up sadly compelling evidence of this most frightening of human capacities. In the twentieth century alone, the Germans had their Jews, the Soviet and Chinese Communists had their peasants, Pol Pot had his city dwellers, and the Hutus had their Tutsis. Name a genocide, and you will find behind it an ingroup seeking to rid itself of certain outgroups it has placed beyond society's zone of compassion.

In a civilization littered with ideologies which have sought to constrict our zone of altruism to the biological minimum, the Judeo-Christian tradition has been a powerful force to the contrary. This tradition has always stressed the sanctity and equality of all humans. People inspired by this insight have consistently made the most sublime of sacrifices on behalf of their fellow men. The history of altruism in the West is, to a surprisingly large extent, the story of men informed and motivated by the Judeo-Christian idea.

The Judeo-Christian tradition provides a solution to the problem posed by our impoverished biological morality and the Sisyphean nature of our moral progress. The Judeo-Christian tradition offers our best hope of finally getting that boulder to the top of the hill and keeping it there. It is to this tradition and its core message that we now turn.

TWO

The Judeo-Christian Idea: Transcending Our Selfish Genes

Let me say, selfishness in any form is in exact opposite to
religion. . . . The question is does a man make his own interest
the object of pursuit? If so, such conduct is the exact opposite of
that benevolence which Christ manifested, when he laid himself
out for the good of mankind and the glory of God.[1]

—CHARLES GRANDISON FINNEY, AMERICAN EVANGELIST

O N THE EVENING OF March 7, 1965, the ABC television network aired a documentary called *Trial at Nuremberg*. The film tells the story of the famous war crimes trial that took place in Germany after World War II. This account of the trial becomes, inevitably, an account of the Nazi crimes themselves.

Before long, the network interrupted the film with breaking news. Suddenly, images of Germany in 1945 were replaced by pictures of Alabama in 1965. Earlier that day, a group of peaceful civil rights protesters had tried to march across the Edmund Pettus Bridge in Selma. Before they could get to the other side, Alabama state troopers attacked them with clubs, tear gas, and police dogs. The protest became a bloodbath.

Watching from his apartment in New York City, Rabbi Abraham Joshua Heschel immediately grasped the connection between the movie and the breaking news. Heschel had already been a vocal civil rights advocate, making speeches and writing articles in support of the cause. Now he understood that the time had come to do more. When civil rights leaders held a protest march in Alabama later that month, Rabbi Heschel did not watch them on television. Marching in the front row, arm-in-arm with Dr. Martin Luther King, Jr., Rabbi Heschel added the prestige of his name and the moral authority of his faith to the cause of justice.

It was certainly not Dr. Heschel's selfish genes which led him to Alabama that day. Neither he nor anyone in his family was African American. Nor was it merely the parallel pictures of racism broadcast into his home that March night which moved him to action. In Heschel's case, the scenes that played out on his television screen were merely catalysts that ignited something much deeper.

Like Dr. King himself, Rabbi Heschel loved the Hebrew prophets and their passion for social justice. In fact, Heschel had recently completed writing a book about the prophets that stressed the relevance of their message to a world which seemed to be turning from it. In his introduction to *The Prophets,* Heschel explained exactly what would later propel him to march:

> The situation of a person immersed in the prophets' words is one of being exposed to a ceaseless shattering of indifference, and one needs a skull of stone to remain callous to such blows.[2]

Heschel's skull was not made of stone. Nor, as the baton blows demonstrated, were the skulls of the civil rights protesters who could well have stayed at home. These men marched because this powerful Judeo-Christian message had entered their minds and moved them to embrace a cause larger than themselves. These men marched because for them, it was personal.

Upon his return from Alabama, Heschel reflected on his experience. "I felt a sense of the Holy in what I was doing," he wrote, "Even without words our march was worship. I felt my legs were praying."[3]

⌒

EVOLUTIONARY BIOLOGY HAS done an excellent job of identifying the problem. We all enter this world with an impoverished genetic morality. Our human nature drives us to care for ourselves and the small circle of family and useful friends who surround us. Yet we remain largely indifferent to the larger world beyond. Indifferent, that is, until the interests of others inevitably conflict with our own, at which point apathy turns into enmity. Whether one calls it the selfish gene, the evil inclination, or original sin, the evil in the world comes from inside us.

The central mission of the Judeo-Christian tradition has always been to overcome this fundamental flaw of human nature. Millennia before science recognized our innate selfishness, Judaism and Christianity identified this core human problem and provided a path towards overcoming it. The Judeo-Christian idea has always stressed the need to transcend our impoverished moral instincts and expand our zone of compassion. It has always sought to shatter our indifference and inspire us to action on our brother's behalf. Simply put, the Judeo-Christian tradition has introduced into the world a powerful ethic of love.

The Jewish Idea

If one were to summarize Judaism's core message in one word, the answer would be as easy as it is surprising. That one word is "love." The Jews discovered love. Not that they were the first people to love their families or their friends; almost every society has demonstrated such basic, instinctive love. But the Jews were the first to expand the circle of love beyond the home, the village, and even the nation to include all of humanity. Judaism was, at its core, a revolutionary theology of love.

Describing Judaism in these terms will no doubt strike many as mistaken. In the popular imagination, Christianity is the religion of love. Judaism, on the other hand, is widely perceived as a religion of cold law and obsessive ritual. Yet the stereotype gets it terribly wrong. When Jesus spoke of love, he was preaching the Jewish faith of his fathers.

⟶

THE BOOK OF LEVITICUS relates that after their dramatic exodus from Egypt, the Children of Israel camp at the foot of Mount Sinai. Now that they are safely outside of Egypt and its corrupting culture, God provides them with an extended discourse on the proper way to live. And it is here, in this first and most direct series of instructions to his people, that God commands the Children of Israel not to "hate your brother in your heart" but rather to "love your neighbor as yourself."[4]

Lest any of the Children of Israel be tempted to interpret this word "neighbor" narrowly, to mean merely a family member or a fellow Israelite, God quickly clarifies the revolutionary universality of his message. A few lines later God commands:

> When an alien lives with you in your land, do not mistreat him. The alien living with you must be treated as one of your native-born. Love him as yourself.[5]

The love demanded of Jews is so universal, in fact, that they are even commanded to love their enemies. That's right, even the very "Christian" idea of loving one's enemies is rooted in the Hebrew Bible. In the book of Exodus, the Children of Israel are instructed:

> If you encounter an ox of your enemy or his donkey wandering, you shall return it to him repeatedly. If you see the donkey of someone you hate crouching under its burden, would you refrain from helping him?—you shall help repeatedly with him.[6]

This commandment of universal love is a stunning departure from what the Hebrews had experienced all of their lives as slaves in Egypt. It was a revolutionary concept. And it quickly became the beating heart at the center of the emerging Jewish religion.

⟳

THE TALMUD* TELLS a famous story about Hillel, one of the most influential rabbis in Jewish history. Hillel is approached by an inquisitive gentile. "I'm ready to become a Jew," the gentile announces, "but only if you can teach me the whole Torah while I stand on one foot." Given the length of the Torah, this request has typically been interpreted as an attempt to mock the good rabbi. But Hillel rises to the challenge. He provides the young man with the distilled essence of Judaism:

> What is hateful to you, do not do to your fellow man. That is the whole Torah, and the rest is just a commentary. Go then and learn it.[7]

Hillel provides two momentous insights here. First, he plucks Leviticus's call to love our neighbor from a long list of laws and recognizes it as the core commandment of the faith. At the same time, he rephrases this commandment in a way which specifies how it must be fulfilled. Hillel's words make it clear that the love the Bible demands must be expressed not merely through emotions or words, but through action. He focuses entirely on what we *do.*

Hillel is not alone in summarizing Judaism this way. Rabbi Akiva, another giant of Jewish history, reached the exact same conclusion. Akiva taught that Leviticus's commandment to love our neighbors as ourselves is "the great, all-inclusive, fundamental principle that sums up the Torah."[8] Elsewhere in the rabbinic literature, a story is told about Akiva which is almost identical to the Hillel story:

> One day a donkey driver came to Rabbi Akiva and said to him, "Rabbi, teach me the whole Torah all at once." Akiva

---

*The Talmud, a compendium of Jewish law and ethics, is the most important text in Judaism after the Torah.

answered, "My son, if our teacher Moses ... required forty days and forty nights on the mountain before he was able to learn the whole Torah, how can you expect me to teach it to you in one session? But know, my son, that the principle behind the whole Torah is this: What you yourself hate, do not do it to your fellow man."[9]

Both Hillel and Akiva are saying something profound about the Jewish message of love. They are not just saying that loving one another is an important commandment, or even the most important commandment. They are saying that this is the commandment which contains within it the substance of all the others. Their point is that every other law in the Torah is simply teaching us *how* to love one another.

∾

IN JUDAISM, THE commandment to love one's fellow man is reinforced by a second, seemingly unrelated commandment. The book of Deuteronomy relates that before the Israelites cross the Jordan River into the Land of Israel, Moses addresses them one last time. It is here, during these final moments together, that Moses shares with them the commandment to "love the Lord your God with all your heart and with all your soul and with all your might."[10] Moses then underscores the importance of this commandment to love God. He issues a series of rules designed to ensure that the Israelites will be reminded of this commandment throughout the course of their every day:

These commandments that I give you today are to be upon your hearts. Talk about them ... when you lie down and when you rise. Bind them as a sign upon your arm and let them be ornaments between your eyes. And write them upon the doorposts of your house and upon your gates.[11]

Judaism has most faithfully, and literally, followed these rules. The Jewish prayer repeating these very words about loving

God—the *Shema*—is the core statement of the Jewish creed and the most important prayer in Judaism. As commanded, Jews recite this prayer twice daily, before they lie down in the evening and after they rise in the morning. In addition, observant Jews fasten small boxes called *tefillin* on their arms and between their eyes every morning. These boxes contain the text of the Shema prayer. Observant Jews also affix a small case called a *mezuzah* to the doorposts and gates of their homes. The mezuzah likewise contains the text of the Shema prayer.

WE NOW ARRIVE at a third core Jewish concept which connects the commandment to love God with the commandment to love our fellow man. This key insight is provided in the beginning, in the very first chapter of the Bible's first book. Genesis relates that in making man, God was unusually explicit about his blueprint. "Let us make man in our image, in our likeness," God says. The narrator then relates that God carried out this plan: "God created man in his own image, in the image of God he created him."[12]

These short lines from Genesis contain within them what may well be the single most revolutionary idea in all of human history. This was the first declaration that every single human has an intrinsic value regardless of his status, wealth, or utility to society. The belief that we are created in God's image lifts us above all the animals, places us on a pedestal, and imbues us with inestimable worth. It is the foundation beneath all human rights.

This creation story not only establishes the supreme value of each human life, but also the equality of all humans. According to the Bible, the man that God created in his image—Adam—was the father of all humanity. This is a crucial point. Adam was not the first Jew. Nor was he the first Caucasian. He was the first man from whom all of the other people of the earth are descended. This means that every person on the planet shares equally this most sublime of human attributes.

The Bible actually goes to great lengths and much detail to emphasize this universality. Most modern readers of the Bible are immediately bored and baffled by the long genealogies interspersed in the text. Why the endless lists of who begat whom? Yet these genealogies serve at least one important purpose: they provide detailed support for the claim that Adam was indeed the first man from whom all other humans have descended. Centuries later, racist thinkers would struggle to find a way to escape the implications of universal equality which flow from the creation story. They would claim that certain "inferior" races were not descended from Adam but from lesser progenitors. Yet these ideas could never be fully reconciled with the Judeo-Christian tradition. The Bible is simply too specific.

Finally, the creation story makes clear that the "man" created in God's image was not just Adam and the males who would follow him. In what strikes many as a curious and poorly written passage, the Bible adds a third line to the two lines of the creation story we have already reviewed:

> God created man in his own image,
> In the image of God he created him;
> Male and female he created them.[13]

It is hard to imagine any reason for such an awkward formulation other than the obvious: the Bible is placing clarity above chronology. Even though Eve has yet to be created, the Bible is stressing that both men and women were created in the image of God and thus share all of the implications that flow from that origin. Any possibility that only the male of the species enjoys such a lofty provenance is eliminated at the outset.

This idea that all humans are created in the image of God requires that believers not only respect their fellow man, but love him. The powerful message at the heart of the creation story is that the closest any of us will come to seeing God in our lifetimes is when we look into our neighbor's eyes. If we love God completely, then this love will naturally extend to the most direct manifestations of God we encounter: our fellow men. Thus, through the creation story, the commandment to love God of which Jews are reminded throughout their every day becomes a prolific source of love for their fellow man.

Finally, when it comes to acting on this love of God, Judaism establishes mankind as the sole beneficiary. It is significant that in summarizing the essence of Judaism, both Hillel and Akiva focus entirely on loving our fellow man and neither mentions loving God. Both of these great rabbis were certainly well aware of the commandment to love God and its centrality to the Jewish faith. They are therefore understood to be teaching that the way to love God is to love the image of God incarnate: our fellow human beings.

Action in the Name of Love

The overriding commandment of Judaism is to love one another. But what exactly does this mean? Does thinking positive thoughts about our neighbors fulfill the commandment? A daily hug, perhaps?

As we've seen, Judaism sets the bar of love much higher. It demands not merely the emotion of love, but action in the name of that emotion. Judaism has, from its inception, been an unabashedly works-based faith. In the Jewish view of the world, what one believes or feels is of little ultimate consequence. It is important to have faith in God. It is good to study the Bible. But what truly matters is whether one acts on this faith and this knowledge to make the world a better place.

Yet Judaism does not command love as a general call to action which each individual can fulfill as he sees fit. For Jews, loving is far too serious a business to be left to individual discretion. In fact, the Torah sets forth a list of 613 commandments that Jews are expected to observe. This list includes 248 positive commandments, or acts that people must perform. The remaining 365 are negative commandments, or acts from which people must refrain. Yet whether positive or negative, almost all of these commandments focus on our actions. Very few tell us what we should think or how we should feel.*

As Hillel and Akiva stressed, every one of these commandments is meant to serve the ultimate goal of instructing us how to love our fellow man. This greater purpose is sometimes obvious, as in the case of the commandment that farmers not reap the corners of their fields so that food will be left for the poor. At other times the connection is more subtle, as with the commandment forbidding gossip. Still other commandments run counter to the popular perception of "love," such as the obligation to rebuke the sinner so that he will sin no more. "Tough love" is hardly a modern invention.

It is just such tough love that the Hebrew prophets provided to their people in abundance. The prophets recognized that their fellow Israelites were failing to observe these commandments and passionately pleaded with them to start doing so. Their overriding message was that words and rituals are irrelevant, even offensive, unless they are accompanied by loving actions. In the words of the prophet Amos:

> I hate, I despise your religious feasts,
> I cannot stand your assemblies.
> Even though you bring me burnt offerings and grain offerings,
> I will not accept them. . . .
> But let justice roll down like waters,
> And righteousness like a mighty stream.[14]

The prophets demanded a more compassionate society. They repeatedly urged their fellow Israelites to care for the most vulnerable among them: the widow, the orphan, and the stranger.

---

*The strongest suggestion that faith is central to Judaism is found in the writing of the Jewish scholar Maimonides. Maimonides wrote that the core tenets of Judaism include the belief that God gave man the Torah and the faith that the Messiah will one day come. Both of these beliefs would, of course, tend to have enormous implications for one's actions.

From the mouths of the Hebrew prophets came some of Western civilization's most fiery calls for social justice. But all along they were simply asking their fellow Jews to fulfill the commandment of love at the very core of their faith.

⟼

ACCORDING TO THE BIBLE, God chose the Jewish people and shared his law with them not only for their own good, but for the benefit of all humanity. Jewish theology has stressed from the outset that the Jews have a global mission. They are tasked with being such compelling role models of better living through God that their example will inspire the nations of the world to seek God and follow His laws. In the book of Genesis, God refers to this mission when he says to Abraham, "through you all the nations of the world will be blessed." The prophet Isaiah reminds the Jews of this responsibility when he stresses that God has called upon them to be "a light unto the nations."

The Jews originally did much to fulfill this global mission. At the time of Jesus's birth, Jews constituted between ten and fifteen percent of the population of the Roman Empire. Approximately eight million Jews lived not only in Judea, but also in Rome, Alexandria, and the Empire's other major cities.[15] Those Jews living outside of Judea generated great interest in their religion among their gentile neighbors. Many gentiles actually converted to Judaism. Many more were drawn to the Jewish faith but stopped short of formal conversion. Yet these "God-fearers," as they were called, studied with the Jews, attended their synagogues, and embraced their morality. Before the birth of Christianity, the Jewish idea was spreading rapidly.

Then, at least from the Jewish perspective, things fell apart. With the birth of Christianity, a rival emerged which would quickly eclipse Judaism in size and influence. For the God-fearers unwilling to make the leap into Judaism, Christianity offered a compelling alternative. Even many Diaspora Jews were drawn to this new faith which shared so much with their own. Once

Christianity was made the official religion in the Roman Empire in the late fourth century, it rapidly displaced paganism as the West's majority faith. As a consequence, Christianity became the primary vehicle by which the Jewish idea was transmitted to the West. In the words of Christian writer Paul Johnson:

> Ethical monotheism was an idea whose time had come. It was a Jewish idea. But the Christians took it with them to the wider world, and so robbed the Jews of their birthright.[16]

As Christianity gained momentum, some of its leaders and institutions embraced an anti-Judaism that developed into full-blown anti-Semitism. Faced with increasing persecution, the Jews of Christian lands could no longer safely or legally share their religion with their gentile neighbors. Instead, these Jews had to devote their full energies to simply keeping their faith alive. The Jewish "light unto the nations" was hidden behind doors shut tight against the mob.

Given these setbacks, it may appear that the Jews failed in their global mission. When viewed from a broader perspective, however, it is clear that the opposite is true. Today, the Jewish idea does in a very real sense light the world. Judaism's monotheism and morality have come to dominate vast expanses of the earth. It may not have happened in the way the Jews themselves originally foresaw or would have preferred. But out of Judaism grew two great faiths—Christianity and Islam—which have indeed spread the core Jewish concepts to billions across the globe. When it comes to the Western world—the focus of this book—Christianity has been a stunningly successful messenger of the Jewish idea.

Many Christians recognize the Jewish roots of their faith. They understand that Christianity was built on a foundation of Jewish texts and beliefs. They acknowledge that the morality they seek to share has a Jewish provenance. In fact, most Christians see their faith as the means by which Isaiah's words about being a "light unto the nations" are being fulfilled.

Jews have often had a harder time acknowledging Christianity as an ally in the spread of Jewish ideas. Especially during periods of Christian anti-Semitism, it was difficult indeed for Jews to see in Christianity a kindred religion of love. Yet over the centuries many Jews were able to look past such betrayals to recognize that Christianity was bringing the core Jewish message to the far corners of the globe. In the twelfth century, no less a figure than Maimonides wrote:

> All these teachings of Jesus the Nazarene and the Ishmaelite
> [Mohammed] who arose after him were intended to pave the
> way for the coming of King Messiah and to prepare the whole
> world to worship God together as one.... For by then, the
> world will already be filled with the idea of Messiah, and
> Torah, and commandments, even in far-off islands and in
> closed-hearted nations, where they engage in discussions on
> the Torah's commandments.[17]

After the Holocaust, Jewish-Christian relations entered a new era of mutual respect. In this more benign environment, Jewish leaders have been increasingly willing to acknowledge the role Christianity has played in disseminating the Jewish idea. Here is how one American Jewish leader, Rabbi Irving Greenberg, recently summarized this Christian achievement:

> Christians not only brought to billions of people the good
> news of the loving God of Israel who seeks the redemption of
> humans and the ethic/commandment to love your neighbor
> as yourself. Christian faith also brought the Bible and Jewish
> values and thinking to bear in the formation of Western civilization, thus magnifying Jewish importance manifold.
> Judaism's claim to be a world religion, and Jewry's self-understanding as a singled out people central to history, as well as
> planetary witnesses to God, would be far more marginal were
> it not for Christianity's teaching.[18]

The Christian Idea

The Jewish tradition is not alone in featuring probing questions from impatient interlocutors. The New Testament tells the story of a Pharisee who approaches Jesus and asks him, "Rabbi, which is the greatest commandment in the law?" The answer that Jesus gives closely parallels the responses of the great Jewish sages to similar questions. Jesus replies:

> Love the Lord your God with all your heart and with all your soul and with all your mind. This is the first and greatest commandment. And the second is like it: "Love your neighbor as yourself." All the law and the prophets hang on these two commandments.[19]

Here Jesus combines the central commandment of the Shema prayer—to love God—with the core commandment of Leviticus 19 and the golden rule—to love your neighbor—in a powerful summation of the Judeo-Christian idea. Like Hillel before him and Akiva after him, Jesus is saying that love is the ultimate goal of his faith toward which everything else leads.

Elsewhere in the Bible, Jesus summarizes his creed with a different formulation. "So in everything," Jesus tells his disciples, "do to others what you would have them do to you, for this sums up the law and the prophets."[20] Here Jesus's words are strikingly similar to those of Hillel and Akiva. Like these two great rabbis, who were his contemporaries,* Jesus is saying that we must express our love for our neighbors through our actions. He likewise reiterates the key insight that the commandment to love our fellow man subsumes within it every other commandment in the Bible, including even the commandment to love God.

Jesus's apostles rose to heights of eloquence in their efforts to place this commandment of love at the core of their nascent faith. The Apostle John, sometimes called the "apostle of love,"

---

*Hillel died in approximately 10 CE. Akiva was born in approximately 50 CE.

famously wrote of love in his letters to several early Christian congregations. "God is love," John wrote, adding that "whoever lives in love lives in God, and God in him."[21] John also stressed the connection between love of God and love of one's fellow man when he wrote:

> If anyone says, "I love God," yet hates his brother, he is a liar. For anyone who does not love his brother, whom he has seen, cannot love God, whom he has not seen.[22]

As the Apostle Paul preached Jesus's message to the gentiles, he consistently stressed the supreme importance of love. As Paul famously wrote to the church he planted in Corinth:

> If I speak in tongues of men and of angels, but have not love, I am only a resounding gong or a clanging cymbal. If I have the gift of prophecy and can fathom all mysteries and all knowledge, and if I have a faith that can move mountains, but have not love, I am nothing. If I give all I possess to the poor and surrender my body to the flames but have not love, I gain nothing.[23]

Later in this letter, Paul summarizes his point as follows: "And now these three remain: faith, hope and love. But the greatest of these is love."[24]

⁓

THERE ARE, OF COURSE, significant differences between Christianity and Judaism. The Jews still wait for their Messiah, while the Christians believe that he has already come. Jews believe that God is one indivisible entity, while Christians believe in one triune God. The two faiths differ markedly in their views on human nature, the nature of evil, the path to righteousness, the details of the afterlife, and a host of other issues.

Yet when we look beyond such issues to focus solely on the question of morality, these differences fade away. The fact is that Judaism and Christianity share moral codes which are identical in their fundamentals. Both Judaism and Christianity teach the sanctity and equality of all humans. Both Judaism and Christianity share a core commandment to love these fellow human beings. Both Judaism and Christianity assert that everything else they teach—all of their laws and commandments and rituals—are intended to further this ultimate goal of love. When we speak of the "Judeo-Christian idea," it is to these central principles that we refer. And when it comes to describing these core ideals, the adjective "Judeo-Christian" is not merely appropriate, it is imperative.

Christianity not only shares Judaism's core morality but has been a most effective marketer thereof. Jesus took the message of love from the Hebrew Bible and the Jewish sages and preached it with a sharp focus and a transformative passion. Jesus spread the Jewish idea of love not only with his eloquent words, but also by his sacrificial deeds. Jesus gave Jewish love a face and a narrative. In so doing, he led much of the world to embrace it.

Action in the Name of Love

Like Judaism, Christianity stresses the need to act in the name of the love that it preaches. In fact, Jesus provides some of the Bible's most compelling teachings on the centrality of compassionate action. Perhaps the most powerful of these passages is found in the book of Matthew. Here, Jesus sits with his disciples and describes for them the scene that will unfold when he returns to earth to judge the nations. Jesus tells them that he will gather all of the nations of the earth before him. He will then divide them up, sending the saved to sit on his right side and the damned to sit on his left. Using the royal third-person, Jesus reveals what he will say to the saved:

> Then the King will say to those on his right, "Come, you who are blessed by my Father; take your inheritance, the kingdom prepared for you since the creation of the world.

"For I was hungry and you gave me something to eat, I was thirsty and you gave me something to drink, I was a stranger and you invited me in, I needed clothes and you clothed me, I was sick and you looked after me, I was in prison and you came to visit me."

Then the righteous will answer him: "Lord, when did we see you hungry and feed you, or thirsty and give you something to drink? When did we see you a stranger and invite you in, or needing clothes and clothe you? When did we see you sick or in prison and go to visit you?"

The King will reply, "I tell you the truth, whatever you did for one of the least of these brothers of mine, you did it for me."[25]

Like the Hebrew prophets before him, Jesus is singling out action on behalf of society's most vulnerable as the highest expression of Judeo-Christian love.

Jesus's brother James later returned to this theme with his own passionate formulation. In a letter to his fellow Jewish believers in Jesus, James writes:

What good is it, my brothers, if a man claims to have faith but has no deeds? Can such faith save him? Suppose a brother or sister is without clothes and daily food. If one of you says to him, "Go, I wish you well; keep warm and well fed," but does nothing about his physical needs, what good is it? In the same way, faith by itself, if it is not accompanied by action, is dead.[26]

∿

CHRISTIANITY PROVIDES PERHAPS the ultimate example of action in the name of love in the story of the crucifixion of Jesus. As the Apostle John put it, "For God so loved the world that he gave his one and only Son, that whoever believes in him shall not perish but have eternal life."[27] Out of this same love, Jesus willingly went to the cross.

Yet in this very sentence about the significance of action, we also see a fundamental emphasis on *faith* that was never present in Judaism. Who shall have eternal life? Whoever *believes* in Jesus. In this one sentence, therefore, we find the tension between "faith" and "works" that has persisted in Christian theology ever since the crucifixion. This emphasis on faith has at times obscured the ongoing centrality of action to the Christian faith.

The promise of eternal life is bound up with the key Christian concept of "salvation." Christians believe that those who are "saved" will receive eternal life in the world to come. They also believe that the saved enjoy transformational benefits in this world: they enter into a personal relationship with Jesus, experience his unlimited love, and achieve an elusive peace. For Christians, salvation is the overriding goal and an all-encompassing priority.

When it comes to achieving salvation, Christianity makes faith a prerequisite. Almost all Christians believe that without faith in Jesus, there is no salvation, no entrée to heaven. Christians disagree, however, as to whether acts of charity and kindness—typically referred to as "works"—are also required for salvation. This is no mere academic question. It was a disagreement over this very issue that led Martin Luther to break with the Catholic Church and pave the way for Protestantism.

The prevailing Catholic and Eastern Orthodox belief is that salvation is the product of both faith and works. Faith may be a prerequisite for entering heaven, but faith alone won't get you there. Martin Luther took exception to this view. He believed that men are saved by faith and faith alone. Luther placed the doctrine of salvation by faith alone—*sola fide* in the Latin—at the center of what became Protestant theology. This key difference between Protestantism and Catholicism continues down to the present day.

Roman Catholics and other Christians who believe that salvation requires works as well as faith have a clear and compelling motive to act in this world. Whether or not they love their neighbors and care for society's most vulnerable will have a direct impact on their own lives, now and forever. For Protestants, however, the ongoing relevance of works has at times been less obvious. For those who believe in salvation by faith alone, this ultimate Christian goal is effectively delinked from action. Once such a Christian possesses the requisite faith, what motive remains for him to perform the commanded actions?

The Protestant theologian John Calvin offered an answer to this riddle when he described works as the "fruit" of salvation. Once Christians are saved, Calvin taught, their hearts are filled with love for their fellow man and this love is manifested through good works. He thus recognized good works as a consequence of salvation, not a prerequisite thereto.

In practice, this clear doctrinal line between cause and effect has tended to get blurred. Those seeking salvation have often sought its fruits with equal zeal. Indeed, as the sociologist Max Weber observed, the stakes of salvation are so high that many Christians long for confirmation that they are indeed among the saved. Such individuals thus have a powerful incentive to devote themselves to good works and other behaviors indicative of this desired state. Behaving like saved people becomes the best assurance they will ever have that they are, in fact, saved.[28]

Yet despite such doctrines, the Protestant focus on faith has at times engendered a suspicion of works. Many Protestant theologians, including Calvin himself, believed passionately that men are powerless to affect their own salvation. They came to fear that preaching the importance of works might create a "works righteousness" which blinded people to their absolute dependence upon God. Thus, while Protestantism has always retained the Christian focus on action, there have been periods when this message was purposely deemphasized.

Then, in the eighteenth century, evangelical Christianity swept through England and America. As this movement transformed Protestant life in these countries, it helped to restore the

Christian commandment of love to its rightful place at the heart of the faith.

Evangelical Love

Evangelical Christianity emerged in England and America through the uncoordinated efforts of a diverse group of thinkers and preachers. Yet history recognizes three men in particular as the fathers of the evangelical movement. John Wesley was an English churchman who spent considerable time preaching in America. George Whitefield, another Englishman, was nevertheless the leading evangelist of America's Great Awakening. And Jonathan Edwards of Massachusetts became the foremost American theologian of the era. These three men started a phenomenon that swept the English-speaking world and, eventually, the entire globe.

All three of these leaders preached and practiced good works. Two in particular—Wesley and Edwards—created a central space for such works in their theology. In the process, they put Christian love, and action in the name of this love, at the core of their nascent movement.

John Wesley's Holy Love

In 1729, a group of Oxford students started coming together for intense Christian fellowship. They devoted three hours every night to studying the Bible and the classics in Greek. They avoided parties, pubs and vice. They never missed church. Their classmates derisively called them the "Holy Club." The name stuck, and this band of students is remembered to this day as the "Oxford Holy Club."

From the outset, the members of the Oxford Holy Club dedicated themselves to fulfilling the commandment to love their neighbors. The students visited the sick and poor in the nearby villages and the prisoners in the local jails. They saved money by denying themselves the luxuries so enjoyed by their fellow students, from fancy clothes to running tabs at the local pub. They even fasted to keep their food costs low. They used these savings to provide food, clothing, and medicine to the people they met in their visits outside the university gates.

While it never exceeded twenty-seven members, the Oxford Holy Club launched the careers of some of the most important churchman in Protestant history. Three members in particular—John Wesley, his brother Charles, and George Whitefield—went on to preach with enormous success in England and America. Enjoying great gifts of charisma and leadership, they developed a following that turned into a movement, Methodism, which swept the English-speaking world. Methodism was the first evangelical movement in England. It is to this day one of the largest Protestant denominations in America.

Especially for John Wesley, the Holy Club's charitable activities were no mere outburst of youthful idealism. Wesley placed such active Christian love at the center of his growing ministry. For the rest of his life, Wesley continued to visit the sick, the poor, and the imprisoned and to devote himself to their care. When resources grew tight, Wesley's determination to continue his humanitarian efforts led him to become an early philanthropic innovator.

When he visited the sick, Wesley aspired to do more than pray for their recovery. Since he couldn't afford to pay doctors to accompany him on his rounds, he decided that he needed to learn enough to care for the sick himself. Wesley cobbled together the requisite skills by attending medical lectures and sitting long hours with local physicians and pharmacists. He also created London's first free medical dispensary.

When visiting the poor, Wesley wished to do more than give alms. Concluding that the best way to help those in economic distress was to find them jobs, Wesley started an employment service. When he couldn't find any job openings, Wesley simply created the jobs himself: he bought bales of cotton and employed women in processing and knitting. Wesley even pioneered the field of micro-credit, starting a fund to provide interest-free loans to the poor.

Even his visits to prisons left Wesley dissatisfied. He knew that his gifts of food, blankets, and clothes to the poorest of the prisoners would do little to offset the appalling conditions so prevalent in British prisons at the time. Wesley responded by becoming an early pioneer of prison reform.[29]

To motivate his flock to similar compassion and action, Wesley became a most eloquent apostle of love. Wesley stressed that true Christianity is "the love of God and all mankind."[30] He summarized Christianity's moral law as the "law of love, the holy love of God and of our neighbor."[31] He described God as "the great ocean of love."[32] Wesley stressed that:

In a Christian believer, love sits upon the throne, which is
erected in the inmost soul; namely, love of God and man,
which fills the whole heart, and reigns without a rival.[33]

Wesley emphasized that such love demanded action in its name. For Wesley, faith without works was "the grand pest of Christianity."[34] He urged his followers to:

Do all the good you can,
By all the means you can,
In all the ways you can,
In all the places you can,
At all the times you can,
To all the people you can
As long as ever you can.[35]

Wesley never abandoned his belief in salvation by faith alone. He simply found a way to integrate faith and works into a complete Christian whole in which works remained central. In the tradition of Calvin, Wesley maintained that once saved by faith, a Christian experienced the unlimited love of God poured into his heart. Now bursting with love for his fellow men, the believer would instinctively do good works for them. Thus while faith came first, good works would follow naturally and inevitably like fruit from a tree. In Wesley's formulation, the tension between faith and works is transformed into the most complementary of relations:

> O, when it comes to faith, what a living, creative, active, powerful thing it is. It cannot do other than good at all times. It never waits to ask whether there is some good work to do; rather, before the question is raised, it has done the deed, and keeps on doing it. A man not active in this way is a man without faith.[36]

Jonathan Edwards's Disinterested Benevolence

Jonathan Edwards is probably best remembered today for his sermon "Sinners in the Hand of an Angry God." In what has quite literally become a textbook example of fire-and-brimstone preaching, Edwards famously warned his congregants that "the God who holds you over the pit of hell, much as one holds a spider, or some loathsome insect, over the fire, abhors you."[37] So much for a loving God.

The real Jonathan Edwards bore little resemblance to this caricature. Edwards was the leading Christian theologian of his era. From his pulpit in New England he played a central role in the Great Awakening that transformed American Christianity in the mid-eighteenth century. And at his core, Jonathan Edwards was a champion of Christian love.

One of Edwards's most important works is a book entitled *The Nature of True Virtue.* Here Edwards wrote that Christians should view the key challenge of their lives as attaining "virtue." He then elaborated on what he meant by this term. "True virtue," he noted, "most essentially consists in benevolence to Being in general."[38] Throughout the work, Edwards equated "benevolence" with "love" and used these words interchangeably. Simply put, Edwards embraced love as the core Christian goal.

Centuries before the field of sociobiology was born, Edwards recognized its key insight. In *The Nature of True Virtue,* he noted that we all have an instinctive love for ourselves and those closest to us. He then clarified that the love he was urging is something far larger. True virtue, Edwards wrote, is "universal benevolence," the love of all humanity, regardless of proximity or utility.

When it comes to our narrow love of our own kith and kin, Edwards made a crucial point. He noted that such "private affection" for a closed circle of people is not only insufficient but actually "against general benevolence" and "of a contrary tendency." Such selfish love, Edwards explained, will cause one to favor certain individuals over others and thus "set a person against general existence and make him an enemy to it."[39] For Edwards, the task of transcending our selfish genes and broadening our zone of compassion was an urgent one.

❧

ONE OF JONATHAN EDWARDS'S most enthusiastic students, Samuel Hopkins, went on to become a leading theologian in his own right. Hopkins played a key role in systematizing Edwards's theology and spreading it to a broader audience. In the process, Hopkins helped to keep Edwards's concept of benevolence at the core of the growing evangelical movement. When it came to Christian love, Hopkins was a most zealous disciple.

Benevolence was so central to his system that Hopkins wrote his own book on the topic, *An Inquiry into the Nature of True Holiness*. Whereas Edwards defined the ultimate Christian goal as "virtue," Hopkins urged his readers to aspire to "holiness." Yet while the terms were different, their meaning was entirely the same. Hopkins equated holiness with love. Paraphrasing Jesus's answer to the question of which commandment is the greatest, Hopkins wrote that:

> all obedience to the law of God is reduced to one thing, LOVE, love to God and our neighbor, including ourselves; this is the whole that is required. Therefore this is the whole of true holiness; it consists in this love and nothing else.[40]

But any old love won't do. Like Edwards before him, Hopkins emphasized that the love he urges is *universal* love. Hopkins defined the love in which true holiness consists as follows:

> This is love to God and our neighbors, including ourselves; and is universal benevolence, or friendly affection to all intelligent beings. This universal benevolence, with all that affection or love which is included in it, and inseparable from it, is the holy love which God's law requires, and is the whole of true holiness.[41]

Like Edwards, Hopkins stressed that our instinctive love for ourselves and our small circle of intimates doesn't merely fall short of universal love, but inexorably sets one in opposition to it. Such self-love, he wrote, is "enmity against God" and is "the fruitful source of every exercise and act of impiety and rebellion against God." Hopkins warned that the self-loving man will turn against humanity as soon as his private good clashes with the universal good, as it inevitably will. Given his particular emphasis, Hopkins updated Edwards's formulation of "universal benevolence." The true Christian goal must be, in Hopkins's words, the exercise of "universal *disinterested* benevolence."

Hopkins stressed that any Christian seeking to practice disinterested benevolence should look toward its ultimate exemplar: Jesus. Jesus's love was so universal that it included even his enemies. His lack of self-love was so complete that he willingly sacrificed himself for the greater good of humanity. There is, with Hopkins, a feeling of closing the circle. The message and example of Jesus's love was always there. But now it was once again being placed front and center for a new generation of Christians who would go on to profoundly influence American history. It is under this banner of "universal disinterested benevolence" that the greatest American social movements would later form and march.

∼

SAMUEL HOPKINS WAS blessed with a long enough life that he was able to participate in two historic religious events. In the mid-eighteenth century, Hopkins was a stalwart of the First Great Awakening alongside his teacher Jonathan Edwards. Then, at the century's close, Hopkins contributed to the early stages of America's Second Great Awakening. Like its precursor, the Second Great Awakening was a dramatic religious revival that swept across America. Preaching in churches, under tents, or in open fields, charismatic churchmen inspired millions of Americans to embrace a more active and largely evangelical Christian faith. Yet unlike their predecessors decades earlier, the leaders of the Second Great Awakening preached and produced social activism on a prodigious scale. It was in this great outpouring of activism that the ideas of disinterested benevolence taught by Wesley, Edwards, and Hopkins found their full expression.

Yet the social engagement that characterized this revival was not fueled by memories of these prior teachers alone. Disinterested benevolence was placed at the center of the Second Great Awakening by its most influential preacher, Charles Grandison Finney. An attorney with little theological training, Finney overcame his academic liabilities with an oratorical force that transfixed and transformed his listeners. He would deeply influence the course of the Awakening and, through it, the nation.

Finney warmly embraced the Edwards-Hopkins doctrine of disinterested benevolence and made it his own. "The law of God," he stressed:

> requires perfect, disinterested, impartial benevolence, love to God and love to neighbor. It requires that we should be actuated by the same feeling, and to act upon the same principles that God acts upon; to leave self out of the question as uniformly as he does, to be as much separated from selfishness as he is.[43]

Like Edwards and Hopkins, Finney saw an enormous danger in our instinctive selfishness:

Let me say, selfishness in any form is in exact opposite to religion. It makes no difference as to the type which selfishness puts on. The question is does a man make his own interest the object of pursuit? If so, such conduct is the exact opposite of that benevolence which Christ manifested, when he laid himself out for the good of mankind and the glory of God. . . . Indeed, everywhere, both in the law and the gospel, religion— true religion—is presented to us as disinterested benevolence.[44]

Most of all, Finney stressed that disinterested benevolence meant action in the name of love. He encouraged Christians to make themselves "useful in the highest degree possible" by contributing their energy and their money to the pressing social causes of the day. He taught that:

if filled with the Spirit you will be useful . . . All preaching should be *practical*. . . . Anything brought forward as doctrine, which cannot be made use of as practical, is not preaching the gospel. . . . It is not the design of preaching, to make men easy and quiet, but to make them ACT.[45]

When it came to such action, Finney led by example. He went further than anyone else in linking the revivals of the Second Great Awakening with social action. One notable example involved Finney's embrace of the temperance movement, which was a popular evangelical response to the alcoholism so rampant among the era's poor and working classes. When he arrived in Rochester, New York, to hold a massive revival in 1830, Finney found himself in what must have felt like the belly of the beast. Rochester at this time was a grain-processing center that was home to some of the nation's largest distilleries and breweries. Yet rather than downplay what was bound to be an unpopular position, Finney chose to take his stand in the very heart of liquor country. At his Rochester revival, Finney went so far as to suspend regular preaching and evangelism to focus exclusively on a temperance campaign.[46] Social action had taken center stage.

⟶

THE LEADERS OF THE Second Great Awakening not only preached benevolence, but they also practiced what they preached by creating a "benevolent empire" of societies dedicated to taking action in fulfillment of Christian principles. Many of these societies focused on spreading the Christian faith. There were Bible societies to distribute Bibles, tract societies to distribute Christian literature, missionary societies to send Christian preachers to distant lands, and Sunday-school societies to better educate Christian youth. Other benevolent societies focused on social welfare and justice. Societies were founded to feed and clothe the poor, rescue and reform prostitutes, and rehabilitate prisoners. Reflecting the deep evangelical concerns about alcoholism at that time, temperance societies sprang up throughout the country.

As the nineteenth century progressed, however, this broadly diffused benevolent energy grew increasingly focused. The benevolent empire's massive network of organizations and activists provided the base from which arose a new movement dedicated to overcoming America's greatest evil. As we will see, the benevolent energies unleashed by the Second Great Awakening found their ultimate outlet in the American abolition movement.

God Is Love

On January 25, 2006, Pope Benedict XVI released his first encyclical. For new popes, the first encyclical provides an opportunity to identify what they believe to be the great challenge of their day and sound the grand themes of their pontificate. Pope John Paul II, for example, assumed his position at a time when the cold war still raged and factions within the Church were preaching a "liberation theology" that many considered tanta-mount to Communism. Thus Benedict's predecessor used his first encyclical to declare that true liberation was to be found not through Communism or its cousins, but through the Catholic Church.

It is thus of enormous significance that Pope Benedict chose to devote his first encyclical to the topic of love. The strong implication is that the pope has identified love—or the lack thereof—as a key challenge of our time. His response, an encyclical entitled *God Is Love,* seeks to meet this challenge by reminding the Church and the world that love is Christianity's core value.

Pope Benedict takes the title of his encyclical from the First Epistle of John. As we saw earlier, John wrote that "God is love, and he who abides in love abides in God, and God abides in him." Commenting on John's formulation, Benedict writes: "These words . . . express with remarkable clarity the heart of the Christian faith: the Christian image of God and the resulting image of mankind and its destiny."[47]

What follows is a remarkable discourse on the importance and the meaning of Christian love. Benedict recognizes at the outset that "in acknowledging the centrality of love, Christian faith has retained the core of Israel's faith."[48] He spends a good portion of his analysis noting the "unbreakable bond" between love of God and love of one's neighbor. In Benedict's words, "love of neighbor is a path that leads to the encounter with God," while "closing our eyes to our neighbor also blinds us to God."[49]

Benedict also highlights the fact that true love is manifested in action on behalf of our fellow man. In fact, he devotes the second section of this two-part encyclical to what he calls "The Practice of Love." Benedict opens this section by quoting St. Augustine's pithy formulation, "If you see charity, you see the Trinity."[50] Benedict then declares unequivocally:

> Love for widows and orphans, prisoners, and the sick and needy of every kind is as essential to her [the Church] as the

ministry of the sacraments and preaching of the Gospel. The Church cannot neglect the service of charity any more than she can neglect the sacraments and the Word.[51]

Benedict ends his encyclical with a powerful summation of Christian love:

> Love is the light—and in the end, the only light—that can always illuminate a world grown dim and give us the courage needed to keep living and working. Love is possible, and we are able to practice it because we are created in the image of God. To experience love and in this way cause the light of God to enter into the world—this is the invitation I would like to extend.[52]

Like John Paul II before him, Pope Benedict has clearly recognized the great challenge of his times. Communism has been defeated and liberation theology largely abandoned. Today, the great challenges facing the West are more private than public. We are increasingly turning inward, cutting our social ties, shrinking our circles down to their barest biological base. We "bowl alone," and when we lock ourselves into our homes at night we no longer read the same books or even watch the same television programs as our neighbors.

Our selfish genes are at it again, forever narrowing our zone of altruism and attachment. So far, this most recent constriction has produced not a focused antipathy but merely a vague apathy. We are not targeting any particular outgroup as the scapegoat for our discontent. Yet, ironically, there is an undeniable and escalating anger being directed toward the primary source of the very transcendence so many seek: the Judeo-Christian tradition. Christianity, Judaism, and religious faith in general are increasingly being stereotyped as the cause of the world's hate rather than as antidotes to it. In such an environment, Pope Benedict's reminder of the ideas at the core of the Judeo-Christian tradition could not be more urgent.

∼

THIS CHAPTER HAS focused on the Judeo-Christian theology of love. It is an impressive literature. The rhetoric soars and the words touch the heart. Yet no matter how prolific or poignant, such loving prose is largely meaningless if it fails to inspire action in the world.

Reasonable people can differ as to whether there is a God and whether this God gave man the Bible. But when it comes to what people who believe in God and the Bible actually do in the world, we move beyond questions of faith to questions of fact. There is an historical record that can provide objective answers.

The thesis of this book is that the Judeo-Christian tradition has been the primary means by which Westerners have been able to rise above their impoverished genetic morality and make ethical progress. Few other Western ideologies have shared the Judeo-Christian emphasis on universal love, and no others have been able to inspire sustained action in the name of this love. To the truth of this proposition, the pages of history provide the most eloquent of testimony. It is to this testimony that we now turn.

THREE

The Judeo-Christian Idea Against Genocide

Aristotle, farewell! From Christ, the eternal truth, we have the commandment "You must love your neighbor as yourself."[1]

—BARTOLOME DE LAS CASAS, DOMINICAN FRIAR

OF ALL THE CRIMES perpetrated by man, genocide is the most evil. And of all the genocides perpetrated by man, the largest in absolute terms occurred neither in Europe nor in Africa, but right here in America. Only in America were so many entire nations completely wiped out. And only in America were so many others reduced to tiny, dispossessed remnants. Like so many things in America, our genocide was of truly continental proportions.

In contrast to the conventional wisdom, pre-Columbian America was not a sparsely populated land waiting forlornly to be "discovered" by Europeans. To the contrary: the America to which Columbus first sailed had a population which *exceeded* that of Europe. Recent studies have estimated that the population of the Americas on the eve of Columbus's arrival was somewhere between seventy-five and one-hundred million,[2] while Europe's population was between sixty and seventy million.[3] The population of central Mexico alone—approximately twenty-five million souls—was seven times larger than the population of England.[4]

Fifty years later, there were only ten million American Indians left.[5] The other tens of millions had been killed off by war, massacres, disease, and slavery.* While this initial half-century of conquest claimed the largest number of Indian victims, the decimation continued until late in the nineteenth century. By the twentieth century, Europeans had killed close to 100 million American Indians.[6]

When we narrow our focus from the continental to the regional, the data is equally startling. In Central Mexico, the Aztec Empire's pre-Columbian population of close to twenty-five million was reduced by almost ninety-five percent, to 1.3 million, by the close of the sixteenth century. In South America, the Inca Empire's pre-invasion population of nine million plummeted to fewer than half a million by the end of the century.[7] The island of Hispaniola (currently divided between Haiti and the Dominican Republic) had a population of approximately eight million when Columbus first landed on its shores. By 1508, the island's Indian population had plummeted to fewer than one hundred thousand. By 1535, it had been completely wiped out.[8]

Genocide in Latin America

In his account of the Spanish conquest of the Americas, Friar Bartolome de Las Casas tells the story of an Indian chief from the island of Hispaniola, which had the misfortune of being

---

*Epidemics of European diseases against which the Indians had no antibodies were major factors in the collapse of Indian populations. Yet the role of these diseases is often discussed in a way that removes all responsibility from the Europeans who first introduced them. It is important to stress, therefore, that these diseases were introduced in conjunction with the European conquest, enslavement, and starvation of the Indians, which left the native population exceptionally weak and vulnerable to disease. Without these intentional assaults, it is doubtful that the unintentional epidemics would have done nearly as much damage.

Spain's first New World conquest. To escape the massacres and enslavement that befell the island's other tribes, the chief fled with his people to the neighboring island of Cuba. When the Spanish landed in Cuba years later, the chief called together his people to warn them of the great troubles that were coming their way.

Waxing philosophical, the chief tried to explain to his tribe why the Spanish were so bloodthirsty. "They have a God whom they worship and adore," he told them, "and it is in order to get that God from us so they can worship Him that they conquer and kill us." As he spoke, the chief was standing beside a basket filled with gold. He gestured toward the basket and finished his point: "Here is the God of the Christians."[9]

This chief saw more clearly than many Spaniards what drove their conquests and their cruelty. The Spanish naturally sought rationalizations for their behavior. They invoked both philosophy and religion to excuse their deeds. But underneath these cover stories, human greed was the mighty engine that drove their crimes in the New World. And for the Spanish in this time and place, greed took the form of a mad hunt for gold.

This lust for gold was only thinly veiled, and often quite explicit. When he was pitching his earliest expeditions to King Ferdinand and Queen Isabella, Columbus stressed to the cash-poor monarchs that he expected to find abundant supplies of gold across the ocean. Columbus recognized that the men joining him on his expeditions shared similar objectives. He wrote of his compatriots that "owing to the greed for gold, everyone will prefer to seek it rather than engage in other necessary occupations."[10] In his account of the Spanish conquest, Las Casas reached a similar conclusion about his fellow Spaniards:

> The reason the Christians have murdered on such a vast scale
> and killed anyone and everyone in their way is purely and
> simply greed. They have set out to line their pockets with gold
> and to amass private fortunes as quickly as possible so that

they can assume a status quite at odds with that into which they were born. Their insatiable greed and overweening ambition knows no bounds.[11]

The Spanish invaders enjoyed an enormous military advantage over the Indians. There was therefore little standing between them and their goal of gold. It is in the presence of such an imbalance of power that human avarice can find its full expression. With neither fear nor defeat to stop them, the Spanish proceeded to destroy an entire world in their quest for gold.

IN THIS TIME OF untrammeled greed, the only people to rise in defense of the Indians were devout Christians inspired by the Judeo-Christian idea. Only religious Christians were able to look beneath the superficial differences of skin color, language, and culture to see in the Indian neither a savage nor a slave, but a brother. And only religious Christians were able to transcend their selfish genes in the face of temptations of the most corrupting kind to place the welfare of these brothers above their own.

The fact that the Indians' only defenders were religious Christians does not mean that all religious Christians defended the Indians. Far from it. During the Spanish conquest of America, even Christian clergy were subject to overwhelming pressure to compromise their principles. Those churchmen who were willing to excuse the conquistadors' behavior, or at least not obstruct it, were embraced by their communities and given the opportunity to accumulate life-changing wealth. Those who insisted on being true to their Christian ideals could expect only relentless attacks on their careers and even their lives. Under these circumstances, only a minority of the faithful were able to rise above their self-interest and live up to the high ideals of their creed. Thus it has always been in challenging times.

Antonio de Montesinos

On the Sunday before Christmas, 1511, a Dominican friar named Antonio de Montesinos ascended to the pulpit of the first church built in the first Spanish settlement in the New World. Before him sat an unusually sin-stained flock. The settlement on Hispaniola was a frontier community more rugged than anything the American West would later produce. The conquistadors who made their way to the New World were a callous crew of ex-soldiers, ex-convicts, and assorted failures from various fields of endeavor back in Spain. These men were united by only their greed for gold and their willingness to stop at nothing to acquire it. The ongoing massacre of the island's Indians and the enslavement of the survivors had already provided bloody testimony to the power of self-interest to trump morality and mercy.

The congregation had been told that an important sermon would be delivered that morning. The colonists thus packed the church, no doubt expecting to hear a theological rationalization of their crimes that would salve whatever conscience they had left. But no such absolution was forthcoming. What the colonists heard instead was a passionate Christian voice calling upon them to live up to the Judeo-Christian idea. Montesinos got right to the point:

> In order to make your sin against the Indians known to you I have come up on this pulpit, I who am the voice of Christ crying in the wilderness of this island, and therefore it behooves you to listen, not with careless attention, but with all your heart and senses, so that you may hear it; for this is going to be the strangest voice that ever you heard, the harshest and the hardest and most awful and most dangerous that you ever expected to hear....
>
> This voice says that you are in mortal sin, that you live and die in it, for the cruelty and tyranny you use in dealing with these innocent people. Tell me, by what right or justice do you

keep these Indians in such a cruel and horrible servitude? On what authority have you waged a detestable war against these people, who dwelt quietly and peacefully on their own land? ...

Why do you keep them so oppressed and weary, not giving them enough to eat nor taking care of them in their illness? For with the excessive work you demand of them they fall ill and die, or rather you kill them with your desire to extract and acquire gold every day.[12]

And then, in this straw hut of a church that served as the outpost of the Judeo-Christian idea in the lawless New World, Montesinos set forth the core of his ancient creed. Echoing the words of Hillel, Jesus, and Akiva in this distant and dangerous place, Montesinos made the following plea on behalf of the Indians:

Are these Indians not men? Do they not have rational souls? Are you not obliged to love them as you love yourselves?[13]

～

HISTORY RECORDS THAT the men who heard Montesinos that morning neither stopped their conquests nor freed their slaves. Instead, an angry mob of conquistadors left the church and marched directly to the Dominican monastery. There they confronted the local vicar, Pedro de Cordoba, and demanded that Montesinos be expelled from the island for what he had said.

But Montesinos had not acted alone. Led by Cordoba, all of the colony's Dominican clergymen had agreed that the time had come to stop the atrocities they witnessed daily. They had drafted the sermon as a group; Montesinos was merely the messenger. Cordoba told the conquistadors that he would neither expel nor discipline the friar. He promised only that Montesinos would preach on the same topic the following Sunday. Presuming that they would be hearing a retraction in a week's time, the mob left in peace.

When Montesinos rose to the pulpit the following Sunday, however, he not only defended his prior sermon but gave it the sharpest of teeth. He told the assembled crowd that he and the other friars would no longer receive them for confession or absolution of their sins so long as they continued to massacre or enslave the Indians.[14] For the believer, there are few penalties more severe; the denial of these rites threatened eternal damnation. Eventually, most of the Dominican clergy throughout the New World instituted this policy of denying confession to anyone who owned Indian slaves.*

WHATEVER THEIR FAILURES back in Spain, the conquistadors were the lords of all they surveyed in the New World. They had dreamt of gold, and they were living their dream. But they also wanted God—or at least the moral balm of a god who was blind to their sins. The conquistadors refused to let this small band of Dominicans deny them their moral sanction. They quickly sent a delegation to Spain to denounce Montesinos as a heretic. Montesinos responded by returning to Spain to refute the charges and request the outright abolition of Indian slavery.

Upon arriving in Spain, Montesinos requested and received an audience with King Ferdinand. He was determined to inform the king of the excesses being committed in his name across the ocean. The king had no doubt heard all about the conquistadors' repeated victories in battle, and he had certainly received his share of the unparalleled riches they were accumulating as a consequence. But before Montesinos it is likely that no one had ever detailed the price being paid for this treasure in Indian blood. Montesinos exposed the dark side of the gold rush.

---

*Not all Dominicans played such an honorable role. A leading friar named Domingo de Betanzos was for many years a prominent proponent of the view that the American Indians were unredeemable "beasts" incapable of Christianity and unworthy of human rights. He later recanted these views on his deathbed in a Dominican monastery.

Montesinos's intervention was astonishingly effective. Despite the powerful interests and vast fortunes arrayed against him, the cleric convinced the king that unacceptable atrocities were being perpetrated in America and must be stopped. In 1512, King Ferdinand extended royal protection to the American Indians by promulgating the Laws of Burgos. These laws limited the number of hours that Indians could be forced to work and required that they be provided with sufficient food, clothing, and beds.[15] They further stipulated that "no one may beat or whip or call an Indian 'dog' or any other name unless it is his proper name."[16]

The outcome of Montesinos's efforts to lobby the king set a precedent that would be repeated for years to come. The king was naturally reluctant to cut off a boundless new source of wealth by halting Spain's advance in the New World or denying his subjects Indian labor. Yet to a surprising extent he and his successors were also unwilling to ignore the humanitarian and theological concerns raised by the Indians' Christian defenders. Thus while Spain's kings never stopped the process of colonization for very long, they repeatedly sought to regulate the conquests and protect the Indians.

The Vatican

As significant as they were, the Laws of Burgos failed to stop the murder and mistreatment of the Indians. In response to these ongoing abuses, another Dominican friar, Bernardino de Minaya, eventually followed Montesinos's lead and returned to Spain from the New World to lobby for additional protection for the Indians. By this time—the mid-1530s—the king had delegated the administration of his American colonies to a body called the Council of the Indies. So it was before this body that Minaya appeared.

Minaya received a chilly reception. Since the Council's creation, the conquistadors had been aggressively lobbying for the repeal of the Laws of Burgos. To rebut the Dominicans' Bible-based attack on Indian slavery, the conquistadors invoked classical philosophy. They were particularly fond of Aristotle, who, as we will see, had elaborated a detailed theory to justify the Greek practice of enslaving their supposedly less-rational neighbors. Applying this theory to the New World, the conquistadors claimed that the Indians were an inferior breed of men who lacked the rationality of Europeans. Such people, they asserted, were incapable of self-rule and were therefore intended by nature to be conquered and enslaved.

During this period, the Italian Renaissance was restoring classical philosophy to a position of prestige throughout southern Europe. By the time Minaya arrived in Spain, most of the members of the Council of the Indies were more enamored with Aristotle than with the Bible. They refused to act on the Indians' behalf. Alarmed by their apathy, Minaya resolved to go over their heads. He set out for Rome on foot to petition Pope Paul III.[17]

At about the time that Friar Minaya was walking to Rome, the pope received a letter from Bishop Julian Garces, another Dominican living in America. Garces had lived and worked with the Indians for over ten years. In his letter, Garces invoked his first-hand experience to directly confront the Aristotelian claim that the Indians were an inferior breed of men destined for servitude. He informed the pope that the Indians possessed an advanced culture and great aptitude, noting specifically that Indian children wrote Latin and Spanish better than Spanish children. Garces assured the pope that the Indians are "justly called rational," "completely intelligent," and "possessed of judgment."[18] He dismissed arguments to the contrary as:

> truly the voice of Satan, determined that our religion and honor shall be destroyed, but this is a voice which comes from the avaricious throats of Christians, whose greed is such that in order to slake their thirst for wealth they insist that rational creatures made in the image of God are beasts and asses.[19]

Minaya and Garces were neither well-heeled nor well-connected. Neither man had spent time in the corridors of power in Rome or the halls of study in Europe's leading seminaries. Both were simple country preachers who had gone to great lengths to challenge the fashionable theories of their day regarding Indian inferiority. And when confronted with their views, the pope wasted little time in taking their side. In 1537, Pope Paul III issued a landmark bull entitled *Sublimis Deus.* Here the pope officially recognized the Indians' humanity and rationality, writing:

> We ... consider . . . that the Indians are truly men and that they are not only capable of understanding the Catholic faith but, according to our information, they desire exceedingly to receive it.[20]

Having rejected the theoretical basis upon which some had justified Indian slavery, the pope proceeded to prohibit such slavery in the clearest of terms:

> Notwithstanding whatever may have been or may be said to the contrary, the said Indians and all other peoples who may later be discovered by Christians are by no means to be deprived of their liberty or the possession of their property, even though they are outside the faith of Jesus Christ; and that they may and should, freely and legitimately, enjoy their liberty and the possession of their property; nor should they be in any way enslaved; should the contrary happen it shall be null and of no effect.[21]

With this bull, Pope Paul III elevated the arguments of a small band of Christian human-rights activists to the status of Christian canon law. It was an unequivocal triumph.

Yet as dramatic as this declaration was, it did little to stop the genocide still ongoing in America. The Vatican simply lacked the power to enforce its edicts. As author Rodney Stark has noted, "The problem wasn't that the Church failed to condemn slavery;

it was that few heard and most of them did not listen."[22] Men with treasure in their grasp rarely pause for theology.

⟶

WITH THE FAILURE of this victory at the Vatican to change the facts on the ground in America, the Indians' Christian defenders returned their focus to the seat of temporal power: the Spanish court. In the years that followed, Christian clerics and thinkers repeatedly lobbied Spain's kings and the Council of the Indies to outlaw Indian slavery and provide greater protection to these persecuted people. This historic effort was led by a slaveholder turned Dominican friar named Bartolome de Las Casas.

Bartolome de Las Casas

In 1502, Bartolome de Las Casas arrived in the New World to seek his fortune. As his ship arrived in the port of Hispaniola, settlers ran down to the docks to ask for the latest news from Spain. The passengers aboard the boat responded with their own questions about what awaited them onshore. One of the settlers enthusiastically reported, "Found a big hunk of gold, and there's a great war going on, get us a lot of slaves. Great stuff!"[23] Thus even before he first stepped foot in Spain's American colonies, Las Casas was introduced to their dominant ethos.

At first, Las Casas pursued conquest, slaves, and fortune like almost all of his fellow countrymen. But little by little, his thinking began to change. He was almost certainly in church the day Montesinos first preached on the humanity of the Indians. Years later, after he had moved to the island of Cuba, Las Casas was himself denied confession by a Dominican implementing Montesinos's policy of refusing absolution to slaveholders. Las Casas eventually sailed back to Europe, studied theology, and entered the clergy. Yet even when he returned to the New World as a priest, he did not immediately free his slaves or protest the treatment of the Indians.

As Las Casas related in an autobiographical sketch, his transformation from slaveholder to abolitionist was finally triggered
by reading the Bible. While preparing an Easter sermon in 1514,
he found himself focusing on the following passage from the
book of Ecclesiasticus:[24]

> Unclean is the offering sacrificed by an oppressor. [Such]
> mockeries of the unjust are not pleasing [to God]. The Lord is
> pleased only by those who keep to the way of truth and justice.
> The Most High does not accept the gifts of unjust people, He
> does not look well upon their offerings. Their sins will not be
> expiated by repeat sacrifices.
>
> The one whose sacrifice comes from the goods of the poor
> is like one who kills his neighbor. The one who sheds blood
> and the one who defrauds the laborer are kin and kind.[25]

Las Casas wrote that this particular formulation of the Judeo-
Christian idea finally pierced his hardened shell of self-interest.
He was suddenly overwhelmed by memories of all the atrocities
he had witnessed and all the anti-slavery preaching he had
ignored. At once, the implications of his creed became clear to
him. Las Casas freed his slaves, returned his land holdings to the
governor, and joined the Dominican order that had so distinguished itself in its opposition to Indian slavery.[26] He would
devote the rest of his life to fighting for justice for the American
Indian.

At first, Las Casas tried to protect the Indians through
preaching. He also implemented the Dominican policy of refusing absolution to colonists who enslaved or otherwise mistreated
Indians.* When these efforts failed to make a difference, Las

---

*Early in his career, Las Casas proposed the introduction of African slaves to the New
World to spare the Indians such heavy labor. Yet once he learned that these Africans
were also unjustly captured and enslaved, he abandoned this view. For the rest of his
life, Las Casas was a vocal opponent of both Indian and African slavery. See Francis
Patrick Sullivan, *Indian Freedom: The Cause of Bartolome de Las Casas* (Kansas City,
MO: Sheed & Ward, 1995), 159–165.

Casas changed his tactics. Like devout Christians before and after him, Las Casas realized that he needed to take his faith and his morality outside church walls and into the corridors of power. We remember Las Casas today because he became—for lack of a better term—a full-time lobbyist on behalf of the Indians.

ᘙ

EARLY ON, LAS CASAS realized that the greatest problem he faced in defending the Indians was a vast information gap. Most Spaniards simply had no idea that the Indians were being mistreated, let alone systematically destroyed. Thus Las Casas threw himself into the project of chronicling all that had befallen the Indians since Columbus first landed in the New World. In 1539, Las Casas published his work under the title *A Short Account of the Destruction of the Indies.* He dedicated the book to one of the people he most hoped to influence, Spain's Prince Phillip II.* At about the same time, Las Casas returned to Spain and devoted most of the years that followed to advocating for greater protection of the Indians at the king's court and before the Council of the Indies.

Through the impact of the *Short Account* and his perpetual lobbying, Las Casas eventually won an astonishing victory. In 1542, King Charles V issued a series of laws providing the Indians with revolutionary new rights and protections. These "New Laws" stipulated that no additional Indians could be enslaved under any circumstances. They required that any Indians illegally held as slaves be immediately released. And they provided that all legally held slaves be freed upon the death of their cur-

---

*The *Short Account* was both a work of history and a piece of political propaganda. It was intended to rouse Spain's leaders from their ignorance of and apathy toward the Indian genocide. The book is now believed to exaggerate some numbers and embellish certain stories. Yet it is still a most valuable guide to the disaster it chronicles.

rent owner. Free Indians were to become Spanish subjects equal in legal status to the conquistadors themselves.[27] The countdown to a radical transformation of Spain's American colonies had begun.

Decades earlier, the conquistadors had refused to suffer a sermon that offended them. They were certainly not going to accept laws which, if implemented, would cripple their ability to acquire wealth and bequeath it to their children. The colonists immediately sent representatives to Spain to lobby for the repeal of the New Laws. These lobbyists came armed with the carrot of bribes and the stick of threatened rebellions. They also engaged on an intellectual level, and came prepared with fashionable philosophical arguments to support their position.

Any celebrations over the passage of the New Laws were thus short-lived. Outraged colonists immediately protested to the king, and a band of conquistadors staged an armed revolt in Peru that overthrew the king's viceroy. By 1545, the colonists and their allies had secured the repeal of key provisions of this legislation, including the sections that would have phased out slavery. Feeling that the momentum had shifted to their side, the colonists now pressed their advantage and sought passage of a law which would grant them perpetual title to their land and slaves. Las Casas and his allies mounted a vigorous opposition.

The Dispute at Valladolid

Eventually, King Charles despaired of resolving the competing claims before him. He instead resorted to the favorite tool of leaders facing intractable issues: the commission. On April 16, 1550, the king appointed a panel of fourteen theologians, jurists, and scholars to review the legality of Spain's conquests and behavior in the New World. This body met in Valladolid, and the disputation that took place there is best known by the name of this town.

After appointing this commission, King Charles issued a second decree that exhibited far more courage. He ordered that all Spanish conquests in the New World be suspended until the Valladolid commission ruled on their legality. As historian Lewis Hanke has noted:

> Probably never before, or since, has a mighty emperor—and
> in 1550 Charles V, Holy Roman Emperor, was the strongest
> ruler in Europe, with a great overseas empire besides—
> ordered his conquests to cease until it was decided if they were
> just.[28]

Las Casas was asked to make the case against the conquest and enslavement of the Indians before the commission in Valladolid. A leading philosopher and scholar named Juan Gines de Sepulveda was asked to present the arguments in favor of continued conquest and slavery.

The commission's proceedings began in August 1550 and continued for almost a month. There are no transcripts of the sessions at Valladolid. Yet in addition to whatever oral arguments they made before the commission, both Las Casas and Sepulveda distributed book-length versions of their views in an effort to influence the judges, the monarchs, and the ruling classes in general. These manuscripts survive, and thus we know to a large extent the case made by each side.

Sepulveda's Argument

Sepulveda seemed to agree with the Dominicans and the pope that the Bible did not sanction the wholesale conquest and enslavement of the Indians. Unlike apologists for American slavery centuries later, Sepulveda did not rest his defense of Indian slavery on the Bible. Instead he based his argument primarily upon the philosophy of Aristotle.

Sepulveda was uniquely positioned to bring classical thought to bear on the great issues of his time. He was a leading Renaissance scholar and humanist thinker, and he was quite likely the foremost living expert on the philosophy of Aristotle. Shortly before the disputation at Valladolid, in fact, Sepulveda had completed the monumental task of translating Aristotle's *Politics* into Latin.

It is in his *Politics* that Aristotle set forth in greatest detail his theory of natural slavery. In Aristotle's view, all men were most definitely not created equal. He argued instead that humanity could be divided into two broad groups. One group, which included the Greeks, consisted of men who were endowed with strong powers of reason and could use this reason to control their passions. Aristotle asserted that such people were meant to govern themselves and others. Lower on the ladder were men who lacked such rationality and were thus ruled by their passions. Aristotle concluded that these people were "natural born slaves" who were intended by nature to serve their more rational superiors.

Sepulveda's core argument was that the American Indians—all of them—were barbarians lacking in reason who therefore fit into Aristotle's category of "natural born slaves." He supported this assertion by citing the most sensational accounts about some Indians as scientific truths applying to all Indians. He wrote with horror of the Indians' "incredible sacrifices of human beings, their horrible banquets of human flesh, and their impious worship of idols." In some passages, he accused the Indians of being bloodthirsty warriors who never tired of battle. Elsewhere, he criticized them for being cowards "who fled like women" from the Spanish conquistadors.

On the basis of this collection of exaggeration and stereotypes, Sepulveda rendered the following fateful judgment of the Indians:

> In wisdom, skill, virtue and humanity, these people are as inferior to the Spaniards as children are to adults and women to

men; there is as great difference between them as there is between savagery and forbearance, between violence and moderation, almost—I am inclined to say—as between monkeys and men.[29]

Applying Aristotle's theory, Sepulveda went on to conclude that these inferior Indians required:

by their own nature and in their own interests, to be placed under the authority of civilized and virtuous princes or nations, so that they may learn from the might, wisdom, and law of their conquerors to practice better morals, worthier customs and a more civilized way of life.[30]

In other words, Sepulveda claimed, it was in the best interests of the Indians that the Spanish conquer and enslave them.

What is perhaps most shocking about Sepulveda's position is the fact that he had never set foot in America and most likely had never met an Indian. With a stunning disregard for objective facts, Sepulveda was willing to condemn the people of an entire hemisphere to perpetual slavery on the basis of second-hand accounts. Even worse, it appears that Sepulveda relied almost exclusively upon the reports of one Indian critic—a man who once made his living branding Indian slaves[31]—while completely ignoring the numerous reports coming from more objective observers describing the high level of Indian art, architecture, language, and government.

Thus Sepulveda's conclusions flowed from an unhappy marriage of fashionable philosophy and stunningly unscientific fact-finding. It was a most perilous precedent. Centuries later, European philosophers would once again join bad ideas with sloppy science to reach similarly dangerous conclusions about the inferiority of other peoples. These modern racists would, like Sepulveda before them, provide the philosophical justification for genocide in their time.

Las Casas Responds

It has long been recognized that Western civilization is the product of two primary cultural streams, one with its source in Athens and the other with its source in Jerusalem. In fact, Western culture has mixed classical philosophy with Judeo-Christian morality so thoroughly that it is often difficult to trace the roots of certain of our most cherished ideals. At Valladolid, however, the contrast between Athens and Jerusalem was on clear display. Sepulveda drew his arguments almost entirely from the ideas of Athens. Las Casas responded by invoking the morality of Jerusalem.

Las Casas refuted Sepulveda's claim of Indian inferiority by citing the core principles of the Judeo-Christian idea. Las Casas emphasized that:

> if we want to be sons of Christ and followers of the truth of
> the gospel, we should consider that, even though these peoples
> may be completely barbaric, they are nevertheless created in
> God's image.... They are our brothers, redeemed by Christ's
> most precious blood, no less than the wisest and most learned
> men in the whole world.[32]

Unlike Sepulveda, Las Casas had lived in the New World and had worked closely with Indians. He was therefore able to buttress his theological position with first-hand observations. Drawing from his years of experience, Las Casas argued that the Indians not only met Aristotle's criteria for rationality, but possessed intellects that were in many ways superior to those of the Greeks, the Romans, and the Spaniards themselves.

Having established Indian humanity, Las Casas reminded his readers how they must treat these fellow human beings. Invoking the golden rule of Hillel, Jesus, and Akiva, Las Casas stressed that:

> we are commanded by divine law to love our neighbor as our-
> selves, and since we want our own vices to be corrected and

uprooted gently, we should do the same to our brothers, even if they are barbarians.[33]

That Las Casas had a low opinion of Aristotle is clear throughout his discourse. Earlier in his life, Las Casas had described Aristotle as "a pagan now burning in Hell, whose principles should be accepted only insofar as they conform to our Christian religion."[34] While he had tempered his critique over the years, Las Casas directly confronted Aristotle and his theory of natural slavery:

> Therefore, although the Philosopher, who was ignorant of Christian truth and love, writes that the wise may hunt down barbarians in the same way as they would wild animals, let no one conclude from this that barbarians are to be killed or loaded like beasts of burden with excessive, cruel, hard and harsh labor and that, for this purpose, they can be hunted and captured by wiser men.[35]

Las Casas closed his argument with a dramatic rejection of classical philosophy in favor of his Christian creed:

> Good-bye, Aristotle! From Christ, the eternal truth, we have the command "You must love your neighbor as yourself."[36]

∽

FOR ALL PRACTICAL purposes, Las Casas and Sepulveda debated each other to a draw. The Valladolid commission never issued a decision. The panel seemed to shrink from instructing the king to forever cease his New World conquests. But while Las Casas did not win any immediate victories, his performance at Valladolid held the line against further erosion of Indian rights. Before these sessions, the colonists and their advocates in Spain were enjoying great momentum: they had won the repeal of key provisions of the New Laws of 1542 and were making progress toward securing perpetual ownership of their slaves and estates.

After Valladolid, this campaign for perpetuity lost support and was soon abandoned.

Beyond stopping the further degradation of Indian life in his day, Las Casas's arguments, books, and ideas likely contributed to a significant posthumous victory. Less than twenty-five years after Valladolid, in 1573, King Philip II promulgated a new ordinance regulating all future Spanish discoveries and conquests. Like some of the prior colonial laws, this ordinance required that indigenous peoples be treated fairly and humanely. Unlike prior legislation, this ordinance explicitly prohibited their enslavement.

What Went Wrong?

In their attempts to lobby leaders in Europe, Montesinos, Las Casas, and their allies were astonishingly successful. This small band of religious Christians convinced both the Spanish throne and the Vatican to issue statutes and decrees protecting the American Indian. They did so at a time when the Spanish monarchy was in desperate need of the gold that flowed from their conquest and enslavement. It is impossible to imagine so small a band of religious activists winning so complete a legislative victory at the expense of a nation's vital economic interests in the present day.

Yet when it came to the situation on the ground in America, these victories were hollow. Despite all of the positive enactments to the contrary, the conquests proceeded, slavery continued, and a genocide of continental proportions took an ever-increasing toll. Las Casas himself summed up the scope of the failure:

> So many laws already issued, so many decrees, so many harsh threats, and so many statutes conscientiously enacted by the Emperor Charles and his predecessors have been ineffective in preventing so many thousands of innocent men from perishing by sword, hunger, and all the misfortunes of total war, and

extensive areas of their highly civilized kingdoms and most fertile provinces from being savagely devastated.[37]

In the final analysis, the problem was not one of intentions but one of power. The Spanish conquistadors were not a traditional army under the king's command. They are more accurately seen as a league of mercenaries who had been authorized to conquer in the king's name. As they amassed life-changing wealth, the conquistadors were blinded by self-interest to all other considerations. They could not be deterred by new laws from Spain or threats of excommunication from Rome. These people who lived by the sword would yield only to the sword.

Yet no authority had sufficient force to confront these bands of heavily armed conquistadors so far away. The pope's Swiss Guards could barely defend the Vatican, let alone impose his will upon such distant lands. Even the Spanish kings lacked the ability to project the requisite power across an ocean. It would have taken a great armada and a massive army to curb the conquistadors. If any of Spain's kings had the will for such a battle—a questionable proposition—the cash-starved monarchs most definitely lacked the way.

In the absence of sufficient military power, the Spanish monarchs tried to manage their vast new colonies by promulgating laws and sending royal agents to enforce them. Yet the hapless bureaucrats who tried to implement these unpopular laws—such as those protecting the Indians—were at best ignored and at worst physically attacked. Spain's first viceroy in Peru, for example, tried to enforce the New Laws abolishing the perpetuation of slavery. He was captured and killed in the course of an armed conquistador revolt.

The body responsible for administering Spain's American colonies for the crown, the Council of the Indies, was well aware of both the problem and its cause. Writing of the laws protecting the Indians, the Council noted:

> We feel certain that these laws have not been obeyed.... The greed of those who undertake conquests and the timidity and humility of the Indians is such that we are not certain whether any instruction will be obeyed.[38]

Genocide and slavery have been stopped only when governments both embrace a moral agenda and commit sufficient force to its implementation. In sixteenth-century Spain, a group of Christian activists achieved monumental legislative victories that proved to be meaningless in the absence of such governmental resolve. In nineteenth-century America, another group of Christian activists would achieve a similarly hollow humanitarian victory.

Ethnic Cleansing in North America

In the early decades of the 1800s, a small band of Cherokee Indians living in what is today the State of Georgia converted to Christianity and began to translate the New Testament into their native tongue. When they had completed translating the Gospel of Matthew, the group shared their work with one of their chiefs, a man named Yanugunski. As they had hoped, the Chief was greatly impressed with what he read. "Strange," he observed, "that the white people are not better after having had it for so long."[39]

Chief Yanugunski's assessment of European morality echoes that of the Caribbean chief who centuries earlier had concluded that Christians worshipped gold. Despite all of the years and miles that separated them, it is hardly surprising that these two Indian leaders reached such similar conclusions. Like the Spanish settlers before them, the British settlers who colonized North America were men completely in thrall to their own greed. While the Spanish hungered for gold, the British craved land. In the rush to secure more Indian land for the needs of an ever expanding settler community, Christian morality was the first casualty.

Even those Cherokees who converted to Christianity and sought to save their civilization through assimilation recognized that the settlers' greed posed an insurmountable hurdle to their progress. In reflecting on the efforts to remove him and his fellow Cherokees from their ancestral lands, a Christian Cherokee leader named Elias Boudinot observed:

> Cupidity and self-interest are at the bottom of all these difficulties. A desire to possess the Indian land is paramount to a desire to see him established on the soil as a civilized man.[40]

∼

THE AMERICAN INDIAN genocide was not a crime perpetrated by Spaniards alone. Most of the North American continent was colonized by the British and their descendants. In their treatment of the Indians they encountered, British disdain for human life rivaled that of the Spanish.

The British had even less reason than the Spanish to concern themselves with Indian survival. In their quest for Indian gold, the Spanish needed to leave some Indians alive to mine it. But in their pursuit of Indian land, all the British colonists and their American progeny wanted of the Indians was their removal from it. What began as ethnic cleansing often waxed genocidal when the Indians dared to fight back.

In absolute terms, the Indian population of what became the United States and Canada was far smaller than that south of the Rio Grande. There were simply fewer Indians for the British settlers to kill. But in per-capita terms, the Anglo-American genocide of the Indians was every bit as thoroughgoing as the Spanish. Between the time of the first European settlements in North America and the close of the seventeenth century, more than ninety-five percent of the eastern Indians (i.e., those tribes that came into contact with the Europeans) were wiped out through wars, massacres, and disease.[41]

∼

LIKE THE SPANISH before them, many Anglos justified such behavior by arguing that some nations or races were inferior to others and thus were not endowed with certain fundamental human rights. The Spanish based such claims upon Aristotle and his theory of natural slavery. The Americans invoked more modern philosophical support. As we will examine in greater detail in Chapter Nine, contemporary philosophers elaborated the concepts that enabled Americans to ethically cleanse Indians and enslave Africans with few moral qualms.

Many of America's leading thinkers and politicians were at the forefront of this campaign against the Indians. Thomas Jefferson defended the physical and mental abilities of the American Indian when doing so served his ultimate goal of proving that North America was a healthy place for human habitation. But when these same Indians stood in the way of his country's westward expansion, Jefferson's benevolence evaporated. In this context, Jefferson wrote that the Indians were to be given a simple choice—to remove themselves from the path of European settlement or be "extirpated from the earth."[42] He later wrote of those Indians still living within the borders of the United States that the government must "pursue them to extermination, or drive them to new seats beyond our reach."[43]

President Andrew Jackson was an equally outspoken advocate of ethnic cleansing and genocide. In fact, he made Indian removal one of his administration's top priorities. In his second annual message to Congress, Jackson stated that people should not grow "melancholy" over Indians being driven to their "tomb," since "true philanthropy reconciles the mind to these vicissitudes as it does to the extinction of one generation to make room for another."[44] Even after leaving office, Jackson recommended that American troops kill Indian women and children in order to eradicate the population. Failure to do so, he wrote, was equivalent to pursuing "a wolf in the hammocks without knowing first where her den and whelps were."[45]

Such genocidal thinking remained prevalent in America into the late nineteenth century. Theodore Roosevelt described the extermination of the Indians and the expropriation of their lands as both "inevitable" and "beneficial." He explained that such conquests:

> are sure to come when a masterful people, still in its raw barbarian prime, finds itself face to face with the weaker and wholly alien race which holds a coveted prize in its feeble grasp.[46]

Roosevelt added, "I don't go so far as to think that the only good Indians are dead Indians, but I believe nine out of ten are, and I shouldn't like to inquire too closely into the case of the tenth."[47]

The author L. Frank Baum is best remembered today for his children's classic *The Wizard of Oz*. But when the subject shifted to the American Indian, Baum's writing was far less heartwarming. In the winter of 1890, he observed:

> The nobility of the Redskins is extinguished, and what few are left are a pack of whining curs who lick the hand that smites them. The Whites, by law of conquest, by justice of civilization, are masters of the American continent, and the best safety of the frontier settlements will be secured by the total annihilation of the few remaining Indians. Why not annihilation? Their glory has fled, their spirit broken, their manhood effaced; better that they should die than live the miserable wretches that they are.[48]

Looking behind the curtain can be disappointing indeed. As author David Stannard has noted, Baum reflected well the views of his time. Ten days after Baum wrote these words, hundreds of Lakota Indians were massacred at Wounded Knee. Women and children accounted for two-thirds of the Indian dead.

At a time when ethnic cleansing and genocide made for popular political platforms, the only people to stand in defense of the

Indians were devout Christians acting on the Judeo-Christian idea. Only religious Christians were able to pierce the rampant racism of the day and see the Indians not as obstacles to be removed but as brothers to be protected. And only religious Christians were able to overcome their impoverished genetic morality to stand with these brothers against their fellow Americans in an unpopular fight. While the masses saw westward territorial expansion as America's "manifest destiny," millions of Christians maintained that America's true destiny was to be a moral beacon to a dark world.

Cherokee Removal

America's victory in the War of 1812 ushered in a period of tremendous economic expansion in what at that time was called the "West": the lands between the eastern seaboard and the Mississippi River. Roads and canals were completed throughout these territories, enabling local farmers to reach a national market. Rising commodity prices ensured that these sales brought in record returns. Lured by these new opportunities, Americans began to pour into these areas in unprecedented numbers.

In the first decade following the War of 1812, the new states of Indiana, Illinois, Mississippi, and Alabama joined the Union. In the two decades following the war, the states of Ohio, Tennessee, and Georgia saw their populations more than double.[49] As populations swelled and economies boomed, the demand for arable land reached unprecedented heights.

While America's European settlers were confined largely to the eastern seaboard, they had put enormous pressure on the local Indians to leave. Under a series of treaties with the federal government, these coastal tribes finally abandoned their ancestral lands in exchange for guarantees of self-rule over large new holdings further inland. As a consequence, Indians now owned millions of acres of fertile land in the heart of this westward expansion. As European settlement intensified around these Indian outposts, history began to repeat itself. The states started demanding that the federal government once again intervene to force the Indians further west.

When the federal authorities failed to act quickly enough, the states started to take matters into their own hands. Georgia was the most aggressive in its pursuit of Indian land. The state was in the midst of a cotton boom but was running out of land on which to grow it. And there, occupying nearly five million fertile acres in northwest Georgia, sat the Cherokee Nation. Instead of seeking to remove them by force, Georgia embarked upon an effort to make the Cherokees' lives so difficult that they would voluntarily leave for points west.

In order to harass the Cherokees, however, Georgia first needed to acquire legal authority over them. Despite the federal treaties granting the Cherokees self-rule, the Georgia Assembly passed a law in 1828 subjecting the Cherokees to the state's civil and criminal jurisdiction. The law was set to go into effect on June 1, 1830. All eyes looked to Washington to see how the federal government would react.

Fortunately for Georgia, the White House was at this time occupied by a champion of Indian removal. Prior to entering politics, Andrew Jackson had been a major general in both the Tennessee militia and the United States Army. He was a veteran of a series of Indian wars in which he had earned a reputation as a fierce Indian fighter. In this capacity, Jackson had personally negotiated treaties with the Creeks, Choctaws, Chickasaws, and Cherokees under which these tribes surrendered millions of acres of land in the American Southeast.

Immediately upon taking office, President Jackson made it clear that he intended to make Indian removal a top priority. In his first message to Congress on December 8, 1829, Jackson spoke out strongly in favor of removing all Indians to points west of the Mississippi River. Jackson's first legislative recommendation to Congress was a bill to facilitate this removal. Jackson's fellow Democrats, who controlled both houses of Congress, were quick to introduce Jackson's bill and schedule votes.

This bill, the Indian Removal Act, authorized the president to set aside an "Indian Territory" on land west of the Mississippi (present-day Oklahoma) for the settlement of Indians from the East. It further empowered the president to offer portions of this new land to the eastern tribes in exchange for their current holdings. Those Indians who accepted the trade were to be given perpetual title to their new land, payments for improvements they had made on their old land, and financial support for their first year west of the Mississippi.

The removal contemplated by this legislation was purely voluntary. The act offered a series of carrots to those tribes which chose to leave their land and go west. Yet all involved understood that the states were waiting in the wings with sticks—like Georgia's legislation—to ensure that the Indians would not refuse.

The Evangelical Response

At this perilous juncture for the Cherokees, a most unlikely champion emerged. Jeremiah Evarts was a Boston-based administrator of a missionary society who had never been active in politics. Yet Evarts had sent missionaries to the Cherokee territory, was sympathetic to the tribe's plight, and was deeply disturbed by what his country was trying to do to them. With no one else stepping forward to fight the Indian Removal Act, Evarts mounted his horse and set off for Washington.

Evarts was a pure product of the Second Great Awakening. He studied at Yale University at a time when that institution was one of the Awakening's intellectual hotbeds. Like most Yale students of his day, Evarts came under the influence of the University's illustrious president, Timothy Dwight. Dwight, who was Jonathan Edwards's grandson, put Edwards's disinterested benevolence at the center of Yale's curriculum and culture. "In whatever sphere of life you are placed," he urged his students, "employ all of your powers and all of your means of doing good as diligently and vigorously as you can."[50]

Like so many of the Awakening's inspired converts, Evarts enthusiastically embraced the mission of disinterested benevolence. After graduating from Yale, he searched for a cause to which to devote his boundless benevolent zeal. Evarts was first drawn to the temperance movement, and he helped to found the Massachusetts Society for the Suppression of Intemperance. From there he moved to the society to which he would devote the rest of his professional life: the American Board of Commissioners for Foreign Missions. Among the "foreign missions" maintained by the Board was a mission to the Cherokee Nation.

For Evarts, the Indian Removal Act was a most troubling sign. Evarts believed that building a virtuous republic was far more important than building a large one. Yet it was now apparent that the nation's greed for land was blinding it to fundamental morality. He insisted that the best way to respond to this failure was not just to pray for better policy, but to seek to influence those who formulated it. Like Montesinos and Las Casas before him, Evarts believed in mixing religion and politics.

〜

TAKING ON A POPULAR president is never easy. And Evarts did so with limited resources and few allies in Washington. Alone, this one man would never have been able to resist the wave of greed and racism that came crashing over Washington. But Evarts did not wage this battle by himself. He entered the fray at the head of a powerful evangelical army. The Second Great Awakening that had so deeply transformed Evart's life had likewise touched millions of his fellow Americans. Evarts believed that a defense of the Cherokees based on an appeal to disinterested benevolence would resonate deeply with Christians across America. To a surprising extent, he was right.

Although new to politics, Evarts designed and implemented a sophisticated, multi-pronged campaign. His core mission was to personally lobby Congress. Evarts rented a room near the Capitol and became a fixture in its halls and offices. He spent months meeting with representatives on both sides of the aisle in both legislative houses. By the time the debate on the Indian Removal Act began, he had lined up friendly congressmen to lead the opposition to the bill and persuaded many more to support them.

In addition, Evarts was one of the first lobbyists to see the value of supplementing his Washington advocacy with a grassroots campaign. Although he lacked a pre-existing political organization, Evarts had access to millions of evangelical activists through the vast network of benevolent societies that had been formed during the Second Great Awakening. Through a constant stream of letters, pamphlets, and speeches, Evarts appealed to this constituency with faith-based arguments against the Indian Removal Act and urged them to speak out against it. In response, evangelicals across America inundated their congressmen with a record number of petitions and memorials opposing the act.

Finally, Evarts launched a media campaign through the dominant medium of his day: newspapers. He wrote a series of twenty-four essays opposing the Indian Removal Act and secured their publication in the country's leading political newspaper, the *National Intelligencer*. He then convinced forty more newspapers to reprint these essays. Evarts also published his essays in a book that he distributed to opinion leaders throughout the country. When the Senate began its debate on the act, a copy of Evart's book of essays sat on every senator's desk.[51]

Like all good political writers, Evarts placed the issue of the Indian Removal Act in a broader context. He stressed that the issue before the nation was no mere land dispute, but a moral challenge of the highest order. Invoking the Judeo-Christian idea, he warned:

> Most certainly, an indelible stigma will be fixed upon us if, in the plentitude of our power, and in the pride of our superiority, we shall be guilty of manifest injustice to our weak and defenseless neighbors.[52]

For Jeremiah Evarts, the golden rule was a standard of behavior not only for individuals but also for nations.

∼

AMONG EVARTS'S GREATEST assets in his campaign was the fact that one of his most passionate evangelical allies happened to be a sitting United States senator. New Jersey senator Theodore Frelinghuysen was, like Evarts, a devout product of the Second Great Awakening. Frelinghuysen was likewise a most enthusiastic proponent of disinterested benevolence. Before coming to the Senate, Frelinghuysen had been the president of no less than four Christian benevolent societies, and he had served as an officer for "all of the rest."[53] Senator Frelinghuysen was referred to by friend and foe alike as "the Christian senator."

When the debate on the Indian Removal Act began, Senator Frelinghuysen took the Senate floor and delivered a six-hour speech against the bill. Given the secular setting, he devoted much of his time to elaborating the Indians' compelling legal case. He walked his colleagues through the long series of treaties between the United States and the eastern tribes. In clear language and in return for enormous concessions, he stressed, the United States had given the Indians full right and title to the lands in which they now lived.

Frelinghuysen then addressed the greed and racism which was driving most of his colleagues to ignore these legal claims. He reminded his fellow senators of the vast tracts that had already been taken from the Indians and chided them for the fact that "like the horse-leech, our insatiated cupidity cries give! give! give!"[54] He challenged his colleagues with what must have been one of the first pleas for racial justice ever heard in the Senate chamber:

> Do the obligations of justice change with the color of the skin? Is it one of the prerogatives of the white man, that he may disregard the dictates of moral principles when an Indian shall be concerned?[55]

Frelinghuysen was speaking in 1830, almost three centuries after the famous dispute at Valladolid. Yet he nevertheless found it necessary to repeat some of the very same arguments made by Las Casas back in 1550. He reminded his colleagues that when the Europeans first encountered the Indians, they were not "a wild and lawless horde of banditti," but lived under an organized government. He challenged the still-prevalent view that the Indian was an inferior breed of man:

> I believe . . . it is not now seriously denied that Indians are men, endowed with kindred faculties and powers with ourselves; that they have a place in human sympathy, and are justly entitled to a share in the common bounties of a benign Providence.[56]

Frelinghuysen acknowledged that his efforts to defeat the Indian Removal Act might fail. Yet he concluded his speech with an eloquent rebuke to those who put greed above principle:

> Defeat in such a cause is far above the triumphs of unrighteous power—and in the language of an eloquent writer—"I had rather receive the blessing of one poor Cherokee, as he casts his look back upon his country, for having, though in vain, attempted to prevent his banishment, than to sleep beneath the marble of all the Caesars."[57]

On April 26, 1830, Frelinghuysen was handed the defeat he had anticipated. The Senate passed President Jackson's Indian Removal Act by a vote of 29 to 19 in a largely party-line vote.

The battle moved next to the House of Representatives. Here Evarts's grassroots efforts had a much stronger impact. A number of Democrats from districts with large evangelical populations announced that they would oppose the act. President Jackson was forced to personally lobby House Democrats to prevent more defections. In a refrain that would be repeated by so many of his successors facing close congressional votes, Jackson told wavering Democratic members that he "staked the success of his administration upon this measure."[58]

The Indian Removal Act passed the House by a vote of 102 to 97.

On May 28, 1830, President Jackson signed the act into law. In the battle between the president and the missionary, the president had won the first round. But Jeremiah Evarts was not prepared to concede defeat.

❧

WITH THE PASSAGE of the Indian Removal Act, a formal mechanism was in place for Indians to relocate west of the Mississippi. All that was needed now was for the Indians to conclude that it was in their best interest to do so. The State of Georgia wasted little time in seeking to influence this decision. On June 1, 1830, the legislation extending Georgia's legal jurisdiction over the Cherokee Nation went into full effect. Shortly thereafter, Georgia began to exercise this new authority by giving away parcels of Cherokee land through public lotteries open to all adult white citizens of the state.

With life getting harder for the Cherokees and no help forthcoming from the other two branches of the federal government, Jeremiah Evarts and the Cherokee leadership decided to petition the United States Supreme Court. The Cherokees requested an injunction preventing the State of Georgia from extending its laws to Cherokee land. They argued that, according to binding federal treaties, the Cherokees were a "foreign nation in the sense of our constitution and law," every bit as independent as Mexico or Canada. Thus, they asserted, the State of Georgia had no right to subject them to its jurisdiction.

The Supreme Court refused to grant the injunction. Four of the six justices concluded that the Cherokees were not a foreign nation and that the Court therefore lacked the jurisdiction to review the case.* But chief justice John Marshall, who wrote the

---

*Since cases involving "foreign nations" come under the Supreme Court's original jurisdiction, the Court can automatically hear them. For the Court to hear other categories of cases, however, another source of jurisdiction must be found. The most common source of such jurisdiction is the appeal of an "existing case or controversy" from a lower court.

majority opinion,[59] made it clear that the Cherokees had a strong argument on the merits. He explained that while the Cherokees were not a foreign nation, they were a "domestic dependent" nation and as such came under federal, not state, control. Marshall indicated that if the Cherokees could find a relevant case that would come under the Supreme Court's jurisdiction, they would likely prevail in their quest for protection from Georgia's escalating encroachments.

~

THE STATE OF GEORGIA soon provided the Cherokees with the case they needed. Georgia passed a law prohibiting white men from entering the Cherokee Nation after March 1, 1831, unless they first obtained a license from the state. The law was intended to exclude missionaries like Jeremiah Evarts, who were rallying the Cherokees to fight their removal.

A group of eleven white missionaries decided to test the new law and refused to leave Cherokee land. Once the deadline passed, they were all arrested, put on trial, and found guilty. The next day, the judge sentenced the eleven to the state penitentiary, "there to endure hard labor for the term of four years."[60]

Eventually, nine of the eleven defendants accepted pardons from the governor in return for their pledge to never return to the Cherokee Nation. But in order to have a case to appeal to the Supreme Court, two of the missionaries rejected the pardon. Thus Samuel Worcester and Elizur Butler reported to the state penitentiary at Milledgeville to begin serving their prison terms.

The Cherokees now had a concrete case they could use to challenge the extension of Georgia's jurisdiction over their territory. They appealed the conviction of the two missionaries to the Supreme Court. The Cherokees argued that they were a "domestic dependent" nation and that subjecting them to Georgia law therefore violated both federal treaties and the U.S. Constitution. This time the Supreme Court determined that it did have jurisdiction over the case. And this time, the Court ruled in the Cherokees' favor.

Writing for the majority, Chief Justice Marshall recognized the Cherokee Nation as a self-governing community "in which the laws of Georgia can have no force, and which the citizens of Georgia have no right to enter, but with the consent of the Cherokees themselves." He thus declared the Georgia legislation under which the missionaries had been convicted to be "void, as repugnant to the constitution, treaties, and laws of the United States." He ordered that the convictions be "reversed and annulled."[61]

With the case decided and nothing to be gained from staying in jail, Worcester and Butler accepted pardons from Georgia's governor. After sixteen months at hard labor, they left prison. Both men would follow their beloved Cherokees west and continue to serve them for the rest of their lives.*

∼

LIKE LAS CASAS centuries earlier, Jeremiah Evarts and his colleagues had taken a lonely stand in favor of persecuted Indians and won an important victory at the highest level of government.** And also like Las Casas, Evarts had presided over a triumph of little practical value because the body issuing the ruling lacked the power to enforce it.

---

*It is worth noting that these missionaries were serving people who largely rejected their religious message. Despite the efforts of missionaries from many different denominations, less than ten percent of the Cherokees had joined Christian churches by the time of their removal to the West. See Theda Perdue and Michael Green, *The Cherokee Nation and the Trail of Tears* (New York: Viking, 2007), 32–33.

**This victory was a posthumous one. Evarts died in 1831. Most accounts attribute his death to exhaustion from overwork in his campaign against the Indian Removal Act. Shortly before his death, he had written to Worcester and others recommending the appeal strategy that ultimately prevailed.

When informed of the Supreme Court's decision in favor of the Cherokees, President Jackson is famously said to have declared, "John Marshall has made his decision; now let him enforce it."[62] Historians still debate whether Jackson actually spoke these words. But spoken or not, they capture well his response to the ruling. Because of his support for Indian removal and his fear of exacerbating anti-federal sentiment in the South, Jackson refused to take any steps to enforce the Court's decision. Georgia was thus free to ignore it.

The Trail of Tears

Between 1831 and 1833, the Georgia legislature gave away all of the Cherokees' land to white settlers through a lottery. In 1836, Georgia authorized the lottery winners to take possession of their winnings. Soon, whites were showing up at Cherokee homes and fields and claiming them as their own. Even the tribe's chief, John Ross, returned home from a trip to Washington to find a white family living in his house. Since their testimony was not permitted in Georgia's courts, the Cherokees had no way to legally challenge the strangers who had taken their property.

Eventually, a group of young Cherokees decided that there was no future for their people in their ancestral land and that the wisest course was to secure the best deal possible in exchange for their relocation to the West. This band proceeded to negotiate a final settlement with the Jackson administration in the name of their tribe. Although this "treaty party" included none of the tribe's official leaders and represented a minority point of view, the Jackson administration did not hesitate to make a deal with them.

Under this treaty, the Cherokee Nation ceded to the United States all of its territory east of the Mississippi for the sum of five million dollars and an interest in lands west of the Mississippi. The United States agreed to pay for removing the Cherokees to their new land and to support them there for one year. Full removal was to be completed within two years of ratification. Congress ratified the treaty on May 23, 1836. The clock began ticking.

When the two-year grace period ended in May 1838, only two thousand Cherokees had voluntarily left for the West.[63] President Jackson's successor, Martin Van Buren, immediately ordered that remaining Cherokees be removed by force. Federal troops entered the Cherokee villages, forced the Cherokees from their homes at gunpoint, and sent them to eleven camps erected to hold them prior to their transport west. Within a single week, some eighteen thousand Cherokee men, women, and children were rounded up and put into what can only be called concentration camps.[64]

In June, the transports started. The first group of one thousand Cherokees were packed into railroad boxcars so tightly that many died from asphyxiation. After this incident, the use of trains was abandoned. Thirteen detachments of over a thousand Cherokees each were instead forced to make the nearly one-thousand-mile journey to their new homes by foot. They marched in bitter cold and heavy snow. They marched with little food after corrupt vendors stole most of what the government had agreed to supply. They marched weakened by the diseases that spread through each detachment.[65]

Of the approximately eighteen thousand Cherokees who were removed, at least four thousand—almost one in four— died in the camps, on the trains, or along the trail.[66] Some estimate that the death toll was closer to eight thousand.[67] In June 1838, the head of the Georgia militia declared that not a single Cherokee remained in the state of Georgia.[68]

⟿

THE STORY OF THE Cherokee removal is just one example of the fate of the North American Indian. Only about ten percent of the Indians who crossed the Trail of Tears from the Southeast to

Oklahoma were Cherokees.[69] Most Choctaws, Creeks, Chickasaws, and Seminoles had already endured this ordeal. By the close of President Jackson's eight years in office, approximately forty-five thousand American Indians had been relocated west of the Mississippi River.[70] By the end of the nineteenth century, over sixty eastern tribes had been removed to Oklahoma.[71]

Even taken as a whole, Jackson's Indian-removal efforts were by no means the great assault. They were merely the mopping-up operation. Almost every tribe that walked the Trail of Tears had already been decimated by European attacks and diseases decades earlier. The Indians subjected to this march were, historically speaking, the lucky ones. They were the remnant who had survived long enough to be expelled.

～

ALMOST ALL OF AMERICA's Indian defenders were evangelical Christians who derived their morality and motivation from their faith. But this certainly doesn't mean that all American Christians defended the Indians. As was the case in the age of Las Casas—and as would be the case in the future struggle over slavery—most Christians failed to live up to the high calling of their creed. Some leading clergymen actually campaigned in favor of Indian removal. The large majority simply didn't get involved.

Jeremiah Evarts's lament about most of his fellow Christians could apply equally well to any other era:

> How tame and timid, and how vacillating and inconsistent—
> how yielding and compromising—nine tenths of even the
> religious people are on all political questions which involve
> moral and religious considerations.[72]

～

BOTH EVARTS AND FRELINGHUYSEN had overtly brought their Christianity to bear on one of the most contentious issues of their time. Even in the first half of the nineteenth century, such faith-based activism was extremely controversial. Supporters of President Jackson attacked the "politico-ecclesiastical coalition"[73] that opposed Jackson's Indian removal policy. Georgia senator Wilson Lumpkin, one of the leading proponents of Indian removal, raged against the "Christian party in politics" and the "fanatics" who opposed his state's efforts to remove the Cherokees.[74]

During the debate on the Indian Removal Act, South Carolina senator Robert Y. Hayne took the Senate floor to speak in support of the legislation. He quickly turned his attention to Jeremiah Evarts and his colleagues. Hayne castigated them for wanting to "regulate the affairs and duties of others." Referring to the Judeo-Christian ethic driving their activism, he warned:

> It is a spirit which has long been busy with the slaves of the
> South, and is even now displaying itself in vain efforts to
> drive the government from its wise policy in relation to the
> Indians.[75]

Hayne urged his colleagues to resist this spirit, which had filled the land with "thousands of wild and visionary projects, which can have no effect but to waste the energies and dissipate the resources of the country."[76]

⌒

SHORTLY AFTER SENATOR Frelinghuysen made his famous speech against the Indian Removal Act, an idealistic young Christian was moved to write a poem entitled "To the Hon. Theodore Frelinghuysen, on Reading His Eloquent Speech in Defense of Indian Rights." The poem praised Frelinghuysen's eloquence and morality and mourned the fact that his efforts to protect the Indians were fruitless in the face of "grasping avarice that never relents." Yet the final stanza looked forward to future victories:

> Be not dismayed. On God's own strength relying,
> Stand boldly up, meek soldier of the Cross;
> For thee ten thousand prayers are heavenward flying,
> Thy soul is purged from earthly rust and dross.

Patriot and Christian, ardent, self-denying,
How could we bear resignedly thy loss?[77]

It is a very good thing indeed that this aspiring poet kept his day job. Thus he was spared starvation, and the nation was delivered from one of its greatest evils. This poem was written by a then little-known Christian activist named William Lloyd Garrison. Garrison and thousands like him were inspired by the efforts of Evarts and Frelinghuysen to take their Christian morality into politics to end a great national sin. They would soon build a far larger Christian movement to challenge another great national sin: slavery.

FOUR

The Judeo-Christian
Idea Against Slavery

*Among the evils corrected or subdued, either by the general
influence of Christianity on the minds of men, or by particular
associations of Christians, the African Slave Trade appears to
me to have occupied the foremost place.*[1]

—THOMAS CLARKSON, ENGLISH ABOLITIONIST

A FTER KILLING OFF THE large majority of America's Indians, the Spanish conquistadors proceeded to enslave most of the survivors. Yet these colonists quickly grew dissatisfied with their Indian slaves. The Indians proved to be rebellious and could too easily flee into the surrounding countryside they knew so well. They were also highly susceptible to European diseases. White indentured servants proved to be no better. They were expensive, often unreliable, and without any resistance to the tropical diseases prevalent in the hemisphere's most important agricultural areas.

Early on, therefore, European colonists in the Americas turned to African slaves as a reliable source of labor. As the colonial economy increasingly focused on cultivating labor-intensive crops for export, the demand for these slaves exploded. From the time the first African slaves were brought to the New World in the early 1500s until the final abolition of slavery in the hemisphere in 1868, slave ships transported approximately ten million African captives across the Atlantic. It is estimated that an additional five million Africans died from the brutal conditions en route.[2] During the first three centuries of European settlement in the Americas, the number of African slaves arriving in the New World actually exceeded the number of European immigrants.[3]

In Britain's American colonies, African slavery was the engine that drove a vast agricultural enterprise cultivating sugar and other valuable cash crops. For most of the eighteenth century, the British spent more on imports from their relatively small colonies in the West Indies than they did on goods from Asia, Africa, Latin America, and even North America. During the early years of the nineteenth century, goods from these Caribbean colonies alone constituted over thirty percent of Britain's non-European imports.[4] As author Adam Hochschild observed of the British West Indies:

> Think of them as the Middle East of the late eighteenth century. Just as oil drives the geopolitics of our own time, the most important commodity on European minds then was sugar, and the overseas territories that mattered most were the islands so wonderfully suited for growing it.[5]

Thus the Europeans enslaved Africans for the same reason that they had massacred and enslaved Indians: greed. The gold was largely gone, but there were vast sums of money to be made through slave-based agriculture. And the selfish gene had been passed down undiminished through the generations.

～

WHEN THE ENGLISH abolitionists first began their campaign to end the Atlantic slave trade in the late 1780s, many of them were confident that they would enjoy a quick victory over this indefensible commerce. But those with a deeper understanding of human nature did not share this optimism. Just as greed had driven the conquistadors to fight the abolition of Indian slavery, it would fuel a vicious opposition to abolition of African slavery centuries later.

John Wesley, the founder of Methodism and the dean of England's evangelicals, immediately recognized what the abolitionists were up against. He wrote to an evangelical abolitionist warning him that he should expect:

> all the opposition which can be made by men who are not encumbered by either Honor, Conscience or Humanity ... who will rush on through every possible means, to secure their great Goddess, interest.[6]

Indian chiefs were not the only ones to recognize that the Europeans worshipped Mammon. Many Christian observers shared the complaint and mourned the reality.

Abolition in Britain

In 1785, Cambridge University selected a provocative topic for its famous annual Latin essay contest. Students were asked to answer the question: "Is it lawful to make slaves of others against their will?"

That year, the winner of the contest was a twenty-five-year-old divinity student named Thomas Clarkson. Clarkson was the son of an Anglican minister, and thus far he was following in his father's footsteps. He had already been consecrated as a deacon in the Church of England, and he had a pastoral position waiting for him upon his graduation.

When Clarkson began his research for the essay, he had no agenda beyond simply winning the contest. Like almost everyone in England at the time, he knew next to nothing about slavery and had never concerned himself with it. But as Clarkson delved further into the topic, he was forever changed by what he learned.

After the contest was over, the burdens of conscience remained. While riding from Cambridge to London to start his career in the ministry, Clarkson was suddenly overwhelmed by the horrors of which he was now so painfully aware. He got off his horse, fell to his knees, and resolved that "it was time that some person should see these calamities to their end."[7] As much as he might have wished it to be otherwise, Clarkson understood that he would have to be that person.

Clarkson recognized from the outset that a newly minted Cambridge graduate would not be able to end slavery by himself. He therefore approached the most obvious allies for his mission: the Quakers. The Quakers were a small denomination of devout Christians who took the Bible's language about human equality and the golden rule quite literally and most seriously. The Quakers had already voted to free their slaves and to bar any Quaker who did not do so from their meetings. Having abolished slavery in their own community, they set out to do the same in the rest of the country. In 1783, the English Quakers formed a committee to outlaw the British slave trade.

This Quaker abolition effort faced long odds. There were fewer than twenty thousand Quakers in England, and they were in every way outsiders, disconnected from the Anglican elites who controlled the government and the culture. The Quakers understood that the only way to accomplish their goals would be to enlist Anglicans in their cause. When Thomas Clarkson showed up at their door, he was received as if heaven-sent.

Thus it came to pass that on May 22, 1787, twelve men met in the London shop of a Quaker printer and established the Society for the Abolition of the African Slave Trade. These twelve founders were all men of deep Christian faith: nine were Quakers, and three others, including Clarkson, were Anglicans.[8]

⁓

THIS FIRST HISTORIC meeting of the Abolition Society was followed by action on a prodigious scale. Each of the members of this small band performed vital tasks that projected their influence well beyond the print shop's walls. The Quakers provided the Society with key organizational and financial support. With members and meeting places in cities and towns across Britain, the Quaker network formed the backbone of a budding grass-roots movement. Many Quakers had achieved a measure of economic success, and their steady stream of donations sustained the abolitionists during good times and bad. Even the print shop which hosted the group's first meeting continued to play a central role, turning out a constant supply of anti-slavery literature.

Clarkson was the movement's chief field organizer and researcher. For many years, he was the movement's *only* field organizer and researcher. Clarkson believed in the power of information. Learning about the horrors of slavery had changed his life, and he maintained that these facts would have the same effect on others. One of his first initiatives was to translate his prize-winning essay from Latin to English. He later supplemented this core text with a series of updates further documenting the brutal reality of slavery.

Writing such literature proved to be the easy part. To distribute his pamphlets and appeal to his countrymen in person, Clarkson set out on an endless series of trips on horseback. By his own estimate, Clarkson traveled over thirty-five thousand miles in the course of visiting almost every city, town, and village in England.[9] In the process, he built the tiny Abolition Society into a national grassroots movement. At certain key junctures in the abolition debate, this network was capable of generating over one million signatures on anti-slavery petitions to Parliament. The total British population at the time was only fourteen million.

Like any grassroots movement with a political objective, the Abolition Society needed an insider to take up their cause in the halls of power in London. The choice proved to be an easy one. It so happened that just as the abolitionists were looking for a leader in Parliament, an influential young member of Parliament was searching for a cause to lead.

William Wilberforce

William Wilberforce had it all. He was a Cambridge-educated heir to a trading fortune. He was a rising star in British politics known for his extraordinary eloquence. He belonged to all five of London's leading social clubs, where his boisterous charm and rapier wit were always in high demand. He was Prime Minister William Pitt's best friend and closest advisor. And he was only twenty-four years old.

Then everything changed. In the fall of 1784, Wilberforce decided to escape the gloom of the London winter by traveling to the French Rivera. He invited his friend Isaac Milner, an up-and-coming member of the Cambridge faculty, to join him. Wilberforce knew that Milner was an engaging and often hilarious conversationalist who would provide good company on the hours of carriage rides that lay ahead. What he did not know was that Milner was also a devout evangelical Christian. When the subject of their travel banter turned to religion, the jokes stopped and a serious dialogue began. Wilberforce returned from France changed, spiritually disturbed, and set on the path that would soon lead to his embrace of evangelical Christianity. He would for the rest of his life refer to the transformation sparked that winter as his "Great Change."

For Wilberforce, this change was not entirely welcome. In fact, it threatened the very things he cherished most. Wilberforce loved life on society's A-list, where he was a prized guest at an endless series of dinners and parties. Yet London's social elites shared a deep-seated disdain for evangelical Christians. They were unlikely to continue associating with one.

Even more troubling to Wilberforce, however, were the implications of his "Great Change" for his career. Wilberforce was thriving in Parliament. But he initially accepted the conventional wisdom that the only way to serve God was to leave the "world" and restrict oneself to the life and community of the Church.

Wilberforce feared that embracing his newfound faith would require abandoning his cherished vocation.

Struggling with his dilemma, Wilberforce showed up at the door of one of England's leading evangelical pastors: the Reverend John Newton. Newton was a former slave-ship captain who decades earlier had abandoned the slave trade to seek ordination by the Church of England. Wilberforce had known Newton as a young boy and had grown more pious in his presence. But as he matured, Wilberforce gravitated toward the secularism so popular among his peers. He had ignored Newton all the years he was living the life of a Cambridge partier and political wonder boy. Now, Wilberforce needed his old pastor's help.

John Newton is famous in his own right. Over the course of his clerical career, he wrote hundreds of Christian hymns. One of these, "Amazing Grace," is among the most beloved and widely recorded songs ever composed. But Newton's most important contribution to posterity may well have been the advice he gave William Wilberforce at this critical juncture. Contrary to Wilberforce's expectations, Newton did not demand that he flee the sinful world of politics. Newton instead told him that he had an obligation to remain in Parliament and to serve God from this position of power. Newton later wrote Wilberforce, "It is hoped and believed ... that the Lord has raised you up for the good of His church and for the good of the nation."[10]

What Newton told Wilberforce that day was revolutionary, and it is advice which continues to be controversial down to the present day. He did not tell Wilberforce that it was merely acceptable to mix religion and politics; he told him that it was imperative to do so. He instructed his young charge to take his faith, and all of the values and compassion with which it filled him, straight back into Parliament. Wilberforce took his advice. And in so doing, he changed the world.

⤳

THE STORY OF HOW William Wilberforce went on to move his reluctant nation to abolish the slave trade could be the stuff of a Hollywood movie. And indeed it was. The 2006 feature film *Amazing Grace* took the title of Newton's hymn as the emblem of Wilberforce's life and achievement. The film was groundbreaking in that it portrayed a man of deep Christian faith not as a crazed villain, but as a cultured hero. Even so, it is quite easy to walk away from *Amazing Grace* believing that Wilberforce's Christianity was merely coincidental to his hatred of slavery. The movie depicts a man who happens to be a believing Christian and who also happens to be a passionate abolitionist. No connection is ever made between these two aspects of his personality.

Yet the relationship between Wilberforce's faith and his activism was not one of coincidence; it was one of cause and effect. Wilberforce's Christianity was the driving force behind his decades-long abolitionist campaign. It was his faith which gave him the moral clarity to see the evil of slavery, the compassion to want to end it, and the courage to take on the fight.

The Campaign

After deciding to stay in Parliament, Wilberforce searched for a cause to which he could devote his newfound benevolent zeal. It was at this juncture that he read Clarkson's Cambridge essay and was greatly moved by it.[11] When Clarkson and his colleagues asked him to lead the fight against the slave trade in Parliament, Wilberforce immediately agreed.

In 1789, William Wilberforce introduced his first bill to abolish the slave trade in the House of Commons. It was not a popular measure. For the next two years, the Caribbean planters and their allies blocked a vote on the bill by demanding that hearings be held. In the 1791 session of Parliament, Wilberforce reintroduced his bill and secured a vote. The bill was rejected by a margin of 88 to 63. In 1792, Wilberforce introduced his bill yet again. This time, to widespread astonishment, the bill passed the House of Commons. But the House of Lords called for additional hearings on the measure and the session ended without a vote.

Thus it went, year after year. For the remainder of the 1790s and into the new century, Wilberforce introduced his abolition bill at the beginning of each new session of Parliament. And each year his bill went down to defeat by parliamentary maneuver or lost votes. Slavery was too deeply entrenched and far too profitable to be eliminated without a struggle.

It would take almost twenty years of tireless effort and heartbreaking disappointments for Wilberforce and his colleagues to achieve their objective. But in 1807, they finally prevailed. That year both houses of Parliament passed a bill to abolish the slave trade throughout the British Empire. Wilberforce, Clarkson, and their band of evangelical and Quaker abolitionists had accomplished the impossible. A trade which had annually transported close to eighty thousand Africans to lives of slavery in the New World was no more.

〜

THE MOVIE *Amazing Grace* ends on a high note with this long-awaited victory. But while the movie stops here, Wilberforce, Clarkson, and their allies did not. The slave trade may have been outlawed, but slavery itself was still legal. Throughout Britain's colonies, over a half-million slaves and their descendents still faced lifetimes of servitude.

Thus, after the briefest of celebrations, the abolitionists started the process all over again. The Quakers inked up their printing press. Clarkson got back on his horse. And William Wilberforce introduced bills before Parliament to abolish the institution of slavery. As Wilberforce grew older and his health began to deteriorate, he recruited another evangelical member of Parliament, Thomas Fowell Buxton, to lead the day-to-day legislative effort. But Wilberforce always remained abolition's principal personality.

These abolitionists would go on to labor for another twenty-six years until they accomplished this second great objective. In

1833, Parliament finally passed legislation abolishing slavery and freeing all of the slaves in the British Empire. William Wilberforce literally refused to depart this world until he knew that the institution of slavery would not survive him. He died the day after the abolition bill passed the House of Commons.

⌇

IT WOULD BE DIFFICULT to overstate the enormity of this accomplishment. Any objective observer would have given this small band of religious misfits little chance of changing the policy of an empire. Commenting on the abolitionists' ultimate victory, no less an observer than Alexis de Tocqueville wrote: "If you pore over the histories of all peoples, I doubt that you will find anything more extraordinary or more beautiful."[12]

When the English abolitionists began their efforts, slavery was an accepted fact of life not only in England but throughout the world. The institution had existed since the dawn of human history, and few people had ever questioned its validity. As author Adam Hochschild has noted, on the day the Abolition Society first met in the Quaker print shop "well over three-quarters of all people alive were in bondage of one kind or another, not the captivity of striped prison uniforms, but of various systems of slavery or serfdom."[13] Beyond African slavery in America, this worldwide bondage included Russian serfdom, Indian debt bondage, African slavery in Muslim lands and in Africa itself, and the slavery practiced by certain American Indian tribes.

The institution of slavery was buttressed not only by its universality, but also by its profitability. Almost all of Britain's slaves lived in its West Indian colonies, where they were essential to the cultivation of the Empire's most valuable cash crops. England's planters and shipping interests believed that abolition would destroy their lucrative enterprises, and they were ferocious in their opposition to it.

These crops were the source of enormous revenue not only for the businessmen who grew and shipped them but also for the

British crown which taxed their sale. The implications of abolition thus extended beyond economics to geopolitics. The unilateral abolition of slavery threatened a crucial source of revenue at the very time that Britain was locked in a bitter global rivalry with France. Defenders of the Empire thus joined with vested economic interests in determined resistance to any such reform.

It turns out that those who predicted that abolition would result in enormous economic losses were not exaggerating. The fiscal impact of abolition was so great, in fact, that historian Seymour Drescher characterized the British abolition of slavery as voluntary "econocide."[14]

The Motives

This small band of evangelical Anglicans and Quakers devoted their lives to helping a group of people of a different race, from distant lands, whom they had never even met. Every one of these abolitionists overcame their impoverished genetic morality to champion the liberty of strangers as passionately as they would have their own. And every one of them was motivated to do so by the Christian faith they shared. The English abolition movement was a thoroughly Christian conspiracy.

Throughout these long years of struggle, it was the Judeo-Christian idea that informed, motivated, and sustained the abolitionists. These activists believed that all men are created in the image of God and therefore share an inestimable value and fundamental equality. They likewise sought to honor the golden rule that demanded that they love these fellow humans as themselves. Thus at a time when so many Enlightenment thinkers were rationalizing slavery and most of polite society breezily accepted its perpetuation, these Christian men and women could not rest until it was abolished.

Wilberforce was a member of Parliament seeking to persuade fellow legislators who were largely skeptical of his faith. He therefore tended to express his ideas in the language of politics and policy. Yet on a number of occasions, Wilberforce was surprisingly frank about his religious motives. Even in his first and most famous speech in Parliament against the slave trade, Wilberforce confessed his Christian core:

Policy . . . is not my principle, and I am not ashamed to say it. There is a principle above everything that is political. And when I reflect on the command that says, "Thou shalt do no murder," believing the authority to be divine, how can I dare set up any reasonings of my own against it? And, Sir, when we think of eternity, and of the future consequences of all human conduct, what is here in this life which should make any man contradict the principles of his own conscience, the principles of justice, the laws of religion, and of God?[15]

On another occasion Wilberforce contrasted his perspective with the views of so many of his secular-minded peers. Christianity, he said:

assumes her true character . . . when she takes under her protection those poor degraded beings on whom philosophy looks down with disdain or perhaps with contemptuous condescension.[16]

Most of the philosophers of his era did indeed look down upon the slaves. Wilberforce would not.

Thomas Clarkson likewise sought to persuade the broader English public by attacking slavery in universal terms. But the Judeo-Christian idea that drove his activism was never far from the surface. Even in his award-winning Cambridge essay, Clarkson had emphasized that "slavery is incompatible with the Christian system."[17] He illustrated this point by noting of his faith:

The first doctrine which it inculcates is that of brotherly love. It commands good will toward men. It enjoins us to love our neighbors as ourselves, and to do unto all men, as we would that they should do unto us. And how can any man fulfill this scheme of universal benevolence, who reduces an unfortunate person *against his will,* to these *most insupportable* of all human conditions; who considers him as his *private property,* and treats him not as a brother, nor as one of the same parentage as himself, but as an *animal of the brute creation.*[18]

Clarkson added that those who practice slavery:

violate that law of universal benevolence, which was to take away those hateful distinctions of Jew and Gentile, Greek and Barbarian, bond and free, which prevailed when the gospel was introduced.[19]

Finally, Clarkson confessed another common Christian motive: the fear of divine retribution for national sin. He wrote that the failure to end slavery must:

draw down upon us the heaviest judgment of Almighty God, who made of one blood all the sons of men, and who gave to all equally a natural right to liberty; and who, ruling all the kingdoms of the earth with equal providential justice, cannot suffer such deliberate, such monstrous iniquity to pass long unpunished.[20]

The Price

In the enthusiasm of his early days as an evangelical politician, William Wilberforce visited the home of a wealthy nobleman and shared with him his desire to use his position in Parliament to reform the nation's morality. The nobleman was unimpressed. "So you wish to be a reformer of men's morals," he began. "Look then, and see what is the end of such reformers." With this, the man pointed to a painting of the Crucifixion.[21]

While Wilberforce and his colleagues were spared such a fate, they were often the object of serious attacks. As we've seen, in seeking to abolish the slave trade and slavery itself, the abolitionists were taking on some of Britain's most powerful interests. Those who opposed the abolition movement were quick to target the small band of religious activists who led it.

Wilberforce was challenged to duels and threatened with lawsuits. He received death threats which he took seriously enough to employ bodyguards. He was also publicly denounced by some of Britain's leading personalities. The country's most beloved military hero, Lord Nelson, declared that he would battle any threat to "our West Indian possessions . . . while I have an arm to fight in their defense, or a tongue to launch my voice against the damnable doctrine of Wilberforce and his hypocritical allies."[22]

James Boswell, the famous biographer of Samuel Johnson, spoke for many in the secular ruling class when he wrote the following verses deriding Wilberforce's faith-based activism:

> Go Wilberforce with narrow skull,
> Go home and preach away at Hull.
> No longer in the Senate cackle
> In strains that suit the tabernacle;
> I hate your little whittling sneer,
> Your pert and self-sufficient leer.
> Mischief to trade sits on your lip.
> Insects will gnaw the noblest ship.
> Go Wilberforce, begone, for shame,
> Thou dwarf with big resounding name.[23]

Modern-day critics of religion in politics may no longer take the time to write rhyming couplets. But the fundamental complaint remains the same.

While Thomas Clarkson was spared the barbs of such famous opponents, he often faced more dangerous assaults. To get the latest facts about the slave trade, Clarkson often rode his horse right into the lion's den of large slave ports such as Liverpool and Bristol. These cities were literally built from the profits of the slave trade and were perilous places for a man so publicly seeking to cut this income off at its source. Clarkson received repeated death threats. On one occasion, a group of officers from a slave ship tried to kill him by pushing him off a shipping pier.

Another leading evangelical abolitionist, Charles Ramsay, was the victim of a vicious character assassination. Ramsay had been a doctor in the Caribbean and was thus able to provide crucial firsthand accounts of the reality of slavery. As his reports proved increasingly effective, the plantation owners and their agents resolved to neutralize him. They planted stories in friendly newspapers claiming that Ramsay had robbed from his church and abused the sick slaves given to his care. Members of Parliament beholden to slave interests repeated these charges in their speeches. Ramsay was deeply distressed by these repeated attacks on his good name. He died of a massive gastric hemorrhage in the middle of the abolition debate at the age of fifty-five.

ᨒ

AFTER ITS HUMBLE beginnings in the Quaker printing shop, the Society for the Abolition of the African Slave Trade later moved to larger headquarters on London's Old Jewry Street. The street was so named because it had once been lined with synagogues before England expelled its Jews in 1290.

The location could not have been more appropriate. There, on Old Jewry Street, men steeped in the Judeo-Christian tradition spent their days applying that tradition's highest ideals of love and brotherhood in an effort to end the greatest atrocity of their time. Their success provided ultimate vindication for the ghosts of Old Jewry's expelled Jews. Centuries after they had been forced to leave, their most cherished values had returned and, through the efforts of a band of devout Christians, had conquered England from within.

ᨒ

JOHN WESLEY, THE founder of Methodism, worked his entire life to ensure that Christians in England and America not only recognized the love at the core of their faith but acted in the name of this love to help society's most vulnerable. He was instrumental in placing benevolent action at the heart of evangelical theology. It was just such Christian benevolence that drove Wilberforce and his colleagues to devote themselves so completely to the welfare of others.

Taking his theology to its logical conclusion, John Wesley became one of England's earliest and strongest opponents of slavery. Wesley preached against slavery both at home and abroad, making abolition a central theme of his Methodist movement. In 1774, he made a powerful case against the institution in a tract called *Thoughts on Slavery.*

In 1791, as he lay on his deathbed, Wesley's thoughts turned once again to slavery. He wrote what was probably the last letter of his life to William Wilberforce. In it he shared the following words of warning and encouragement with this young abolitionist leader:

> I see not how you can go through your glorious enterprise in opposing that execrable villainy which is the scandal of religion, of England, and of human nature. Unless God has raised you up for this very thing, you will be worn out by the opposition of men and devils; but if God is with you, who can be against you? Are all of them stronger than God? Oh, be not weary in well doing. Go on, in the name of God and in the power of His might, till even American slavery, the vilest that ever saw the sun, shall vanish away before it.[24]

Wilberforce and his colleagues did go on. They persevered until the slave trade and then slavery itself were abolished. And then, as Wesley had hoped, the righteous zeal unleashed by this band of English abolitionists crossed the Atlantic Ocean to America.

Abolition in America

Throughout his life, William Wilberforce suffered long bouts of ill health. These episodes only worsened as he aged. After retiring from Parliament, he began spending extended periods in Bath, an English spa town where the water was believed to restore health. Thus when a young American abolitionist named William Lloyd Garrison arrived in England in 1833, it was to Bath that he set off in hopes of meeting this ailing legend.

Although only twenty-eight years old, Garrison was already emerging as the leading American abolitionist. Garrison was the founder and publisher of *The Liberator,* America's most prominent abolitionist newspaper. He was also one of the founders of the New England Anti-Slavery Society. Shunning gradualism, Garrison was known for his zeal for the immediate abolition of slavery in America and his impatience with anyone who did not share it.

Garrison's one great hero and shining example was William Wilberforce. Wilberforce had not only proved that a small band of Christian brothers could transform society, but he had provided the blueprint for how to accomplish it. In almost every speech he gave, Garrison told the story of Wilberforce and the British abolitionists. In the pages of his newspaper, Garrison shared his dream of a day when Americans would finally overcome their racism, elect a black president, and change the name of their capital from "Washington" to "Wilberforce."[25]

Wilberforce took an immediate liking to this fiery young American. Despite Wilberforce's poor health, the two talked for hours. Before letting Garrison leave, Wilberforce took him aside and gave him his blessing.[26]

⤳

IT TURNED OUT that Garrison's trip to England coincided with two historic events. It was during Garrison's visit that the House of Commons finally passed the bill abolishing slavery in the British Empire. It was also during Garrison's trip, only days after their meeting, that William Wilberforce died. Garrison walked in the funeral procession of his fallen hero. In a very real sense, Garrison returned to America as Wilberforce's heir.

Garrison arrived home more determined than ever to replicate Wilberforce's successful campaign. He immediately pushed for the creation of a national abolition society modeled on the movement Wilberforce had led in England. A mere two months later, in December 1833, Garrison presided over the founding of the American Anti-Slavery Society in Philadelphia.

There is no record of whether Wilberforce and Garrison discussed their faith at their historic meeting in Bath. If they had done so, they would have found a deep bond. These two men were not simply abolitionists who happened to be Christian. They were abolitionists only because they were Christians who believed that their faith demanded their activism. Among the many similarities between the English and American abolition movements was the fact that they both consisted almost entirely of devout Christians seeking to implement the core principles of the Judeo-Christian idea.

The Movement

In February 1834, a theology student at Ohio's Lane Seminary named Theodore Weld decided that the time had come to enlist his fellow seminary students in the abolitionist cause. He secured permission from the school's administration to hold a series of public discussions on the question: "Ought the people of the slaveholding states to abolish slavery immediately?" For eighteen days, the students huddled together and debated this question long into the night.

Given the diverse backgrounds of the students, it is a wonder that these "Lane Debates" did not explode into violence. Among the participants were Weld and other abolitionists, white Southerners whose families owned slaves, and an ex-slave named James Bradley who had purchased his freedom.[27] But guided by Weld and his passionate appeals to their shared theology, these sessions yielded a surprising unity of vision. At the end of the debate, the students voted unanimously in support of immediate abolition.

Like Thomas Clarkson in England, these students not only understood that the time had come to stop the sin of slavery but recognized that they were the ones who would have to accomplish the task. The Lane students immediately created a campus abolition society. Many also began to work in the community of freed slaves that lived in nearby Cincinnati.

Lane Seminary's conservative trustees were horrified. Abolition was still the most controversial of causes, and they feared that these student activists would alienate both the seminary's financial supporters and its white neighbors. The Board of Trustees quickly passed a resolution banning the students' abolition society. All but a handful of Lane students responded by leaving the seminary. As the members of the abolition society noted in a letter to the faculty, they believed they had done nothing which "duty to God, and love to man, did not require."[28] They would compromise neither.

After dropping out of the seminary, many of the Lane students devoted themselves full-time to activism. Weld went to work for Garrison's American Anti-Slavery Society. Two other students opened a school for Cincinnati's free black population. One of the Southern students withdrew from Lane for an even more revolutionary purpose. His theological studies had been supported by the labor of his slaves back home. He resolved not only to free his slaves, but to find a job so that he could support them while they began their own studies.[29]

∽

IF WILLIAM LLOYD GARRISON can be seen as the American Wilberforce, then Theodore Weld was the American Thomas Clarkson. Like Clarkson before him, Weld was a minister's son who was studying to become a minister. Also like Clarkson, Weld abandoned these plans when he discovered the cause of abolition. Through their burning passion and indefatigable work, each man did more than any of his fellow citizens to build grassroots abolition movements in their respective countries.

In 1834, Weld became a full-time field agent for the American Anti-Slavery Society. Eventually, he persuaded thirty of the fifty-four members of Lane Seminary's abolition society to join him in this work.[30] These Lane students now dominated the Anti-Slavery Society's grassroots efforts and would continue to do so for the remainder of the decade.

Weld spent most of 1835 and 1836 building local abolition societies in Ohio, western Pennsylvania, and western New York. Yet even in Northern states such as these, abolition was a deeply unpopular cause. Weld encountered hostility almost everywhere he went. Some townsfolk simply shouted and heckled. Others threw rotten eggs and fruit. But Weld learned that if he kept speaking through it all, night after night, his opponents would eventually tire and start listening to what he had to say. Once they did so, he was often able to win them over to the cause of abolition. Many of the towns which most abused Weld upon his arrival formed the most active abolition societies after his departure.

Garrison and the other leaders of the Anti-Slavery Society were deeply impressed by the progress that Weld and his fellow students were making. They realized that these students were accomplishing far more in the field than they had been able to achieve by printing newspapers and pamphlets from their offices back East. In 1836, the Anti-Slavery Society decided to abandon the distribution of written materials and devote their full resources to putting more men in the field under Weld's leadership.

In the Gospel of Luke, Jesus appoints seventy of his followers to go into the world and spread his message. Following this example, the Anti-Slavery Society decided to expand Weld's band to seventy full-time field agents. Weld was put in charge of selecting and training the new recruits. "The Seventy," as this group came to be known, would leave an indelible mark on America's political landscape. Almost all of the abolitionist districts in America were communities which had been visited and organized by one or more of these agents.

Beyond his field work, Weld also wrote extensively against slavery. Two of his books became literary pillars of the abolition movement. In *The Bible Against Slavery,* Weld made a theological case for abolition. He detailed the many significant ways in which slavery as practiced in America differed from the type of servitude sanctioned by the Bible. He then set forth a compelling argument that American slavery was "the highest possible violation" of core Christian commandments such as those prohibiting theft and kidnapping.

In his second book, *Slavery As It Is,* Weld moved past theology to focus on the harsh reality of slavery. Like Clarkson, Weld believed that the public's apathy toward slavery was due largely to the fact that most people had no idea how brutal the institution really was. Thus Weld used mostly public sources to compile a long list of abuses and tortures that characterized slavery in America. *Slavery As It Is* became one of the abolition movement's most effective tools.

⌇

WHEN WELD AND HIS fellow students were engaged in their historic debate at Lane Seminary, the daughter of the seminary's president would often sit and listen.[31] This young evangelical Christian proved to be no more immune to Theodore Weld's righteous charisma than his fellow students. She embraced the cause of immediate abolition along with everyone else in the room.

This young woman would turn out to be the most important of Theodore Weld's converts. Her name was Harriet Beecher, and when she married Calvin Stowe she added his last name to her own. Her 1852 book *Uncle Tom's Cabin* became a national and international bestseller and one of the most influential abolitionist texts ever written.

Uncle Tom's Cabin was not a work of theology or history, but a novel about the ordeal of slaves in the American South. Yet Stowe's story was so compelling that it was able to pierce the prevailing indifference to slavery in a way that facts and logic alone never could. Suddenly, millions of Americans were able to see the cruelty and injustice of slavery, and they abhorred it. No less a figure than President Lincoln recognized the transformative impact of *Uncle Tom's Cabin*. When the president met Stowe at the White House during the Civil War, he is said to have greeted her with the words, "So you're the little woman who wrote the book that started this great war."[32]

Stowe never experienced slavery first-hand. But she remembered the stories the Southern students had told during the Lane debates years earlier. She had also closely read Theodore Weld's book *Slavery As It Is* and incorporated many of its examples into her plot.[33] Harriet Beecher Stowe thus delivered Theodore Weld's abolitionist message to a far larger audience than Weld himself could ever reach.

～

THE AMERICAN ABOLITION movement was managed and staffed by a surprisingly small band of evangelical activists. When it came to the movement's financial support, the cast was smaller still. To a very large extent, American abolitionism was funded by two evangelical brothers: Arthur and Lewis Tappan.

The Tappans made a fortune in the silk trade. As products of the Second Great Awakening who believed in the centrality of disinterested benevolence to their faith, they spent most of this wealth bankrolling a number of the era's most important benevolent societies. Along with most of the evangelical activists they funded, however, the Tappans eventually narrowed their focus and their financing to one cause in particular: abolition.

The Tappan brothers funded Garrison's newspaper, *The Liberator*. They funded the American Anti-Slavery Society. They funded the Lane Seminary where Weld and his fellow activists studied. They funded the field work of The Seventy. When the slaves aboard the ship *Amistad* staged a mutiny and were arrested upon landing in New York, the Tappans were the ones who paid for the lawyers who eventually won them their freedom.

The Motives

Garrison, Weld, the Tappans and almost all of the leaders of the American abolition movement were products of the Second Great Awakening. It was this massive religious revival which deepened their faith and placed the mission of disinterested benevolence on their hearts. Their efforts consisted largely of preaching the principles of the Second Great Awakening in the language of the Second Great Awakening to the converts of the Second Great Awakening. The American abolition movement was to a great extent the political arm of this massive religious revival.[34]

The movement's religious character was on clear display in the work of Weld and his fellow field agents. Weld and his colleagues rarely, if ever, spoke in town squares or private homes; they spoke in churches. Their speeches were not lectures so much as sermons in which they preached an abolitionist message closely linked to core Christian principles. Given the religious nature of their work, Weld recruited his agents from the leading evangelical institutions of his day. In fact, the Seventy was composed almost entirely of seminary students and clergymen who had left their posts to preach abolition to the nation.[35]

Writing about the American abolition movement, historian Gilbert Barnes concluded:

> From the beginning the movement had been inextricably bound up with the churches. The churches were its forums and the houses of its local organizations; from the churches it drew its justifying inspiration. It was an aspect of the

churches, non-sectarian in organization but evangelical in character—a part of the benevolent empire. . . . Everywhere in the organization clergymen were in control. In every aspect, the agitation was "a moral movement—a religious movement" drawing its life from the churches.[36]

⁓

WILLIAM LLOYD GARRISON's transformation from idealistic youth to abolitionist leader was the fruit of seeds sown by three Christian leaders. Shortly after his arrival in Boston in late 1826, Garrison began attending services at Lyman Beecher's Hanover Street Church. Beecher was one of the leading preachers of the Second Great Awakening. Like Jeremiah Evarts, Beecher was a Yale graduate and a protégé of Yale's president, Timothy Dwight. Also like Evarts, Beecher had enthusiastically embraced Dwight's message of disinterested benevolence. Beecher told his congregation that "the way to get good was to do good,"[37] and he urged them to enlist in a "moral militia."[38] Garrison thus learned the importance of disinterested benevolence directly from one of its most prominent proponents.

Having embraced benevolence as his goal, Garrison began searching for his cause. In 1828, he went to the Federal Street Baptist Church in Boston to listen to a speech by a Quaker abolitionist named Benjamin Lundy. At a time when slavery was a rarely questioned fact of American life, Lundy rejected all compromise and gradualism. He told his listeners that they had a Christian duty to abolish slavery and the power to do so. Garrison was so moved by Lundy's speech that he followed him back to Baltimore and went to work for his abolitionist newspaper. William Lloyd Garrison had found the cause to which he would devote the rest of his life.

In his early years as an activist, Garrison encountered the third significant influence on his life: the Reverend George Bourne. Bourne was a Presbyterian minister and outspoken abolitionist who made a powerful biblical argument against slavery in his 1816 work *The Book and Slavery Irreconcilable*. Here, Bourne based his anti-slavery argument on Genesis 21:16, which reads, "He that stealeth a man and selleth him . . . shall surely be put to death." Modern Bible translations typically substitute the word "kidnap" for "stealeth." Bourne argued that since America's slaves had originally been kidnapped from Africa, slavery as practiced in America constituted the gravest of sins.

Referring to Bourne's book, Garrison stated, "Next to the Bible, we are indebted to this work for our views of the system of slavery."[39] Throughout his career, Garrison would use the biblically charged term "man-stealing" to describe slavery. Even the mission statement of the American Anti-Slavery Society, written by Garrison, prominently proclaimed that "every American citizen, who retains a human being in involuntary bondage, is a MAN-STEALER."[40]

Garrison's loyalty to the Bible was absolute. He declared that in all of his actions he would "consult no statute book than the Bible."[41] Even if the Bible's requirements conflicted with those of the secular law, Garrison had little doubt which authority he would follow. In such a case, Garrison wrote, he would violate the secular law and "submit to the penalty, unresistingly, in imitation of Christ, and his apostles, and the holy martyrs."[52] As we will see, Garrison had ample opportunity to demonstrate the sincerity of these words.

After Charleston, South Carolina fell to Union forces in 1865, Secretary of War Stanton honored Garrison by inviting him to speak at a flag-raising ceremony at nearby Fort Sumter. Afterward, Garrison made his way to Zion Church, where he received a hero's welcome from several thousand former slaves. It was here, addressing those to whom he had devoted his life, that Garrison most eloquently expressed the Judeo-Christian idea that had moved him. Garrison told the former slaves:

> It was not on account of your complexion or race, as a people, that I espoused your cause, but because you were the children

of a common Father, created in the same divine image, having the same inalienable rights, and as much entitled to liberty as the proudest slaveholder that ever walked the earth.[43]

⌇

IT TOOK THEODORE WELD a long time to finish college. Throughout his extended student career, national events repeatedly conspired to pluck him off campus and place him on the national stage. It is a testament to Weld's love of learning that he kept trying to escape the spotlight and go back to school.

Among the institutions of higher learning that Weld abandoned was Hamilton College in upstate New York. Weld was studying at Hamilton when Charles Finney, the most popular preacher of the Second Great Awakening, held a major revival in nearby Utica. Hamilton students flocked to Finney's meetings and came back to school still buzzing about his charismatic persona and dramatic style. Weld was not impressed. "This man is not a minister," he said of Finney, "and I will never acknowledge him as such."[44]

Weld's aunt had other ideas. She tricked her nephew into attending a church service in which Finney made an unannounced appearance. Finney was fully briefed on Weld's skepticism, and he focused his entire sermon on winning over this young leader. Preaching on the theme of how "one sinner destroyeth much good," Finney stared directly at Weld as he spoke. "And yes, you'll go to college," Finney concluded, "and use all your influence against the Lord's work."[45]

Weld was furious. He later accosted Finney in a market and publicly denounced him "with all the vocabulary of abuse the language afforded."[46] Finney offered little protest. By nighttime, Weld's rage had turned to shame. He went to apologize to Finney. Surprised to see Weld at his door, Finney asked, "Is it not enough? Have you followed a minister of the Lord Jesus to his own door to abuse him?" Weld told him no, that he had come "for a very different purpose."[47]

Before Weld could finish his sentence, Finney threw his arms around the young man's neck and lowered them both to their knees where they sobbed and prayed. "That put an end to my studying," Weld later recalled. "I was with him in his meetings, speaking and laboring, all that summer."[48]

Finney was the leading preacher of the Second Great Awakening and, as we've seen, its most passionate proponent of disinterested benevolence. Weld thus imbibed his zeal for benevolent action directly from its greatest contemporary source. Before long, he left Finney's side to devote himself full-time to the cause of disinterested benevolence in the form of the abolition movement.

〜

EVANGELICAL THEOLOGY OFFERED not only carrots to reward Christian efforts to confront sin but also sticks to punish the failure to do so. Most abolitionists were motivated by both. Many expressed the fear that failing to end the sin of slavery would bring divine retribution upon the United States. William Lloyd Garrison repeatedly warned that such divine punishment would take the form of a violent slave uprising. When Nat Turner led a bloody slave revolt in 1831, Garrison saw it as the first sign that his dark prophecy was being fulfilled. He wrote, "The first drops of blood, which are but the prelude to a deluge from the gathering clouds, have fallen."[49]

In December 1835, a massive fire destroyed most of downtown Manhattan, including the Tappan brothers' store and warehouse. Theodore Weld feared that this conflagration was nothing less than a warning from God. "My brother," he wrote to Lewis Tappan, "I can't resist the conviction that this terrible rebuke is but a single herald sent in advance to announce the coming of a host."[50] He told his patron that only redoubled efforts to free the slaves and feed the hungry could save America from this impending doom.

Harriet Beecher Stowe likewise lived with a sense of dread that a just God would punish her nation for the sin of slavery.

Writing in her journal, she revealed that this fear was among her main motives for writing *Uncle Tom's Cabin*:

> I wrote what I did because as a woman, as a mother, I was oppressed and brokenhearted with the sorrows and injustice I saw, because as a Christian I felt the dishonor to Christianity, and because as a lover of my country I trembled at the coming day of wrath.[51]

Despite her efforts to forestall it, Stowe believed that this day of wrath eventually came in the form of the Civil War. She concluded that "it was God's will that this nation—the North as well as the South—should deeply and terribly suffer for the sin of consenting to and encouraging the great oppressions of the South."[52]

Even Abraham Lincoln saw God's hand in this national tragedy. In his second inaugural address, he described the Civil War as a "woe" being suffered because of the "offense" of slavery. Although victory was merely days away, Lincoln declared:

> If God wills that it continue until all the wealth piled by the bondsman's two hundred and fifty years of unrequited toil shall be sunk, and until every drop of blood drawn with the lash shall be paid by another drawn with the sword . . . so still it must be said the judgments of the Lord are true and righteous altogether.

The Price

In pressing for the immediate abolition of slavery, Garrison, Weld, and their colleagues provoked the intense enmity of some of the most powerful interests in America. Even in the North, large segments of the economy depended upon slavery and the revenues it produced. New England's ships dominated the bustling international trade in plantation produce. Massachusetts' textile factories prospered from their access to cheap Southern cotton. In New York, bankers, manufacturers, and retailers alike relied upon the patronage of Southern planters. In fact, it was estimated that at least one-third of the price of a bale of cotton ended up being transferred to New York merchants.[53] Even the Northern working class had strong reasons to fear abolition. It was widely believed that once liberated, free blacks would migrate to the Northern cities en masse to compete with them for jobs.

At a deeper level, many Americans feared the abolition movement because they sensed just how intractable the dispute over slavery really was. They realized that any serious effort to abolish slavery would lead to the secession of the Southern states from the Union and, quite possibly, civil war. Rather than blame the slaveholders, many Northerners attacked the abolitionists with a rage that can only be generated by the deepest of fears.

ᶜᵛ

WHILE WORKING FOR Benjamin Lundy's abolitionist newspaper in Baltimore, William Lloyd Garrison wrote an article disclosing that seventy-five slaves had been transported from Baltimore to New Orleans on a ship owned by a New England merchant named Francis Todd. Garrison criticized Todd for making his money in so unscrupulous a fashion.

Todd did not appreciate the publicity. Since Maryland was a slave state, Todd was able to persuade sympathetic local authorities to indict Garrison on the criminal charge of having published a "gross and malicious libel." Garrison was found guilty and sentenced to pay a fifty-dollar fine or spend six months in jail. Unable to afford the fine, Garrison entered Baltimore Jail on April 17, 1830. He served forty-nine days of his sentence before Arthur Tappan paid his fine and secured his release.

Even after he returned north to Boston, Garrison's efforts continued to meet with hostility. In September 1835, abolition opponents erected a nine-foot-high gallows in front of his home. The following month, Garrison's enemies progressed from threats to action.

On October 21, Garrison arrived downtown to address a meeting of the Boston Female Anti-Slavery Society. A large mob quickly assembled outside and called for Garrison to be lynched. The event was cancelled and the women left. Garrison fled the building through a back window and hid in the loft of a nearby shop.

The leaders of the mob soon found Garrison's hiding place. They tied a rope around his waist and made him crawl out the window and down a ladder into the crowd of thousands waiting below. As they pulled Garrison down the street by the rope, the ringleaders debated what to do with their despised captive. Some wanted to lynch him. Less homicidal souls wanted merely to dye his hands and face in black ink and then tar and feather him.

Garrison was saved from both of these fates by a quick-witted sheriff. The lawman arrested Garrison for "disturbing the peace" and brought him to the safety of prison. Finding himself behind bars once again, Garrison reflected that it was "a blessed privilege thus to suffer for Christ."[54]

In 1838, Garrison and other abolitionist leaders were invited to address an anti-slavery meeting in Philadelphia. The meeting took place in Pennsylvania Hall, a brand-new structure built to serve as a center for the city's abolition movement. Pennsylvania Hall had been constructed and financed largely by contributions from working-class activists, who proudly called their building the "hall of the people."

Word of the abolitionist meeting spread quickly, and soon a mob of thousands had gathered outside. The abolitionists finished their speeches despite the rocks crashing through the windows and the need to shout to be heard above the din of the crowd below. Then they exited through the front door and navigated a gantlet of shoves and taunts. Once the audience had departed, the mob broke down the doors, ransacked the building, and set it on fire. Pennsylvania Hall, the "hall of the people," had been open for all of four days before it was burned to the ground.[55]

When the threats against his life were at their worst, Garrison shared with his wife the source of his courage. He wrote to her, "There is a whole eternity of consolation in this assurance—he who loses his life for Christ's sake shall find it."[56]

～

AS THEODORE WELD went from city to city preaching abolition, he grew accustomed to the constant barrage of insults, eggs, and rotten fruit. But sometimes the locals would throw rocks instead of eggs, and sometimes they would hit him with clubs instead of tomatoes. Weld wrote that in Troy, New York, the stone-throwing was so frequent that his entire body was "one general, painful bruise."[57]

The residents of Troy were so violent toward Weld that he was certain he would be killed if he continued preaching abolition. Weld insisted upon continuing to speak every night. But he also took the precaution of drafting a farewell letter expressing his willingness to "fall and die a martyr" for the cause. "God gird us all to do valiantly for the helpless and innocent," Weld wrote. "Blessed are they who die in the harness."[58]

～

ALTHOUGH THEY WORKED largely behind the scenes, even the Tappans found themselves under attack for their support of abolition. In 1834, Lewis Tappan's home was burned to the ground by arsonists. To prevent a similar fate from befalling their business, Arthur Tappan armed his clerks and announced that he would meet violence with violence.[59] Southern governors demanded that Arthur Tappan be extradited and tried for fomenting rebellion.

～

THEODORE WELD SPENT most of 1835 speaking in churches across Ohio as an agent of the American Anti-Slavery Society. During this time, Weld made a deep impression upon a young Ohio attorney named Joshua Giddings. Giddings went on to lead the local abolition society and was elected to Congress on an anti-slavery platform. When he arrived in Washington, Giddings rented a room in the boardinghouse of Mrs. Ann Sprigg. He shared the house with eight other congressmen who also boarded there, including a newly elected representative from Illinois named Abraham Lincoln.

In their leisure time back at the boardinghouse, Giddings and Lincoln held many long conversations about slavery. Giddings explained to Lincoln that the incidents of slave abuse they witnessed together in Washington were not aberrations, but the certain consequences of an evil institution.[60] Giddings stressed that these evils could not be eliminated through reform or other half-measures, but only by the immediate abolition of slavery. Thus, through the person of Joshua Giddings, Theodore Weld's anti-slavery message reached the ears of the man who would one day end slavery in America.

FIVE

Falling Backwards:
The Abandonment of the Judeo-Christian Idea and the Return of Slavery and Genocide

If I were asked today to formulate as concisely as possible the main cause of the ruinous [Russian] Revolution that swallowed up some sixty million of our people, I could not put it more accurately than to repeat: "Men have forgotten God; that's why all this has happened."[1]

—ALEKSANDR SOLZHENITSYN, SOVIET DISSIDENT

IN THE EARLY 1930s, Soviet leader Joseph Stalin starved millions of Ukrainian peasants to death. Throughout this period, it was forbidden to take food from the cities to the people starving in the countryside. Likewise, the peasants were not allowed to leave the countryside for the cities to seek food. Yet the postal service still dutifully delivered the mail between these two worlds. Thus, in the middle of the famine, a young Jewish reporter for a Communist Party newspaper in Moscow was able to receive a letter from his father back in the Ukrainian countryside. The letter read, in part:

> My beloved son, this is to let you know that your mother is dead. She died from starvation after months of pain. I, too, am on the way, like many others in our town. . . . Your mother's last wish was that you, our only son, say *Kaddish** for her. Like your mother I, too, hope and pray that you may forget your atheism now when the godless have brought down heaven's wrath on Russia.[2]

Kaddish is the prayer that Jews recite when mourning the death of a loved one.

Stalin was starving this reporter's parents not because they were Jews, but because they were peasants. In the Soviet Union, the peasants were a hated class enemy. Even if they had survived Stalin's famine, however, this couple would have won only a temporary reprieve. A decade later, when the Nazis invaded Ukraine, they almost certainly would have been murdered along with nearly all of Ukraine's other Jews. At this later date, they would have been killed not because they were peasants but because they were Jews.

This young Communist reporter likely dismissed his father's explanation for the Soviet Union's problems as an embarrassing peasant superstition. But his father was right. He was able to penetrate the pall of Communist propaganda to identify the true source of his own suffering. Divine intervention aside, this man and millions like him were being starved to death because the Soviet Union had abandoned the core principles of Judeo-Christian morality.

Had this man survived Stalin's famine to be murdered by the Nazis a decade later, the same insight would have explained his fate. The Jews of Ukraine were lined up in rows and machine-gunned into mass graves because the Nazis had likewise rejected the Judeo-Christian idea.

～

AT THE DAWN OF THE twentieth century, there was reason for measured optimism about the future of Western civilization. In the prior century, people informed and motivated by the Judeo-Christian idea had led mass movements to end the West's greatest atrocities. The noble but ultimately unsuccessful Christian efforts to save the American Indian from ethnic cleansing were replicated and applied to the problem of slavery. First in England and then in America, Christian movements led the fight to abolish the slave trade and then slavery itself. Millions of Christians on both sides of the Atlantic saw through the fog of racism that had descended on their cultures to recognize the sanctity and

equality of all humans. They then transcended their impoverished genetic morality to love their persecuted neighbors as
themselves. The West's zone of compassion was growing ever
wider.

Then things went horribly wrong in a hurry. With the intellectual freedom of the post-Enlightenment era, modern philosophies emerged that rejected the Judeo-Christian idea and
passionately promoted new divisions of mankind. Communism
replaced the brotherhood of man with a class-based worldview
in which only the workers possessed human rights. Nazism
rejected the brotherhood of man for a race-based worldview in
which only "Aryan" life was sacred.

In the early decades of the twentieth century, political parties
based on these new ideologies seized power in Russia and Germany. Suddenly, new regimes with guns and armies went to
work aggressively implementing their modern theories about
humanity and progress. As they did so, they opened wide the
doors of Western civilization to the very atrocities that the
Judeo-Christian activists had so recently helped to expel.
Through these doors walked the worst mass murderers and
slave-drivers that human history has ever known.

〜

THE FACT THAT A book defending religious faith includes a chapter on these modern secular atrocities is predictable to the point
of cliché. Those seeking to condemn religion as the great source
of human violence will inevitably cite the Crusades and the
Spanish Inquisition. Those seeking to defend religious faith and
place the blame for human atrocity elsewhere will invariably
respond by pointing to the Holocaust and the Gulag.

The purpose of this chapter, however, is not to demonstrate
shared guilt. This is not an exercise in filling in the other side of
the ledger. To note that secular regimes have also committed
atrocities is, quite frankly, a pathetic defense of religious faith.
The purpose of reviewing these episodes is not merely to note

that they occurred, but to make a deeper point about *why* they occurred.

At the root of all of these atrocities, whether they are classified as "religious" or "secular," we find neither religion nor ideology. These atrocities, and all atrocities, are the product of human nature. It is our inborn inclination to pursue our own self-interest and to disregard the interests of those outside our particular ingroup—our selfish gene—that drives humans to enslave and kill. And it is because all humans are born with this evil inclination that genocide and slavery have been so common in so many cultures for so long.

The great insight of the Judeo-Christian tradition is that we are the source of the evil in this world. The great promise of the Judeo-Christian tradition is its power to inspire men to overcome the evil in their hearts. The West has yet to produce another system that has enabled so many people to so effectively transcend our impoverished genetic morality.

Modern ideologies such as Nazism and Communism, by contrast, did not seek to transcend human nature, but to empower it. These new ideologies turbo-charged our natural selfishness and encouraged it as the greatest good. Elevating and unleashing humanity's most dangerous impulses was a perilous enterprise. Genocide was as certain as the sunrise.

The point is this: Communism and Nazism were not evil ideologies that coincidentally rejected the Judeo-Christian idea. These ideologies were evil precisely *because* they rejected the Judeo-Christian idea.

Adolf Hitler and the Nazis: From the Brotherhood of Man to the Aryan Reich

In 1862, a newly minted doctor of zoology named Ernst Haeckel accepted the position of professor of comparative anatomy at the University of Jena, in Germany. These were exciting times to be entering this particular field of study. Charles Darwin's revolutionary book *On the Origin of Species* had been published just a few years earlier. It suddenly seemed that the biological sciences could help unlock mankind's deepest mysteries.

For Haeckel, in fact, the implication of Darwin's views extended well beyond science. In an 1864 letter to his father, a devout Christian, Haeckel wrote:

> I share essentially your view of life, dear father, only I value human life and humans themselves much less than you.... The individual with his personal existence appears to me only a temporary member in this large chain, as a rapidly vanishing vapor ... Personal individual existence appears to me so horribly miserable, petty, and worthless, that I see it as intended for nothing but destruction.[3]

Despite the revolutionary nature of his theory, Darwin was reluctant to apply his ideas beyond the realm of science to questions of morality. Yet many of his students lacked such reservations and were supremely confident that their study of animal development would yield profound ethical insights. Ernst Haeckel became a leader among those applying Darwinism more broadly. By the end of the century, he had taken his belief in evolution to what he believed to be its logical moral conclusion. Ernst Haeckel became an outspoken advocate of eugenics, infanticide, euthanasia, racial inequality, and the murder of the mentally and physically disabled.

By the turn of the century, Haeckel had become Germany's preeminent Darwinist. His books setting forth his views on science and morality were among the era's most popular works of nonfiction. Scores of Haeckel's acolytes adopted and developed his ideas. In the process, Haeckel's interpretation of Darwinism came to dominate the intellectual environment of early twentieth-century Germany.

Among those coming of age in this intellectual milieu was an Austrian art student named Adolf Hitler. There can be little doubt that Hitler was influenced by Haeckel's ideas. A close examination of Hitler's pronouncements on the value of human life, morality, racial competition, and eugenics reveals a similarity with Haeckel's writing that sometimes verges on direct quotation. Whether he studied Haeckel directly or through the many popularizers of his work, Hitler was clearly Haeckel's disciple.*

Hitler no doubt exaggerated and twisted Haeckel's ideas in ways the zoologist never predicted and certainly would not have condoned. But that is precisely the danger inherent in the application of science and philosophy to the basic principles of our morality. Once we venture from the safe harbor of the Judeo-Christian idea, we can drift towards treacherous waters with astonishing speed. Haeckel and his colleagues may not have chosen the ultimate destination. But they were the ones who pulled up anchor and set sail.

Rejecting the Judeo-Christian Idea

Technically speaking, Adolf Hitler was a Christian. He was born to Roman Catholic parents and was baptized into the Roman Catholic Church. It appears that he even received a rudimentary Catholic education. Yet Hitler's rejection of his Judeo-Christian roots could not have been more absolute.

It is no surprise, of course, to learn that Hitler had a negative view of Judaism. Given his pathological hatred of the Jewish

---

*In writing this section on the life and thought of Ernst Haeckel and its influence upon the intellectual climate of early twentieth-century Germany, I have relied in large part on Richard Weikart's book *From Darwin to Hitler*. Some have criticized Weikart for claiming too direct a connection between thinkers such as Haeckel and Nazi ideology. I believe that these critiques are largely unfair. Weikart goes to great lengths to emphasize the limits of his claim. In particular, he recognizes an important distinction between intending and enabling an outcome. Weikart does not claim that Haeckel intended to produce a Hitler or that his ideas led inevitably to the death camps. Weikart merely seeks to demonstrate that Haeckel's ideas, especially as applied and interpreted by others, enabled Nazi thought by providing many of its building blocks. The evidence he cites in support of this chain of causation is compelling.

people, he could never have acknowledged that they contributed anything of value to the world. Yet while he wrote and spoke at great length about the evils of Jews, Hitler devoted relatively little time to attacking their religion. He did not seem to take Judaism seriously enough to invest the effort in a detailed critique. Instead, Hitler merely projected what he believed to be the faults of the Jews onto their faith. He dismissed Judaism as "nothing but an instrument for his [the Jew's] business existence."[4] Elsewhere, he referred to Judaism as the worship of "the golden calf" and claimed that the faith had no foundation "but the most repulsive materialism."[5]

In dismissing Judaism, Hitler was well within the mainstream of contemporary German anti-Semitism. When it came to Christianity, however, the ranks of the German anti-Semites were divided. While some rejected their Christianity, others sought to salvage their faith by disconnecting it from what they saw as its tainted Jewish roots.

Toward this end, a group of Protestant Nazi sympathizers formed a denomination, the *Deutsche Christen* (German Christians), which worked to systematically extirpate all things Jewish from their faith. They advocated removing the "Jewish" Old Testament from the Bible, as well as barring all non-Aryans from becoming Christian ministers or teachers. In 1939, the German Christians formed an official body with a name that made its mission quite clear: the Institute for the Research and Removal of Jewish Influences on the Religious Life of the German People.

By all accounts, Hitler refused to make such fine distinctions. He never demonstrated any real interest in Christianity outside of efforts to co-opt it for his political purposes. Once Hitler had consolidated his grip on power, his anti-Christian remarks grew more frequent.[6] Most of all, it seems that Hitler simply refused to embrace a tradition swaddled in so Jewish a cloth. Seeing Christianity as an inherently Jewish philosophy, Hitler associated it with everything he hated most. According to Hitler:

> The heaviest blow that ever struck humanity was the coming
> of Christianity. Bolshevism is Christianity's illegitimate child.
> Both are inventions of the Jew.[7]

Hitler's Race-Based Morality

Hitler's rejection of the Judeo-Christian tradition did not render him a nihilist. He never abandoned the concepts of good and evil; he simply twisted them into a hideous new ethic of his own making.

In constructing his alternative morality, Hitler did not innovate so much as synthesize and exaggerate. Hitler borrowed almost all of his fundamental assumptions from his era's most popular intellectuals. In fact, almost every idea Hitler appropriated, and twisted, can be traced back to the Enlightenment and the Romantic movement's response thereto.

Hitler claimed to share the Enlightenment's overriding faith in the power of human reason. He stated that National Socialism's one ambition must be "to scientifically construct a doctrine that is nothing more than an homage to reason."[8] Hitler's doctrine will stand, instead, as a cautionary tale forever warning us of the limits of reason.

Hitler also shared the Enlightenment's deep reverence for nature. He believed that "salvation" came from accepting "the laws of nature."[9] When it came to discovering these laws, Hitler embraced both Darwin's theory of evolution and the crude social Darwinist interpretations of this theory that were so popular in Germany at the time. He passionately believed that Darwin's insights not only explained human development over the ages but could also prescribe social policy in the present. Hitler turned the social Darwinist thesis into the most absolute of faiths.

Hitler believed that human reason applied to the study of nature and evolution had unlocked the key to a millennial future. At the root of everything Hitler did was his belief that humanity would be perfected through a series of racial struggles. In Hitler's words, "the triumphal march of the best race" was the "precondition for all human progress."[10] And Hitler had no doubt about which race was the best. He wrote:

> All the human culture, all the results of art, science, and tech-
> nology that we see before us today are almost exclusively the
> creative product of the Aryan. . . . He is the Prometheus of
> mankind from whose bright forehead the divine spark of
> genius has sprung at all times, forever kindling anew that fire
> of knowledge which illuminated the night of silent mysteries
> and thus caused man to climb the path to mastery over the
> other beings of this earth. Exclude him—and perhaps after a
> few thousand years darkness will descend on the earth, human
> culture will pass, and the world turn to a desert.[11]

Yet Hitler was not content to wait for nature to refine human-ity through a gradual Aryan triumph. He sought to speed the process by which the Aryans would come to dominate their infe-rior neighbors by military conquest, ethnic cleansing, and geno-cide. From the Nazi perspective, World War II and the Holocaust would simply accelerate the inevitable outcome of the struggle for survival.

In addition to the struggle *between* races, Hitler also recognized a second Darwinian struggle *among* the stronger and weaker members of each individual race. For Hitler, this internal struggle was also crucial for humanity's forward march. This was the force which would ultimately perfect the Aryan race from within.

In this context as well, Hitler was not content for nature to slowly work its magic. He sought to accelerate the purification of the Aryan race by eliminating the weakest Germans, namely the mentally and physically disabled. Hitler thus embraced infanti-cide, euthanasia, and eugenics. He wrote that preventing "defec-tive people" from having "equally defective offspring" represented "the most humane act of mankind."[12] He described the urgency of such policies in messianic terms:

Here the state must act as the guardian of a millennial future in the face of which the wishes and the selfishness of the individual must appear as nothing and submit. It must put the most modern medical means in the service of this knowledge. It must declare unfit for propagation all who are in any way visibly sick or who have inherited a disease and can therefore pass it on, and put this into actual practice.[13]

⌐

HITLER'S MORAL CODE followed logically from his Darwinian worldview. Hitler's goal was nothing less than the perfection of humanity. He believed that this goal would be achieved through the "triumphal march" of strong Aryans over their inferiors, both foreign and domestic. Therefore, anything that promoted Aryan progress in this march was inherently good. Anything that retarded this Aryan advance was innately evil. As Hitler put it, he refused to "grant the right to existence even to an ethical idea if this idea represents a danger for the racial life of the bearers of higher ethics [the Aryans]."[14]

Hitler's evolutionary ethics represented a complete departure from the Judeo-Christian tradition. In fact, Hitler's ethics were not merely an alternative to the Judeo-Christian idea; they were its diametric opposite. For every core tenet of Judeo-Christian morality, Hitler offered a dark antithesis.

The Judeo-Christian tradition maintains that all humans are created in the image of God. Hitler believed that only Aryans embodied the divine image. Employing biblical language to describe his contrary views, Hitler referred to the Aryan race as the "highest image of the Lord." He warned that anyone who attacked Aryans "commits sacrilege against the benevolent creator of this miracle and contributes to the expulsion from paradise."[15] For Hitler, God was an Aryan.

The Judeo-Christian idea insists upon the sanctity of all humans. Hitler valued only the lives of Aryans. For Hitler, "All who are not of good race in this world are chaff."[16] Elsewhere, he stressed the limited value of all human life, even that of Aryans, by reference to his great exemplar, nature:

> The life of the individual must not be set at too high a price. If the individual were important in the eyes of nature, nature would take care to preserve him. Against the millions of eggs a fly lays, very few are hatched out—and yet the race of flies thrives.[17]

The Judeo-Christian tradition recognizes the equality of all humans. Not only did Hitler reject the principle that all men are created equal, but he viewed the very suggestion of such equality as a dangerous heresy that could impede Aryan progress. In Hitler's words, "As soon as the idea was introduced that all men were equal before God, that world was bound to collapse."[18]

In his autobiography, *Mein Kampf*, Hitler elaborated on his rejection of human equality, noting that his philosophy:

> by no means believes in an equality of the races, but along with their difference it recognizes their higher or lesser value and feels itself obligated, through its knowledge, to promote the victory of the better and stronger, and demand the subordination of the inferior and weaker in accordance with the eternal will that dominates the universe. Thus, in principle, it serves the basic aristocratic idea of Nature and believes in the validity of this law down to the last individual. It sees not only the different value of the races, but also the different value of individuals.[19]

Hitler highlighted just how deep he believed this racial inequality to be when he argued, like so many racists both before and after him, that "the gulf between the lowest creature which can still be styled man and our highest races is greater than that between the lowest type of man and the highest ape."[20]

Flowing from its recognition of the sanctity and equality of all humans, the Judeo-Christian tradition has always emphasized the importance of loving one's neighbor. Jesus and the Hebrew prophets stressed the need to focus this love with particular intensity on the most poor and vulnerable among us. Hitler utterly rejected such Judeo-Christian compassion for the weak. In Hitler's view:

> a stronger race will drive out the weak, for the vital urge in its ultimate form will, time and again, burst all the absurd fetters of the so-called humanity of individuals, in order to replace it by the humanity of Nature which destroys the weak in order to give his place to the strong.[21]

For Hitler, Judeo-Christian charity was not merely unnecessary, but downright dangerous. He believed that supporting the weak would slow the inevitable course of the struggle for survival, thus obstructing this sacred source of human progress. In Hitler's words, "Humaneness is therefore only the slave of weakness and thereby in truth the most cruel destroyer of human existence."[22] Elsewhere he warned that:

> the law of selection justifies this incessant struggle, by allowing the survival of the fittest. Christianity is a rebellion against natural law, a protest against nature. Taken to its logical extreme, Christianity would mean the systematic cultivation of the human failure.[23]

Hitler stressed that the "best and strongest in the world" had a "right to victory."[24] Thus, his social policy was a simple one:

> Those who want to live, let them fight, and those who don't want to fight in this world of eternal struggle do not deserve to live. Even if this were hard—that is how it is![25]

For Hitler, the meek most definitely did not inherit the earth.

Finally, Judaism and Christianity have always stressed the importance of overcoming the selfish drive inherent in our human nature, be it called the evil impulse or original sin. For Hitler, who so worshipped nature, the idea that we should seek to overcome nature—human or otherwise—was nothing more than "Jewish nonsense."[26] He warned that:

when man attempts to rebel against the iron logic of Nature, he comes into struggle with the principles to which he himself owes his existence as a man. And this attack must lead to his own doom.[27]

Hitler's Toll

When Hitler cut his society loose from Judeo-Christian morality, he unleashed and encouraged the very worst in human nature. His new evolutionary ethics opened the door wide to some of the most abhorrent practices in human history. These horrors returned almost instantly.

Slavery came first. Shortly after coming to power, the Nazis built their first forced-labor camps and filled them with political opponents and Jews. When the outbreak of World War II dramatically increased their need for forced labor, the Nazis exploited the large number of prisoners of war coming into their hands. Beginning with the Poles and continuing later with the Soviets, the Nazis forced millions of captured soldiers to work in massive new labor camps.

When their appetite for forced labor outstripped their supply of POWs, the Nazis proceeded to enslave civilians in the regions they occupied. During the war years, the Nazis deported at least 1.5 million Polish civilians and nearly three million Soviet civilians to German territory and forced them to work without pay in industry and agriculture.[28] By August 1944, more than 7,500,000 non-Germans were registered as working in the German Reich. The overwhelming majority of these foreigners were forced laborers.[29]

The Nazis also turned all of Poland into one giant slave-labor camp. In the fall of 1939, the German occupation authorities in Poland issued orders requiring all Polish and Jewish males to perform unpaid forced labor for the Reich. Most of these slaves were employed in the hundreds of factories the Nazis built in

Poland to produce goods for the German war effort. In the Lodz ghetto alone, for example, the Germans built over ninety-six such plants.[30]

Yet the Nazi hatred for certain races was so blinding that they often placed a higher priority on killing them than enslaving them. Aided by modern technology, Hitler brought back genocide with a ruthless efficiency. The Nazi Holocaust is the most infamous modern genocide. The six million Jews the Nazis murdered represented two-thirds of Europe's Jews and over one-third of all Jews on the planet. This genocide was not a byproduct of Nazi greed for Jewish land or money; it was an end in itself.

The Nazis also targeted other nationalities for murder. They killed at least 1.9 million non-Jewish Polish civilians[31] and approximately two hundred thousand Roma or "Gypsy" civilians.[32] By holding them in the most inhumane of conditions, the Nazis also killed between two and three million Soviet prisoners of war.[33] The death toll goes on.

Multitudes of Germans likewise fell victim to Hitler's Darwinian madness. Shortly after seizing power in 1933, the Nazis passed a eugenics law which established "Hereditary Health Courts" throughout the country. These courts were staffed by panels of doctors who reviewed the files of people believed to have physical and mental defects to determine whether they should be permitted to have children. All those deemed unworthy of reproduction were sent to be sterilized. Over 350,000 Germans were forcibly sterilized through this process.[34]

For disabled people living in Nazi Germany, however, there were fates worse than sterilization. In 1939, the Nazis began their euthanasia program to systematically murder people who were institutionalized due to physical or mental defects. At first, the Nazis killed their victims through drug overdoses and starvation. But as the program expanded, they developed more efficient methods. Before they gassed their first Jew, the Nazis had built six centralized gassing installations where they killed disabled Germans with carbon monoxide. By the end of the war, over two hundred thousand Germans, including five thousand children, had been killed in the euthanasia program.[35]

Beyond slavery and the genocide, Hitler's ideology sparked and sustained the most massive war in human history. In a very real sense, every casualty in the European theater of World War II was a victim of Hitler's evolutionary ethics. While estimates vary widely, it is safe to say that Hitler's race-based war killed well over 35 million soldiers and civilians.

Marx and Lenin: From the Brotherhood of Man to the Dictatorship of the Proletariat

Early in 1865, Abraham Lincoln received a letter from some European admirers congratulating him and the American people on his recent reelection. "If resistance to the Slave Power was the reserved watchword of your first election," the letter dramatically declares, "the triumphant war cry of your re-election is Death to Slavery."[36]

This energetic anti-slavery rhetoric continues for another few paragraphs. Then the letter concludes by noting how auspicious a sign it was that:

> it fell to the lot of Abraham Lincoln, the single-minded son of the working class, to lead his country through the matchless struggle for the rescue of an enchained race and the reconstruction of a social world.[37]

This letter was written by Karl Marx, and it was signed by the Central Council of the International Workingmen's Association. The anti-slavery sentiments these Communists expressed to the American president were quite sincere. The Communists saw America's black slaves as the most wretched victims of the capitalist class, and they applauded their emancipation as a great victory for all the workers of the world.

Indeed, Marx did more than just congratulate Lincoln after the fact. He had been a vocal supporter of the Union cause throughout the Civil War. Living in London at the time, he repeatedly and publicly criticized the many British leaders who expressed anti-Union sentiments. Marx also encouraged the German socialists living in America to support the Union cause, and many responded enthusiastically to the call.[38]

⁓

SEVENTEEN YEARS BEFORE writing this letter to Lincoln, Marx had written the *Communist Manifesto*. Here Marx took his opposition to slavery to what he believed to be its logical conclusion. He argued that the world's industrial workers, while ostensibly free, were for all practical purposes the slaves of the capitalists. Just like the slaves in the American South, these workers had no choice but to toil for masters who stole the fruits of their labor while leaving them with barely enough to survive. Marx closed the *Communist Manifesto* with the stark symbolism of slavery by declaring, "The proletarians have nothing to lose but their chains."[39]

Yet while Marx may have seen himself as continuing and extending the abolitionists' mission, he in fact rejected their core insights and worked to undermine their key accomplishments. Wilberforce, Garrison, and the other leading abolitionists were motivated by the Judeo-Christian idea of the sanctity and equality of all humans. They dedicated their lives to expanding the zone of altruism to include all men. Marx, by contrast, embraced the division of mankind into classes and dedicated his life to narrowing the zone of altruism to the only one of these classes he valued: the workers. In word and deed, Marx and his followers stripped all other people of their humanity and any protections which may have flowed from it. As a result, Marx, the self-styled abolitionist, opened the door to the return of slavery and genocide on the most massive scale.

Rejecting the Judeo-Christian Idea

From a purely ethnic perspective, Karl Marx was a Jew. Both Marx's father and mother were Jewish, and each came from a long line of rabbis. From a religious perspective, Marx was a Christian. Marx's father had converted to Christianity shortly before Karl's birth. Karl Marx was baptized at the age of six.

Yet Marx had nothing but contempt for both his Jewish heritage and his nominal Christian faith. Marx derived his worldview from a very different source: he was a child of the Enlightenment. He had been a philosophy student and a member of the Young Hegelians, a group of intellectuals who embraced and developed the core ideas of German philosopher Georg Wilhelm Hegel. When Marx later broke with this group, he continued to view the world through a largely Hegelian lens.

A better writer and deeper thinker than Hitler, Marx dismissed religion with a now-famous formulation:

> Religion is the sigh of the oppressed creature, the feeling of a heartless world, and the soul of soulless circumstances. It is the opium of the people.[40]

While Marx's contempt for religion may sound benign, his next words, less frequently quoted, revealed his more radical agenda:

> The abolition of religion as the illusory happiness of the people is the demand for real happiness. The demand to give up the illusions about their condition is a demand to give up a condition that requires illusion. The criticism of religion is therefore the germ of the criticism of the valley of tears whose halo is religion.[41]

Marx not only denigrated religion in general, but disdained the Judeo-Christian tradition in particular. Despite his Jewish background—or perhaps because of it—Karl Marx saw nothing of value in the Jewish faith. Like Hitler, Marx dismissed Judaism as a mere cover under which Jews pursued their economic interests:

> What is the implicit and explicit basis of the Jewish religion? Practical need, egoism. . . . The god of practical need and self-ishness is money. Money is the jealous god of Israel before whom no other god may stand.[42]

Also like Hitler, Marx denounced Christianity by stressing its Jewish roots:

> Christianity had its origin in Judaism. It has dissolved itself back into Judaism. The Christian was from the beginning the theorizing Jew; the Jew is therefore the practical Christian, and the practical Christian has become the Jew again.[43]

While recognizing their differences, Marx saw an unavoidable unity between these two faiths. He even went so far as to suggest that they were collaborators in some sort of ancient capitalist conspiracy. According to Marx, Christianity worked to alienate man "from himself and from nature." Once this was accomplished, Judaism could "attain general domination" and reduce man to being "a prey to the slavery of egoistic need and the market."[44]

❧

MARX'S IDEAS MAY well have remained confined to the realm of obscure philosophy clubs were it not for Vladimir Lenin. Lenin was the first Communist to lead a successful revolution and to apply Marx's theories to the governance of a nation. Thus Lenin's interpretation of Marx's thought determined the reality of Communism in practice.

When it came to religion, Lenin faithfully embraced Marx's views and even repeated his words. Lenin observed that:

> those who toil and live in want all their lives are taught by religion to be submissive and patient while here on earth, and to

take comfort in the hope of a heavenly reward. . . . Religion is opium for the people. Religion is a sort of spiritual booze, in which the slaves of capital drown their human image, their demand for a life more or less worthy of man.[45]

Lenin believed that Communism would free the workers from their need for such myths. According to Lenin, the enlightened worker:

casts aside religious prejudices, leaves heaven to the priests and the bourgeois bigots, and tries to win a better life for himself here on earth. The proletariat of today takes the side of socialism, which enlists science in the battle against the fog of religion.[46]

The Class-Based Morality of Marx and Lenin

While Marx and Lenin may have rejected Judeo-Christian morality, they were not without an ethos of their own. Like Hitler, the Communists defined right and wrong in the most rigid of terms and were unforgiving of those they believed to be in the wrong. Hitler believed that humanity would advance toward perfection through a series of racial struggles, and thus he embraced a race-based morality. Marx and Lenin believed that mankind would be perfected through a series of class struggles, and thus they espoused a class-based morality.

Early in his *Communist Manifesto*, Marx writes that "the history of all hitherto existing society is the history of class struggles."[47] Marx described a process in which feudalism had led inevitably to capitalism, and in which capitalism was now beginning to show the signs of its own inevitable demise. According to Marx, the day was soon coming when the workers would rise up, take over the factories in which they worked, and usher in the end of history.

Marx used messianic terms to describe the new society he believed would emerge following this ultimate victory in the class struggle. Once the workers were in power, he wrote, they would create a perfectly just society without the exploitation of labor and the poverty it produced. In so doing, they would eliminate the root cause of all violence and crime. As a new age of brotherhood dawned, police forces, jails, and even governments would be rendered obsolete. When the Communists spoke of creating a workers' paradise, they meant it literally.

Yet the path to paradise would flow with blood. Marx understood that the capitalists were not simply going to hand over the keys to their factories. If the workers wanted Marx's new world, they would have to take it by force. In Marx's words:

> Revolution is necessary . . . not only because the ruling class
> cannot be overthrown any other way, but also because the
> class overthrowing it can only in a revolution succeed in rid-
> ding itself of all the mush of the ages and become fitted to
> found society anew.[48]

When Marx spoke of "revolution," he was not merely waxing metaphorical. He was speaking of an armed revolt against the ruling class. In fact, Marx was quite explicit about his belief that social change would come only through the barrel of a gun. He wrote that the Communists' objectives "can be attained only by the forcible overthrow of all existing social conditions."[49] He encouraged the workers to perpetrate acts of terrorism and to "compel" the less enlightened of their colleagues to "carry out their present terrorist phrases." Marx welcomed such violence not only in the name of the revolution, but also in the name of vengeance:

> Far from opposing so-called excesses, instances of popular
> revenge against hated individuals or public buildings that are
> associated only with hateful recollections . . . must not only be
> tolerated but the leadership of them taken in hand.[50]

In elaborating this view that society would progress only by means of violent conflict, Marx found corroboration in the views of one of his contemporaries: Charles Darwin. While Marx may have replaced the survival of the fittest with the class struggle, he saw a strong theoretical connection between the two concepts. As Marx wrote to a friend, "Darwin's book is very important and serves me as a natural-scientific basis for the class struggle in history."[51] In a letter to his collaborator Friedrich Engels, Marx further observed:

> It is remarkable how Darwin recognizes among the beasts and plants his English society with its division of labor, competition, opening up of new markets, "inventions," and the Malthusian struggle for existence.[52]

Thus Marx and Hitler agreed that human progress would come only through violent struggle. It was only on the nature of this struggle that they differed.

⁓

MARX'S ETHICS FOLLOWED logically from his belief that such enormous good would be unleashed by the triumph of the workers. For Marx, anything that furthered the workers' revolution was good. Anything that impeded this revolution was evil.

Marx's new class-based ethics were evident in everything he wrote. Yet Marx's rejection of traditional morality was so complete that he refused to borrow its concepts. He never elaborated a new moral code, and did not even use the words "morality," "right," or "wrong." It was thus left to Lenin to make explicit the morality at Communism's core. Speaking after the October Revolution which brought the Communists to power in Russia, Lenin emphasized that:

> the class struggle is continuing and it is our task to subordinate all interests to that struggle. Our communist morality is also subordinated to that task. We say: morality is what serves to destroy the old exploiting society and to unite all the working people around the proletariat, which is building up a new, a communist society. Communist morality is that which

serves this struggle and unites the working people against all exploitation, against all petty private property.[53]

Lenin also emphasized that this class-based morality could in no way coexist with Judeo-Christian morality:

> We reject any morality based on extra-human and extra-class concepts.... We say that our morality is entirely subordinated to the interests of the proletariat's class struggle. Our morality stems from the interests of the class struggle of the proletariat.[54]

The Toll of Marx and Lenin

During a visit to Prague after the fall of the Soviet Union, author Anne Applebaum observed an interesting phenomenon. She saw American and western European tourists eagerly buying Soviet collectibles still readily available in this former Eastern Bloc city. Referring to these shoppers, Applebaum wrote that:

> All would be sickened by the thought of wearing a swastika. None objected, however, to wearing the hammer and sickle on a T-shirt or hat.... While the symbol of one mass murderer fills us with horror, the symbol of another mass murderer makes us laugh.[55]

To this day, the West has not fully recognized or internalized the enormity of the Soviet Union's crimes against humanity.*

---

*Marxism's toll of death and human suffering is actually far higher than this chapter suggests. Since this book is about Western civilization, this chapter focuses on the West's leading Marxist regime: the Soviet Union. In the East, two other Marxist regimes—those of China and Cambodia—infamously implemented their own versions of Marxism and in the process perpetrated genocide on a massive scale. The policies of China's Mao Zedong killed tens of millions of Chinese, largely through execution, starvation, and overwork. The policies of Cambodia's Pol Pot killed an estimated two million Cambodians (out of a total population of seven million) by similar means.

When Ronald Reagan famously called the Soviet Union an "evil empire" in 1983, his words sparked a firestorm of criticism. The president's statement was seen as an exaggerated indictment of a legitimate, albeit different, system. Today, similar value judgments about the former Soviet Union are still perceived as expressions of ideology rather than statements of fact. When it comes to the Soviets, a residual respect remains.

Yet Soviet ideology was strikingly similar to Nazi ideology. Both flatly rejected the Judeo-Christian idea of the sanctity and equality of all humans. Instead, each recognized a favored category of humans—the proletariat on the one hand, Aryans on the other—and very narrowly defined moral behavior as anything that benefitted this ingroup. Those who did not belong to the elect were exiled from humanity and stripped of all value and protection. In both the Soviet Union and Nazi Germany, belonging to such outgroups was often a death sentence.

The parallels between the Soviet and Nazi regimes extend beyond ideology to atrocity. In each case, these regimes acted on their theories to the exclusion of any external morality. Each enslaved millions. Each murdered millions. By almost any metric of human suffering, the crimes of the Soviets rival those of the Nazis.

These Soviet crimes also reinforce a larger point. They demonstrate that the Nazi regime was hardly an historical aberration. The Nazis did not concoct some rare formula for evil that is unlikely ever to be replicated. Instead, the Soviet record confirms that the danger lay not only in the ideas people embrace, but also in those they reject. When our civilization abandons the Judeo-Christian idea, we open the door to the return of slavery and genocide. These evils enter by means of a Trojan horse; they have been hiding inside of us all along.

Soviet Slavery

Slavery was so widespread in ancient Greece and Rome that even the government owned slaves. These "state slaves" were sent to perform the difficult and dangerous tasks that were shunned by free people, from building roads to extracting silver from deep mines.

After an interlude of centuries, the Soviet Union revived the institution of the state slave. From its first days, the Soviet government carried out mass arrests of its political opponents. As soon as the Communists seized power in 1918, Lenin ordered that "unreliable elements" and "class enemies" be sent to prison camps. By 1921, there were already eighty-four such camps spread out over forty-three Russian provinces.[56] The infamous Gulag, the enormous network of prison camps which dotted the Soviet countryside, was not a perversion of the Soviet system— it was one of its original sins. When Stalin emerged as Lenin's successor in the late 1920s, he merely accelerated the Gulag's rate of growth. Like Lenin, Stalin used the Gulag as a dumping ground for his political opponents and anyone else suspected of inadequate personal loyalty or insufficient Communist ardor.

Stalin was the first to exploit these Gulag prisoners as a vast pool of forced labor. Anne Applebaum goes so far as to conclude that under Stalin, the "primary purpose" of the Gulag was to provide a source of state slaves.[57] Just like ancient Greece and Rome, the Soviet Union used these slaves to perform the most backbreaking tasks. Gulag prisoners were sent to mine coal and precious metals under hazardous conditions. They were also forced to work on construction, infrastructure, and lumber projects in the brutal Siberian cold. The development of Russia's vast northern provinces was advanced almost exclusively by slave labor.

The number of Soviet citizens condemned to slavery under this system ran into the multi-millions. From its inception after the 1918 revolution, the Gulag grew at a steady pace until the early 1950s. At its height, the Gulag consisted of at least 476 separate camp complexes which together contained thousands of individual prison camps.[58] These camps typically held a combined total of approximately two million prisoners. Since the death rates in the camps were so high, and since those who survived the camps were released at the end of their terms, a steady supply of new prisoners was needed to maintain the Gulag's population at this level. It is estimated that between 1929 and 1953, the Gulag's peak years, some eighteen million people served time in these camps.[59]

Yet even this massive number understates the true extent of slave labor in the Soviet Union. Millions of those condemned to labor for the state were not sent to the Gulag but were instead "exiled" to Soviet outposts in the freezing snows of Siberia or the barren deserts of Kazakhstan. During Stalin's reign, it is estimated that at least six million Soviet citizens were exiled from their homes to live out the rest of their lives in these harsh, distant lands.[60] Even though they were not surrounded by barbed wire, these exiles were hardly free, and their conditions were at times even worse than those in the Gulag. Thousands of Soviet exiles died in remote villages to which they were sent with neither food nor the means to grow sufficient crops before they starved.

Even the combined total of Gulag prisoners and exiles—twenty-four million people—grossly understates the true number of Soviet state slaves. An important insight into the actual size of the Soviet forced labor corps is provided by the slang popular among the Gulag prisoners. These prisoners did not divide the Soviet population into camp inmates such as themselves and free men on the outside. Instead, they distinguished between Gulag prisoners locked in the "small prison zone" and every other Soviet citizen residing in what they referred to as the "big prison zone."[61]

Indeed, by what standard were any Soviet citizens free? The government had the power to tell them where to work and where to live. All of their information—from their books and newspapers to radio and television—was censored. They were not allowed to criticize their rulers in the public square or even in the privacy of their own homes. The violation of any of these restrictions could lead to swift and severe punishment. In a very real sense, every single citizen of the Soviet Union was a state-owned slave whose life and labor were controlled by a brutal, totalitarian master.

Soviet Genocide

Under Soviet morality, the urban industrial worker was the only full human. All other classes were viewed with the contempt that other Europeans had reserved for American Indians or Africans. These classes were outside the zone of compassion, without human rights, and expendable. In the Soviet Union, this meant that they could be enslaved. It also meant that they could be murdered.

While the capitalists may have been Soviet enemy number one, they were far from being the only suspect class. Communist ideologues also hated the great masses of peasants who dominated the Soviet countryside. Although these rural folk were every bit as poor and exploited as urban workers, they were nevertheless believed to lack sufficient "revolutionary consciousness." In particular, they were suspected of clinging too tightly to their limited private property—small farms, homes, and livestock—as well as to their religion and their nationalism. The Soviet leadership believed that if they were going to achieve their workers' paradise, they would first have to break the reactionary peasants.

Shortly after the October Revolution brought the Communists to power, Lenin tried to move the peasants off of their private property and onto large, state-owned collective farms. But Lenin was quick to abandon these efforts when they met with determined resistance. Recognizing the scope of the challenge, Stalin initially ignored the peasants and concentrated on consolidating his power. Once he was firmly in control of the government, however, Stalin turned his full focus and ferocity to bending the peasants to his will.

Stalin launched a two-pronged assault on the Soviet peasantry. At one level, he worked to decapitate the peasant class by eliminating its leadership. This group, derogatively referred to as "kulaks," was the rural bourgeoisie: those peasants in each community who had the largest farms and the most power. Like any other Soviet term, "kulak" was hardly applied in a scientific fashion. This damning label was slapped on anyone the local Communists deemed to be overly rich or insufficiently cooperative.

Yet no matter how imprecise its application, the kulak designation was practically impossible to reverse or escape. When it came to such outgroups, Communist dogma went so far as to embrace a sort of biological determinism. Soviet ideologues claimed that class members possessed a certain "class essence," which they retained even if they relinquished their property or lost their status. Like an African in the American South or a Jew in Nazi Germany, the kulak was branded for life with a stigma he could never remove.

While Soviet propaganda portrayed the kulak as a subhuman class enemy, Soviet policy proposed a radical remedy. In December 1929, Stalin publicly announced his new approach:

> We have gone over from a policy of limiting the exploiting tendencies of the kulak to a policy of liquidating the kulak as a class.[62]

This was no mere rhetorical flourish. A month after this announcement, the Soviet Politburo promulgated strict orders for implementing this "liquidation" policy. The kulaks were divided into three categories. The first group, those guilty of "counter-revolutionary activities," were to be executed or sent to prison camps. Their families were to be dispossessed and deported to Siberia or the deserts of Kazakhstan. The second group, called the "arch-exploiters," were to be dispossessed and deported. The third category, kulaks thought to be loyal to the regime, were to be stripped of their property and moved to the poorest quality land.[63] Yet the kulak label typically proved too strong a stigma to overcome, and most of the people in this third category were eventually exiled as well.[64]

The original plan was for approximately one million kulak families—an estimated six million people—to be "dekulakized" in this manner.[65] Yet the number of people actually condemned as kulaks far exceeded these numbers. In addition to those executed outright, close to four million people were imprisoned and between ten and twelve million people were deported under this policy. In their effect, these prison terms and deportations were often death sentences. Soviet prisoners had notoriously short life spans, and between a quarter and a third of the deportees quickly died in exile. A large proportion of these exile fatalities were children who could not survive the harsh new climates to which they were sent. In total, it is estimated that Stalin's dekulakization program killed 6.5 million people.[66]

While he was eliminating their leaders through dekulakization, Stalin began implementing the second prong of his attack on the peasantry: collectivization. Communism abhorred private property. In the cities, the private ownership of factories and shops had been outlawed immediately after the October Revolution. Now, Stalin decided that the time had finally come to eliminate the private ownership of farms and livestock in the countryside. Unlike Lenin, Stalin was determined to overcome peasant resistance no matter what the price.

Stalin's goal was to transform the Soviet Union's millions of private farms into a network of large, state-owned collective farms. Stalin thus ordered that all peasant land and livestock be confiscated and transferred to the collectives. The peasants were then forced to live and work in these collective farms, producing food for the state. As wrenching as this massive transformation was, Stalin pushed to accomplish it on the most compressed of time scales. In a frenzy of expropriation over five months in early 1930, over half the peasant households in the Soviet countryside were collectivized.[67]

This wave of confiscations and dislocations instigated peasant revolts throughout the country. Stalin suppressed this dissent, sent millions more to the Gulag and into exile, and then resumed his aggressive program. Before the collectivization effort began in 1929, there had been approximately twenty million family farms in the Soviet countryside. By the end of 1934, these had largely been replaced by 240,000 collective farms which accounted for nine-tenths of the Soviet Union's sown acreage.[68] Within the space of a few short years, the Soviet countryside had been transformed into a vast Communist collective.

∽

NOW THAT HE controlled the means of agricultural production, Stalin sought to put the country's agricultural output in the service of his most burning priorities: building Soviet industrial and military might. Stalin issued a series of large new grain quotas to extract food from the collective farms and bring it under state control. He sent the majority of this grain to feed the workers and the soldiers. Most of what remained was exported to raise the hard currency needed to purchase factory machinery and arms.

Such grain requisitions were not new, and reasonable quotas could have been safely met while leaving enough food to feed the peasants. The problem was that in the summer of 1932, the Soviets set the grain procurement targets far too high. The government demanded that farmers deliver more food than they were actually able to produce. Even in the face of increasing evidence that these targets were unrealistic, Stalin continued to enforce his draconian quotas with an iron fist. He focused his harshest measures on the Soviet Union's breadbasket, Ukraine. Stalin considered the Ukrainian peasants especially dangerous since they were believed to combine a fondness for their private farms with the dual sins of Ukrainian nationalism and Christian faith.

A month after these new grain targets were set, Stalin sent a stark reminder to the peasants that they no longer owned the food they grew. He issued a decree formally classifying everything on the collective farms, including grain and cattle, as state property. The decree further stipulated that those who in any way interfered with the collection of state property were enemies of the people who were to be shot in the absence of extenuating circumstances. When extenuating circumstances were found to exist, the penalty could be reduced to imprisonment of not less than 10 years.[69] The Soviet government sent armies of Communist officials into the countryside to enforce these decrees.

By early March 1933, almost all of the food produced by the collective farms had been removed, and the Ukrainian countryside was starving. Peasants started to leave the farms by the thousands in search of food. Stalin responded by issuing internal passports and strictly enforcing regulations against unlicensed travel. No food was allowed into the villages, and no peasants were allowed out.[70]

Witness reports captured the horrors that ensued. In town after town, peasants simply lay in their huts with swollen bellies, unable to move. Most of the victims died quietly in their homes. People were often too weak to bury the dead. Instead, starving peasants sometimes ate the dead in their desperate struggle to survive. Starvation was so widespread that anyone who didn't exhibit its physical signs immediately aroused suspicion.

In 1932, the Ukrainian farm population had been close to twenty million. Of these, an estimated five million peasants*— approximately one out of every four—died in the famine.[72] Another three million people died from the famines that resulted from the pursuit of similar policies in Kazakhstan, the

---

*These are Sovietologist Robert Conquest's figures, which are based on his extensive archival research. While the actual death toll from the Ukrainian famine is still the subject of debate, no one disputes that millions died. Ukrainian president Victor Yushchenko has claimed that the mass starvation killed "an estimated seven to ten million Ukrainians, including up to a third of the nation's children." (Victor Yushchenko, "The Holodomor," *Wall Street Journal,* November 26, 2007) Historian Nicolas Werth estimates that four million Ukrainians died during the famine, along with two million Soviet citizens in the northern Caucasus and in Kazakhstan. (Robert Gellately, *Lenin, Stalin and Hitler* (New York: Knopf, 2007), 235) Others argue that the death toll in Ukraine was closer to three million.

northern Caucasus and elsewhere in the Soviet Union. When the death toll from these famines is added to that from the dekulakization program, we see that Stalin's rural policies killed a combined total of approximately 14.5 million peasants.[72]

As these peasants starved to death, the grain, potatoes, and other food they had grown ended up being put to a number of less-than-urgent uses. In addition to the large quantities exported for hard currency, grain continued to be sent to distilleries to produce vodka. Some of the countryside's produce actually remained in local granaries, where it was theoretically being saved for "emergencies" but was never released to the starving peasants. Finally, given the ever-present Soviet inefficiencies, grain and potatoes often rotted in the fields before they could be transported elsewhere. Witness accounts tell of people starving to death close to the rotting crops they dared not eat.

◇

STALIN NEVER ACKNOWLEDGED that his policies were starving millions to death. Throughout the famine, the Communist Party line was that the grain quotas were reasonable and there was plenty of food in the countryside. Stalin blamed the failures to meet the quotas on peasant sabotage and hoarding.

Since the peasants were allegedly hoarding food, it followed that they did not need any shipments of food to sustain them. Thus when the starvation was at its height, Stalin's chief deputy in charge of collectivization in Ukraine specifically ruled out sending food to the villages. Like Pharaoh ordering the Hebrews to make bricks without straw, he announced that the state would not even provide seed corn for planting a new crop.[73] The peasants would have to find their own seed.

The scene unfolding in Ukraine was so distressing, and so greatly at odds with the party line, that many Soviet officials in the field felt compelled to report the reality to their superiors. One after another these dutiful officials were replaced, shot, or exiled. Before word got out that such accurate reporting was criminal, almost half of all collective farm chairmen were removed.[74]

When it came to public relations, the Soviets initially stuck to their policy of denying that there was a famine. Later, as stories of the mass starvation trickled to the outside world, the Soviets and their apologists admitted that there was a famine, but suggested that it was caused by drought or the peasants' refusal to work the land. Foreign reporters were banned from the famine zone. Since the Soviets controlled most of the information coming out of the region, it was difficult for observers to prove anything to the contrary.

Yet a tragedy of this magnitude could not be kept secret for long. Reports about the famine began to leak out after Stalin's death, and the pace of these disclosures accelerated with the fall of the Soviet Union. Historians such as the Hoover Institution's Robert Conquest have combed through Soviet records and pieced together a much clearer picture of the tragedy that befell Ukraine's peasants. As a result, it has become increasingly difficult to view this famine as anything other than an intentional genocide perpetrated against a hated class of people.*

There is strong evidence that Stalin knew from the start that his grain quotas were excessive and that he planned to starve the Ukrainian peasants into submission. But even if one is willing to overlook this evidence and believe that Stalin did not initially intend to commit genocide by starvation, it is far more difficult to find a benign explanation for Stalin's continued enforcement of the quotas and exports of grain once news of the famine was widespread.

Robert Conquest makes a convincing case that all of the leading Communist officials in Moscow and Ukraine were aware of the famine. Stalin's successor Nikita Khrushchev, for example,

---

*Please see the extended note at the end of the endnote section regarding the debate over whether the Ukrainian famine was an intentional act. Some scholars argue that the mass starvation was merely the unintentional result of Stalin's failed policies.

wrote the following about this episode in his memoirs: "I can't give an exact figure because no one was keeping count. All we knew was that people were dying in enormous numbers."[75] These officials would have reported these facts to Stalin, at least until it became clear that Stalin was literally shooting the messengers. Conquest cites numerous accounts of Stalin being informed of the scope of the starvation from a variety of sources, including his wife, high-ranking Communist officials, and the Soviet intelligence services.[76] In the face of this knowledge, Stalin's refusal to change course was a death sentence for millions.

Writing in 1985, Conquest summed up the Soviet famine with the following analogy to the Nazis' Bergen-Belsen concentration camp:

> Fifty years ago . . . the Ukraine and the Ukrainian Cossack and other areas to its east—a great stretch of territory with some forty million inhabitants—was like one vast Belsen. A quarter of the rural population, men, women and children, lay dead or dying, the rest in various stages of debilitation with no strength to bury their families or neighbors. At the same time (as at Belsen), well-fed squads of police or party officials supervised the victims.
>
> This was the climax of the revolution from above, as Stalin put it, in which he and his associates crushed two elements seen as irremediably hostile to the regime: the peasantry of the USSR as a whole, and the Ukrainian nation.[77]

Both Communism and Nazism rejected the Judeo-Christian idea and replaced it with creeds that removed its humanitarian shield from vast numbers of people. The proponents of these two ideologies hated each other and fought an all-out war against one another. But in the final analysis, they both produced the same hell on earth.

〜

IN THE POST-SOVIET era, it is becoming increasingly difficult to imagine that class hatred could run as deep as more ancient hatreds such as racism and anti-Semitism. After all, people of different classes commonly share the same skin color, speak the same language, and pray to the same God. Yet the human capacity for hate is strong enough that such superficial differences are by no means necessary. The Soviet Union was able to dehumanize people belonging to the wrong class every bit as effectively as other regimes have stigmatized those belonging to the wrong race, religion, or nationality.

Thus while some Communist officials took pity on the starving peasants, many more despised this class so deeply that they were incapable of sympathy for them. One witness summed up the behavior typical of Communist Party officials in the countryside as follows:

> They would threaten people with guns, as if they were under a spell, calling small children "kulak bastards," screaming "bloodsuckers!" . . . They had sold themselves on the idea that the so-called "kulaks" were pariahs, untouchables, vermin. They would not sit down at a "parasite's" table; the "kulak" child was loathsome, the young "kulak" girl was lower than a louse. They looked on the so-called "kulaks" as cattle, swine, loathsome, repulsive: they had no souls; they stank; they all had venereal diseases; they were enemies of the people and exploited the labor of others.[78]

A Communist official who served in the countryside during the famine later confessed to having had just such a mindset:

> With the rest of my generation I firmly believed that the ends justified the means. Our great goal was the universal triumph of Communism, and for the sake of that goal everything was permissible—to lie, to steal, to destroy hundreds of thousands and even millions of people, all those who were hindering our work or could hinder it, everyone who stood in the way. . . .

In the terrible spring of 1933 I saw people dying from hunger. I saw women and children with distended bellies, turning blue, still breathing but with vacant, lifeless eyes. And corpses—corpses in ragged sheepskin coats and cheap felt boots; corpses in peasant huts, in the melting snow . . . . I saw all this and did not go out of my mind or commit suicide. Nor did I curse those who had sent me out to take away the peasants' grain in the winter, and in the spring to persuade the barely walking, skeleton-thin or sickly-swollen people to go into the fields in order to "fulfill the Bolshevik sowing plan. . . ." Nor did I lose my faith. As before, I believed because I wanted to believe.[79]

The faith of which he speaks is, of course, faith in the truth of Communism. What is so chilling about this passage is that this man's views so closely tracked official Communist ideology. Marx and Lenin had introduced a new moral code in which even the most brutal of crimes were deemed virtuous so long as they were performed in the service of the working class. This official—and millions of his comrades—internalized these new ethics with astonishing ease. Whatever preexisting morality they may have possessed was quickly overwritten. As Soviet culture went bad, Soviet atrocity went mainstream.

Another official who participated in the famine more succinctly summarized the Communist ethos that prevailed at this time. When asked after the fact how she could have enforced such cruel orders against clearly starving people, the party official responded: "What I said to myself at the time was 'they are not human beings, they are kulaks.'"[80]

This statement is the mantra of every perpetrator of every genocide throughout human history. Genocide becomes possible once those in the victim class have been dehumanized to the point where they no longer qualify for even our limited genetic compassion. Replace the word "kulak" in her statement with

"Jew" or "Indian" or the name of any other victim group, and you have the creed that enabled that group's massacre.

〜

WHEN THE SPANISH conquistadors invaded Cuba in 1512, they enslaved the island's Indians and forced them to work in the gold mines. The Spanish left those who couldn't work—the elderly and the children—behind in the villages to starve to death. Las Casas described the devastation that resulted:

> I sometimes heard, back then when I traveled the island, as I would enter a village, voices calling forth from the huts. When I went to find out what they wanted, they answered, Food! Food! There was not a man or woman able to stand on two legs that they did not drag off to the mines. As for the new mothers with their small boy and girl children, their breasts dried: they had so little to eat, so much work, they had no milk left, the babies died.[81]

Over four hundred years later, Soviet Communists confiscated all of the food harvested in the Ukrainian countryside. They left the people who had grown this food behind to starve to death. A Communist official described the suffering that followed:

> The most terrifying sights were the little children with skeleton limbs dangling from balloon-like abdomens. Starvation had wiped every trace of youth from their faces, turning them into tortured gargoyles; only in their eyes still lingered the reminder of childhood. Everywhere we found men and women lying prone, their faces and bellies bloated, their eyes utterly expressionless.[82]

Such parallels of human suffering are hardly unique. We could list many more in disturbing detail. Yet while the atrocities share many similarities, the ideologies that drove them appear, at least on the surface, to be starkly different. It would be difficult to imagine worldviews more dissimilar than those of a sixteenth-century Spanish conquistador and a twentieth-century Communist apparatchik. And neither would have much in common with an American slaveholder or a Nazi commandant. Indeed, the Nazis and Communists harbored an enmity for one another so deep that it sparked a war.

Yet despite their superficial differences, these ideologies produced such similar atrocities because they shared the same fundamental flaw. Each of these systems rejected the core Judeo-Christian idea of the sanctity and equality of all humans. Each replaced this ethic with one which exiled certain groups of people from the zone of compassion and stripped them of the protections traditionally afforded our fellow humans. Each thus unleashed and empowered the worst impulses of our selfish genes toward these outgroups. In the final analysis, the only significant difference between these ideologies is which group of people they placed in the role of villain and victim.

SIX

The Rising: The Judeo-Christian Idea in the Post-War World

*We have before us the glorious opportunity to inject a new
dimension of love into the veins of our civilization. There is still
a voice crying out in terms that echo across the generations,
saying: "Love your enemies, bless them that curse you, pray for
them that despitefully use you, that you may be the children of
your Father who is in Heaven."*[1]

——MARTIN LUTHER KING, JR.

When Martin Luther King, Jr. moved to Montgomery, Alabama in the spring of 1954, he was planning on a busy but peaceful life. He had accepted a job as pastor of the Dexter Avenue Baptist Church and was confident that he could win over this sometimes elitist flock. He had finished his coursework for a doctorate in theology from Boston University, though he still had a thesis to write. And he had a young bride and plans to start a family.

King's idyllic days lasted for a little over a year. Then, on December 1, 1955, an African American woman named Rosa Parks refused to give up her seat on a Montgomery city bus to a white passenger who had boarded after her. In so doing, she violated the city's segregation laws. Parks was removed from the bus and arrested.

The arrest of such an upstanding woman for such an insulting reason sparked an increasingly restless community to action. The following evening, King hosted an emergency meeting of Montgomery's most prominent African Americans at his Dexter Avenue Church. By night's end, this group had agreed upon their response. They called on their fellow blacks to boycott Montgomery's buses until the city agreed to a set of demands, including seating on a first-come, first-served basis. These leaders announced that they would hold a meeting at the Holt Street Church a few nights later to explain the boycott to the public and rally support.

When they assembled for the second time, shortly before this public meeting, the organizers decided to form an official body—the Montgomery Improvement Association (MIA)—to coordinate and guide the boycott. Quick to spot talent in their ranks, they unanimously elected King to be the MIA's president.

King's fist act as a civil rights leader was to address the gathering that night. Having had little time to write a speech, King stepped up to the podium and spoke from his heart to the overflow crowd:

> We are not wrong in what we are doing. If we are wrong, the
> Supreme Court of this nation is wrong. If we are wrong, the
> Constitution of the United States is wrong. If we are wrong,
> God Almighty is wrong. If we are wrong, Jesus of Nazareth
> was merely a utopian dreamer that never came down to earth.
> And we are determined here in Montgomery to work and
> fight until justice runs down like water and righteousness like
> a mighty stream.[2]

In his very first civil rights speech, King invoked the name of Jesus and quoted from the Hebrew prophets as he reached his rhetorical climax. This was a pattern he would follow until his very last speech almost thirteen years later.

As soon as King's new position was announced, the death threats began. A month into the boycott, King recalled, he was getting as many as forty threatening phone calls a day. A white friend warned King that he had heard from a reliable source that a group of segregationists were plotting to kill him.[3]

At first, King was able to ignore the threats and the danger. Then he finally reached his breaking point. As he later related, he was lying in bed one night after a long day when the phone rang. An angry voice threatened: "Listen, nigger, we've taken all we want from you; before next week you'll be sorry you ever came to Montgomery."[4] Something about this call finally penetrated his psyche. Unable to sleep, King rose and paced around his house. He thought about the danger to his wife and his infant daughter. As fear began to seize him, he decided that he could take no more. He began searching for a way to resign from his leadership position "without appearing a coward." He finally turned to prayer. As King recalled:

> With my head in my hands, I bowed over the kitchen table and prayed aloud. The words I spoke to God that midnight are still vivid in my memory: "Lord, I'm down here trying to do what's right.... But Lord, I must confess that I'm weak now, I'm faltering. I'm losing my courage. Now, I am afraid. And I can't let the people see me like this because if they see me weak and losing my courage, they will begin to get weak. The people are looking to me for leadership, and if I stand before them without strength and courage, they too will falter. I am at the end of my powers. I have nothing left. I've come to the point where I can't face it alone."
>
> It seemed as though I could hear the quiet assurance of an inner voice saying: "Martin Luther, stand up for righteousness. Stand up for justice. Stand up for truth. And lo, I will be with you. Even until the end of the world."
>
> I tell you I've seen lightning flash. I've heard the thunder roar. I've felt sin breakers dashing trying to conquer my soul. But I heard the voice of Jesus saying to fight on. He promised never to leave me alone. At that moment I experienced the presence of the Divine as I had never experienced Him before. Almost at once my fears began to go. My uncertainty disappeared. I was ready to face anything.[5]

For King, his Christian faith was far more than a source of soaring rhetoric. It was the boundless reservoir of the colossal courage he would need to risk his life day after day for the freedom of his people and the soul of his country.

This courage was quickly put to the test. Three nights after King's epiphany, he left his wife and daughter at home to attend a public meeting on the bus boycott. As he prepared to speak, he noticed a commotion in the pews and people pointing in his direction. When King demanded to know what had happened, he was informed that his house had been bombed. No one in the church knew whether his wife and daughter were still alive. King later recalled his reaction:

> Strangely enough, I accepted the word of the bombing calmly.
> My religious experience a few nights before had given me the
> strength to face it. I urged each person to go straight home
> after the meeting and to adhere strictly to our philosophy of
> nonviolence.[6]

As King approached his home, he saw an angry crowd of his supporters gathering outside. Inside, to his relief, he found his wife and daughter unharmed. He also found the mayor, the police commissioner, and some white reporters sitting around his dining room table. As the crowd outside grew larger and louder, the whites became frightened to leave. King walked out onto his front porch to defuse the tension. The crowd instantly hushed as he began to speak:

> We believe in law and order. Don't get panicky. Don't do any-
> thing panicky at all. Don't get your weapons. He who lives by
> the sword will perish by the sword. Remember this is what
> God said. We are not advocating violence. We want to love our
> enemies. I want you to love our enemies. Be good to them.
> Love them and let them know you love them.[7]

With these words from their leader, the crowd's rage melted into a chorus of "Amen's" and "God bless you's." King later reflected that "the spirit of God was in our hearts, and a night that seemed destined to end in unleashed chaos came to a close in a majestic group demonstration of nonviolence."[8]

A year later, almost to the day, a wave of bombings struck the churches and homes of Montgomery's civil rights leaders. King was once again lucky; a faulty fuse prevented the twelve sticks of dynamite placed on his front porch from exploding. As news of the bombings spread, an angry crowd once again gathered outside King's home. And once again, King stepped out onto his porch and overcame every normal human emotion to declare:

> We must not return violence under any condition. I know this
> is difficult advice to follow, especially since we have been the
> victim of no less than ten bombings. But this is the way of
> Christ; it is the way of the cross. We must somehow believe
> that unearned suffering is redemptive.[9]

Then, since it was Sunday morning, King urged everyone to go home "and get ready for church."[10]

Christians are supposed to strive to emulate Jesus. On these two nights in Montgomery, and on so many other occasions during a long and dangerous struggle, Martin Luther King rose to this challenge in a way matched by few leaders in Western history. King transcended his selfish genes and his human anger to express love for the very people who had tried to kill him and his family. King embodied the love at the core of the Judeo-Christian tradition, and to a miraculous extent, his followers overcame their own human nature to follow his example. And in their transcendent embrace of the Judeo-Christian idea, they transformed a nation.

The Civil Rights Movement: The Judeo-Christian Idea Against Oppression in America

The success of the civil rights movement stands as a powerful rebuke to all who seek to deny the enormous contribution of the Judeo-Christian idea to Western civilization. Unable to question this movement's accomplishments, many secular critics have instead sought to deny its Christianity. Yes, they will concede, Dr. King and other civil rights leaders may have employed religious rhetoric to appeal to certain traditional elements within their constituency. Yet such rhetoric aside, they assert, the civil rights leaders were actually secular men who led a largely secular movement to achieve purely secular goals. One author recently went so far as to declare that "in no real as opposed to nominal sense . . . was he [King] a Christian."[11]

It is true that some civil rights leaders and many civil rights activists were thoroughly secular. The earliest civil rights organizations, such as the NAACP and CORE, were purely secular in their leadership and orientation. But during the height of activism from the mid-1950s until the mid-1960s—the period we typically have in mind when we speak of the "civil rights movement"—the religious element was not merely pronounced, it was dominant.

The direct action movement that defined this decade was sparked by the Montgomery bus boycott. As we've seen, the Montgomery boycott was literally born in a church. Its key leaders came from the pulpits, and most of its grassroots army came from the pews. Throughout the year-long effort, churches served as its primary meeting places, staging areas, and recruitment centers. Ministers even comprised the bulk of the volunteer drivers who worked overtime to provide alternative transportation to boycott participants.

In January 1957, King and other civil rights leaders from across the South met in Atlanta's Ebenezer Church and decided to expand the Montgomery boycott into a region-wide integration movement. These leaders created an organization called the Southern Christian Leadership Conference (SCLC) to organize and guide the effort. King was elected as the SCLC's first president, a position which he held until his assassination in 1968. For the rest of King's life, and for some years beyond, the SCLC was the dominant organizational force behind the civil rights movement.

As the name they chose indicates, the SCLC's founders intended that this larger movement would replicate the Montgomery boycott's close link to the black churches. "Almost all" of the participants in this inaugural meeting were Christian ministers, and the organization they created was often referred to simply as the "ministers group."[12] Four of the five original officers of the SCLC were ministers. After King's death, three of the following four SCLC presidents were likewise ministers, the exception being King's son.

As the movement spread across the South, a "seemingly endless"[13] list of churches opened their doors to host its meetings and house its activists. Summarizing the sense of applied theology that permeated the organization, the SCLC's fifth president, the Reverend Fred Shuttlesworth, maintained that the civil rights movement gave "the Christian Church its greatest opportunity in centuries to make religion real in the lives of men."[14]

Of the core group of activists who founded the SCLC, only Bayard Rustin lacked this deep Christian core. Rustin was a secular Northerner raised outside of the faith and culture of the black churches. Yet while he did not share it, Rustin recognized the importance of this Christian fervor to the struggle. He noted that:

> the high moral tone of the Baptist preacher well suited the movement. . . . The movement needed an emotional dimension to whip up the enthusiasm of people who might soon be faced with economic hardship or physical danger. And no one could bring a crowd to an emotional pitch like the black preacher.[15]

⟶

ON FEBRUARY 1, 1960, four black freshmen at North Carolina A&T College in Greensboro went to their local Woolworth's store to purchase school supplies. When they finished shopping, they sat down at the store's lunch counter and ordered coffee. Yet while the store was open to all, the lunch counter was segregated—as was the case in similar stores across the South. When the students were denied service, they refused to leave. News of this "sit-in" quickly spread, and it inspired other black students to do likewise. Within three months, there were similar sit-ins in over fifty Southern cities.[16]

The students who led these protests decided to create a new, national organization to orchestrate their efforts. Meeting in April 1960 at Shaw University in North Carolina, these student delegates formed the Student Nonviolent Coordinating Committee (SNCC). For the remainder of the decade SNCC was not only the dominant civil rights organization on America's college campuses but also a significant force on the national stage.

In its early years, SNCC worked closely with the SCLC, serving in many ways as its student arm. The students of SNCC often appealed to their elders in the SCLC for funds, speakers, advice, and infrastructure. And, as its name highlighted, the students of SNCC embraced the nonviolent tactics and ethos of the SCLC leaders.

SNCC grew out of the campuses, not the churches, and thus lacked the direct Christian connection of the SCLC. Yet from the start, SNCC was "anchored in the language, imagery, and energies of the church."[17] In its heyday, SNCC's most prominent leaders were seminary students who had left school to join the movement. SNCC's first chairman, James Lawson, was a theology student at Vanderbilt when he began to organize sit-ins. It was Lawson who drafted SNCC's original "statement of purpose," which expressed the organization's commitment to "a social order permeated by love and to the spirituality of nonviolence as it grows from the Christian tradition."[18]

SNCC's second chairman, John Lewis, was a student at a Baptist seminary when he began to participate in the sit-ins. Lewis described the goal of the civil rights movement as "nothing less than the Christian concept of the Kingdom of God on Earth."[19] When he was arrested for the first of what would be over forty times, Lewis explained to his mother that he was "acting according to my Christian faith and my conviction."[20] Reflecting on his career in civil rights, Lewis observed that, "Faith in God was at the heart of all I did."[21]

Over time, however, SNCC began to betray these Christian roots. After suffering political defeats at the 1964 Democratic convention and witnessing the violence of the 1965 Watts riots, many SNCC members lost patience with the ideals of nonviolence and integration. Instead, increasing numbers of students embraced "black power" as their goal and expressed their determination to achieve this goal by "any means necessary." Malcolm X began to eclipse Martin Luther King as the student movement's hero.

In 1966, Stokely Carmichael, one of the leaders of SNCC's militant wing, ousted John Lewis and took control of the organization. In 1969, SNCC changed its name to the "Student National Coordinating Committee" to eliminate the word "nonviolence." That same year, SNCC expelled all of its white members. By the end of the decade, SNCC had practically ceased to exist.

SNCC's decision to cut its structural and ideological ties to the black churches, and the rapid disintegration that followed, dramatically highlights the centrality of faith to the civil rights movement. For the militant students, self-interest had replaced the Judeo-Christian idea as their driving motive. Yet while self-interest spiked with anger could generate protests, it could not long sustain the patience, courage, and love of enemy that would eventually win the war. Disconnected from its Judeo-Christian roots, the student movement turned violent and, before long, impotent.

∽

MANY READERS WILL no doubt bristle at the notion that the non-violence of the civil rights movement was inherently Christian. Just as the conventional wisdom has recast Martin Luther King as a secular activist, it has likewise traced his passion for nonviolence to a non-Christian source. It is now widely believed that King's nonviolence was inspired by Mahatma Gandhi, the Indian activist who led his countrymen in a peaceful campaign to win independence from the British. As one secular commentator claimed, "Although Martin Luther King was a Christian, he derived his philosophy of non-violent civil disobedience from Gandhi, who was not."[22]

There can be no doubt that during the long years of his struggle, King took both instruction and inspiration from the example of Gandhi. King studied Gandhi's writings and campaigns. Portraits of Gandhi occupied prominent positions on the walls of both King's home and office. In 1959, at the height of the civil rights movement, King flew to India to see the country in which his hero had lived and taught.

Yet those who claim that King's nonviolence was primarily an Indian product exaggerate the point. When King helped to launch the Montgomery bus boycott, he actually knew very little about Gandhi. A review of his earliest pronouncements on the topic makes clear that when it came to nonviolence, King's original example and inspiration was Jesus. As King reminded the angry crowd gathered in front of his home in Montgomery, it was Jesus who commanded his followers to reject the sword and love their enemies.

It was only after the Montgomery boycott had begun, and after King had insisted upon nonviolence as the movement's method, that King learned more about the Indian leader. Once the boycott was national news, nonviolent activists from across the country flocked to King's home. They typically came bearing advice and reading material. One of these advisors, the Reverend Glenn Smiley, later recalled a conversation he had with King at this time:

I said to Dr. King, "I'm assuming that you're very familiar with and have been greatly influenced by Mahatma Gandhi." And he was very thoughtful, and he said, "As a matter of fact, no. I know who the man is. I have read some statements by him, and so on, but I will have to truthfully say . . . that I know very little about the man."[23]

In his own writing, King was quite clear about the evolution of his thinking on nonviolence. Although he and others came to refer to their tactics with terms first made popular by Gandhi, such as "passive resistance" and "nonviolent resistance," King wrote that he did not originally use such phrases. Instead, he explained:

the phrase most often heard was "Christian love" It was the Sermon on the Mount, rather than a doctrine of passive resistance, that initially inspired the Negroes of Montgomery to dignified social action. It was Jesus of Nazareth that stirred the Negroes to protest with the creative weapon of love.[24]

Once he started to study Gandhi, moreover, what King learned was not the *philosophy* of nonviolence but the *technique* of nonviolence—the way in which a leader could best implement this philosophy to achieve political goals. As King explained:

Nonviolent resistance had emerged as the technique of the movement, while love stood as the regulating ideal. In other words, Christ furnished the spirit and motivation while Gandhi furnished the method.[25]

⌒

NOT ONLY WAS King's Christian philosophy of nonviolence not based on Gandhi's teachings, but there is evidence that the converse may have been true. To a surprising extent, Gandhi's nonviolence had Christian roots. Gandhi was profoundly moved by the theological works of Russian writer Leo Tolstoy. Gandhi wrote in his autobiography that "Tolstoy's *The Kingdom of God is Within You* overwhelmed me. It left an abiding impression on me."[26] Gandhi credited "Tolstoy by his book, *The Kingdom of God is Within You*" with being one of three "moderns" who "left a deep impress on my life."[27]

In *The Kingdom of God Is Within You*, written in 1893, Tolstoy set forth what he calls the "doctrine of non-resistance to evil by force." Tolstoy wrote this book after coming to a deep Christian faith. His thesis is that the use of force cannot be reconciled with the teachings of Christ, and he builds his case for nonviolence on a thoroughly biblical base.

Gandhi read the book while he was living in South Africa, years before he had returned to India to struggle for his home-land's independence. When Gandhi embarked upon a series of nonviolent protests against the South African government, he gave the name "Tolstoy Farm" to the commune that served as his base of operations. Later in his autobiography, Gandhi credited two additional books by Tolstoy, *The Gospels in Brief* and *What to Do?*, with helping him "to realize more and more the infinite possibilities of universal love."[28]

Yet the roots of the philosophy of nonviolence do not end in Russia. They actually extend all of the way back to American soil. In *The Kingdom of God Is Within You*, Tolstoy wrote at length about an American practitioner of nonviolence who had deeply influenced him: the abolitionist William Lloyd Garrison. According to Tolstoy:

> The work of Garrison ... convinced me of the fact that the departure of the ruling form of Christianity from the law of Christ on non-resistance by force is an error that has long been observed and pointed out, and that men have labored, and are still laboring, to correct.[29]

⁓

ONE OF THE LEADERS of the civil rights movement in Mississippi was a sharecropper named Fannie Lou Hamer. Mrs. Hamer had lived forty-four years without ever getting involved in politics. Yet when SNCC workers came to her church looking for volunteers to register to vote, she immediately answered the call. When her first efforts to register resulted in termination from her job, expulsion from her home, and escalating threats of violence, she never wavered in her commitment to the cause. As she calmly told a friend in the midst of a particularly dangerous period, "Well, killing or no killing, I'm going to stick with civil rights."[30]

In 1963, on the trip home from a voter registration training session in South Carolina, Mrs. Hamer and her colleagues pulled into a rest stop in the town of Winona, Mississippi. They sat down at the lunch counter and asked to be served. Despite federal rulings outlawing segregated transportation facilities, the local authorities were outraged. The group was arrested and taken to the Winona County Jail. There, the police took the civil rights activists one by one to a back room and brutally beat them.

As the police were beating one of her colleagues, Annelle Ponder, Mrs. Hamer sat in her cell and listened to the screams. Eventually, Annelle Ponder stopped screaming and began praying. It was not for herself that she prayed, however, but for the guards who were abusing her. As Mrs. Hamer later recalled, "She started prayin' for 'em, and she asked God to have mercy on 'em because they didn't know what they was doin'."[31] Ponder, of course, was echoing the words of Jesus, who during his crucifixion asked God to forgive his tormentors, "for they know not what they do."

Later in the day, the guards came for Fannie Lou Hamer. They beat the length of her body with a blackjack. Every time she proved unable to comply with their orders not to scream, they punched her head. After the ordeal, Mrs. Hamer was unable to walk for days. She suffered permanent kidney damage and a blood clot which threatened the vision in her left eye.

The very next day, Mrs. Hamer showed the spiritual grandeur that would transform her into one of the movement's most beloved leaders. Ailing and alone in her cell, she started singing spirituals. Her colleagues heard her strong voice, and joined her in song. Soon the halls of the Winona Country Jail were reverberating with a song about the Apostle Paul and Silas, who had been arrested while doing God's work but were quickly freed by divine intervention.

A couple of days later, Mrs. Hamer struck up a conversation with the jailer's wife, who described herself as a Christian. Mrs. Hamer told the woman that she needed to read Acts 17:26. The jailer's wife must have certainly understood Mrs. Hamer's point when she opened her Bible to this section and read the following words: "God hath made of one blood all nations of men for to dwell on the face of the earth."

Reflecting on the experience, Hamer later remarked, "It wouldn't solve any problem for me to hate whites just because they hate me. Oh, there's so much hate, only God has kept the Negro sane."[32] Unbowed and undeterred, Fannie Lou Hamer continued to work for civil rights and nonviolence for the rest of her life.

～

THE CATHOLIC THINKER Thomas Merton described the American civil rights movement as the greatest example of Christian faith in action in the social history of the United States.[33] When one reads the stories of civil rights leaders such as Martin Luther King and Fannie Lou Hamer, one begins to grasp Merton's point. It is simply impossible to comprehend how these and so many other heroes were able to persevere in their struggle without falling victim to despair, hate, or violence without understanding the deep Christian faith which inspired and sustained them.

The White Churches: From Apathy to Engagement

Before the Civil War, Christian clergy in the South frequently invoked the Bible to defend slavery. In so doing, they largely neutralized the power of Christianity to overcome the blinding self-interest that sustained this institution. Abolition had to be imposed upon the South by force of arms.

When it came to segregation a century later, Southern churches provided no such theological cover. Very few Christian clergy publicly supported segregation, and this already small number dwindled as the 1950s gave way to the 1960s. In the absence of any real biblical support, those churchmen who did endorse segregation typically offered secular rationales for doing so.[34]

There were surprisingly few exceptions to this rule. A small number of segregationist pastors sought to justify their stand by invoking Acts 17:26, which speaks of God "determining the boundaries" of the various nations. Segregation, they claimed, was merely one such divine boundary between different peoples. Yet this argument had a fatal flaw. The first part of that very same Bible verse contains the language so beloved by Fannie Lou Hamer and other civil rights leaders, the proclamation that God "made of one blood all the nations of men."[35]

To the extent that they got involved in the issue at all, the South's leading denominations and preachers intervened to oppose segregation. In the mid-1950s, the South's two largest Christian denominations—the Southern Presbyterians and the Southern Baptists—both passed resolutions supporting desegregation and calling on their members to comply with the laws and court decisions implementing it. The Baptist resolution in support of desegregation passed by a vote of roughly nine thousand to fifty.[36] During the same period, both of these denominations integrated their Southern seminaries and elected strong opponents of segregation as their presidents.

As early as 1954, the most famous evangelical preacher of the era, the Reverend Billy Graham, refused to permit segregated seating at his crusades.[37] In 1957, Graham invited Martin Luther King to share the stage with him at his New York crusade in Madison Square Garden. There Graham praised King and his "social revolution."[38]

One segregationist clergyman accurately summarized the state of play when he complained that:

> when religion is brought into the question, it seems to be tentatively assumed that segregation must be done away with, and that it is the will of Jesus to do so. Because He said that we must love one another, racial distinctions and racial barriers must be destroyed. Religion is so intimately tied in with ... brotherly love and concern for the underprivileged that many people seem to assume without question that desegregation should be the position of the Church, and that ... they should do all they can to support it, or ... at least not oppose it.[39]

⌒

UNFORTUNATELY, THIS theological embrace of integration did not typically translate into participation in the civil rights movement. With some limited exceptions, African Americans fought for their civil rights alone throughout the 1950s and into the first years of the 1960s.

The silence of the South's white churches during the civil rights struggle is yet another example of the perpetual pull of self-interest. Just like their black counterparts, those Southern white clergy who joined the civil rights movement risked and sometimes lost their lives. In addition, unlike their black counterparts, white clergy who supported the civil rights movement risked and often lost their jobs. Time after time, white churchmen who spoke out in support of integration and civil rights were forced from their pulpits and their homes by segregationist pressure and threats.

Fannie Lou Hamer observed that "most black preachers had to be dragged kicking and screaming into supporting the movement."[40] What was true of black preachers was even truer of white ones. For whites, the cause of civil rights was further removed from their well-being and that of their families. It therefore required an even greater leap for them to overcome their natural obsession with self and enter the fray. As has been the rule throughout history, few people proved willing to risk their lives or even their livelihoods on behalf of someone else's rights.

Martin Luther King famously lamented the resulting apathy in his letter from the Birmingham Jail:

> In the midst of blatant injustices inflicted upon the Negro, I have watched white churches stand on the sideline and merely mouth pious irrelevancies and sanctimonious trivialities. In the midst of a mighty struggle to rid our nation of racial and economic injustice, I have heard so many ministers say, "Those are social issues with which the gospel has no real concern."[41]

⌒

THE AUGUST 1963 March on Washington is widely seen as the defining moment of the civil rights movement. Here, standing in front of the Lincoln Memorial, Martin Luther King reached the height of his eloquence in his iconic "I Have a Dream" speech. Before him stood approximately three hundred thousand blacks and whites who had made their way to Washington to participate in this historic outpouring of support for civil rights.

The very next day, most newspapers marveled at King's eloquence as well as the size and civility of the crowd that came to hear him. But writing in the *New York Times,* veteran journalist James Reston struck a more sober note. "The first significant test of the Negro march on Washington," he predicted, "will come in the churches and synagogues of the country this weekend." One of the central goals of the march was to demonstrate support for President Kennedy's landmark civil rights legislation then pending before Congress. Yet the success of the march by no means ensured passage of the bill. As Reston explained:

> It is no good waiting for a political reaction in Congress, for if there is no effective moral reaction out in the country, there will be no effective political reaction here.
>
> This whole movement for equality in American life will have to return to first principles before it will "overcome" anything. And as moral principles preceded and inspired political principles in this country, as the church preceded the Congress, so there will have to be a moral revulsion to the humiliation of the Negro before there can be significant political relief.[43]

Marches and speeches aside, the only way that Congress was going to pass landmark civil rights legislation was if a significant segment of the white population demanded it. As Reston recognized, those whites most likely to rise to this moral challenge were those most closely connected to the Judeo-Christian idea through their churches and synagogues. In order for America to fulfill King's dream and "live out the true meaning of its creed," America's white churches would first have to live out the true meaning of theirs. They would have to take their faith into politics. Luckily for America, they finally did.

~

IN MANY WAYS the March on Washington marked a turning point, the moment when the civil right movement ceased to be a lonely black struggle. The National Council of Churches co-sponsored the march, and many white denomination heads and clergymen were among the organizers. It is estimated that over two hundred white religious leaders brought approximately forty thousand white church and synagogue members to Washington to participate. After the march was over, white church leaders were prominent among those who met with President Kennedy and lobbied their members of Congress on behalf of Kennedy's civil rights legislation.[44]

When the civil rights bill finally began to move through Congress, white religious leaders organized a series of public events in Washington to press for its passage. On April 19, 1964, Protestant, Catholic, and Jewish seminary students from across the country launched a round-the-clock vigil at the Lincoln Memorial in support of the legislation. They maintained this vigil uninterrupted until the bill was passed in June. Also in April, the National Council of Churches initiated a daily worship service for supporters of the bill at a church across the street from the Capitol. These services were held every day until the bill's passage.[45]

On April 28, over six thousand church and synagogue leaders attended an interfaith rally at Georgetown University in support of the civil rights bill. Washington's Archbishop Patrick O'Boyle summarized well the Judeo-Christian creed shared by everyone in attendance when he noted that "we are diverse in religious heritage, but together we proclaim that all men are equal under God."[46] The following day, almost two hundred religious leaders met with President Johnson to urge passage of the bill.[47]

These Washington events were backed up by an effective grassroots effort. Most notably, the National Council of Churches launched a campaign to generate support for the civil rights bill in the Midwest. This region included large rural districts where the other core members of the civil rights coalition—African Americans and labor unions—lacked numbers and influence. The NCC, on the other hand, had thousands of sympathetic pastors and lay leaders in these regions. The NCC updated this network as the civil rights legislation progressed through Congress, and alerted them when action was needed. NCC staff traveled throughout the region holding workshops on the bill and how best to support it.[48]

This "Midwest strategy" proved to be extremely effective. Midwestern senators and congressmen received a "deluge" of letters, telegrams, and personal visits from church groups urging them to support the civil rights bill. The *Wall Street Journal* estimated that "almost half" of the mail some Midwestern lawmakers received in favor of the legislation "reveals church influence."[49]

When votes were held in both the House and the Senate, a large number of pivotal Midwestern Republicans ended up voting in favor of the bill. Their support ensured its passage in both chambers. On July 2, President Johnson signed the Civil Rights Act of 1964 into law.

～

WHILE IT IS impossible to measure exactly how effective these efforts were, both friends and foes of the Civil Rights Act credited the churches with having played a pivotal role in its passage. Senator Hubert Humphrey, one of the bill's most prominent supporters, wrote: "I have said a number of times, and I repeat it now, that without the clergy, we couldn't have possibly passed this bill."[50]

One of the bill's leading opponents, Georgia senator Richard Russell, concurred in this assessment. He declared that the bill passed because "those damn preachers had got the idea it was a moral issue."[51] He also complained that thousands of ministers had sought to "coerce" people into accepting their religious views. As Senator Russell saw it, "Such a philosophy of coercion by the men of the cloth ... is the same doctrine that dictated the acts of Torquemada in the infamous days of the Spanish Inquisition."[52]

Senator Russell's condemnation of these Christian civil rights activists echoed Senator Hayne's remarks more than a century earlier denouncing Jeremiah Evarts and the Christian activists who had defended the Cherokees. Both senators reprised the attacks that various members of Parliament launched against William Wilberforce and the Christian abolitionists in England. For as long as there have been men moved by their faith to petition their leaders on behalf of humanity, there have been politicians moved by self-interest to condemn such appeals. Lacking any moral case of their own, these critics have angrily advanced the dubious proposition that morality born of faith has no place in politics.

Bono's Campaigns: The Judeo-Christian Idea Against Poverty in Africa

In the mid-1980s, the Irish rock band U2 paid a visit to Chicago's Peace Museum. There, the band members saw an exhibit dedicated to the life and work of Martin Luther King. The Irish visitors had certainly heard of King before, and like most people they knew that he had campaigned for black civil rights. But as they progressed through the exhibit, they were captivated by the man, his message and his methods.

U2's new hero featured prominently in their next album, *The Unforgettable Fire*. The album's lead single, entitled "Pride (In the Name of Love)," is a passionate tribute to King. The song lauds "one man come in the name of love" and closes with an unmistakable reference to King's 1968 assassination:

> Early morning, April Four
> A shot rings out in the Memphis sky
> Free at last, they took your life
> But they could not take your pride.

The closing song on *The Unforgettable Fire* is also dedicated to King. Entitled "MLK," the song is a gentle lullaby sung by the band to the slain leader, closing with the prayer "may all your dreams be realized."

This embrace of King was no passing fancy. For U2, King became an inspirational example of active Christian faith. For the band's lead singer, known to the world by his nickname "Bono," this mission to realize King's dreams would lead from a Chicago museum to the refugee camps of Africa and, eventually, to the corridors of power in America and Europe.

～

BONO WAS BORN Paul Hewson in Dublin, Ireland, to a Catholic father and a Protestant mother. On Sundays his father would attend Catholic mass and then wait for Bono and his mother outside the Protestant church down the street. When it came time to go to high school, Bono chose an experimental school called Mount Temple, which welcomed both Protestants and Catholics with ecumenical Christian themes.

It was during his years at Mount Temple that Bono met his fellow band members and formed U2. Yet during this period another passion competed with music for the attention of Bono and his new friends: religion. It was in high school that Bono and two of the three other members of the band—David Evans (nicknamed "The Edge") and Larry Mullen, Jr.—became born-again Christians. Zealous in their newfound faith, these three gravitated toward an evangelical organization called the Shalom Christian Fellowship. Here, they devoted increasing amounts of their free time to Bible study, prayer, and Christian worship.

The members of U2 never hid their faith. In their early years, they were quite explicit about it. In an interview after the release of their first album, Bono told reporter Bill Graham, "One thing you should know . . . we're all Christians."[53] Early recording sessions were interrupted for prayer. There were no drugs on the back of the U2 tour bus, only Bible study. At one point, Bono and his two religious band mates grew so devoted to the Shalom Fellowship that they seriously contemplated leaving the gritty world of rock music for a more pure devotion to their faith.[54] Like Wilberforce centuries earlier, however, they eventually decided that they could serve God from within their chosen career.

U2's second album, *October*, was labeled a Christian album by critics due to its biblical references and explicit statements of faith. The album's lead single, "Gloria," was one of the band's first hits. Yet few fans realized that the song's chorus sings the praises not of a girl, but of God. "Gloria" is the Latin word for "glory," common in the Catholic Mass. Further invoking Mass Latin, the chorus places this glory squarely "in te Domine"—in you, God.

For years, U2 closed its massive concerts with the song "40." While this song takes its name and most of its words from Psalm 40, it borrows its chorus from Psalm 6. Hundreds of thousands have thus left U2 concerts with the words of the Psalmist ringing in their ears:

> I waited patiently for the Lord
> He inclined and heard my cry
> He brought me up out of the pit
> Out of the miry clay
> I will sing, sing a new song.
> I will sing, sing a new song.

Even U2's tribute to Martin Luther King, "Pride (In the Name of Love)," carries a strong Christian message. The song makes reference not only to King, but also to a second man who "came in the name of love." This second man was "betrayed by a kiss." U2's clear reference to Jesus in a song about King is no accident. Despite the conventional wisdom to the contrary, the band members recognized King as a devout Christian striving to emulate the love and nonviolence of his Savior.

⁀

BY THE TIME they visited Chicago's Peace Museum, U2's three Christian band members had become disillusioned with the Shalom Fellowship. While still passionate about their Christianity, they were growing increasingly skeptical of organized religion and were searching for a way to make their faith more relevant in the world. Whether or not they realized it at the time, this introduction to Martin Luther King would mark a watershed between the band's more conventional Christian past and their new focus on taking their faith beyond church walls. In

King, they found the ultimate exemplar of the active faith to which they now aspired.[55]

U2's desire to take their faith into the world manifested itself in their music. While the band continued to pepper its lyrics with biblical references, it made these references less explicit. Bono once described this new approach as an effort to "draw our fish in the sand." In other words, the fish—a symbol of Christianity—would be softer but still visible for those "who are interested." [56]

This new focus also changed the way the band, and especially Bono, lived outside of the studio. Consciously or not, Bono had chosen a new path. He would become a Christian activist in the spirit of Martin Luther King. He would seek to remind his fellow men of the love at the heart of the Judeo-Christian idea. More importantly, he would strive to serve the most vulnerable among them in the name of this great love. Bono would go on to accomplish far more than anyone would have expected from a sunglass-wearing, earring-studded Irish rock star. But he would do so by joining an effort that was first begun by others.

Jubilee 2000

After Britain abolished the slave trade in 1807, evangelical abolitionist William Wilberforce did not rest. He immediately introduced legislation to abolish the institution of slavery itself. The struggle to pass this legislation would go on for another twenty-five years.

As the years passed, however, Wilberforce grew too old and sick to continue leading this legislative fight. He eventually selected another evangelical member of Parliament, Thomas Fowell Buxton, as his successor. In 1833, Buxton finally won passage of a law abolishing slavery throughout the British Empire. Although far less well known than the charismatic Wilberforce, Buxton earned his place among the heroes of Christian compassion.

A century and a half later, Buxton's great-great-great grand-son, an English professor named Martin Dent, followed in his illustrious forebear's footsteps. In the 1990s, Dent became a leader in an effort to end what he and his colleagues believed to be a modern form of African bondage: the debilitating debts that many African nations owed to the industrialized North. Many of the poorest African countries were paying much more in interest on these debts than they had left to spend on education and healthcare for their people. As these massive payments flowed to the first world, thousands died daily at home for lack of clean water, mosquito nets, and basic medicines. In a very real sense, Dent argued, these Africans were still laboring for European masters rather than for themselves.

Dent believed that the only way these African countries could begin to address their domestic emergencies was if the industrialized nations agreed to forgive their debts. Yet Dent also understood that debt forgiveness must be a strictly limited intervention. If lenders ever came to believe that African debts would be cancelled as a matter of course, they would simply cease extending credit to the continent.[57] Sitting in an Oxford pub one day in 1990, Dent seized upon the biblical concept of "jubilee" as the perfect solution to the problem.[58]

In book of Leviticus, God instructs Moses that every fiftieth year shall be a "Year of Jubilee" in which all slaves were to be freed and all debts were to be forgiven.[59] The Bible thus commanded a radical egalitarian realignment, but one which would occur only twice a century. For Dent, the approaching millennium offered a powerful symbolic date to which to link this historic charitable gesture. Dent began to advocate for a modern jubilee in which the richest nations would forgive the debts of the poorest by the year 2000.

Dent shared his idea with his students and conducted some small demonstrations and letter-writing campaigns. In time, he persuaded a number of Christian charities to join him in his work. In 1996, Dent and his allies launched a debt cancellation campaign called "Jubilee 2000." Their first office was a shed on the roof of the offices of Christian Aid.

Jubilee 2000 was not the first organization to seek to persuade the major industrialized nations to forgive the debts of the world's poorest nations. But these prior efforts had sparked little interest beyond the specialized circles focused on the issues of third world development. Jubilee 2000, by contrast, quickly grew into a popular grassroots movement. The genius of Dent's concept was that it invoked a biblical theme and an approaching deadline—the year 2000—to attract and motivate large networks of religious activists.

Jubilee 2000 expanded rapidly in Europe. When the G7 industrialized nations met in England in May of 1998, the movement was large enough to stage a massive show of support for debt cancellation. Over sixty thousand demonstrators surrounded the convention center in a human chain meant to symbolize the debt which enslaved the poorest nations to these rich ones.[60] When the G7 met the following year in Germany, fifty thousand activists surrounded the meeting to demand debt cancellation. They were joined by a million more activists who took to the streets of their home countries around the world.[61]

By 1999, over five hundred thousand "Cancel the Debt" postcards had been sent to Gordon Brown, who was then Britain's minister of finance.[62] Brown, it turns out, faced pressure not only from without, but also from within. His father, a Church of Scotland minister, personally lobbied him to support debt cancellation.[63] Brown became one of Jubilee 2000's earliest allies in government.

Throughout this effort, Europe's churches were the source of the grassroots army that sent postcards to leaders and demonstrators to the streets. Reflecting on the successes of 1998 and 1999, Jubilee 2000 organizer Jamie Drummond noted that "the church networks have been the bedrock from which everything has come."[64] Campaign founder Charlie Dent agreed. He praised "the leading role of the churches" in Jubilee 2000:

We have derived enormous momentum from the support of all the churches. They have acted like the leaven in the lump to help produce the present extensive level of support for Jubilee 2000. They have been effective inspirers of action in the secular field and have brought to the campaign a dimension of the call for justice and compassion.[65]

Jubilee in America

While the campaign thrived in Europe, however, it was failing to generate much interest in the United States. Jubilee 2000 assigned Jamie Drummond the task of jump-starting the campaign in America. Drummond had worked for Christian Aid in Ethiopia, and he brought a great passion for Africa to the cause. He also brought clear insight into the levers of influence in America. Drummond recognized that the quickest way to get Americans interested in debt relief was to find a celebrity spokesman.

Drummond did not have to look very far to find a star passionate enough about Africa to accept the assignment. He immediately approached Bono.

Bono had already demonstrated an interest in Africa. In 1985, U2 performed in the massive "Live Aid" charity concert which raised over two hundred million dollars for food aid to famine victims in Ethiopia. In the process, Bono's curiosity and compassion were piqued. Unlike so many of the other performers, Bono did not forget about the famine after the concert was over. The following year, he and his wife Ali traveled to Ethiopia and spent a summer working in a refugee camp run by the Christian charity World Vision.

When they first spoke, Drummond used Bono's role in the Live Aid concert to demonstrate the necessity of debt forgiveness. Yes, Drummond noted, Live Aid was a wonderful effort that raised two hundred million dollars for famine relief. But, he asked, was Bono aware of the fact that African nations spent this amount servicing their debts to the industrialized nations *every five days?*[66] The money raised by Live Aid had changed nothing. Only debt cancellation could give Africa the fresh start it needed.

Bono was an instant convert to the cause and immediately overflowed with the convert's zeal. He threw himself into his new mission. Aspiring to do more than pose for photographs, Bono sought out tutors on the issues of debt and development. He sat down for a two-day study session with Harvard economist Jeffrey Sachs. He met with Paul Volker, former chairman of the Federal Reserve; James Wolfensohn, head of the World Bank; and David Rockefeller, former chairman of Chase Manhattan Bank.[67] Bono also solicited advice on the ways of Washington. He reached out to Bobby Shriver, John F. Kennedy's nephew, and forged a friendship which gave the Irish rocker insight and entrée into a town he knew little about.

Once his preparation was complete, Bono turned to his first target: President Clinton. In a meeting with Treasury secretary Lawrence Summers and Clinton economic adviser Gene Sperling, Bono boldly suggested that the Clinton administration cancel one hundred percent of the debts owed to the United States by the world's poorest nations. Bono was dogged in his followup, even visiting the workaholic Sperling in the White House on a Sunday to ensure that debt relief was not forgotten in the press of business.[68]

Summers and Sperling eventually persuaded President Clinton to embrace Bono's goal. In a speech before the World Bank on September 29, 1999, President Clinton announced that the United States would cancel one hundred percent of the six-billion-dollar debt owed to it by the world's poorest thirty-three countries. Suddenly, the United States had become a leader in the effort to forgive Africa's debts.

⌒

BONO WAS OVERJOYED when he received the call telling him about the president's decision. Then his Washington colleagues explained to him that their work had only just begun. Forgiving these debts would require a government expenditure of $545 million, an amount representing the "present value" of the loans at issue. But Congress, not the president, controls the federal purse strings. Thus the only way that the debts could be forgiven was if Congress appropriated the necessary funds.

The odds of securing such congressional cooperation were long. At this juncture, Congress was controlled by Republicans who were fiercely opposed to government spending in general, and to foreign aid in particular. Making matters worse, congressional Republicans had recently impeached President Clinton and remained overwhelmingly hostile to him. They would not be quick to hand him a legislative victory.

Undeterred, Bono began to work the Republican side of the aisle. As expected, he found that many Republicans objected to debt relief for reasons of philosophy and policy. Yet when dealing with Republicans who were also believing Christians, Bono found an effective way to circumvent these ideological obstacles: he appealed directly to their shared Christian faith.[69] Bono invoked the core principles of the Judeo-Christian idea with a passion and focus rarely heard on Capitol Hill. In so doing, he convinced these legislators to apply their faith to politics in a new way. Bono found that Christian compassion could trump fiscal conservatism.

Bono's faith-based appeal was quickly put to its greatest test. North Carolina senator Jesse Helms emerged as the leading opponent of the additional funding for debt relief. Helms, the powerful chairman of the Senate Foreign Relations Committee, was the champion of an aging breed of Southern conservative. Helms had criticized the landmark civil rights legislation of the 1960s, and he was so opposed to a national holiday for Martin Luther King that he conducted a sixteen-day filibuster in an effort to block it. His staunch resistance to foreign aid and other spending programs had earned him the moniker "Senator No." In his late seventies at the time, Senator Helms had never heard of U2. It took the intervention of some of his younger staffers to get Helms to even meet with the Irish rocker.

When their meeting began, Bono could tell that he was making little progress with his standard litany of African statistics. He quickly shifted to the theological imperatives. "I started talking about Scripture," Bono recalled. "I talked about AIDS as the leprosy of our age."[70] He also spoke about the Bible's repeated exhortations to help the poor and the biblical origin of the concept of a jubilee year. Bono's heartfelt invocation of shared faith once again proved effective. Helms eyes began to well up with tears. "I want to give you a blessing," he told Bono as he embraced him, "I want to do anything I can to help you."[71] Helms was so moved by his new friend that he later attended a U2 concert, albeit with his hearing aid turned down.

After the arch-conservative Helms had embraced debt relief, most of the remaining Republican skeptics felt free to support the effort. The last holdout was Alabama congressman Sonny Callahan. Callahan was chairman of the House Foreign Operations Subcommittee, which controlled the foreign aid budget. As far as Callahan was concerned, the budget over which he presided was already too large. Callahan had recently criticized President Clinton for handing out taxpayer money "every time somebody walks in the White House with a turban."[72] As for debt cancellation, he was convinced that it was "money down a rat hole."[73]

This time the breakthrough did not come from persuasion in Washington, but through pressure from back home. Bono and his colleagues mobilized Christian activists in Callahan's Alabama district, who urged the congressman to support the debt relief package. By Callahan's own admission, this grassroots effort is what eventually convinced him to change course:

> Priests and pastors sermonizing on debt relief on Sundays, telling their congregations to tell Callahan to take care of this, including my own bishop. Eventually I gave in.[74]

Bono later shared that the idea of getting Callahan's bishop to contact him was not an original one. He had learned it from Martin Luther King. King, Bono related, had been deeply disappointed by Attorney General Robert Kennedy's failure to provide sufficient federal protection to the civil rights marchers. So King contacted Kennedy's bishop and asked him to appeal to Kennedy with a faith-based case for civil rights.[75]

On October 25, 2000, Congress appropriated the additional $435 million needed for the one-hundred-percent debt cancellation.

~

THE PIVOTAL ROLE played by grassroots Christians in persuading Rep. Callahan to embrace debt relief was no aberration. Bono and his Jubilee 2000 colleagues recognized early on that the reason foreign aid received so little funding was that it had no constituency. Bono also understood that his fame could not overcome this liability. "Politicians aren't afraid of rock stars and student activists," he observed, "they're afraid of churchgoers and soccer moms."[76] When it came to building a constituency to back his efforts, Bono focused on the churchgoers in particular.

The churchgoers quickly responded to the call. Not only did the campaign invoke core biblical themes, but it enjoyed the support of key Christian leaders. As early as 1994, Pope John Paul II issued an apostolic letter in which he recognized a link between the biblical concept of jubilee and the approaching millennium. The pope wrote that the time had come to contemplate "reducing substantially, if not canceling outright, the international debt which seriously threatens the future of many nations."[77]

Bono and his colleagues capitalized on this Vatican support by requesting an audience with the pontiff at the height of their push for debt cancellation. On September 23, 1999, Pope John Paul II held a widely publicized meeting with Bono and other representatives of Jubilee 2000 to express his support for their efforts. At the end of the meeting, the pope gave Bono a rosary.

Lacking a more appropriate gift, Bono gave the pope his trademark wrap-around sunglasses. The pope donned the glasses, a sight so comical that the Vatican refused to release the photos until after John Paul II's death. Bono has worn the pope's rosary around his neck ever since.

Bono also recruited prominent evangelical leaders to the cause. He asked evangelical icon Billy Graham to make a video explaining the importance of Jubilee 2000 and then sent it to a number of key congressmen.[78] Bono also invited Christian broadcaster Pat Robertson to participate in a September 2000 meeting at the White House to organize the final legislative push for debt relief. When it later appeared that Texas senator Phil Gramm might block the debt relief legislation, Robertson took to the airwaves. As Senator Gramm's phone number flashed on the screen, Robertson asked the audience of his popular *700 Club* television show to contact the senator and demand that he permit the bill to pass.[79] Gramm's threatened obstruction never materialized.

Sometimes the grassroots activists were so persuasive that they won allies to the cause without the help of Bono or his lobbyists. An Alabama congressman named Spencer Bachus, for instance, had originally opposed debt forgiveness. A delegation of Presbyterians from his district decided to fly to Washington to change his mind. One of the delegation leaders later recalled that as she began to explain how her Christian faith led her to support debt relief, the congressman's staff members started rolling their eyes. Bachus, however, "perked up and listened."[80] Bachus became an enthusiastic supporter of debt cancellation, proclaiming:

> This bill is a gift of life. Jubilee 2000 is a celebration of the 2000th birthday of Christ.... What more appropriate time to give to these poor countries in celebration of the birth of Jesus, who gave us life?[81]

The AIDS Initiative

Bono did not abandon the cause of Africa after the debt cancellation victory. He and his colleagues viewed debt relief as a structural prerequisite to humanitarian progress but not as a guarantee of such progress. Africa still needed help. Bono was particularly distressed by the millions of Africans dying from "treatable, preventable diseases" such as AIDS and malaria. At the time, an estimated 6,500 Africans were dying *every day* from AIDS alone. For Bono, these deaths represented not a cause but "an emergency."[82]

In early 2002, the Bush administration asked Bono to endorse their new approach to African aid called the Millennium Challenge Account, or MCA. The goal of the MCA was to stop the recurrent waste and theft of foreign aid by providing funds only to transparent regimes which could demonstrate that all aid funds reached their intended destinations. Bono embraced the concept and agreed to appear with the president at a press conference launching the program. But Bono decided to ask for something in return for his support: an historic initiative to prevent and treat AIDS in Africa.[83]

As Bono was being driven to the White House for his first meeting with President Bush, he was still finalizing his pitch for the AIDS initiative. In his search for the words that would move the president to action, he consulted neither policy papers nor scientific studies. With his Bible on his lap and an Irish priest on the phone, Bono was looking for those lines in scripture which best capture the Christian obligation to help those in need. He finally settled on the twenty-fifth chapter of the book of Matthew, where Jesus tells his disciples that whenever they care for the sick, feed the hungry, or welcome the stranger, it is as if they are caring for, feeding, and welcoming Jesus himself.[84] "Whatever you did for the least of these brothers of mine," Jesus tells them, "you did it for me."

⁓

BONO RECOGNIZED THAT his celebrity and powers of persuasion alone would not be able to convince the president to embrace an expensive new initiative. So just as he had done during the debt relief campaign, Bono once again went to work building a constituency to support his objectives. And in building this constituency, he once again looked to the churches.

In December 2002, Bono embarked on what he called the "Heart of America Tour." The weeklong tour included stops in seven Midwestern cities. Instead of playing music, Bono gave speeches urging his audiences to join him in the effort to combat AIDS in Africa. His primary venues were churches and Christian colleges. For the first time in his life, Bono gave Bible-based speeches from church pulpits in the American heartland.

At the outset of the tour, Bono was unsure whether his appeal to the churches would work. He was convinced that the church was a powerful constituency that could move Washington, but he feared that it would remain a "sleeping giant."[85] He worried that the insensitive statements made by some Christian leaders about AIDS might indicate a broader intolerance. Yet the enthusiastic response he received quickly erased these doubts. By the end of the tour, he had signed up thousands of new activists who flooded the White House with calls and letters in support of a major AIDS initiative.

After the tour, Bono happily admitted his mistake:

> I kind of thought the church was asleep . . . but I'm glad to say I was wrong. Particularly evangelicals, who seemed very judgmental to me over the years, turned out to be incredibly generous in their time and support of this effort. I've already had my view of the church turned upside down. . . . It's given me great faith in the church. I have always had it in God.[86]

In his 2003 State of the Union address, President Bush proposed a five-year, $15-billion AIDS initiative in fifteen countries, twelve of which were in Africa. Far from being a throwaway line in a speech, this program was pursued, passed, and fully funded. Through what is billed as "the largest commitment by any nation to combat a single disease in history," the president's Emergency Plan for AIDS Relief has provided treatment to over two million HIV-infected individuals, support for over ten million infected individuals and their families, and a massive education and condom-distribution program to prevent the further spread of the disease.

Bono's Motives

Bono is certainly among the least orthodox of the Christian activists motivated to humanitarian action by the Judeo-Christian idea. Despite his deep faith, he is skeptical of organized religion and has lived his life largely outside of the church and its institutions. Yet despite, or perhaps because of, his unconventional background, Bono has been unusually outspoken about the religious roots of his activism. In the process, he has become one of the most eloquent and effective apostles of the Judeo-Christian idea alive today.

It has become increasingly common in recent years for secular critics to dismiss the radical equality at the heart of the Judeo-Christian idea as obvious and even instinctive. To the extent that they credit this egalitarian insight to any external source, such critics typically acknowledge the Enlightenment or classical Greece. Thus Bono stands against a rather determined conventional wisdom when he notes that "equality is an idea that was first really expressed by the Jews when God told them that everyone was equal in His eyes."[87] Elsewhere Bono has elaborated upon this point:

> I will say this for the Judeo-Christian tradition: we have at
> least written into the DNA the idea that God created every
> man equal, and that love is at the heart of the universe. I
> mean, it's slow. The Greeks may have come up with democ-

racy, but they had no intention of everyone having it. We have to conclude that the most access to equality in the world has come out of these ancient religious ideas.[88]

Bono stresses that, far from being "self-evident," this concept of human equality is actually a "preposterous idea" and one that is "hard to hang on to."[89] This insight has made him far more sensitive than most to the ways in which our civilization fails to live up to this ideal. Of course, Bono notes, "most people accept that women, blacks, Irish, and Jews are equal." But he is quick to add that such acceptance exists "only within our borders." As a consequence, he concludes, "I'm not sure we accept that Africans are equal."[90]

Bono argues that this residual discrimination is manifested not so much in our actions as in our omissions. In the aftermath of the September 11 attacks, he frequently noted that 6,500 Africans were dying every day from AIDS. He emphasized that this number represented "two 9/11's a day, eighteen jumbo jets of fathers, mothers, families falling out of the sky." Yet, he lamented, there are "no tears, no letters of condolence, no fifty-one gun salutes." For Bono, this disparity flowed from the fact that:

> we don't put the same value on African life as we put on a European or an American life. God will not let us get away with this, history certainly won't let us get away without excuses. . . .
>
> If we really thought that an African life was equal in value to an English, a French, or an Irish life, we wouldn't let two and a half million Africans die every year for the stupidest of reasons: money. We just wouldn't. . . . We don't really deep down believe in their equality.[91]

～

DURING THE NINETEENTH-century abolition struggle, many activists warned that divine judgment would befall America if it failed to free its slaves. When it comes to the faith community, such theological sticks still have the power to motivate. Even Bono, the hip apostle of love, has warned that divine judgment will befall America if we fail to come to Africa's aid:

> Now, for all its failings and its perversions over the last 2,000 years ... it is unarguably the central tenet of Christianity that everybody is equal in God's eyes. So you cannot, as a Christian, walk away from Africa. America will be judged by God if, in its plenty, it crosses the road from 23 million people suffering from HIV, the leprosy of the day. What's up on trial here is Christianity itself. You cannot walk away from this and call yourself a Christian and sit in power. Distance does not decide who is your brother and who is not.[92]

In addition to threatening America with divine judgment, he has threatened the church with marginalization. "If the church doesn't respond to this [the AIDS crisis]," Bono warned during his Heart of America Tour, "the church will be made irrelevant."[93] For Bono, it was clear that "Judeo-Christian culture is at stake."[94]

～

IN BONO'S MISSION to realize Martin Luther King's dream, King's example is never far from the surface. Bono has described his efforts to combat AIDS in Africa as "a Civil Rights movement for our generation" since this struggle, just like King's, is "about equality."[95]

During U2's 2005 *Vertigo* tour, Bono took advantage of the sold-out arenas to continue building his grassroots army. In each concert, he sang his tribute to King, "Pride (In the Name of Love)." After the song, Bono asked the crowd to act on King's belief that "everyone is created equal in the eyes of God ... everyone is equal in the eyes of God."[96] Then the massive video screens flashed the web address and contact number for the One Campaign, Bono's latest effort to build a constituency for foreign aid.

Human Trafficking Legislation: The Judeo-Christian Idea Against Modern Slavery

The founder of Jubilee 2000, Martin Dent, analogized the enormous debt burden of many African countries to slavery. Yet slavery exists today not only figuratively, but also quite literally. And while Bono was organizing America's Christians to combat African debt, other religious leaders were appealing to these same grassroots to help abolish modern slavery.

～

TODAY, SLAVERY IS illegal almost everywhere. Yet slavery is nonetheless thriving like never before. Kevin Bales, one of the leading authorities on modern slavery, estimates that there are twenty-seven million slaves in the world today. If his estimate is correct, then there are actually more slaves today than at any other time in history. In addition, as Bales notes, "There are more slaves alive today than all the people stolen from Africa in the time of the transatlantic slave trade."[97]

The majority of this total, an estimated fifteen to twenty million slaves, are bonded laborers in India and Pakistan. These individuals pledged their labor and that of future generations as collateral for small loans that, under their creditors' corrupt accounting, will never be repaid. The remainder of today's slaves are largely concentrated in southeast Asia, northern and western Africa, and parts of South America. Most labor in agriculture. But millions also work in manufacturing and, increasingly, in the sexual slavery of forced prostitution.[98] It is estimated that as many as eighty percent of modern slaves are women.[99]

～

IN THE LATE 1990S, a new abolition movement emerged that was dedicated to combating modern slavery and the modern slave trade, or "human trafficking," that fuels it. Many of these activists focused their efforts on persuading foreign governments to enforce their laws barring such practices. Others tried to free and rehabilitate slaves even in the absence of government cooperation. Still others turned their attention to Congress. They lobbied for legislation which would enlist America's moral and economic power in the effort to curb human trafficking.

Just like its nineteenth-century predecessors, this modern abolitionist campaign was a largely faith-based effort. By all accounts, the man who organized this legislative initiative and constantly prodded it forward was Michael Horowitz, a Jewish public policy expert and "moral entrepreneur."[100] While Horowitz's coalition was dominated by evangelical Christians, it also included major Catholic and Jewish groups. Through their constituencies in America's churches and synagogues, these activists were able to mobilize a vast grassroots army in support of anti-trafficking legislation.

To ensure bipartisan support for the bill, Horowitz reached beyond this faith-based core to recruit human rights and feminist groups to the effort. The broad coalition that eventually lobbied Congress in favor of the anti-trafficking bill included groups such as Human Rights Watch and Amnesty International and personalities such as Gloria Steinem and Jessica Neuwirth.

⁓

AS IN THE ICONIC campaigns of old, these modern abolitionists enlisted sympathetic legislators to champion their cause. In the House of Representatives, Rep. Chris Smith of New Jersey led the fight for the anti-trafficking bill. Smith, a devout Catholic, was elected to Congress after serving as the head of New Jersey Right to Life. Smith attributes his passion for human rights directly to the book of Matthew:

The Gospel message has a very strong social justice component, especially Matthew 25 where Christ asked, "when I was
hungry, did you give me food to eat? Visit me in prison?" And
you know the bottom line to that is he says, "Whatsoever you
do to the least of these my brethren, you do it to me." And
that has been the core, the absolute bedrock of all right-to-life
and human rights work that I've done.[101]

In the Senate, Sam Brownback of Kansas took the lead. A former evangelical Protestant who converted to Catholicism,
Brownback cites William Wilberforce as his role model and great
inspiration. In his autobiography, Brownback relates that as a
young senator he was reading a biography of Wilberforce when
he paused to compare himself to the English politician. Brownback was shaken by his failure to measure up. "When I thought
about the things I had done, particularly in comparison with
what Wilberforce accomplished in his lifetime," Brownback
wrote, "I felt it was of little value. . . . I felt I'd been wasting much
of my time."[102] According to Brownback, this moment was a
major turning point in his life:

> When I put the book down I had tears streaming down my
> face, in part because of the power of the story, but also because
> of the feeling that I needed to rededicate myself to the mission
> God has given me.[103]

ᘒ

IN OCTOBER 2000, Congress passed the Trafficking Victims Protection Act (TVPA) with strong bipartisan support.* The TVPA
placed the full weight of America's diplomatic and economic
clout behind the effort to combat human trafficking.

---

*Liberal icon Paul Wellstone was the Democratic co-sponsor of the TVPA in the Sen-
ate. It was one of the last pieces of legislation he championed before his tragic death in
an airplane crash.

Among the TVPA's key provisions was the creation of an office within the State Department charged with monitoring the anti-slavery efforts of every country in the world. This office is responsible for issuing an annual report ranking countries according to how seriously they are confronting human trafficking within and across their borders. The president may then impose sanctions upon those nations found to be making insufficient efforts. Such sanctions, and often merely the threat thereof, have proven to be extremely effective in prodding otherwise apathetic nations to action.

The TVPA was reauthorized in 2003, 2005, and again in 2008. The 2008 reauthorization legislation was appropriately entitled the "William Wilberforce Trafficking Victims Protection Reauthorization Act."

⟿

MICHAEL HOROWITZ WAS raised as an Orthodox Jew, and he notes that he's "always been a deeply self-identified Jew." For many years, Horowitz relates, he "backslid" in terms of his observance and synagogue attendance. As he worked closely with religious Christians in support of human rights, however, he was moved to return to regular synagogue attendance. According to Horowitz, the experience "brought me much more deeply in touch with my own faith."[104]

In describing the beliefs that drove him to campaign so passionately against modern slavery, Horowitz the Jewish policy wonk sounds almost identical to Bono the Christian rock star:

> The inherent message of Christianity is so clear a call for dignity and freedom and human autonomy as to make it necessarily subversive to tyrants. Our Judeo-Christian faith has taught the most radical political message of all times: the equality of all in the eyes of God.[105]

SEVEN

Myths about Biblical Immorality

*Christianity was the one great religion which had always
declared the diminution, if not the final elimination, of slavery
to be meritorious; no real case for slavery could be constructed,
in good faith, from the Christian scripture.*[1]

—PAUL JOHNSON, HISTORIAN

$\sim$ **A**rticle 1, Section 2 of the United States Constitution provides that congressional representatives shall be apportioned among the several states on the basis of population. It goes on to specify that, for this purpose, the population shall be determined by counting the number of "free persons" and adding to this total three-fifths of "all other persons."

These "other persons," of course, were slaves. This strange census math is the codification of the Constitutional Convention's infamous "three-fifths compromise." The delegates from the slave states wanted to maximize their representation in Congress, so they argued that their slaves should be included in their population. Since any gains in Southern representation would come at their expense, the delegates from the Northern states opposed the inclusion of slaves. The compromise they reached split the difference by counting each slave as three-fifths of a person.

Article 1, Section 9 of the United States Constitution provides that Congress may not prohibit the "importation" of persons prior to the year 1808. This curious language is another codification of a major compromise between North and South. The delegates from the slave states feared that Congress might abolish the slave trade, and they demanded a guarantee that this would not happen. Most of the Northern delegates were opposed to limiting congressional power when it came to such a controversial issue. The two sides finally agreed that this horrific trade would be allowed to continue for at least another two decades.

Article 4, Section 2 of the Constitution provides that:

> no person held to Service or Labor in one State ... escaping
> into another, shall ... be discharged from such service or
> labor, but shall be delivered up on claim of the party to whom
> such service or labor may be due.

This is the fugitive slave clause. The Southern delegates used their leverage at the Constitutional Convention to address their longstanding complaint that the Northern states were obstructing their efforts to recover runaway slaves. With this language, the Framers enshrined in the Constitution the requirement that runaway slaves be returned to their masters.

After the Civil War, the Thirteenth Amendment was ratified and slavery was officially abolished in America. Yet amendments do not delete Constitutional language; they simply supersede it. Thus these peculiar relics of slavery remain in the Constitution's text to this very day.

No matter how troubling these provisions may be, however, it would be a mistake to judge America's founding documents on the basis of this language alone. These texts contain much more than cynical compromises. They also express our society's highest ideals and aspirations. In one stirring sentence in the Declaration of Independence, the Founders summarized the ethos at the heart of our democracy in a way that continues to shape the nation. Supplementing the Judeo-Christian idea with the Enlightenment's language of natural rights, they famously asserted:

We hold these truths to be self-evident, that all men are created equal, that they are endowed by their creator with certain
unalienable rights, that among these are life, liberty, and the
pursuit of happiness.

In time, this overpowering idea of equality prevailed over the
detailed compromises with slavery. The larger principles of our
founding had a force and a logic which eventually swept away
our nation's original sin. America was not born perfect. It has
taken the course of our nation's history for Americans to live out
the true meaning of our creed. But we have, albeit too slowly and
at too high a price, rendered irrelevant our Constitution's peculiar compromises. Of all people, we Americans should understand that a document can both sanction sin and at the same
time point the way forward toward the abolition of that sin.

ᕈᔣ

WHEN OUR FOUNDING FATHERS gathered in Philadelphia to draft
the Constitution, Thomas Paine was not among them. Paine was
an Englishman who had moved to America and written a pamphlet—*Common Sense*—that inflamed the colonists' passion for
independence. But Paine was by his own description more of a
revolutionary than a statesman. After the Revolution was won
and the Founding Fathers settled down to the task of governing,
Paine left for France. There he had another monarchy to attack
and another revolution to foment.

Later in his life, Paine set his sights on the ultimate monarch
of them all: God. In a book entitled *The Age of Reason*, Paine set
forth the Enlightenment's most forceful critique of religious
faith. While other Enlightenment thinkers made similar arguments, none did so with the focus and ferocity of Paine.

Paine's complaint was not that God's words had been per-
verted by the fallible humans to whom they had been entrusted.
He took issue with the words themselves. Paine argued that the
defects in Christianity and Judaism flowed from their flawed

foundational text. In a passage indicative of his approach, Paine complained about the Bible:

> Whenever we read the obscene stories, the voluptuous debaucheries, the cruel and tortuous executions, the unrelenting vindictiveness with which more than half the Bible is filled, it would be more consistent that we call it the word of a demon than the word of God. It is a history of wickedness that has served to corrupt and brutalize mankind; and, for my part, I sincerely detest it, as I detest everything that is cruel.[2]

In post-September-11 America, Paine has enjoyed a renaissance. This evil perpetrated by the extremist adherents of one religion has fostered an intellectual environment inimical to all religion. Suddenly, there are packs of latter-day Paines recycling his attacks on the Bible and the great faiths that revere it. These modern efforts rarely rise to the level of Paine's original. Yet what these critics lack in originality and intellectual depth they often make up for in mass appeal. Today's atheists are populists.

Like their hero, many of these modern critics trace the flaws they see in the Judeo-Christian tradition back to its core text. Attacks on the Bible are thus central to their argument. The following quotations from the recent literature indicate the level of the discourse:

> The idea that the Bible is a perfect guide to morality is simply astounding given the contents of the book.[3]

> Those who wish to base their morality literally on the Bible have either not read it or not understood it.[4]

> The Bible may, indeed does, contain a warrant for trafficking in humans, for ethnic cleansing, for slavery, for bride-price, and for indiscriminate massacre.[5]

If these Bible critics have a consistent theme, it is that when it comes to morality the Bible gets it terribly wrong. Read the text, they urge, and you will see that it promotes the greatest of evils, including slavery and genocide. For such critics, all of the Bible's talk of love and brotherhood is merely wrapping paper on a ticking bomb. If we wish to elevate human morality, they argue, the Bible cannot be part of the solution, because it is the root of the problem.

As superficial as these critiques may be, they happen to be based on a foundation of fact. Someone who picks up the Bible and reads it for the first time will indeed confront some disconcerting language. There are multiple passages in the Bible which seem to contradict our modern morals and offend our contemporary sensibilities.

Finding these controversial biblical injunctions is hardly a major discovery—the faithful have been grappling with them for centuries. Indeed, the problem with these critiques of the Bible is not that they lack a basis in the text, but that they have no connection to the tradition. The Bible has been subject to century after century of exegesis and hermeneutics. Both Judaism and Christianity have long histories of wrestling with this rich and multi-layered document. These interpretations—and not the neophyte's first impressions—have governed how Bible believers have acted in the world. Thus when it comes to gauging the Bible's impact on Western morality, Jewish and Christian interpretations are not merely relevant; they are dispositive.

In a very real sense, the Bible, like the Constitution, is a living document. The Constitution has an amendment process, and it has been amended to outlaw slavery. The Bible has an interpretation process, and it has been interpreted by both Christianity and Judaism as prohibiting slavery and other objectionable practices it was once seen to sanction. In each case, core principles have come to override temporal specifics. Like our own Constitution, the Bible contains the means of its own perfection.

The Bible and Genocide: Confronting Our Evil Inclination

The parting of the Red Sea is one of the Bible's dramatic high points. With Pharaoh's army in hot pursuit, the Children of Israel walk across the seabed to Sinai. Then God allows the waters to crash down and drown Pharaoh's troops.

But danger lurks even on the far side of the Red Sea. As they begin their years of desert wandering, the Israelites are attacked by a tribe called the Amalekites. Once again God intervenes, and once again the Hebrews triumph, but only after they have fought a bloody battle.

Once the battle is won, God promises Moses that he—God—will "completely blot out the memory of Amalek from under heaven."[6] Forty years of desert wandering later, however, the responsibility for this blotting out shifts from God to the Israelites themselves. In his farewell message to the Children of Israel, Moses instructs them that "you shall blot out the memory of Amalek from under heaven. Do not forget!"[7]

As the years passed, this commandment to blot out Amalek grew even more explicit and ferocious. The book of Samuel relates that when Israel becomes a monarchy under King Saul, the prophet Samuel visits the king to share with him new divine instructions:

> This is what the Lord Almighty says: "I will punish the Amalekites for what they did to Israel when they waylaid them as they came up from Egypt. Now go, attack the Amalekites and totally destroy everything that belongs to them. Do not spare them: put to death men and women, children and infants, cattle and sheep, camels and donkeys."[8]

This is nothing less than a call for genocide—and worse, actually. The Israelites are commanded to kill not only every last Amalekite, but all of their animals as well. The book of Samuel goes on to report that, with an assist from Samuel, this grisly task is accomplished.

Nor are the Amalekites the only tribe condemned to such a fate. In his farewell speech, Moses lectures the Israelites on how they are to live when they cross the Jordan River into their Promised Land. Here he provides an explicit set of instructions for how to deal with the people already living in this land, the Canaanite nations. When it comes to the Canaanites, there are no exhortations to "love the stranger." On the contrary, Moses instructs the Children of Israel in genocide:

> In the cities of the nations the Lord your God is giving you as an inheritance, do not leave alive anything that breathes. Completely destroy them—the Hittites, Amonites, Canaanites, Perizzites, Hivites and Jebusites—as the Lord your God has commanded you.[9]

The book of Joshua relates that Joshua and the Israelites under his command largely comply with this bloody decree.

The Judeo-Christian Interpretation

It is not difficult to see where the Bible critics are coming from. This is extremely bloody stuff. And yet there is, at the outset, a serious problem with viewing these passages as a "warrant for genocide" today. The Bible is quite specific about whom the Israelites are to destroy: seven ancient Middle Eastern tribes that no longer exist.

When it comes to the six Canaanite tribes, Moses's commands were long ago rendered moot. By the time the Talmud was written (approximately 500 CE), Jewish authorities were in agreement that the Canaanite tribes had long before assimilated into the surrounding nations and disappeared as distinct peoples. Thus the commandment to kill them has been a dead letter since ancient times.

The case of the Amalekites, however, proved trickier. Despite the biblical passages indicating that the Israelites wiped out the entire tribe, there is a long-standing Jewish tradition that the

Amalekites somehow lived on. In fact, the Talmud teaches that Haman, the villain in the book of Esther who seeks to murder the Jews of Persia, was actually an Amalekite. If the Amalekites survived, then must the Jews still kill them?

This question was not debated for very long. The Talmud eliminated any chance that this commandment might be taken literally by removing its racial component. The Talmud reasons that what made the Amalekites evil was their behavior, not their blood. Righteous Amalekites would therefore cease to be "Amalekites" for purposes of this particular decree. And evil people, no matter what their ethnicity, would now be "Amalekites" in this context. A commandment to eliminate a specific tribe was thus transformed into a commandment to confront evil people in general.

The Talmud underscores its rejection of any race-based enmity for the Amalekites in the most powerful way possible: it notes that some Amalekites had become Jews. In fact, the Talmud teaches that "the descendants of Haman [an Amalekite] studied Torah in B'nai Brak [an ancient rabbinic center]."[10] To further emphasize the point, a rabbinic tradition identifies one of these Amalekite descendants who studied in B'nai Brak as none other than Rabbi Akiva, one of the most beloved rabbis in the Jewish tradition. Thus the people the Jews were supposed to kill had become, by Talmudic times, their fellow Jews and most revered teachers.

Elsewhere, the Talmudic sages go further still in reinterpreting the injunction to kill Amalek. They actually transform the story of Amalek from a command to kill the stranger into a lesson on the importance of loving the stranger. The Bible notes that the nation of Amalek descended from a gentile princess named Timna.[11] The Talmud later provides an interesting background story. According to the Talmud, Timna had approached the early patriarchs and expressed a desire to convert to Judaism, but they turned her away. Thus rebuffed, Timna instead became a concubine to Esau's son and gave birth to the nation of

Amalek.[12] The Jewish people thus suffered the enmity of Amalek because of their own failure to properly love and respect an outsider. So much for genocide.

By medieval times, leading rabbis began to allegorize the story of Amalek more broadly. In particular, Amalek was no longer seen as an external evil, but as an internal one. Judaism teaches that we are all born with an evil inclination that drives us toward selfishness and the gratification of our base desires. The commandment to blot out Amalek was increasingly understood as a commandment to confront and overcome this evil inclination.[13]

Today, defining Amalek as our personal evil inclination is the favored view of even the most orthodox of Jews. The interpretation of the Chabad Lubavitch movement illustrates the point. The Chabad are not merely religious Jews, they are ultra-Orthodox Jews. When it comes to interpreting the Bible, they tend to be among the most literal. Yet here is how official Chabad literature describes the commandment to destroy Amalek:

> In time the Amalek nation assimilated into the people around them.... But this doesn't mean that Amalek has disappeared. Amalek is alive and well today, albeit in a different form. No longer a foreign nation, today's Amalek is an internal enemy. We each have an Amalek lurking within our very self. The inner Amalek is unholy cynicism. That little voice inside us that derides, belittles and attacks truth and goodness; our irrational tendency to mock people who act morally, to be cynical when we see altruism, to doubt our own or others' sincerity— these are the modern day Amalekites. They wage a lethal war with our soul. If we let it, cynicism can kill our every attempt to improve ourselves and smother every move towards refining our character and expressing our soul.[14]

Thus whatever the original meaning of the commandment to eliminate Amalek, it was centuries ago transformed into something completely different. First, it was stripped of its racial component and turned into a commandment to battle evil in the world. Then it was internalized and understood as a commandment to battle our own evil inclinations. To find in these lines of the Bible a warrant for genocide, one must overlook centuries of interpretation by the very people who take this language most seriously.

～

CHRISTIANS HAVE TYPICALLY not felt the need to wrestle with the commandments to wipe out Amalek and the Canaanite tribes. Christian theology maintains that the arrival of Jesus and his sacrificial crucifixion created a new covenant in which believers could achieve salvation without having to follow all of the laws of Moses. While Christians may debate which Mosaic laws apply to them and which do not, they all agree that they are no longer bound by those commandments which are clearly limited to the specific geography or circumstances of ancient Israel. Thus while Judaism slowly reinterpreted many of the laws of Moses through biblical exegesis, Christianity instantly abandoned many of them through its early doctrine.

Yet while they were released from the literal commandment to destroy Amalek, many Christians nevertheless embraced the concept of Amalek as a personal evil inclination. Most famously, John and Charles Wesley incorporated this idea into a number of their popular hymns. One such hymn begins:

> Jesus, we dare believe in Thee
> Against this Amalek within
> He soon extirpated shall be.[15]

Another Wesley hymn includes the line, "Too well that Amalek I know, who still maintains the war within."[16]

After the September 11 attacks, a group of evangelical scholars revisited the topic of how Christians should relate to these commandments. They were troubled by the way the terrorists had justified their actions by citing lines from the Qur'an. Does our own Bible, they asked, contain any doctrines that could be seen to sanction similar atrocities? Answering this question led these scholars to focus on the most obvious call for violence in the Bible: the commandment to eliminate the Canaanite tribes.

The 2003 book *Show Them No Mercy*[17] offers an analysis of this issue from four evangelical scholars representing different biblical perspectives. All four agree that the commandment to obliterate the Canaanites no longer has any ongoing relevance for Christians. Their reasoning reflects the thinking that has long kept this issue at the far margins of Christianity. Two focus on the larger theme of "discontinuity" between the faith of ancient Israel and that of the Christian church. They stress that the commandment to eliminate the Canaanites is simply one of a large number of Mosaic commandments which were rendered superfluous by the coming of Jesus. The other two scholars focus more on the rather limiting specificity of this particular commandment. As one of them notes, this commandment is "unique" to its time, place, and circumstances, and these limitations "preclude any possible justification for modern genocide for any reason."[18]

The Bible and Slavery: From Tolerance to Abolition

The Bible does not ban slavery. On the contrary: the Bible acknowledges and explicitly permits this most evil of institutions. It is certainly not difficult to find the sanction for slavery of which the Bible critics speak.

Unlike the Constitution, the Bible calls slavery by its name, or at least by its Hebrew and Greek names. In the book of Leviticus, the Israelites are told:

> Your male and female slaves are to come from the nations around you; from them you may buy slaves. You may also buy some of the temporary residents living among you and members of their clans born into your country, and they will

become your property. You can will them to your children as inherited property and can make them slaves for life.[19]

Like the Hebrew Bible before it, the New Testament nowhere abolishes the institution of slavery. On the contrary, the New Testament contains passages which encourage slaves to obey their masters. For instance, in his letter to the Ephesians, Paul writes:

> Slaves, obey your earthly masters with respect and fear, and with sincerity of heart, just as you would obey Christ. Obey them not only to win their favor when their eye is on you, but like slaves of Christ, doing the will of God from your heart. Serve wholeheartedly, as if you were serving the Lord, not men, because you know that the Lord will reward everyone for whatever good he does, whether he is slave or free.[20]

The Apostle Peter provides similar instructions:

> Slaves, submit yourselves to your masters with all respect, not only to those who are good and considerate, but also to those who are harsh.[21]

Such acceptance of slavery did not end with the Bible. Some of the greatest thinkers in the Christian and Jewish traditions continued to sanction slavery for centuries thereafter. St. Augustine saw slavery as "the result of sin" and stressed that the subjugation of one man by another would not happen "save by the judgment of God, with whom there is no unrighteousness, and who knows how to award fit punishments to every variety of offense."[22] In the Jewish world, the great medieval scholar Maimonides condoned slavery and reiterated the view that non-Hebrew slaves could be worked "with rigor."

The Judeo-Christian Interpretation

Despite this language and history, it is simply inaccurate to claim that the Bible in any way sanctioned the form of slavery that came to be practiced in the modern West. Anyone wishing to make such a claim must ignore the important limitations the Bible placed on this institution. They must also overlook the way in which the Judeo-Christian tradition has interpreted and applied these passages over time. Most of all, they must focus on the letter of the Bible to the exclusion of its overriding spirit.

Just because the Bible sanctioned an institution called "slavery" does not mean that the Bible likewise sanctioned any institution, no matter how different, that might have been called by that name. The fact is that the slavery permitted by the Bible bears little resemblance to the slavery that was practiced in America. As the *Canada Christian Advocate* noted in 1861, "No two things on earth can be more unlike, both in principle and in practice, than Hebrew and Negro slavery."[23]

Western slavery was a most peculiar institution. For starters, it was thoroughly racist; only Africans and their descendants could be slaves. These Africans started their journey into slavery when they were kidnapped from their native villages. They were then transported across the Atlantic in conditions so appalling that a significant percentage of the captives died en route. Finally, the survivors were sold to owners who faced few limits on the treatment of their new property. The physical torture and mental abuse of slaves was widespread.

The slavery sanctioned by the Bible shared none of these characteristics. First of all, biblical slavery was not racist. Slaves could come from among the Israelites themselves or from neighboring tribes, without regard to skin color. While it is true that Israelite slaves received special protections, the members of any race or tribe could and did become Israelites. As Abraham Lincoln noted in his debates with Stephen Douglas. "Whenever you establish that slavery was right by the Bible, it will occur that that slavery was the slavery of the white man—of men without reference to color."[24]

Next, the Bible never contemplated or permitted the practice of kidnapping people to serve as slaves. In fact, the Bible forbids kidnapping anyone for any reason. This crime—typically translated as "man-stealing"—was so reviled that it was punishable by death.[25] The Bible envisioned slaves being obtained from other sources, namely those who chose to sell themselves to pay off debts or escape poverty. The African slave trade was thus a gross violation of one of the Bible's strictest prohibitions.

Just as the Bible did not permit slaves to be obtained through kidnapping, it did not permit them to be retained through kidnapping. In the West, it was common for escaped slaves to be hunted down, captured, and returned to their masters in chains. As we have seen, an obligation to return fugitive slaves is even enshrined in the United States Constitution. The Bible, on the other hand, actually had a reverse fugitive slave law. It commanded that when a runaway slave sought refuge, he should neither be returned to his master nor oppressed.[26]

The Bible further commanded that slaves be treated humanely. Masters were required to let their slaves rest on the Sabbath. And masters were not permitted to injure their slaves. In fact, a master who beat his slave hard enough to cause him bodily injury—such as knocking out a tooth—was obligated to set that slave free.[27] A master who beat his slave to death was to be severely punished.[28]

When it came to Hebrew slaves—i.e., slaves who were themselves Israelites—the rules were even more strict. In fact, the institution to which the biblical Israelites were subject is more accurately described as indentured servitude than slavery. A poor Israelite could sell himself to another man, but his service was strictly limited to a term of six years. In the seventh year, the servant had to be set free.[29]

During these six years of servitude, the master was required to treat his servant well. The Bible states repeatedly that a master must not treat his Hebrew servant "ruthlessly."[30] In addition, the master was required to provide the servant with food and living conditions at least equal to his own. And when the six years had passed, the master was required to send the servant away with livestock and "liberal" amounts of food and wine.[31] It is for these reasons that the rabbis of the Talmud concluded that "whoever buys a Hebrew slave, he buys a master for himself."[32]

These rules governing the treatment of Hebrew servants set a standard which in time was applied more broadly. Jewish theologians eventually began to urge that non-Hebrew slaves be treated similarly. Writing in the twelfth century, Maimonides acknowledged that it was permitted to work a non-Hebrew slave "with rigor." But he quickly added that:

> although this is the law, the way of the pious and the wise is to be compassionate and to pursue justice, not to overburden or oppress a servant, and to provide them from every dish and every drink. . . . You should not denigrate a servant, neither physically nor verbally. . . . Do not treat him with constant screaming and anger, rather speak with him pleasantly and listen to his complaints.[33]

The New Testament likewise encouraged humane treatment of slaves. After Paul urges slaves to obey and respect their masters, he goes on to address the masters:

> And masters, treat your slaves the same way. Do not threaten them, since you know that he who is both their Master and yours is in heaven, and there is no favoritism with him.[34]

Later Paul reiterates this admonition:

> Masters, provide your slaves with what is right and fair, because you know that you also have a Master in heaven.[35]

In his letter to the Galatians, Paul writes that all believers in Christ are equals: "There is neither Jew nor Greek, slave nor free, male nor female, for you are all one in Christ Jesus."[36] In the brief epistle to Philemon, Paul sends a runaway slave back to his master but urges the master to accept him "no longer as a slave, but better than a slave," since he is now a "brother in the Lord."[37]

ᴧ

THE BIBLE DID NOT permit the racism, kidnapping, and cruelty of slavery as practiced in the West and thus in no way sanctioned the American form of this institution. But even more important than the letter of the Bible is its spirit. Simply put, there is a significant difference between what the Bible permits and what it encourages.

Every major principle of the Bible points to slavery's ultimate abolition. Slavery contradicts the core principle of the sanctity and equality of all humans that is established by the creation story in Genesis. Slavery violates the golden rule of Hillel, Jesus, and Akiva. Slavery betrays the disinterested benevolence of Edwards, Hopkins, and Finney. As one American minister noted in 1845, opposition to slavery "blazes from every page of God's book which is a wall of fire around the rights of the poor."[38]

These big ideas are the ones that motivate men. Once they are introduced into the world, they have the power to soften hearts, change minds, and alter history. As these ideas spread and gain momentum, the details that accompanied their introduction tend to fade into the background. It was only a matter of time before Jews and Christians lived out the true meaning of their creed and rejected slavery altogether.

These key Judeo-Christian principles are what motivated the English and American abolitionists to take their stand against slavery. These abolitionists, in turn, eloquently invoked these same core principles when seeking to persuade their countrymen to do likewise. The most compelling arguments that slavery is antithetical to the spirit of Christianity come to us from the pens and lips of the abolitionists themselves.

In his 1785 Cambridge essay on slavery, for example, English abolitionist Thomas Clarkson wrote that "slavery is incompatible with the Christian system." He traced the source of this incompatibility to, among other things, the fact that slavery ran counter to the commandment "to love our neighbors as ourselves, and to do unto all men, as we would that they should do unto us."[39]

In an 1841 open letter to the clergy "in the slave states of America," Clarkson again cited the golden rule, arguing that those who own slaves "violate it deliberately, not only every day, but every hour of every day."[40] After all, Clarkson wrote:

> is there a planter who would wish to be a slave? Or rather, is there any planter, who would not think it the heaviest affliction that could befall him in his life, to be a slave? Why then does he do that to another, which he would not wish to be done, and which God says, should not be done, unto himself?[41]

Another English abolitionist, the Reverend G. W. Conder, seized upon a similar theme when he publicly criticized an American apologist for slavery in 1855:

> Christianity, as I understand it, tells us that we are to love our neighbors as ourselves. You, Dr. Adams, tell us that we may buy our neighbor—sell our neighbor, as so much property;— that we may flog him, drive him to work like a brute; that we may maim and mutilate him, tear him from all he loves; lacerate his heart as well as his flesh; and finally kill him, if it suit our purpose.[42]

Moving on to another core biblical principle, Conder further rebuked this defender of slavery:

> Christianity, as I understand it, tells me that God hath made of one blood all nations, for to dwell on the face of the earth, and that in Jesus Christ all souls are equal in the sight of God. You and the abettors of slavery, and its most iniquitous laws, give the lie to this. You tell us that the slave is inferior to you, and that God's law permits you to do so. You fly in the face of every precept and all the spirit of Christianity.[43]

In *The Bible Against Slavery*, American abolitionist Theodore Weld wrote that two of the Ten Commandments "deal death to slavery." Weld argued quite convincingly that slavery is a violation of the eighth commandment, "Thou shalt not steal":

> The eighth commandment forbids the taking of *any part* of that which belongs to another. Slavery takes the *whole*. Does the Bible which prohibits the taking of *any* thing, sanction the taking of *every* thing? Does it thunder against the man who robs his neighbor of *a cent,* yet commission him to rob his neighbor of *himself?* Slaveholding is the highest possible violation of the eighth commandment.[44]

Weld also argued that slavery violates the tenth commandment, "Thou shalt not covet anything that is thy neighbor's." Weld explains that this commandment forbids having the state of mind behind all stealing. He then asks, "Who ever made human beings slaves without coveting them?"[45]

A Canadian Christian commenting on American slavery in 1865 summed it up best when he wrote:

> If there is in my view anything incontestable, it is that slavery is from all points of view the direct negation of two great principles that Christianity has brought into the world: first, equality before God for all members of the human family; second, charity, or the love of others taking the place of love of self. Slavery is the most absolute violation of these two fundamental principles of all religion and all morality.[46]

⌒

THE BIBLE'S SANCTION of slavery raises an obvious question. If the larger principles of the Bible have pointed toward the abolition of slavery all along, then why did the Bible permit slavery in the first place? Wouldn't a more efficient approach have been to simply ban the practice at the outset?

How one answers this question depends on one's view of the Bible's provenance. For those who believe that the Bible is a man-made document, the answer is quite simple. Just like our

Constitution, the Bible was written by fallible men who were hobbled by the limits of their own vision and the need to accommodate the imperfect societies they sought to influence. Yet also like our Constitution, the genius of the Bible is not that it was perfect, but that it was perfectible. The Bible has maintained its moral force in the world because it contained within it powerful ideas that would in time overshadow the relics of its flawed origins.

Those who believe that the Bible is divinely authored or inspired face a more difficult challenge. They must explain why an omniscient God did not simply abolish slavery from the outset. Naturally, the faithful have confronted and sought to answer so obvious a question. The most common answer is that God recognized the limitations of the humans to whom he gave the Bible and did not seek to change their behavior more quickly than they could tolerate. Instead, God permitted certain entrenched practices, regulated them, and introduced the principles by which they would ultimately be eliminated. In other words, the Bible met men halfway.

In the Jewish world, Maimonides was the leading proponent of this idea of divine gradualism. He elaborated the concept in considerable detail in his discussion of animal sacrifice. Unlike slavery, the Bible not only permits animal sacrifice but *requires* it. Yet Maimonides maintained that, despite such clear sanction, animal sacrifice was merely a concession to human nature that God always intended to eliminate.

In his *Guide for the Perplexed*, Maimonides wrote that when God gave his laws to the Jews, animal sacrifice was a deeply entrenched custom in the Middle East. Along with the other peoples of the region, the Israelites had developed a profound emotional attachment to this mode of worship. Thus, according to Maimonides:

> he [God] did not command us to give up and discontinue all these manners of service; for to obey such a commandment

would have been contrary to the nature of man, who generally cleaves to that to which he is used.[47]

Instead, Maimonides maintained, God permitted animal sacrifice. But he placed so many limitations and restrictions on the practice that it gradually became easier to abandon. By the time the Second Temple was destroyed, the Jews had progressed to the point where they were ready for sacrifice to be replaced by prayer.

Jewish tradition takes a similar view of many other practices permitted in the Bible but ultimately abandoned, including monarchy and polygamy. Some rabbis even claim that the Bible's sanction of meat-eating was merely a temporary concession to our carnivorous nature. They argue that the Bible points the way for mankind to become vegetarian. In their view, the many restrictions that Jewish law places around the eating of meat are meant to make it easier for Jews to eventually give up the practice altogether.

Christianity has also adopted the concept that the Bible made certain compromises with human nature and culture. John Calvin, for instance, wrote that "because we are not yet participants in the glory of God, thus we cannot approach him; rather, it is necessary for him to reveal himself to us according to our rudeness and infirmity."[48] Thus, in Calvin's succinct phrasing, "revelation is an act of divine condescension."[49]

Thomas Clarkson expressed this gradualist view in his Cambridge essay against slavery. Here he wrote that one of the "proofs" that Christianity was the product of "infinite wisdom" was the fact that:

> though it did not take such express cognizance of the wicked national institutions of the times, as should hinder its reception, it should yet contain such doctrines as, when it should be fully established, would be sufficient for the abolition of them all.[50]

Misuses of the Bible

On the occasion of his second inauguration, Abraham Lincoln made one of the shortest and most profound political speeches in American history. With a bloody civil war nearing its end, Lincoln rejected a triumphal tone for one of remorse. Referring to the two sides in the war, he noted:

> Both read the same Bible and pray to the same God, and each invokes His aid against the other. It may seem strange that any men should dare to ask a just God's assistance in wringing their bread from the sweat of other men's faces, but let us judge not, that we be not judged.

Here Lincoln highlighted a painful truth about the American slavery debate. Those who claimed the Bible as their moral guide were not all on the side of abolition. Apologists for slavery commonly cited the Bible in defense of their "peculiar institution." Their arguments resonated across the South and beyond.

Those who used the Bible to defend slavery may well have had the easier job. They did not need to delve into the details of exactly what kind of "slavery" the Bible allowed. Nor did they have to remind listeners of the overriding moral message shining forth from between the Bible's temporal concessions. Slavery advocates could simply cite the many lines from the Bible that sanctioned an institution called "slavery" and rest their case.

Many pro-slavery preachers took full advantage of this rhetorical edge. In a widely publicized sermon, for example, a South Carolina preacher named Richard Fuller cited the many biblical passages that sanction slavery. He then took ironic aim at the abolitionists:

> Here, then, we have the Author of the gospel, and the inspired propagators of the gospel, and the Holy Spirit . . . all conniving at a practice which was a violation of the entire moral principle of the gospel![51]

〜

IN HER NOVEL *Uncle Tom's Cabin,* the evangelical author Harriet Beecher Stowe provided a crucial insight into the motives of pro-slavery preachers. She did so through one of her characters, a slaveholder named Augustine St. Clare, who asks the following question:

> Suppose that something should bring down the price of cotton once and forever, and make the whole slave property a drag in the market, don't you think we should have another version of the Scripture doctrine? What a flood of light would pour into the church, all at once, and how immediately it would be discovered that everything in the Bible and reason went the other way![52]

Here Beecher highlights the real motive behind the biblical apologies for slavery: self-interest. As Edwards, Hopkins, and Finney all recognized, self-interest turns men into enemies of humanity. It was self-interested people who used every tool at their disposal—from their faith to their very lives—to preserve their lifestyle, their prerogatives, and their peculiar institution of slavery. Not everyone who searched the Bible for its position on slavery sought the whole truth. Many sought only those passages that would support their own narrow agenda.

Most of the people who invoked the Bible to defend slavery were, quite naturally, Southerners. They were the slaveholders, the merchants who owed their livelihood to the slave economy, and the pastors who owed their positions to such men. Their self-interest in preserving slavery was obvious.

Southerners were hardly alone in making Bible-based defenses of American slavery. Many Northerners offered similar arguments. It is often assumed that these Northerners were objective observers, free from the kind of self-interest that prejudiced their Southern allies. Yet this was rarely, if ever, the case.

The Northern economy was linked to the slave economy far more than is generally recognized. As we've seen, some of the largest Northern cities depended upon the supply of cheap raw materials grown by slaves, the sale of manufactured goods to wealthy slave-owners, and all the trade thus generated. These economic ties generated enough self-interest in the perpetuation of slavery to blind men to moral truths. As a well-known French writer observed at the time, pro-slavery preaching was rare in the North "except in seaports, and especially in New York," where "the interests of this great city are bound up to such a degree with those of the cotton States."[53]

Yet it would be a mistake to see selfish motives only among those Northerners with economic connections to the slave economy. As America debated abolition in the years leading up to the Civil War, a broader fog of self-interest descended upon the North and clouded the judgment of all but the most idealistic of abolitionists. The South was not prepared to give up the practice of slavery under any circumstances. Thus if the abolitionists ever achieved their goal, the inevitable result would be Southern secession, war, or both. And everybody knew it. Thus every Northerner who craved peace and prosperity for himself more than justice for others had a profound incentive to embrace rationalizations for slavery. So long as they could obscure the compelling morality of abolition, they could both keep the peace and salve their consciences.

Given the enormous price that would have to be paid to end slavery, it is easy to understand why so many Christians were willing to accept the pro-slavery narrative. The only surprise is that so many other Christians nevertheless saw the truth, answered the call, and stood up against the great evil of their day. It is a testament to the power of the Judeo-Christian idea that it—and it alone—was able to inspire and sustain a mass abolition movement in so hostile an environment.

∽

WHEN IT CAME to slavery, therefore, few Americans were truly disinterested. To find truly objective observers, it is necessary to look outside the United States. Christians in Canada and Europe had far less of a stake in the outcome of America's slavery debate, and thus they were far less likely to be swayed by self-interest or fear.

These objective foreign Christians shared a broad consensus that the Bible did not sanction slavery. Even the most theologically conservative and literal-minded of them tended to believe that their faith required its abolition. As we've seen, evangelical Christians were often the most vehement in expressing moral outrage against slavery and the most zealous in organizing efforts to combat it. As historian Mark Noll has noted, when it came to Protestants abroad, "there was only contempt for efforts to defend slavery on the basis of the Bible."[54]

Even when the focus narrowed to the thorny issue of slavery in America, this anti-slavery consensus endured. According to Noll, the commentaries on American slavery written by European and Canadian Protestants, as well as by liberal Roman Catholics,* were characterized by "intense religious conviction about the evils of slavery and the urgent need to end the slave system in the United States."[55] Noll further observes that this foreign commentary:

> is noteworthy literature for revealing much stronger opinions *against* slavery than *for* the North. It is also noteworthy for providing almost no evidence, even from the most theologically conservative sources, that these non-Americans endorsed what so many American Protestants believed concerning the Bible's legitimization of slavery.[56]

⌒

WE CONTINUE TO live in a world in which slavery is practiced and genocides are perpetrated. Thus the challenge of identifying the source of such atrocities is a most urgent one. Those of us who

---

*Noll writes that conservative Catholics did not share these views.

are truly interested in combating human brutality need to engage in this analysis without the distorting burden of angry agendas. We must objectively investigate the motives not only of those who commit these atrocities but also of those who seek to stop them.

The easy answers of the Bible critics contribute little to this effort. Focusing on the Bible text to the exclusion of how that text has been interpreted and applied by its most fervent believers may make for effective rhetoric, but it obscures far more than it reveals. We cannot place all of our sins on the scapegoat of religion and send it off into the desert. The goat will depart, but our troubles will remain. We are the source of the evil we fear.

If human nature is the source of the poison, then the Judeo-Christian idea is a most potent antidote. In the West, the Judeo-Christian tradition has been a singularly powerful tool in the struggle to transcend our impoverished genetic morality. Time after time throughout history, the people who have stepped forward to fight our civilization's greatest evils have been inspired and sustained by this tradition. This noble record of activism, and not the cynical attacks, is the best gauge of the Bible's true meaning.

EIGHT

Myths about
Judeo-Christian Atrocities

*Whoever touches a Jew to take his life
is like one who harms Jesus himself.*[1]

—BERNARD OF CLAIRVAUX, SPIRITUAL LEADER OF THE SECOND CRUSADE

In 1482, the Spanish Inquisition was still in its early years. Yet news of its excesses had already begun to spread. These reports prompted a prominent observer to issue a scathing public condemnation. "The Inquisition," he complained, "has for some time been moved not by zeal for the faith and the salvation of souls, but by lust for wealth." He then listed some of the Inquisition's uglier abuses:

> Many true and faithful Christians ... have without any legitimate proof been thrust into secular prisons, tortured and condemned as relapsed heretics, deprived of their goods and property and handed over to the secular arm to be executed, to the peril of souls, setting a pernicious example, and causing disgust to many.[2]

This critic of the Inquisition was none other than Pope Sixtus IV. And the medium in which he leveled this critique was the most public one at his disposal: an official papal bull.

The pope's outrage at the mistreatment of "Christians" should not be mistaken for a cold-hearted refusal to acknowledge the Inquisition's Jewish victims. At this stage and throughout its first fifty years, the Inquisition's victims were almost exclusively Christians who had converted from Judaism. Jews who had never converted did not come under the Inquisition's jurisdiction. Thus the pope was not ignoring the issue. He was issuing a full-throated rebuke of the Inquisition's primary work.

At first blush, it seems highly schizophrenic that the pope would condemn an institution that he had personally authorized and purportedly controlled. But the reality of the Inquisition is very much at odds with the conventional wisdom. The Inquisition was not a top-down persecution of Jews orchestrated and directed by the Catholic Church. It was, on the contrary, a bottom-up persecution of Jewish converts to Christianity demanded by Spain's anti-Semitic masses. Far from instigating the Inquisition, the pope and the Church often acted as its brakes and critics-in-chief.

～

CRITICS OF THE Judeo-Christian tradition have never limited their attacks to the text of the Bible. They have also targeted the alleged atrocities of the faithful. According to their narrative, not only does the Bible exhort its readers to barbarism, but those who seek guidance from the Bible too often follow its dangerous dictates. To so many of these critics, Christianity, Judaism, and other religions are the gushing source of division and violence in the world. Reject religion, they argue, and the world will live as one.

Thomas Paine was among the first to make this argument. In his famous polemic against the Judeo-Christian tradition, *The Age of Reason,* Paine attacks not only the Bible but the faiths based upon it. Rising to his full hyperbolic mode, Paine blames religion for all of history's greatest evils:

> The most detestable wickedness, the most horrid cruelties,
> and the greatest miseries that have afflicted the human race
> have had their origin in this thing called revelation, or

revealed religion. It has been the most dishonorable belief against the character of the Divinity, the most destructive to morality and the peace and happiness of man that ever was propagated since man began to exist....

Whence arose all the horrid assassinations of whole nations of men, women and infants, with which the Bible is filled, and bloody persecutions and tortures unto death, and religious wars, that since that time have laid Europe in blood and ashes—whence rose they but from this impious thing called revealed religion, and this monstrous belief that God has spoken to man?[3]

Paine thus set forth the exaggerated mantra that critics of the Judeo-Christian tradition have repeated, albeit less eloquently, down to the present day. Fueled by their horror at the religion-inspired attacks of September 11, a cabal of new atheists have stepped forward to loudly proclaim that religion is the root of all atrocity. Typical of the discourse are the following quotes:

A glance at history, or at the pages of any newspaper, reveals that ideas which divide one group of human beings from another, only to unite them in slaughter, generally have their roots in religion.[4]

Only religious faith is a strong enough force to motivate such utter madness in otherwise sane and decent people.[5]

As I write these words, and as you read them, people of faith are in their different ways planning your and my destruction, and the destruction of all the hard-won human attainments that I have touched upon. *Religion poisons everything.*[6]

It is, of course, undeniable that the pages of history are drenched in blood spilled in the name of religion. It's likewise true that atrocities continue to be committed in the name of religion. Yet when one scratches ever so slightly beneath the surface of this history of violence, clear distinctions begin to emerge.

For starters, it has been centuries since Christianity and Judaism have sanctioned violence in their name. As a result, remarkably few Christians and Jews have spilled blood in fulfillment of theology in modern times. Those who have were quickly criticized and effectively marginalized. Given the fact that there are over two billion Christians in the world, and that almost half of the world's approximately thirteen million Jews live under the constant threat of terrorist attack, this record is nothing short of miraculous.

To the extent violence is committed in the name of religion on a consistent basis today, it is committed in the name of one interpretation of one religion. Militant interpretations of Islam do call for violence in fulfillment of theology, and legions of the faithful have, tragically, answered this call. September 11 was merely one example of what has become an international phenomenon threatening Christians, Jews, and—most of all—innocent Muslims. Yet to condemn all Muslims, let alone the adherents of other faiths, because of the actions of such extremists is a leap that defies all logic.

~

SINCE SO MANY blithely seek to obscure it, the distinction at the heart of this analysis bears emphasizing. Religious faith can accurately be seen as a source of violence only when people do violence in its name—that is, when they spill blood in fulfillment of theology. Faith is not the problem if theology is merely coincidental to, or actually a brake upon, such violence. A suicide bomber who shouts "God is great!" before blowing himself up in a crowd while anticipating his heavenly reward of seventy-two virgins is most definitely committing religious violence. The Christian Inquisitors who condemned men to death for heresy were guilty of the same.

Yet such purely theological violence is not nearly as widespread as is commonly suggested. For as long as there have been humans, there has been human violence perpetrated by members of ingroups against those believed to belong to outgroups. And for as long as there have been religions, religious differences have joined the tribal, national, linguistic, racial, and myriad other distinctions which serve as the bases for separating ingroups from outgroups. Yet the fact that religious differences often feature in such line-drawing between groups does not necessarily transform all violence between such groups into "religious" violence. Quite often, the religious differences merely add an additional layer of rhetoric to conflicts that are fundamentally driven by other factors.

The Arab-Israeli conflict illustrates this point well. Israel is a Jewish state surrounded by Arab Muslim neighbors. Yet when Israel battled these neighbors in a series of conventional wars from 1948 until 1973, and when it confronted Yasser Arafat's PLO terrorism, the conflict was not primarily "religious." During this period, the fighting was fueled largely by competing secular nationalisms. The Arab leaders called upon their armies to destroy Israel in the name of pan-Arab nationalism. Yasser Arafat built the PLO on the basis of a narrower Palestinian Arab nationalism. Israel's leaders invoked Jewish nationalism—Zionism—to create their nation and rally the people to its defense. These soldiers and terrorists did not kill for Allah or God. They killed for country.

In recent years, however, the emergence of groups such as Hamas and Hezbollah has injected a decidedly religious element into this conflict. Hamas is based in the Gaza Strip and the West Bank, and its members are Palestinians. Hezbollah is based in Lebanon and its ranks are entirely Lebanese. Yet Palestinian and Lebanese nationalism is often incidental to their programs. When Hamas and Hezbollah leaders send their followers out on suicide missions or to launch rockets into Israel, they invoke the doctrines of militant Islam. These terrorists do not kill merely for homeland or nation. They kill for Allah.

By this more precise definition, more people are often killed in the name of militant Islam in one day than have been killed in the name of Christianity or Judaism in the past decade, and quite possibly the past century. This record presents modern atheists with a serious evidentiary hurdle. They boldly assert that religion *in general* is to blame for the world's worst violence. Yet so broad an allegation cannot be supported by examples from only one faith.

To obscure this disparity, these critics desperately search for religious atrocities perpetrated by Christians and Jews. Most frequently, they supplement the record with one or two medieval Christian outrages and hope that no one focuses on the fact that these events are centuries old. Other times they seek greater currency by recycling the same few examples of universally condemned modern Christian or Jewish murders.

Such rhetorical sleight of hand cannot hide the yawning violence gap that exists between the three great monotheistic religions. These blanket indictments of religion fail to acknowledge the real record of Christianity and Judaism in the modern era. They likewise are an unfortunate slander of those Muslims who are working to win their faith back from the extremists. This intellectual laziness does a great disservice to all who seriously wish to confront the problem of violence in the world today.

This is not to say that the world has become any less violent in modern times. Man remains the same flawed creature he has always been. We are born with selfish genes which drive us to care only about ourselves and a small circle of intimates around us. We have a chilling capacity for demonizing outsiders. We remain quick to resort to violence whenever our perceived interests conflict with those of such outgroups. War, genocide, and slavery all preceded the birth of Judaism, Christianity, and Islam. They would most certainly survive their demise.

Human nature is the mother of violence. It is human nature which, to borrow a phrase, "poisons everything." It is also human nature which leads us to seek an external scapegoat to blame for our evil instead of doing the far more difficult work of overcoming that evil.

This search for scapegoats is a terrible distraction. And it is also a great danger. Time after time throughout history, we have sacrificed such scapegoats for our sins. Yet time after time our troubles persist. It turns out that the Jews were not the source of all of our problems. Neither were the capitalists. Neither is religion.

Christian Atrocities: Ancient Examples Exaggerated

To find examples of Christian atrocities, we must look to the distant past. In particular, critics of faith have made a mantra of two infamous medieval episodes: the Crusades and the Spanish Inquisition. These two events have become Exhibits A and B in any argument that Christian zeal turns inevitably into bloodshed.

It is of course true that both the Crusades and the Inquisition involved the torture and murder of thousands of innocents. It is also true that Christian theology featured prominently in each disaster. These are instances where the Christian gospel of love took the form of a sword drawn in fury. It is incumbent upon every person of faith to study these atrocities and learn the lessons they teach about the peril of theology delinked from love and humility.

Justice demands that these atrocities be recognized and remembered. Yet justice also demands that they be put into proper perspective. Those who list these episodes as among the greatest of humanitarian disasters often exaggerate their actual magnitude. More importantly, the tendency to blame these atrocities entirely on the Catholic Church or Christian theology has obscured a more instructive understanding of the true forces driving them. To study the Crusades and the Inquisition is to appreciate the wide gap between rhetoric and reality when it comes to these and many other "religious" atrocities.

As we will see, Europe's Jews were the primary victims in each of these cases. It is therefore important to note that this chapter is not intended to be a detailed treatment of, or apology for, the long history of Christian anti-Semitism. There can be no denying the relentless discrimination and violence that generation after generation of Jews suffered in Christian Europe. There is likewise no denying that certain Christian teachings and churchmen—both Catholic and Protestant—contributed to this dark history of anti-Semitism. Instead of wrestling with this larger history, the more modest goal of this chapter is to review two of its most notorious episodes and better understand the role that Christian faith played in each.

The Crusades

To those who would assert that Christianity is essentially a religion of peace and love, critics have at the ready a one-word rebuttal. And that word is: "Crusades." Over time, the word "Crusade" has become a shorthand for violence in the name of religion. Yet contrary to this conventional wisdom, the reality of the Crusades is surprisingly nuanced.

At the outset, the Crusades must be placed in their larger historical context. These military campaigns were hardly a break with otherwise peaceful relations between Christians and Muslims. The Crusades took place during an era of continuous warfare between Christian and Muslim powers that shared a long and rapidly shifting border. In the course of these conflicts, the Muslims were typically the aggressor and were almost always the victor.

After the birth of Islam and its explosion out of the Arabian Peninsula, the Christian world was put on the defensive. Historian Bernard Lewis has summarized this dynamic as follows:

> In the course of the seventh century, Muslim armies advancing from Arabia conquered Syria, Palestine, Egypt and North Africa, all until then part of Christendom. . . . In the eighth century, from their bases in North Africa, Arab Muslim forces, now joined by Berber converts, conquered Spain and Portugal

and invaded France; in the ninth century they conquered Sicily and invaded the Italian mainland. In 846 C.E. a naval expedition from Sicily even entered the River Tiber, and Arab forces sacked Ostia and Rome.[7]

In the eleventh century, a new Muslim power, the Seljuk Turks, began marching westward into the heartland of the Christian Byzantine Empire. In 1071, the Seljuks destroyed the Byzantine armies in the Battle of Manzikert and soon conquered all of Anatolia (modern-day Turkey). As these Muslim armies advanced ever closer to Constantinople, Byzantine Emperor Alexius I sent an urgent appeal to Pope Urban II asking for help in defending this eastern capital of Christendom. It was in this context and in response to this plea that Pope Urban called forth the First Crusade.

Thomas Madden, a leading scholar of this period, has described the Crusades as little more than a blip on the Muslim radar. "From the grand perspective of Muslim history," he writes, "they [the Crusades] were simply tiny and futile attempts to halt the inevitable expansion of Islam."[8] Bernard Lewis has expressed a similar view, characterizing the Crusades as:

> a long-delayed, very limited, and finally ineffectual response to the jihad. The Crusades ended in failure and defeat, and were soon forgotten in the lands of Islam.[9]

The purpose of reviewing this history is not to point the finger of blame at either the Muslim or the Christian armies. It is simply to note that it is a mistake to see the Crusades as a sudden paroxysm of Christian bloodlust and intolerance. The Crusades are more accurately viewed as rounds in a much longer and larger clash between Christian and Islamic civilizations. This clash of civilizations is likewise more properly seen as but one episode in the history of warfare between tribes, nations, and cultures—a history that long predates the birth of either of these particular faiths.

〜

IN THESE CENTURIES of armed conflict between Christian and Muslims, each side was certainly guilty of killing civilians and committing atrocities. Such was the nature of war in that era. But the Crusades produced at least one group of victims who belonged to neither side of this power struggle: Europe's Jews. The goal of the Crusades was to liberate the Holy Land from the "infidel" Muslims. But some of the Crusaders were so passionate about fighting infidels that they could not wait until they arrived in the Middle East to do so. They instead attacked those non-Christians who had the misfortune of living much closer to home.

When critics cite the Crusades as a Christian atrocity, they are often referring in particular to a series of massacres perpetrated upon the Rhine Valley's defenseless Jewish communities. Yet even when the focus is narrowed to these attacks on Europe's Jews, the conventional wisdom regarding the Crusades remains very much at odds with the reality. The Christian atrocity of legend simply fails to materialize.

For starters, there is a tendency to overstate the scale of the violence. Taken as a whole, these outbursts of Crusader violence against Europe's Jews took some three to four thousand lives. Given the small size of the Rhineland's Jewish population, these numbers bespeak an unmitigated disaster. Yet given the superlatives so often applied to the Crusades, it is commonly assumed that the death toll was even larger. Tragically, Jewish history in Europe would be punctuated by pogroms and massacres of far greater proportions.

The second major misconception about the Crusades relates to the identity of those who perpetrated the atrocity. The conventional wisdom holds that the murder of Jews during the Crusades was a top-down affair which the pope and the Catholic hierarchy ordered or at least encouraged. But the reality is that Pope Urban II and the Church leadership never ordered or even suggested violence against the Jews. These massacres are more accurately seen as early pogroms in which anti-Semitic mobs attacked Jews without theological sanction or motive.

The bloodiest assaults on Europe's Jews took place during the First Crusade. Most of these attacks were perpetrated by a militia under the control of one man: Count Emicho of Flonheim. Emicho was a peripheral figure. He was one of many provincial leaders who decided to join the Crusader armies passing through their towns on the way to Jerusalem. Yet unlike most of the others, Emicho and his followers never caught up with the rest of the Crusaders. Instead, he and his band expended all of their energy and resources on their own unique mission: attacking the defenseless Jews who lived nearby.

Emicho and his men began their wave of terror by attacking the Jews in the town of Speyer. In a random and disorganized attack, they ended up killing twelve Jews. By the time Emicho's forces arrived in the nearby city of Worms, they were better organized and more focused. They murdered the city's entire Jewish community of some five hundred souls. Next they arrived in Mainz, where they massacred that city's approximately one thousand Jews. Finally, Emicho's militia entered Cologne, where they tracked down and murdered the many hundreds of Jews living there.[10]

It is important to note that Emicho and his band of Crusaders did not operate alone. In almost every town they entered, Emicho's men found willing collaborators among the local "burghers," the middle-class townsmen engaged in trade and shop-keeping. The burghers' resentment of the Jews ran deep. The burghers viewed the Jews as economic rivals whose business success threatened their livelihood. They also saw the Jews as political competitors whose alliances with the local nobility eclipsed their power. In Speyer, Worms, and Mainz the burghers were involved in every stage of the anti-Jewish violence. In Mainz, the burghers were the ones who opened the city gates that had been locked shut to keep out Emicho and his men.

～

FAR FROM LEADING the charge, the Church leadership actually tried to stop this anti-Semitic violence at every turn. In particular, the archbishops and bishops of the cities and towns on Emicho's route went to great lengths to protect their Jewish communities from his attacks.

Count Emicho and his men started their rampage in the town of Speyer. When Bishop John of Speyer heard that an anti-Semitic mob was approaching, he decided that the best way to protect his Jewish community was to remove them from the Crusaders' path. The bishop sent the Jews to the fortified towns he controlled outside the city proper. When Emicho and his band came looking for Speyer's Jews, few were left. It was for this reason that only twelve Jews were killed there.

Once Emicho's militia had moved on, Bishop John punished some of the local burghers who had collaborated with them by cutting off their hands. While his methods may have been medieval, his message was quite clear. Violence against the local Jewish community would not be tolerated.

As Emicho and his men approached the city of Mainz, the local archbishop ordered the gates of this walled city locked against them. He then invited the Jews to take shelter inside his personal compound, where they would be protected by a second set of fortified walls. Once the Crusaders made their way through both barriers, however, the archbishop and his men fled to save their own lives, leaving the Jews to their fate. While the archbishop's behavior does not provide a profile in courage, he did everything he could to save his Jewish community short of risking his own life.

As Emicho's band approached the city of Cologne, the local archbishop, Herman, sought to protect his Jewish community by replicating the strategy that had worked so well for Bishop John in Speyer. Archbishop Herman hid Cologne's Jews in the fortified towns he controlled outside of the city. Tragically, the tactic failed. This time the Crusaders hunted down and killed the Jews in each of the towns in which they had sought refuge.[11]

In seeking to protect their Jewish communities, these Christian leaders were simply following the mandates of their faith. The fact is that Christian theology explicitly prohibits both the murder and the forced conversion of Jews. No less an authority than St. Augustine introduced the ban on killing Jews in the fourth century. Pope Gregory I issued a prohibition against forcibly converting Jews at the close of the sixth century. The Catholic hierarchy largely honored and frequently reaffirmed both of these prohibitions.

After the massacres of the First Crusade, Pope Calixtus II recognized that these Church doctrines protecting the Jews needed to be once again restated and reinforced. He therefore issued a papal bull in 1120 which condemned physical attacks on Jews, rejected their forced conversion, and promised Jews "the shield of our protection." This bull was reaffirmed and reissued at least twenty-two times by successive popes between the twelfth and fifteenth centuries.[12]

⌒

WHEN THE SECOND CRUSADE began in 1145, it seemed that history was poised to repeat itself. A French monk named Radulf reprised the role played by Count Emicho. Radulf and his band of followers began attacking Jews in some of the same Rhineland communities that had been targeted in the First Crusade fifty years earlier. This time, however, the Crusade's spiritual leader, Bernard of Clairvaux, was still in Europe when the attacks began. He moved decisively to block a repeat of the earlier atrocities. He wrote repeated letters urging the Rhineland's Christians not to harm the Jews. When the violence nevertheless continued, Bernard traveled in person to confront Radulf.

According to one of the leading Jewish chroniclers of the Second Crusade, Bernard said the following to Radulf and his men:

Whoever touches a Jew to take his life is like one who harms Jesus himself. My disciple Radulf, who has spoken of annihilating Jews, has spoken in error, for in the book of Psalms it is written of them: "Slay them not, lest my people forget."[13]

After Bernard's intervention, the attacks on Jews ceased. This time, the Church was more successful in reining in the mob. Anti-Semitic atrocities on the scale of those of the First Crusade were not repeated in the Second or any subsequent Crusade.

The Spanish Inquisition

Like the word "Crusade," the words "Spanish Inquisition" have become synonymous with "religious atrocity." In the popular imagination, the Inquisition was a Church-orchestrated campaign of torture and murder which left a trail of victims rarely matched in human history. Yet much like the Crusades, there is a significant gap between this perception of the Inquisition and the reality.

Perhaps the greatest misconception about the Inquisition involves the number of its victims. The way it is so often selected from centuries of bloody history as a prime example of human cruelty, one would suppose that the Inquisition was responsible for the slaughter of hundreds of thousands, if not millions. This was, however, an atrocity on a smaller scale. Whatever its crimes, the Inquisition was not a violent mob; it was an orderly legal proceeding which required witnesses and testimony before judgments were rendered. Death sentences were the rare exception, not the rule.

As leading Inquisition scholar Henry Kamen has noted:

The overwhelming majority of these [Inquisition defendants] were not in fact brought to trial; they were disciplined as a result of the edicts of grace, and had to undergo various penalties and penances, but escaped with their lives. Trial cases were very much fewer. In them, the penalty of death was pronounced for the most part against absent refugees. Effigies, which were burnt in their place, may form part of the total figures for executions given by the early chroniclers. The direct penalty of death for heresy was in fact suffered by a very much smaller number than historians had thought.[14]

How many people did the Spanish Inquisition condemn to death? Kamen comes to the following conclusion:

> Taking into account all the tribunals of Spain up to about 1530, it is unlikely that more than two thousand people were executed for heresy by the Inquisition.[15]

When the Inquisition was active in Portugal from 1547 to 1580, it executed another 169 souls.[16]

Especially given the small size of the community terrorized by the Inquisition, these numbers disclose an absolute disaster. Yet because the Inquisition is so often cited as being among the greatest of human atrocities, it is commonly assumed that the death toll was even greater. The tragic truth is that pogroms and slaughters on a far larger scale awaited Europe's Jews down the road.

Another major misconception about the Spanish Inquisition concerns the identity of its victims. From a religious perspective, they were not Jews. The Spanish Inquisition, like all other inquisitions, was established to root out heresy among *Christians*. During its most active years, the Spanish Inquisition targeted Jewish converts to Christianity—called "conversos" or "Marranos"—who were accused of still secretly practicing their Judaism. Those Jews who never converted to Christianity were largely beyond the Inquisition's reach.

A third misconception about the Inquisition involves the identity of those who demanded its establishment and expansion. The conventional wisdom holds that the Inquisition was a top-down affair both instigated and implemented by the Catholic Church in furtherance of Christian theology. The reality was far more complex.

Much like the Crusades, the Spanish Inquisition is more accurately seen as a bottom-up phenomenon. Spain's masses demanded the Inquisition in the course of decades of anti-Semitic agitation which featured, for the first time, a significant racial component. For Spain's anti-Semites, the Inquisition was above all a way to overcome the privileges and protection that Church doctrine extended to Jewish converts to Christianity. Yes, the Church did consent to the Inquisition, and it never fully withdrew this official sanction. But far from being the driving force behind this effort, the Church was more often a barrier to be overcome and a brake on the Inquisition's worst excesses.

⁓

THE FIRST SIGNIFICANT steps on the path to the Inquisition were taken decades earlier, in the year 1391, when a series of anti-Semitic riots broke out across Spain. Led by local figures and fueled by mob passion, these rioters killed thousands of Jews and sold even more into slavery.

Like the anti-Semitic outbursts of the Crusades, the 1391 pogroms were an example of the popular anti-Semitism steadily spreading across Europe. The Jews had already been expelled from England in 1290 and from France in 1306. The motives behind these attacks were those which would continue to fuel European anti-Semitism for centuries to come. The Jews were resented for their economic success. They were hated for their roles as tax collectors for, and allies of, unpopular lords and monarchs. Proliferating myths about the nefarious deeds committed by these peculiar outsiders—from poisoning wells to murdering Christian children—overcame what little tolerance remained. In Spain, the massive death toll and economic dislocation resulting from the Black Death and a subsequent series of wars inflamed these already simmering hatreds to the boiling point.[17]

Unlike most who would follow them, however, the anti-Semites who perpetrated the 1391 attacks offered the Jews an escape route. Displaying a perverse Christian sensibility, these rioters largely spared the lives of Jews who agreed to convert to Christianity. As a result, the 1391 pogroms resulted not only in mass murder, but also in mass conversion. This large influx of Jews into the Catholic Church produced unexpected results for both the persecutors and the persecuted.

Like most other European countries of this era, Spain did not permit non-Christians to rise to society's commanding heights. Spain's Jews were thus barred from serving in government, blocked from most professions, and prohibited from marrying Christians. While Spanish Jews did prosper, they did so at the margins of Christian society.

Yet all of these restrictions were drawn on the basis of religion, not race. Christian theology has always recognized the equality of all Christians, and the Catholic Church has consistently opposed any form of discrimination against converts to the faith, regardless of their color or national origin. When it came to defining who was a Christian, even Europe's temporal authorities tended to respect this clear theological imperative.

Thus while Spain's Jews may have entered the Church at the point of a sword, their new status opened wide the gates of integration and opportunity. These originally reluctant Jewish converts now rushed into all of the heretofore prohibited fields. Within a generation, Jewish "conversos" occupied leading positions in Spain's government, business community, and professions. They began to marry into Spain's leading families. And, most ironically of all, conversos quickly rose to prominent positions in Spain's Catholic Church.

While conversion was a surprising boon to the conversos, it was an unmitigated disaster for the anti-Semites. Their original resentment of Jewish economic success and power was only exacerbated by the conversos' rapid rise. The mounting rage of Spain's anti-Semites in this period provides a window into their true motives. Had the pogroms of 1391 truly been about religion, then all should have been forgiven once the Jews converted to

Christianity. Instead, in the decades following 1391, anti-Semitism continued to grow in direct proportion to converso success.

～

FOR THE FIRST HALF of the fifteenth century, the Spanish crown and the Church largely succeeded in holding these rising anti-converso passions in check. But in 1449 the floodgates were opened when a group of rebels seized power in the city of Toledo. The Toledo uprising was a popular revolt led by local nobles who resented the monarchy's ever increasing hold on power. Like so many populist movements in Europe before and since, the Toledo rebels placed anti-Semitism at the heart of their program. They began by attacking the homes of converso tax collectors. Eventually, they targeted all of the city's conversos and Jews.

The Toledo rebels' true agenda was revealed not only by the murders they committed in rage but also by the legislation they enacted after full deliberation. Once in control of the city, the rebels passed a law, the *Sentencia-Estatuto*, meant to address the grievances that had led them to take up arms. Among other things, this law imposed upon the conversos all of the restrictions that had previously applied to them as Jews. The Sentencia barred conversos from holding civil and ecclesiastical office, and it denied them the right to give testimony in the courts. Significantly, the Sentencia applied these prohibitions not only to the first generation of conversos but also to their offspring in perpetuity.[18] In other words, this law penalized a group of people defined not by their religion, but by their race.

Revealing the racism at its core, the Sentencia pioneered the use of the racially charged language that would characterize modern anti-Semitism. The statute identified the conversos as the offspring of the "perverse lineage of the Jews." By contrast, the "Old Christian" community that existed before the mass conversion of Jews is repeatedly referred to as "pure."[19] The doctrine of *limpieza de sangre*—purity of blood—became the mantra of those who wanted to exclude former Jews and their descendants from Spain's institutions and professions.

Once unleashed by the Toledo uprising, this overtly racial anti-Semitism spread throughout Spain. Across the country, people demanded the passage of similar measures to ensure that only "pure-blooded" Christians would be permitted to rise to society's heights. In short, the anti-Semites viewed the conversos as Jews, not Christians. And they wanted these Jews reduced to the status they had held before anti-Semitic attacks forced them to convert in the first place.

∽

THESE EFFORTS TO discriminate against a group of Christians based on their race clearly contravened Christian theology and Church policy. To its credit, the Vatican was quick to react. After the Toledo rebels passed their racist Sentencia law in 1449, Pope Nicholas V issued a Papal bull in which he condemned the racist legislation in the strongest of terms:

> Under pain of excommunication we order each and every Christian of whatever station, rank or condition, both ecclesiastic and civil, to admit each and all of those who were converted, and those who will be converted in the future, either from gentilehood or from Judaism, or from any other sect, as well as the descendants of those converts, both lay and clerical, who live as Catholics and good Christians, to all the dignities, honors, offices, notaryships, the bearing of witnesses and all the other things to which are usually admitted all other Christians who are older in their faith.[20]

The pope backed up this threat of excommunication with action. In another bull issued on the same day, the pope excommunicated the leaders of the Toledo rebellion along with their chief supporters and followers.[21]

The Vatican and the Christian theology which motivated it thus emerged as a serious impediment to the program of Spain's anti-Semites. So long as the conversos were Christians in good standing, the Vatican would insist on protecting them as the full equals of every other Christian. Israeli scholar Benzion Netanyahu described the emerging conflict as follows:

> Violent waves of that gushing current [anti-Semitism] ... were relentlessly hitting the Marranos' [conversos'] shores and yet could not make deep inroads, because they were blocked by a powerful dyke. By the dyke we mean the conversos' Christianity and the powerful system of laws that sustained it and prevented a breakthrough.[22]

Spain's anti-Semites wanted desperately to remove this barrier. They hoped to transform the Church from the conversos' protector to a collaborator in their persecution. The only way to accomplish this was through the charge of heresy. At this time, heresy was still regarded as a most serious offense. While the Church would not sanction the persecution of Jews, it would most certainly participate in the punishment of heretics.

Thus, at roughly the time of the Toledo revolt, allegations of a widespread converso heresy began to be made with increasing frequency. The thrust of the complaint was that the conversos were not sincere converts to Christianity but were still practicing Judaism in secret. The scope of this allegation was conveniently coterminous with its target. The anti-Semites did not claim that some conversos were secret Jews; they insisted that they all were. They demanded the appointment of an inquisition to root out this Jewish heresy.

〜

LIKE SO MANY leaders before and after them, Spain's King Ferdinand and Queen Isabella were by most accounts more concerned with consolidating their control than with any overriding ideological agenda. Thus the monarchs tended to use religion to promote their power more than they used their power to promote religion.[23] As Henry Kamen has noted, "Behind virtually every move of his [King Ferdinand's] concerning the Inquisition, political motives can be discerned."[24]

During these years, the royal couple were obsessed with extending and centralizing their authority at the expense of Spain's provincial nobles and rulers. In this power struggle they found valuable allies in Spain's urban and rural masses, who typically resented their local overlords far more than the distant monarchs. Yet these same masses were the ones now demanding action against the conversos. Rather than confront these anti-Semitic agitators, Ferdinand and Isabella decided to co-opt them. Of all of the mob's demands, appointing an inquisition was the least violent. The monarchs championed the cause.[25]

The Vatican had resisted earlier calls for an inquisition. But once the Spanish throne made the request, the Vatican quickly complied. On November 1, 1478, Pope Sixtus IV issued a papal bull authorizing Ferdinand and Isabella to appoint inquisitors. The Spanish Inquisition had begun.

Now that the Inquisition was authorized and operating, anyone truly concerned about heresy should have been satisfied. Instead, Spain's anti-Semites reacted to the Inquisition in a way that once again demonstrated the racial animus that drove them. They complained bitterly that the monarchy allowed conversos to continue to enjoy all of their new privileges unless and until they were found guilty of heresy. They also continued to agitate for the passage of blood-purity laws which would bar all conversos from the mainstream of Spanish society regardless of their fidelity to the faith.[26] In the decades that followed, these anti-Semitic forces succeeded in securing the passage of a series of such laws that excluded the conversos from "all of Spain's military orders, most of its religious orders, and nearly all of its major colleges and universities."[27]

∾

THE BEHAVIOR AND demands of Spain's anti-Semites thus clearly contradict the view that Christian theology was the driving force behind the Inquisition. Modern Inquisition scholars have found corroborating evidence for this view in the behavior of the conversos themselves. The number of Jewish converts to Christianity who secretly practiced Judaism, it turns out, was very small indeed. The very problem the Inquisition purported to combat was, by most accounts, a rare and dwindling phenomenon.

The Israeli scholar Benzion Netanyahu* sets forth this evidence at great length in his 1995 magnum opus, *The Origins of the Inquisition.* On the basis of a wide range of primary sources, Netanyahu concludes that the conversos were eager converts to Christianity "bent upon a course of complete assimilation."[28] As a result, he contends, the number of conversos secretly practicing Judaism fell rapidly, to the point that they were a small minority when the Inquisition was established in 1481. Netanyahu reasons:

> If only a fraction of the Marranos [conversos] were still Jewish and more and more of them kept becoming Christian, what sense was there in establishing the Inquisition? Surely there was no need to eliminate by force a phenomenon that was disappearing by itself.[29]

Another leading Inquisition scholar, Henry Kamen, agrees that there was little evidence of conversos practicing Judaism. He notes that even the Inquisition itself never uncovered much evidence of the very phenomenon it was established to suppress:

> If the idea that conversos were secret Jews is to be sustained principally by the evidence dug up by the Inquisition during the 1480s, there can be no doubt of the verdict. Very little convincing proof of Jewish belief or practice among the conversos can be found in the trials.[30]

---

*Although he is one of the leading authorities on the Jews of medieval Spain, Professor Netanyahu is probably best known for his famous children. His son Binyamin is currently the prime minister of Israel. His son Yonatan died while leading an Israeli raid on Entebbe, Uganda, to free a group of Israelis who had been aboard a hijacked plane.

Having eliminated Jewish heresy as a possible motive, Netanyahu concludes that the real motive behind the Spanish Inquisition was racism. Those who demanded an inquisition did not hate Jewish heresy. Nor did they hate the Jewish faith. They simply hated Jews. In Netanyahu's words:

> In the midst of a people whose Christian zeal could in no way be doubted, a theory based on racism appeared whose three major articles of faith were: the existence of a conspiracy to seize the government of Spain; the ongoing "contamination" of the "blood" of the Spanish people; and the need to do away with these frightful dangers through a genocidal solution of the converso problem. No less than racism itself, these three postulates were alien to everything Christianity stood for or had ever taught about the Jews. That such a theory could hold its own and, moreover, gain ground against the doctrines of the Church, until it finally overcame the Church's opposition and became an established social principle in Spain, indicates that it was driven by a far stronger force than any obstacle the Church could put in its way.[31]

Another leading Inquisition scholar, Edward Peters, reached a similar conclusion:

> From the mid-fifteenth century on, religious anti-Semitism changed into ethnic anti-Semitism, with little difference between Jews and conversos except for the fact that conversos were regarded as worse than Jews because, as ostensible Christians, they had acquired privileges and positions that were denied to Jews.[32]

The Role of the Vatican

On November 1, 1478, Pope Sixtus IV issued the bull that authorized the Spanish Inquisition. This initial concession would be followed by future concessions, including the Vatican's assent to the appointment of the now-infamous Thomas Torquemada to the position of chief inquisitor. Through actions such as these, the Vatican inextricably linked the Catholic Church to the Inquisition and all that would follow. This is a connection that can be neither overlooked nor excused.

Yet to end the moral accounting here would do a disservice not only to the Church, but also to the truth. As soon as the Vatican learned of the Inquisition's excesses, it intervened to try to stop them. In fact, a succession of popes responded with a series of measures meant to tame the monster that it had helped to create.*

It did not take long for the Spanish clergy and the conversos themselves to report to Rome the abuses committed by the Inquisition in its first years of operation. The pope responded forcefully. In January 1482, Pope Sixtus IV actually revoked his prior authorization of the Inquisition and declared that the inquisitors could only continue to operate if they submitted to the supervision of their local bishops.[33]

In April of that same year, Pope Sixtus attacked the Inquisition once again. This time he issued the bull cited at the beginning of this chapter, in which he strongly denounced the Inquisition's corruption and excesses and ordered a series of reforms. One year later, Sixtus issued yet another bull aimed at reining in the Inquisition. This time he ordered the Inquisition to demonstrate more mercy and stipulated that all appeals from the Inquisition's rulings must be decided in Rome.[34]

Sixtus's successor, Pope Innocent VIII, likewise tried to curb the Inquisition's excesses. He issued two bulls in 1485 demanding that the Inquisition exercise greater leniency. He also ordered the body to make greater use of the practice of secret reconciliation to avoid the public defamation of suspects.[35]

---

*By our modern standards, of course, taming the Inquisition's excesses was hardly sufficient. Even the most lenient of inquisitions still ordered the torture and murder of human beings for their refusal to conform to a religious orthodoxy. Such acts are properly considered religious violence. The point here is not to deny the horrors of the Spanish Inquisition but merely to clarify their sources and scope.

In 1503 another new pope, Julius II, weighed in on Spain's growing anti-Semitism. His particular concern was not the Inquisition, but the racist blood-purity statutes that were being passed throughout the country. The pope was outraged that the Christian descendants of Jews were being barred from so many religious and secular institutions. He therefore issued a bull in which he condemned such race-based policies as "detestable customs and real corruption" and declared "null and void all the rules, regulations, constitutions, and laws, etc., which were enacted for this purpose."[36]

In 1519 yet another new pope, Leo X, turned the focus back to the Inquisition. He issued a series of orders curbing the power of the Inquisition and eliminating certain of its special privileges.[37]

～

TRAGICALLY, ALL OF THESE Papal decrees and pronouncements against the Spanish Inquisition had little practical effect. In some cases, these bulls were simply ignored. In other cases, the Vatican was actually forced to back down and retract them. In no case did the Inquisition stop its pattern of greed, abuse, and violence.

Spain's ability to ignore these papal orders flowed from the gross power imbalance that existed between Spain and Rome at this time. As religious leaders, the popes still had official authority over Spain's churches and souls. But as temporal leaders of the weak Papal States, these popes simply did not have the power to enforce their edicts.

At this juncture, Spain was a rising power, while the Papal States faced strategic threats on two fronts. To the east, an expanding Ottoman Empire menaced the Papal States and much of Europe, and Spain's military might was needed for the defense of Christendom. The Vatican was thus reluctant to alienate a potential defender. To the west, an ascendant Spain itself loomed as a threat to all of its neighbors, including the Papal States. The Vatican was thus loathe to provoke a potential invader. Such fears later proved to be well founded. In 1527, Spain

invaded and occupied most of Italy, sacked Rome, and imprisoned the pope.

The Real Problem

The conventional wisdom is wrong. The Church was not the
driving force behind the anti-Semitic violence of the Crusades or
the Inquisition. On the contrary, the Vatican and its hierarchy
repeatedly sought to curb such violence and protect the Jews. In
so doing, these popes and bishops were hardly improvising; they
were trying to enforce Church laws that clearly forbade killing or
forcibly converting Jews.

Yet as important as it is to debunk the popular myths about
these atrocities, it is equally important not to overlook an underlying reality. While the Church does not bear primary responsibility for the crimes of the Crusades or the Inquisition, it is by no
means free from all responsibility for these and other anti-
Semitic outbursts. After all, the European masses that hated Jews
were *Christian* masses. The European mobs that killed Jews were
Christian mobs. Many lower-level Church officials, priests, and
monks enthusiastically participated in these persecutions in con-
travention of Church law. These facts raise the question of
whether the Church somehow contributed to an environment
in which anti-Semitism resonated so deeply with so many
Christians.

There can, in fact, be little doubt that certain doctrines the
Church taught contributed to the popular anti-Semitism it
fought. Two concepts stand out as particularly problematic. The
first was the doctrine of deicide. The Church taught not only
that the Jews killed Jesus, but that all Jews at all times bore the
responsibility for this most infamous of crimes. The belief that
Jews were Christ-killers was a core component of the popular
anti-Semitism that swept Europe. Few allegations proved to be
more inflammatory.

The second provocative doctrine was replacement theology. The Church taught that because the Jews rejected Jesus as their messiah, God rejected the Jews as his chosen people and replaced them with a new Israel: the Christians. There is a definite danger to teaching that God has cast aside a particular group of people. At the very least, it suggests to men that it would be permissible to do likewise. The idea that the Jews were repudiated by God thus joined the belief that they had murdered God as accelerants on the bonfire of European anti-Semitism.

Neither of these doctrines ever sanctioned or even suggested violence against Jews. Yet there is an obvious tension between the provocative rhetoric about Jews, on the one hand, and the official policy of protecting them, on the other. As historian Robert Chazan has noted:

> The Church's assertion that Jews are deserving of legitimacy and must be allowed to live safely and securely as Jews in a Christian society contrasted severely with its regular reinforcement of the negative Gospel portrait of the Jews. While this combination makes a certain intellectual sense, it strains emotional resources. That periodically Christians might have undone this unstable mix is not difficult to envision.[38]

The trail of causation twists and turns, but it can still be followed. The Church leaders who taught these doctrines understood that they did not justify violence against Jews. Yet the masses upon whose ears they fell were less familiar with the totality of Christian theology and thus were not restrained by it. As author James Carroll summarized it:

> For a thousand years, the compulsively repeated pattern ... would show in bishops and popes protecting Jews—but from expressly Christian mobs that wanted to kill Jews because of what bishops and popes had taught about Jews.[39]

～

TWO ADDITIONAL POINTS must be made be made about these provocative doctrines of deicide and replacement theology. First of all, the Church has finally abandoned them. In 1965, the Second Vatican Council issued a historic declaration entitled *Nostra Aetate* that addressed the Church's relationship with non-Christians. Here the Catholic Church finally rejected the charge of deicide against contemporary Jews, concluding that Christ's passion "cannot be charged . . . against the Jews of today." This document likewise rejected the most negative rhetoric that had accompanied the doctrine of replacement theology, noting that "the Jews should not be presented as rejected or accursed by God." In the decades following the Holocaust, most leading Protestant denominations likewise officially rejected the dangerous rhetoric that had often surrounded their discussions of the Jews.

Yet while these specific teachings may be gone, the larger danger is still clear and present. The Judeo-Christian message is one which offers a path toward transcending the limitations of our human nature. Yet the custodians of this message remain deeply and unalterably human. Thus this elevating idea is vulnerable to corruption by the very human nature it seeks to overcome. When this happens, religion can become an agent for promoting our worst impulses instead of transcending them.

The Crusades and the Inquisition are typically cited in support of a false premise. They do not prove that religion is the great source of human violence. Yet these episodes must nevertheless serve as cautionary tales for all people of faith. These atrocities teach an urgent lesson about the need for constant vigilance and deep humility. The faithful must be forever vigilant lest their faith be corrupted by their flawed human nature. And they must remain profoundly humble in recognition of the possibility that such corruption may have already occurred. It has happened before.

Modern Christian Atrocities

As exaggerated as they may be in the popular imagination, the Crusades and the Inquisition still do provide concrete examples of atrocities committed in the name of Christianity. The modern era offers no such examples. There are over two billion Christians in the world today. Yet remarkably few of these faithful ever commit acts of violence in furtherance of their faith. This record is a most eloquent tribute to Christianity's success in removing from its theology any sanction of violence in its name.

When searching for an example of modern Christian violence, critics typically end up recycling the same few incidents. In the mid-1990s, there were a series of attacks on abortion providers in the United States that left six doctors and clinic workers dead. These attacks culminated in the murder of Dr. Bernard Slepian, an obstetrician and sometime abortion provider.* Dr. Slepian was shot by a sniper while he stood preparing dinner in the kitchen of his home. It turned out that the killers were in most cases religious Christians who claimed to be acting on their belief that abortion is murder.

Madmen can and do perpetrate violence in the name of manifold causes they neither understand nor represent. The important question is not whether these lunatics embraced Christianity, but whether Christianity embraced them. Did the Christian world rationalize and equivocate, or did it condemn these men as murderers? The fact is that Christian leaders from across the theological spectrum rejected these attacks in the

---

*On May 31, 2009, an abortion provider named Dr. George Tiller was murdered while serving as an usher at his Kansas church. A man named Scott Roeder was arrested for the crime shortly thereafter. Roeder later confessed to killing Tiller and claimed that he did so because "preborn children's lives were in imminent danger." On January 29, 2010, Roeder was found guilty of first-degree murder by a Kansas jury. Despite Roeder's history of mental illness and anti-government activism, there can be little doubt that extreme interpretations of Christian teachings against abortion played a role in Roeder's crime.

strongest, most unambiguous of terms. These authorities made it crystal clear that Christianity utterly rejects such violence in its name. No Christian figure with any claim to credibility sought to excuse these crimes. Such moral clarity is no doubt why so few acts of violence are committed in the name of Christianity today.

Jewish Atrocities: Modern Examples Recycled

When it comes to the topic of Jewish atrocities, the record offers little for the conventional wisdom to exaggerate. History records remarkably few episodes in which Jews have resorted to violence in the name of their faith.

The worst examples of Jewish atrocities come to us from a Jewish source: the Bible. As we've seen, the Israelites are commanded to blot out the tribe of Amalek and to utterly destroy the six Canaanite tribes that inhabited the Land of Israel. While there is little in the way of archeological or historical confirmation, the Bible relates that the Israelites largely complied with these genocidal commands.

Outside of the Bible, ancient history records one additional Jewish atrocity with which few people are familiar. A number of historical sources report that when the Persians began their conquest of Palestine from the Byzantines in the early seventh century, thousands of Jews joined the fight on the Persian side. These sources further detail that when this joint army reached Jerusalem in 614 CE, these Jewish soldiers joined with the Persians in massacring the city's Christian inhabitants. Some historians have claimed that as many as ninety thousand Christians were thus killed. Others believe that both this death toll and the Jewish role in this massacre have been exaggerated.[40]

Modern Jewish Atrocities

Once we move into the modern era, the search for Jewish atrocities becomes even more challenging. Despite an enormous temptation to seek vengeance after the Holocaust, and the high tensions between Israel and her Arab neighbors, remarkably few Jews have committed violence in the name of their faith. Judaism long ago eliminated any justification for such behavior.

With such a small number of examples to choose from, critics of faith must resort to recycling the same few incidents. In particular, those seeking to demonstrate that every faith produces dangerous extremists will inevitably cite the two poster children for modern Jewish violence: Yigal Amir and Baruch Goldstein.*

Yigal Amir is the Jewish fanatic who assassinated Israeli prime minister Yitzhak Rabin in 1995. Rabin's death was a national tragedy for Israel, and it may well have contributed, along with a violent spree of Palestinian terror that claimed hundreds of Israeli lives, to derailing the Oslo peace process. Yigal Amir was convicted of murder and is presently serving a life sentence in an Israeli prison.

Baruch Goldstein's story is even more troubling. In 1994, Goldstein entered the Muslim section of Hebron's Tomb of the Patriarchs and began firing his automatic weapon at men bowed in prayer. He killed twenty-nine Muslims before the worshippers beat him to death.

Both Amir and Goldstein were religious Jews, and their interpretations of their faith were central to their actions. But in each case, the entire spectrum of Jewish opinion stepped forward with an immediate and unambiguous condemnation of what these men had done. No one except a few of their lunatic fellow-

---

*While these two examples of Jewish religious violence are the bloodiest and most often cited, they are certainly not the only ones. In recent years, for example, there have been numerous reports of violence perpetrated by West Bank settlers against neighboring Arab villages. While the reports do mention some punching and shoving of people, this violence has been directed primarily against olive trees and other property. No fatalities have been reported. While the motives for such attacks no doubt involve numerous factors, it is quite likely that extreme interpretations of Jewish theology play a role.

travelers sought to justify or rationalize their crimes. No one asked us to understand the "roots" of their rage. The universal Jewish condemnation of these attacks is no doubt an important reason why there are so few examples of such faith-based violence on the Jewish side of the Israeli-Palestinian conflict.

~

THE SEARCH FOR Jewish atrocities beyond these oft-cited examples can become downright desperate. In a 2006 work called *Reckless Rites,* author Elliott Horowitz seeks to write an entire book on a topic better left to a small pamphlet: Jewish violence. In his introduction he wastes no time bringing up Goldstein and Amir. He also mentions the massacre of Jerusalem's Christians in 614.

Then the search for content gets far more challenging. Horowitz fills the rest of the book with examples that are almost comical in light of the very real violence that Jews have suffered for so many centuries. For example, Horowitz makes much of an incident in 1995 when a Jew named Moshe Ehrenfeld "spat conspicuously" as a procession of Armenian priests passed by him in the Old City of Jerusalem. Yet the Israeli authorities refused to take even so harmless an offense lightly. An Israeli court found Ehrenfeld guilty of "interfering with a religious ritual."[41] He was fined and given a suspended prison sentence.

Running out of flesh-and-blood victims, Horowitz devotes an entire chapter to Jewish acts of violence against inanimate objects. It seems that over the centuries they lived in Christian lands, Jews who harbored grudges against Christianity or Christians sometimes vented their anger upon Christianity's most prominent symbol: the cross. For example, Horowitz cites allegations that in eleventh century Rome a number of Jews "mocked" a crucifix. The Jews so accused were executed for this offense. Another example involved a Jew who allegedly "snatched and trampled" a crucifix in 1268 as a church procession passed through a Jewish neighborhood in Oxford. In a case from sixteenth-century Mexico, a farmer of Jewish decent was accused of hanging strings of chili peppers to dry on the arms of a cross.[42] It seems that the only violence to result from these symbolic outbursts befell the Jews who were alleged to have enacted them.

NINE

The Myth of Enlightenment Perfection

Enlightenment, understood in the widest sense as the advance of thought, has always aimed at liberating human beings from fear and installing them as masters. Yet the wholly enlightened earth is radiant with triumphant calamity.[1]

—MAX HORKHEIMER AND THEODOR ADORNO, PHILOSOPHERS

IN 1787, THOMAS JEFFERSON sent a very large and most unusual package to a French scientist named Georges Louis Leclerc. In his cover letter, a proud Jefferson describes the package's contents:

> I am happy to be able to present to you at this moment the bones & skin of a Moose, the horns of the Caribou, the elk, the deer, the spiked horned buck, & the Roebuck of America.[2]

Jefferson then apologizes at length for the size of some of the specimens:

> The horns of the elk are remarkably small. I have certainly seen of them which would have weighed five or six times as much.... I must observe also that the horns of the Deer, which accompany these spoils, are not of the fifth or sixth part of the weight of some that I have seen.[3]

Jefferson concludes the letter by begging Leclerc "not to consider those now sent as furnishing a specimen of their ordinary size."[4]

For Jefferson, it seems, size most definitely mattered.

～

WHILE IT MAY appear that Jefferson was indulging a peculiar passion for animal bones and horns, the stakes were actually much higher. In sending these specimens to France, Jefferson was engaging in a passionate intellectual defense of his country.

Leclerc, more commonly known by his title Count de Buffon, was the most influential naturalist of the era. He had recently completed the definitive work in the young field of natural history, his thirty-six-volume *Histoire naturelle, générale et particulière*. Yet among Buffon's theories was one which deeply troubled Jefferson as a patriot trying to build a new nation in the New World. Buffon had written that the American climate—namely its cold and humidity—was so unhealthy that it caused the "degeneration" of the flora and fauna living there. As a result, Buffon claimed, America's native plants and animals were smaller and weaker than those of Europe. Even plants and animals transported from the Old World to the New would, he argued, eventually degenerate into lesser specimens.

What made this theory of degeneration so very distressing to Jefferson was the fact that Buffon applied it to *all* of America's animals, including America's humans. Referring to the American Indian, Buffon acknowledged that the "savage of the New World is about the same height as man in our world." Nevertheless, Buffon was quite confident that the Indians were not in any significant way "an exception to the general fact that all living nature has become smaller on that continent."[5]

Buffon backed up this claim of Indian degeneration with what he believed to be convincing proof. He noted that the American Indian has "no ardor whatever for his female" and that he has "neither hair nor beard." He claimed that Indians were so lazy that if someone were to relieve an Indian of his hunger and thirst, he would "deprive him of the active principle of all his movements; he will rest stupidly upon his legs or lying down entire days." Finally, Buffon wrote that the Indian "has small organs of generation."[6] It seems that Jefferson was not the only Enlightenment thinker obsessed with size.

Buffon never directly applied his theory of degeneration to the Europeans who migrated to America. But the implications of his theory for such immigrants could not have been clearer. Another prominent French thinker, the Abbé Raynal, was quick to take Buffon's ideas to their logical conclusion. Raynal claimed that the Europeans who moved to America would degenerate along with their animals. As proof of this proposition, Raynal noted that America "has not yet produced one good poet, one able mathematician, one man of genius in a single art or a single science."[7]

～

BUFFON'S THEORY THUS posed a serious challenge to an America that aspired to take its place as an equal alongside Europe's leading powers. Few Europeans would want to invest economically or militarily in the survival of a republic thus stunted in its prospects for advancement. Fewer still would want to immigrate there. For men such as Jefferson who believed that ideas shaped history, Buffon's theory was a dangerous intellectual assault on his country. It was imperative that a gifted scientist and thinker publicly rebut this idea. Jefferson rose to the challenge.

In addition to shipping Moose carcasses across the Atlantic, Jefferson devoted the only book he ever wrote to this topic. The bulk of Jefferson's *Notes on the State of Virginia* is a detailed rebuttal of Buffon's theory of degeneration. Here Jefferson questioned whether America was in fact colder and more humid than Europe. He also challenged the assertion that cold and humidity were necessarily inimical to animal and plant life. On the specific issue of animal size, Jefferson buried Buffon under pages of data that the Frenchman had never bothered to compile. *Notes on the State of Virginia* contains a series of lengthy tables and lists demonstrating that America's animals compared quite favorably in size with those of Europe.

America's animals thus vindicated, Jefferson proceeded to defend the continent's human inhabitants. This effort required that Jefferson become an advocate for those humans who had spent the most time in America: the American Indians. Jefferson brought great understanding and sensitivity to the task. He argued that the American Indian is not "more defective in ardor, nor more impotent with his female, than the white reduced to the same diet and exercise."[8] He expressed great confidence that once allowance is made for the Indians' particular circumstances, "we shall probably find that they are formed in mind as well as body, on the same module with 'Homo sapiens Europeus.'"[9] Supporting this claim of Indian intellectual ability with anecdotal evidence, Jefferson cited a famous speech made by the Indian chief Logan upon the murder of his family by English settlers. He judged it superior to the "orations of Demosthenes and Cicero."[10]

Jefferson likewise defended the minds and bodies of the whites "transplanted" to America from Europe. In response to the Abbé Raynal's charge that America had produced no prominent men of art or science, Jefferson proudly noted the accomplishments of George Washington in war, Benjamin Franklin in physics, and David Rittenhouse in astronomy.[11] He modestly left himself off of this list.

〜

IT TURNS OUT that Buffon never spent much time observing America's flora and fauna. In fact, this eminent naturalist never so much as stepped foot in America. He based his scientific theories upon the most unscientific of evidence, namely the anecdotes of European travelers. It was on this flimsy foundation that Buffon opined so boldly on the inferiority of an entire hemisphere's inhabitants.

The spectacle of the pompous scientist denigrating so many millions on the basis of so few facts in the name of the highest intellectual ideals is almost comical. Almost comical, that is—until one remembers that the consequence of such dangerous ideas was not the embarrassment of the theorists but the genocide of the theorized. The road from philosophy to atrocity can be astonishingly short.

This is not to say that Buffon was responsible for the genocide of the American Indian. This unparalleled human tragedy had already killed multi-millions before Buffon caught his first butterfly. The rationale for the American genocide had in fact come from an older philosophical tradition, that of the ancient Greeks, who claimed that certain peoples were so inferior that they were clearly intended by nature to be slaves. Yet instead of finally discrediting this dangerous idea, Buffon and other Enlightenment thinkers updated it and gave it currency for a new era. The American genocide continued, and new ones followed.

Indeed, this idea—that certain groups of humans are inherently inferior to others—is nothing less than the mother of genocide. Those who have introduced this idea in its various iterations may well have done so with the most benign of intentions. But history demonstrates that this is an idea that inexorably separates, degrades, enslaves, and kills. It is the most dangerous idea that man has ever produced. And it is an idea of thoroughly secular provenance.

⌇

MANY OF THE leading critics of religion live in a reassuringly black and white world. As we've seen, they believe they have identified the dark source of the world's most dangerous ideas: the Bible and the religions based upon it. They likewise think they have discovered the pure wellsprings of the higher ideas with which we can overcome our religion-scarred past: science and philosophy. It turns out that these modern critics of religion have not rejected faith at all. They have simply replaced faith in God with an absolute faith in human reason. They believe, in the face of all evidence to the contrary, that their faith demands less of a leap.

In particular, these critics often possess a special reverence for that eighteenth-century flowering of secular philosophy they have humbly named "the Enlightenment." In their version of history, the Enlightenment philosophers were the heroes who finally broke religion's stranglehold on the human mind. These thinkers are given primary credit for having empowered mankind to overcome slavery, genocide, and all of the other atrocities which the Bible is alleged to have introduced.

Once again, Thomas Paine blazed the trail which so many of the modern critics now follow. In the very title of his seminal attack on religious faith, *The Age of Reason,* Paine identified his new north star. He summarized his creed in the book's second paragraph: "The most formidable weapon against error of every kind is reason," Paine declared. "I have never used any other, and I trust I never shall."[12]

It is difficult to decide if such a declaration demonstrates extreme hubris, gross naiveté, or both. Reason does not exist on some abstract moral plane high above the compromised human reality. Reason exists only in the minds of humans born with limited comprehensions, selfish genes, and evil inclinations. It thus turns out that the fruit of human reason—philosophy—has proven to be every bit as fallible as the people who produce it. Some philosophers have introduced extraordinarily valuable ideas into the world. Yet other philosophers—or sometimes the very same ones—have unleashed some of history's most danger-ous ideas.

Most of these perilous philosophical pronouncements were made with the best of intentions. The most influential modern thinkers have offered their theories in an effort to elevate civi-lization, not destroy it. These ideas often had to be stretched well beyond their original formulations to justify atrocities that their authors neither desired nor envisioned.

Yet such exaggerations may well have been inevitable. Intentions aside, the most dangerous modern philosophies all shared the same fatal flaw: they directly challenged the Judeo-Christian idea. They exceeded the safe boundaries of philosophy and presumed to question the sanctity and equality of all humans. In so doing, they ended up unleashing the worst tendencies of our selfish genes to both narrow our ingroups and persecute outgroups.

It turns out that Paine was only half-right. Reason can be a powerful weapon against error. But reason can also be a prolific source of error. Time after time, fallible humans exercising their limited powers of reason have introduced dangerous ideas that the accumulated wisdom of prior generations had wisely rejected. Reason alone is not the answer. Only reason which respects certain longstanding moral boundaries will advance us.

〜

IN ADDITION TO THE problem of secular ideas, we must also acknowledge the problem of secular action. When hitched to the engine of self-interest, secular philosophy has pulled humanity forward by truly historic lengths. It was precisely this marriage of ideas and interest that propelled the American and French Revolutions, which forever altered the relationship between government and the governed.

But once these lofty ideas are decoupled from self-interest, once the focus shifts to someone else's fundamental rights, fiery revolutionaries too often become the most passive of apologists. It seems that even when secular philosophy embraces the right ideas, it is often impotent to motivate men to implement them. Secular philosophy is good at generating enlightened self-interest. It has a much less impressive record of motivating disinterested benevolence.

〜

IN HIS REBUTTAL OF Buffon's views on the American Indian, Thomas Jefferson was a heroic voice of intellect in defense of humanity. When he turned his attention to African Americans, however, Jefferson not only forgot his critique of Buffon but enthusiastically embraced the Count's flawed logic. In his *Notes on the State of Virginia,* the same book in which he so eloquently asserts Indian equality, Jefferson engaged in a lengthy discourse on black inferiority.

Jefferson suggested that blacks are inferior to whites in intellect, because "one [black] could scarcely be found capable of tracing and comprehending the investigations of Euclid."[13] Jefferson claimed that blacks are inferior to whites in the arts, because "never yet could I find that a black had uttered a thought above the level of plain narration; never see even an elementary trait of painting or sculpture."[14] He asserted that blacks are less attractive than whites because blacks themselves are more attracted to whites "as uniformly as is the preference of the Oranootan for the black woman over those of his own species."*[15] Here, Jefferson's towering intellect stooped to the uncritical embrace of the most ridiculous of myths. On the basis of such impressions and outright fantasies, Jefferson wrote:

> I advance it therefore as a suspicion only, that the blacks ... are inferior to the whites in the endowments both of body and mind. It is not against experience to suppose, that different species of the same genus, or varieties of the same species, may possess different qualifications.... This unfortunate difference of color, and perhaps of faculty, is a powerful obstacle to the emancipation of these people.[16]

How could Jefferson be so stunningly inconsistent in his analyses of Indians and Africans? While it is impossible to explain this disparity with any certainty, Edwards, Hopkins, and Finney

---

*A popular racist myth of the time was that male orangutans mated with African women.

all point the way to the likely source: self-interest. Indeed, it is difficult to ignore Jefferson's clear self-interest in the positions he took. In the case of the American Indians, Jefferson's self-interest required that they be equal to whites. Defending his country as a healthy place for human habitation necessitated defending America's native peoples. When it came to African Americans, however, Jefferson's self-interest demanded their inferiority.

Thomas Jefferson was dependent on the institution of slavery. He was a slave-owner who relied upon his slaves to maintain his cherished estate and lifestyle. He was also a leader of a republic founded on, and still inextricably bound to, compromises which permitted the institution of slavery to flourish. Indeed, Jefferson did not hide the role of self-interest in his thinking. In his most famous quotation on the problem of American slavery, Jefferson candidly confessed: "We have the wolf by the ears; and we can neither hold him, nor safely let him go. Justice is on one scale, and self-preservation on the other."[17]

It is true that Jefferson was deeply conflicted about slavery and wrestled with the morality of this institution throughout his life. It is precisely for this reason that he would have welcomed any rationalization that might salve his troubled conscience. Both self-interest and the national interest required that slavery be rendered morally tolerable by a doctrine of black inferiority. And thus inferior Jefferson made them.

∽

THE IMPERFECTIONS AND outright failures of philosophy in general, and of Enlightenment thought in particular, are brought into sharp focus when we review the role such ideas have played in the two greatest categories of human atrocity: slavery and genocide. When it comes to slavery, the Enlightenment's legacy is surprisingly weak. Yes, some Enlightenment philosophers did oppose slavery. But most either ignored it or justified it. And none embraced the abolition of slavery as their mission in life the way so many Christian activists of that era did.

When it comes to genocide, modern philosophy has an even more troubling record. Far from curbing genocide, European philosophers introduced three ideologies—racism, nationalism, and Communism—that have served as the primary rationales for genocide in our time. When we examine the cultures that have perpetrated the genocides of the twentieth century, we often find Enlightenment ideas—twisted and exaggerated, but still recognizable—at their core.

The Philosophers and Slavery

Slavery was not an aberration that arose only under the unique circumstances of the European colonization of America. On the contrary, slavery has been a constant throughout human history. As sociologist Orlando Patterson has observed:

> There is nothing notably peculiar about the institution of slavery. It has existed from before the dawn of human history right down to the twentieth century, in the most primitive of human societies and in the most civilized. There is no region on earth that has not at some time harbored the institution. Probably there is no group of people whose ancestors were not at one time slaves or slaveholders.[18]

Western civilization has been no exception to this rule. The classical civilizations which we in the modern West so deeply admire were enthusiastic practitioners of slavery. In both Greece and Rome, slaves performed almost all of the difficult physical labor, including farming, construction, and mining. Each of these societies also employed enormous populations of domestic slaves. Almost every household in Athens and Rome had slaves, and the number of slaves in these societies at times outnumbered the free population.[19]

When the leading Greek philosophers applied their powers of reason to the problem of slavery, they arrived at a position of unequivocal support for the institution. Plato, for example, was a

strong proponent of enslaving non-Greeks. The slavery he advocated, moreover, was absolute. Plato wrote that if either parent was
a slave, then their child would be a slave. He also maintained that
slaves were under the complete authority of their masters and
could be punished by them as well as by any other free person.
Regarding Plato's views on slavery, historian David Brion Davis
has written, "No American slave code was so severe."[20]

As we've seen, Plato's student Aristotle adopted and further
developed his teacher's views on slavery. In his *Politics*, Aristotle
noted that some of his contemporaries claimed that the rule of a
master over a slave is "contrary to nature" and therefore unjust.
But Aristotle refuted this claim in the strongest of terms:

> There is no difficulty in answering this question, on grounds
> both of reason and of fact. For that some should rule and oth-
> ers be ruled is a thing not only necessary, but expedient; from
> the hour of their birth, some are marked out for subjection,
> others for rule.[21]

Aristotle added that "the lower sort are by nature slaves, and it is
better for them as for all inferiors that they should be under the
rule of a master." Supporting this assertion by analogy, Aristotle
reminded his readers that animals are better off when they are
ruled over by man, and that the "inferior" female is meant to be
ruled over by the "superior" male.[22]

In case one were to conclude from his words that slaves
retained some element of humanity, Aristotle noted that "the use
made of slaves and tame animals is not very different; for both
with their bodies minister to the needs of life."[23] Elsewhere, in
his *Nicomachean Ethics*, Aristotle employed an even more troubling analogy. He concluded that "the slave is a living tool and
the tool a lifeless slave."[24]

Plato and Aristotle embraced slavery without reservation.
Given how widespread slavery was in their own day, their thinking on this topic was neither hypothetical nor harmless. In addition, as we've seen, these great philosophers articulated a defense

of slavery which would resonate down through the ages with tragic repercussions.

Modern Philosophy and Slavery

Some of the philosophers who have most deeply influenced Western civilization lived and wrote in the two centuries preceding the eighteenth-century Enlightenment. These men developed many of the key concepts that undergird the liberal democracy and civil rights we so cherish today. Yet when it came to slavery, these philosophers merely updated ancient rationales for a new era. As historian David Brion Davis has noted, "The great political theorists of the sixteenth and seventeenth centuries all found justifications for chattel slavery."[25]

The English philosopher Thomas Hobbes is among the most influential thinkers in the history of the West. In his 1651 book *Leviathan,* Hobbes was the first to elaborate some of the core concepts of liberal democracy, including the idea that all men are born with a set of inalienable rights. In the very same book, however, Hobbes also engaged in a vigorous defense of slavery. In fact, Hobbes set forth a rationale for slavery which legitimized it for a new age and justified it at the time of its most explosive growth.

Hobbes judged all institutions by whether or not they improved upon the way humans lived in our original "state of nature." And of this state of nature, Hobbes took a famously dim view. He imagined life in our natural state as "nasty, brutish and short" and "a war of all against all."[26] When Hobbes used the word "war," he was not speaking figuratively. "In the natural state," he wrote, "any one may legitimately subdue or even kill Men, whenever that seems to be to his advantage."[27]

Given this dim view of our starting point, Hobbes saw slavery as a definite step forward. If one man has a right to kill another, Hobbes reasoned, then it certainly follows that this man has a right to spare his victim's life in exchange for his servitude.

For Hobbes, slavery was completely legitimate if the loser of a battle decided to save his own life by making "a promise to the victor or the stronger party to serve him, i.e. to do all that he shall command." He thus envisioned slavery as a contractual arrangement, freely entered into, with the following terms and consideration:

> In this contract the good which the defeated or weaker party
> receives is the sparing of his life, which could have been taken
> from him, in men's natural state, by right of war; and the good
> which he promises is service and obedience. . . . From this
> point on one who is so bound is called a SLAVE, the one to
> whom he is bound is called a MASTER.[28]

The slavery that Hobbes saw as resulting from such a contract was no less absolute than that of the Greeks. Hobbes wrote that a master has "supreme dominion" over his slaves and that he "may say of his slave no less than of any other thing, animate and inanimate, *This is mine.*"[29] Hobbes even compared the ownership of a man to the ownership of an animal, arguing that "right over non-rational animals is acquired in the same way as over the *persons* of men, that is, by natural strength and powers."[30] For Hobbes, these ownership rights included the right to take from the slave everything he possessed, including his children and his very life.

Later in the seventeenth century, John Locke followed Hobbes to philosophical prominence in England. Locke's *Second Treatise of Government* elaborated theories regarding the right to revolution and limited government which would prove pivotal to the future of both England and America. Indeed, some scholars have gone so far as to say that the Declaration of Independence relies "almost exclusively" on Locke's philosophy of natural rights.[31] Yet in the same book in which he set forth these noble ideas, Locke also provided a strong defense of slavery.

When it came to life in the state of nature and the best form of government, Locke vehemently disagreed with Hobbes. When it came to the issue of slavery, however, Locke not only agreed with Hobbes but borrowed Hobbes's logic and embraced his rationale. Locke justified slavery as a humane alternative to death for those defeated in battle. According to Locke, a vanquished soldier has forfeited his life, and thus the victor has every right to "delay to take it [his life] and make use of him to his own service, and does him no injury by it." Locke concluded that "this is the perfect condition of *slavery,* which is nothing else but *the state of war continued, between a lawful conqueror and a captive.*"[32]

~

IN THEORY, HOBBES and Locke were sanctioning slavery only in the narrow context of prisoners of war. Yet in practice they elaborated a rationale large enough to sail a slave ship through. These men and those who adopted their ideas were doing nothing less than justifying the only form of slavery that existed in the Western world at that time: that of Africans in America. The entire trade in African slaves proceeded under cover of the fiction that these captive Africans had originally been taken as prisoners of war in tribal conflicts. Therefore, it was argued, they could legitimately be kept as slaves in Africa or sold to European slave traders.

The reality, of course, was far different. There were simply not enough African wars to produce enough prisoners to meet the growing demand for slaves in the New World. Thus this demand fueled a business dedicated to kidnapping Africans for the sole purpose of selling them to European slave traders. The details of what transpired in these inland villages were easily obscured so that the trade could proceed under its philosophical cover.

Most Europeans involved in the African slave trade knew better than to ask too many questions. Yet this rationale for slavery was important enough to some participants that they did make inquiries into the source of their slaves. As late as 1721, for example, the Royal Africa Company asked its agents to investigate how the slaves they purchased had first been captured. They were specifically instructed to find out whether there was any method of enslavement other than "that of being taken prisoners in war time." The agents were ordered not to buy slaves obtained from such other, forbidden sources. These philosophical concerns may well have been introduced years earlier by one of the investors in the Royal Africa Company, an English philosopher named John Locke.[33]

⟋

THE DAWN OF THE eighteenth century roughly coincided with the beginning of a period of philosophical and scientific ferment which later admirers would call the Age of Enlightenment. This era's leading thinkers enthusiastically expressed ideas about human dignity and liberty which were inherently inimical to slavery. Indeed, the two classic political expressions of Enlightenment philosophy—the American Declaration of Independence and the French Declaration of the Rights of Man and Citizen—both include language which would appear to spell the end of slavery. The Declaration of Independence states:

> We hold these truths to be self-evident, that all men are created equal, that they are endowed by their Creator with certain unalienable Rights, that among these are Life, Liberty and the pursuit of Happiness.

The French Declaration of the Rights of Man provides that all men have a set of "natural, inalienable and sacred rights." These rights include "liberty, property, security and resistance to oppression."

Among the Enlightenment's great accomplishments was to popularize the idea that all people have certain fundamental rights and liberties. Yet at the very time that certain Enlightenment thinkers were elaborating rights which were in theory universal, they or others were introducing the very ideas through which these rights would be denied in practice to great masses of humanity. In particular, theories of human inequality such as those espoused by Buffon and Jefferson became the leading rationales for such disparities.

As a consequence, the Enlightenment tolerated the institution of slavery for far longer than its reputation would suggest or its ideals should have allowed. No one better captures the Enlightenment's ambivalence toward the issue of slavery than the French thinker Montesquieu. Montesquieu was a giant of political philosophy who developed crucial concepts about how best to structure government and preserve liberty. In his 1748 book *The Spirit of the Laws,* Montesquieu introduced the principle of the separation of powers that would be so enthusiastically embraced by America's founding fathers.

In the same book, Montesquieu addressed the question of slavery. He directly confronted, and demolished, the argument of Hobbes and Locke that slavery was justified as an alternative to killing prisoners of war. Shifting the focus from moral hypotheticals to practical realities, Montesquieu reminded his readers that "murdering in cold blood by soldiers after the heat of the action is condemned by all the nations of the world."[35] Instead, Montesquieu observed, the only right that the victors have over their captives is to imprison them for the duration of the conflict so that they can no longer wage war. If soldiers are not permitted to kill their captives, he reasoned, then enslaving them for life ceases to be justifiable as a more humane alternative.

Yet after so promising a start, Montesquieu faltered. In the very chapter in which he rejected the prevailing justification for slavery, he offered up a brand-new one. Montesquieu observed that:

> there are countries where the heat enervates the body and
> weakens the courage so much that men come to perform
> arduous duty only from fear of chastisement; slavery there
> runs less counter to reason.[36]

Montesquieu reasoned that if Aristotle's natural slaves did in fact exist, then they were the people who inhabited these hot climates. Therefore, he concluded, "natural slavery must be limited to certain particular countries of the world."[37]

These words were written at a time when the vast majority of slaves labored in the heat of the Caribbean, Brazil, and the American South. At least in the West, slavery was rare in temperate climates. Thus what Montesquieu provided was nothing less than a rationale for the perpetuation of the dominant form of slavery of his day.

It therefore comes as no surprise that Montesquieu called not for the abolition of slavery but for its regulation. Montesquieu wrote that the laws must seek to eliminate the "abuses" and "dangers" of slavery, and must further ensure that slaves are "nourished and clothed" and "looked after in sickness and in old age." As for abolition, Montesquieu advised only caution, warning that "slaves must not be freed suddenly in considerable numbers by a general law."[38]

Another pillar of the Enlightenment, Voltaire, exhibited a similar ambivalence about the issue of slavery. In his 1764 classic the *Philosophical Dictionary,* Voltaire invoked Montesquieu's critique of the modern justifications for slavery. But elsewhere, in his *Essay on the Manners and Spirit of Nations,* Voltaire echoed the classical justification for slavery:

> We make household slaves only of the Negroes; we are severely reproached for this kind of traffic, but the people who make a trade of selling their children are certainly more blamable than those who purchase them, and this traffic is only proof of our superiority. He who voluntarily subjects himself to a master is designed by nature for a slave.[39]

Other Enlightenment thinkers were less equivocal in their critiques of slavery. In his 1762 masterpiece *The Social Contract,* for example, Jean-Jacques Rousseau attacked slavery on grounds almost identical to those set forth by Montesquieu. "If war does not give the conqueror the right to massacre the conquered peoples," he argued, "the right to enslave them cannot be based upon a right which does not exist." Accordingly, for Rousseau, a claim to own slaves based on such faulty logic was not only illegitimate but "absurd and meaningless."[40] Unlike Montesquieu, Rousseau did not offer up any new rationales for slavery to replace the one he had discredited.

Yet even while criticizing the philosophy behind slavery, neither Rousseau nor those who shared his views demonstrated much indignation over its ongoing reality. At the time they wrote, millions of slaves labored under the most brutal conditions in France's Caribbean colonies. Yet to the extent these philosophers criticized slavery at all, they did so in the abstract. They failed to object to the situation in the Caribbean, let alone undertake concrete efforts to change it.

～

IN THE LATER decades of the eighteenth century, some philosophers finally issued more enthusiastic denunciations of slavery. Among the leading Enlightenment foes of slavery was a thinker and revolutionary named the Marquis de Condorcet. In his 1781 book, *Reflections on Negro Slavery,* Condorcet stated in the clearest of terms that "to reduce a man to slavery, to purchase him, to sell him, to keep him in servitude, these are veritable crimes and they are crimes worse than theft."[41]

Yet when it came to actually stopping these crimes, Condorcet's outrage turned into a most accommodating patience. While Condorcet supported abolition, he proposed that the slaves be freed over the course of many decades:

> We propose ... not to free Negroes the moment they are born, but to grant their masters the right to raise and use them as slaves on condition that they are freed at the age of thirty-five.[42]

Under Condorcet's plan, those slaves already living would continue to serve as slaves for a period of years determined by their age on the date of enactment. Slaves under fifteen years old at the time would be freed at the age of forty. Those older than fifteen would remain slaves until the age of fifty, at which point they would be given the choice of remaining in bondage or being set free. Condorcet estimated that if this policy were enacted, "there would be no more slaves in the colonies in seventy years."[43]

Condorcet deserves much credit. His promulgation of a plan for gradual emancipation was a significant improvement upon the purely abstract musings of his predecessors. Yet Condorcet's patience when it came to securing the freedom of slaves stood in sharp contrast to the urgency with which he sought to vindicate his own. Condorcet did not merely propose a plan by which future generations of Frenchmen might eventually enjoy full political rights. Instead, he played a leading role in the French Revolution through which he and his comrades fought to secure those rights immediately.

Condorcet was an honest enough thinker to recognize this urgency gap, and he sought a rationalization to justify it. Unwilling to invoke racism like so many of his contemporaries did, Condorcet found another excuse. He suggested that the slaves had been incapacitated by the brutal conditions under which they lived, rendering them like any other people who had "been deprived of their faculties through misfortune or illness." Such damaged people, Condorcet explained, "cannot be allowed the full exercise of their rights lest they harm others or themselves."[44] Therefore, he concluded, "the decision not to grant to all the slaves the enjoyment of their rights all at once need not be incompatible with justice."[45]

Only a few years later, France would temporarily abolish slavery. But it did so not because of the philosophers' patient proposals, but as a result of the slaves' own decisive actions. The slaves in France's colony of Haiti were inspired by the French Revolution and its core principles of liberty and equality. Yet they had little patience for the rationalizations by which they were being denied both. They therefore followed the lead of

France's revolutionaries and sought to vindicate their rights by force of arms. While France at first acquiesced in the new reality created by this slave revolt, it would later send warships to Haiti to reinstate by force the slavery it had not yet rejected in principle.

⟞

THE GLARING GAP between the Enlightenment philosophers' high ideals and their actual deeds is perhaps best exemplified by their most famous American counterpart, Thomas Jefferson.

In principle, Jefferson opposed the institution of slavery and advocated its abolition. In his private correspondence, he waxed eloquent on the injustice of slavery and the need to erase its blot from the nation he loved. Jefferson wrote that a just God would in time awaken to the slaves' distress and free them from their bondage. He regretted that his country was so slow to progress toward this crucial reform.

Such reflections aside, however, Jefferson never advocated the immediate abolition of slavery. Instead, like Condorcet in France, Jefferson supported a gradual abolition that would begin at some unspecified point in the future. In his *Notes on the State of Virginia*, as well as in his correspondence, Jefferson elaborated an abolition plan which would free all slaves born after a certain date to be determined. A slave born as late as one day before the magic date, however, would be forced to endure a lifetime of slavery.

Under Jefferson's plan, even those slave children lucky enough to be born after the emancipation date would never be permitted to live as free people in America. Jefferson envisioned that these freed children would be raised by their slave parents until they reached the age of majority. At that point, they would be deported from the United States.[46] Jefferson seems to have favored the idea of sending these freed slaves to agricultural colonies in Africa.[47]

Jefferson justified these proposed deportations on purely racist grounds. He wrote that separation of the races was necessary since "nature, habit, opinion has drawn indelible lines of distinction between them."[48] It was in the context of defending his deportation plan that Jefferson wrote his extended discourse on African inferiority in the *Notes on the State of Virginia.* He also warned of the danger of race-mixing if the freed slaves were permitted to stay. Jefferson noted that America's slaves were not like those of Rome who, once freed, could "mix with, without staining, the blood of [their] master[s]."[49]

Thus Jefferson's preferred plan for emancipation would not have applied to any slaves then living and would have eventually resulted in a purely white United States. Yet even his support for so tepid a program was tentative and easily abandoned. While Jefferson occasionally discussed his proposal in private, he never seriously pursued it in public. Writing late in his life, Jefferson explained his failure to press his plan by claiming that "it was found that the public mind would not yet bear the proposition, nor will it bear it even at this day."[50] Elsewhere he wrote that to push for emancipation too soon would only "rivet still closer the chains of bondage and retard the moment of delivery to this oppressed description of men."[51]

Not only did Jefferson conclude that the moment for abolition had not arrived, but he suggested that it was not even imminent. Days before his death in 1826, Jefferson wrote: "The revolution in public opinion which this cause requires is not to be expected in a day, or perhaps in an age; but time, which outlives all things, will outlive this evil also."[52]

∾

JEFFERSON HAD BEEN far less patient with injustice when he and his fellow whites were the ones suffering it. He didn't merely propose that Britain stop taxing Americans without representation at some unspecified future date. Instead, he risked his life to help lead a revolution to end this practice immediately. Jefferson might well have been commenting on his own behavior when he wrote:

> What a stupendous, what an incomprehensible machine is man! Who can endure toil, famine, stripes, imprisonment & death itself in vindication of his own liberty, and the next moment be deaf to all those motives whose power supported him through his trial, and inflict on his fellow man bondage, one hour of which is fraught with more misery than ages of that which he rose in rebellion to oppose.[53]

Across the ocean in England, contemporaries of Jefferson led by William Wilberforce and Thomas Clarkson were able to rise above the obsession with self Jefferson so ably described and so unfortunately exhibited. While perfectly secure in their own liberty and prosperity, these English abolitionists struggled for decades in the face of vehement opposition to vindicate the rights of their fellow man. Guided by the Judeo-Christian idea, they proved that man can be a most stupendous machine indeed.

The Philosophers and Genocide

Genocide, like slavery, is an ancient evil that has existed from the dawn of human history. Even the classical cultures which we in the West so admire perpetrated genocide. Indeed, the Roman destruction of Carthage has served for centuries as a particularly popular genocidal precedent.

Carthage was a city on the North African coast that prospered in the classical era. Like Rome, Carthage aggressively pursued control of the Mediterranean world, and by the fifth century BCE it had established a network of city-states throughout North Africa and Spain. As they sought to build their empires on the same stretches of land, Rome and Carthage were on a collision course. The two powers eventually fought a series of wars for regional supremacy.

The Roman statesman Cato the Elder grew obsessed with eliminating this competition from Carthage once and for all. The historian Plutarch wrote that in his later years, no matter what topic he addressed, Cato ended his every speech with the words "Carthage must be destroyed."[54]

A few years after Cato's death, in 146 BCE, Rome finally conquered Carthage. But instead of accepting the typical terms of surrender, the Roman army proceeded to fulfill Cato's wish. Roman troops demolished every building in the city and slaughtered half of its inhabitants. Of Carthage's approximately 300,000 residents, at least 145,000 were killed and the remainder were sold into slavery.[55] Carthage was indeed destroyed.

According to author Ben Kiernan, "From the sixteenth century on, advocates of religious or ethnic violence often cited the Carthaginians as a prime precedent of an exterminated people."[56] Tragically, the example of Carthage was invoked not to shock people into vowing "never again," but to inspire them to go and do likewise.

Modern Philosophy and Genocide

Centuries after Carthage was destroyed, the Enlightenment philosophers set forth a vision for humanity that appeared to be quite at odds with Cato's. They spoke about the dignity and equality of men in universal terms. They stressed the right of all men to life and liberty. These ideas should have finally delegitimized any lingering rationales for genocide inherited from darker times.

Yet no so such progress took place. While some Enlightenment thinkers were elaborating the rights of man, they or others were introducing the very theories by which these rights would be denied to large segments of humanity. They justified these distinctions by claiming that certain groups of humans were inherently inferior to others. Thus the key genocidal idea of human inequality was not discredited—it was updated.

Tragically, Enlightenment thinkers actually contributed new variations on the theme of human inequality. In particular, the Enlightenment philosophers and their intellectual cousins introduced into the world's thought-stream three ideas which have served as rationales for genocide. Enlightenment thinkers invented the concept of race. Romantic philosophers, reacting to this concept of race, developed the ideology of nationalism. And philosophers building on the Enlightenment tradition created Communism. All of these concepts were introduced in the name of knowledge and human progress. Yet in practice they served as the ideological foundation for evil in our time.

The Rise of Racism

Enlightenment thinkers were fascinated by nature. Many studied the world's living creatures and made prodigious efforts to classify and categorize them. These men and women created the fields of natural science and anthropology. By subjecting human beings to such classification along with every other animal, these thinkers also invented the concept of race.

Carolus Linnaeus of Sweden was the first modern thinker to create a system for categorizing animal life. Upsetting some of the religious authorities of his day, Linnaeus included human beings in his system as a species in the mammal class of the animal kingdom. In his 1735 work *Systema Naturae,* Linnaeus named the human species "Homo sapiens" and divided it into four different "varieties"—American, European, Asian, and African.[57]

Linnaeus's great rival in the field of natural history was our old friend George Louis Leclerc, the Count de Buffon. For his part, Buffon recognized five main varieties of the human species: Laplanders, Europeans, Americans, Africans, and Oriental Tartars.[58] A third pioneer of this field, Johann Blumenbach, likewise divided humanity into five varieties. Blumenbach identified these as Caucasian, Mongolian, Ethiopian, American, and Malay.[59]

Merely dividing the human family into varieties may not have been dangerous in and of itself. Unfortunately, recognizing different varieties of man almost always leads to ranking them. Not surprisingly, these European naturalists all described the European variety of man as superior to the others. From the outset, the theory of race was muddied by the reality of racism.

Linnaeus described European man as "white, sanguine, muscular," "gentle, acute, inventive," and "governed by laws." He characterized African man as "black, phlegmatic, indolent," "crafty, lazy, negligent," and "governed by caprice."[60] Buffon described Europeans as the "most handsome and beautiful" of the varieties of man, and wrote that all the others had "degenerated" from this ideal.[61] Blumenbach also embraced the view that the Caucasians were the original race from which the others had degenerated. He wrote that the Caucasians were "the most handsome and becoming" of the groups. Blumenbach, who attached particular significance to skull shape, added that Caucasians had "the most beautiful form of the skull."[62]

All three of these scientists accepted the biblical account of creation in which all humans descended from Adam and Eve. Thus they classified all humans as belonging to the same species even while they recognized different categories within this species. Yet this belief in "monogenesis"—that all humans shared one common ancestor—presented a serious intellectual challenge. Its proponents needed to explain how humans could have developed such significant physical differences in the mere thousands of years since the biblical creation took place.

Buffon devoted particular attention to this challenge. It was in the effort to reconcile racial diversity with monogenesis that he developed his theory of degeneration. Buffon reasoned that as Adam's descendants multiplied, they spread out across the globe into many different regions characterized by widely divergent climates. These different climates, Buffon argued, were the powerful agents that acted upon man to produce the different colors and physiques that eventually emerged. A hot sun caused black skin, a weaker sun left the skin white, and so on.

Buffon took this theory to its logical conclusion. He argued that Africans who lived in Europe would eventually turn white, and that Europeans who lived in Africa would in time turn black. Buffon even proposed an experiment to test his premise. He suggested transporting a group of Africans from Senegal to Denmark and then enclosing the Africans "with their women" so as to exclude the possibility of interracial mating. Then, Buffon explained, it would be possible to measure how long it takes for the Africans to "reintegrate" to their original white color.[63] For Buffon, it wasn't a question of *whether* these Africans would turn white, but *when*.

～

BEFORE BUFFON EVER got around to conducting his experiment, the real world was providing sufficient evidence to refute his theory. By the mid-eighteenth century, Africans had been living in Europe and America long enough to discredit Buffon's notion that they would eventually change color. The years passed, but racial characteristics remained unchanged. In many instances, African women in Europe and America were in fact giving birth to babies with lighter skin than their own. Yet only the very innocent were prepared to explain this phenomenon by reference to the climate.

As experience discredited Buffon's climate-based argument, new ideas emerged to take its place. Some thinkers responded to the mounting evidence by rejecting the concept of monogenesis altogether. They proposed in its place the theory of "polygenesis," which maintained that each different racial group descended from its own unique set of ancestors. The creation story in Genesis, they claimed, does not chronicle the creation of all men, but only the creation of European men.

Among the most enthusiastic apostles of polygenesis was the Enlightenment philosopher Voltaire. While more of a philosopher than a scientist, Voltaire was hardly reticent about articulating his rejection of the monogenesis theory which dominated in his day. For example, demonstrating a peculiar fixation on the significance of hair, Voltaire concluded that "bearded Whites, wooly-haired Blacks, yellow-skinned peoples with their long manes, and beardless men do not come from the same man."[64] Elsewhere, he simply asserted that "the negro race is a species of men as different from ours as the breed of spaniels is from that of greyhounds."[65]

Voltaire believed not only that humanity could be divided into different species, but that these species could be ranked in a hierarchy of merit. And in this hierarchy, Voltaire placed Africans toward the bottom of creation, just above "apes and oysters."[66] While other observers focused on white superiority, Voltaire was more interested in detailing African inferiority. He described Africans in the most demeaning of terms:

> Their round eyes, squat noses, and invariable thick lips, the
> different configurations of their ears, their wooly heads, and
> the measure of their intellects, make a prodigious difference
> between them and other species of men; and what demon-
> strates that they are not indebted for this difference to their
> climates, is that negro men and women, being transported
> into the coldest countries, constantly produce animals of their
> own species; and that mulattoes are only a bastard race of
> black men and white women, or white men and black women,
> as asses, specifically different from horses, produce mules by
> copulating with mares.[67]

〜

THOSE WHO STILL embraced the biblical account of creation needed to respond to the challenge of polygenesis, and they needed to do so with a theory which could withstand the emerging evidence of the permanence of racial characteristics. Into the void stepped one of the Enlightenment's most eminent philosophers,

Immanuel Kant. In his effort to meet this intellectual challenge, Kant became the first thinker to define the term "race" and to use it in a consistent fashion to explain human differences. While he may be best remembered today for his theories of reason and morality, Kant actually devoted more of his university lectures to the topic of race than to any other.

Kant wrote that there is only one species of human, but that this species is divided into four varieties: "whites, Negroes, Huns, and Hindus."[68] He called these varieties "races." Kant theorized that all men originally carried within them "seeds" that could develop into any one of these four races. But as the earliest men spread out and settled in a wide variety of climates, the seed most appropriate to that climate took root and grew accordingly. The key to Kant's race theory was that this process of adaptation was irreversible. Once one seed developed, the other three withered away. For Kant, race had an entrance but no exit.

Like his predecessors, Kant did not simply describe four separate but equal races. Instead, he suggested that there were significant differences between the races which extended beyond their physical appearance to include their intellect and morality. Kant thus injected racism into his concept of race from the very start. Not surprisingly, Kant concluded that the white race was superior to the others. He claimed:

> Humanity is at its greatest perfection in the race of whites. The yellow Indians do have a meager talent. The Negroes are far below them and at the lowest point are a part of the American peoples.[69]

Describing himself and his fellow Europeans, Kant wrote:

> The inhabitant of the temperate parts of the world, above all the central part, has a more beautiful body, works harder, is more jocular, more controlled in his passions, more intelligent than any other race of people in the world. That is why at all points in time these people have educated the others and controlled them with weapons.[70]

As his racial hierarchy makes clear, Kant believed that Africans compared quite poorly with Europeans. Kant stressed that the differences between these two races were "as great in regard to mental capacities as in color."[71] In an infamous paragraph in which the philosopher's racism appears to prevail over his misogyny, Kant discussed and then dismissed evidence of an intelligent African:

> Father Labat reports that a Negro carpenter, whom he reproached for haughty treatment towards his wives, answered: "You whites are indeed fools, for first you make great concessions to your wives, and afterward you complain when they drive you mad." And it might be that there was something in this which perhaps deserved to be considered; but in short, this fellow was quite black from head to foot, clear proof that what he said was stupid.[72]

In discussing African inferiority, Kant often invoked and repeated the observations of the giant of the Scottish Enlightenment, David Hume. Hume seemed to embrace polygenesis and clearly embraced racism when he wrote:

> I am apt to suspect the Negroes and in general all the other species of men (for there are four or five different kinds) to be naturally inferior to the whites. There never was a civilized nation of any other complexion than white, nor even any individual eminent in either action or speculation. No ingenious manufactures amongst them, no arts, no sciences. . . . Such a uniform and constant difference could not happen in so many countries and ages, if nature had not made an original distinction betwixt these breeds of men."[73]

Hume then repeated the conventional wisdom of his day that among all of the blacks dispersed throughout Europe and her colonies, there was not a single one who demonstrated "any symptoms of ingenuity." Hume acknowledged having heard talk of a Negro in Jamaica who was a man of "learning." Yet he dismissed the report by concluding that the man was probably "like a parrot who speaks a few words plainly."[74]

Across the Atlantic Ocean, America's leading Enlightenment thinker espoused similar racial views. As we've seen, Thomas Jefferson engaged in an ingenious defense of the American Indian. Yet when it came to Africans, Jefferson simply regurgitated the ideas of Kant and Hume.

∽

AT THE HEIGHT of the French Enlightenment, many of its leading thinkers collaborated in writing an encyclopedia intended to organize all of their newfound knowledge. The entries were written by the likes of Diderot, Jaucourt, Montesquieu, Rousseau, and Voltaire. The work they produced, the *Encyclopédie,* is one of the Enlightenment's defining texts. Demonstrating the faith in reason and knowledge that characterized his era, Diderot declared that this volume would not only make men wiser but also "more virtuous and happy."[75]

The *Encyclopédie*'s entry for "Negro" reflects the Enlightenment's racist consensus. The entry endorses polygenesis by noting that Negroes "appear to constitute a new species of mankind." This is followed by the observation that:

> if one moves further away from the Equator toward the
> Antarctic, the black skin becomes lighter, but the ugliness
> remains: one finds there the same wicked people that inhabits
> the African Meridian."[76]

England's answer to the French *Encyclopédie* was the Encyclopedia Britannica. Britannica's first American edition, published in 1798, likewise contains a racist entry for "Negro." After noting their "ugliness," the entry goes on to say:

> Vices the most notorious seem to be the portion of this
> unhappy race: idleness, treachery, revenge, cruelty, impu-
> dence, stealing, lying, profanity, debauchery, nastiness and

intemperance, are said to have extinguished the principles of natural law, and to have silenced the reproofs of conscience. They are strangers to every sentiment of compassion, and are an awful example of the corruption of man when left to himself.[77]

〜

THERE IS A strong inclination to overlook the Enlightenment's embrace of racism and tolerance of slavery on the grounds that such views were common at the time. It is not fair, some would suggest, to judge these eighteenth-century men by our modern, multicultural standards.

Yet one need not judge these thinkers by our current standards to find them wanting. Men like Jefferson, Buffon, and Kant fall short when judged by the standards of contemporaries such as Wilberforce and Clarkson who unequivocally rejected slavery and racism. These Enlightenment thinkers likewise fall short when judged by the standard set centuries earlier by men like Montesinos and Las Casas, who stressed the brotherhood of man. In the final analysis, the times did not make the Enlightenment philosophers racist. These philosophers helped to make the times racist.

The Rise of Nationalism

One of the first intellectuals to object to this new racial thinking was a young German named Johann von Herder. As a college student, Herder attended a series of lectures given by Immanuel Kant on the division of humanity into races. He was deeply troubled by what he heard. Eventually, Herder publicly challenged his teacher's race theory and the nascent racism which accompanied it. Kant responded in detail. What followed was one of the most famous intellectual debates in eighteenth-century Germany.

With stunning prescience, Herder saw the danger in the idea that there are significant and fixed differences between different groups of humans. Already in his day, such thinking was fueling ugly speculation that Africans were more closely related to apes and monkeys than to Europeans. Herder called upon his fellow Europeans to reject such views:

> You human should honor yourself. Neither the pogo nor the gibbon is your brother, whereas the American [Indian] and the Negro certainly are. You should not oppress him, nor murder him, nor steal from him; for he is a human being just as you are.[78]

Herder then attacked the very idea of dividing humanity into races:

> Finally, I would not like the distinctions that have been interjected into humankind out of a laudable zeal for a comprehensive science to be extended beyond their legitimate boundaries. Some have for example ventured to call four or five divisions among humans, which were originally constructed according to regions or even according to colors, *races*; I see no reason for this name. Race derives from a difference in ancestry that either does not occur here or that includes the most diverse races within each of these regions in each of these colors. . . . In short, there are neither four nor five races, nor are there exclusive varieties on earth. The colors run into one another.[79]

With these words, written in 1784, Johann von Herder both rejected racial divisions and set forth a most beautiful alternative image of human brotherhood.

⁓

WHILE HERDER REJECTED the division of men into races, he did not do so in the name of universalism. He instead proposed his own alternative division of humanity. For Herder, the meaningful distinction between men was to be found not in their biology, but in their nationality. Herder was the father of modern nationalism.

Herder attributed a deep significance to nationality. He believed that each nation developed its own unique *volksgeist*, or national spirit. He described this national spirit as a mystical product that emerged over centuries as a people communed with its native soil and developed its distinctive language, culture, and morality.

Herder believed that this process of organic national development was nothing less than the engine driving human progress. In his view, nations that are able to develop their national spirit free from outside interference produce the great ideas and innovations which inevitably enrich all humanity. When a nation's national development is disrupted, however, the world is denied the flower of their particular national genius.

Herder was not only the first nationalist; he was also the first multiculturalist. While he divided humanity into different nations, he never ranked these nations in any sort of hierarchy. In Herder's view of the world, the nations were very much separate, but they were also very much equal. Each nation had something unique and precious to contribute to the world.

Yet, as we saw with race, any idea that attributes such significance to the divisions between members of the human family opens the door to an inevitable danger. Human nature will insist upon ranking the groups thus created, and it will demand that one's own group come out on top. Within a generation, Herder's tolerant nationalism was transformed into an ugly chauvinism.

As this tolerance evaporated, the danger inherent in nationalism from the start quickly emerged. Herder had defined the nation narrowly, as a native group which had produced a distinctive culture by communing with its local landscape for centuries. But this definition excluded relative newcomers who did not share these ancient bonds of land and language. So fixed a concept of the nation had particularly dangerous implications for the largest ethnic minority in most European countries at the time: the Jews. There was simply no way for a Jew to assimilate into a nation thus defined.

~

IN THE NINETEENTH and early twentieth century, a massive wave of nationalism came crashing down over Europe. A multiplicity of ethnic groups began identifying themselves as nations and demanding the right to develop their national spirit free from outside interference. Efforts by these new nations to win their independence from the larger empires or states to which they belonged began to spark conflicts across the continent. The First World War was triggered when a Yugoslav nationalist named Gavrilo Princip assassinated Austria's Archduke Franz Ferdinand. At his trial, Princip shared his simple motive: "I am a Yugoslav nationalist, aiming for the unification of all Yugoslavs, and I do not care what form of state, but it must be free from Austria."[80]

After World War I, the victors decided that the solution to the problem of nationalism was not to fight it, but to fulfill it. These powers pursued the further division of Europe into smaller states to accommodate the many national groups now seeking independence. American president Woodrow Wilson became a particularly zealous advocate of the view that stability would come to Europe once each of Europe's peoples had their national aspirations satisfied through their own independent nation-state.

Yet while this nationalist program may have made sense in theory, the reality was far more complex. Settlement patterns in Europe were too intricate and intertwined to allow for neat national solutions. There would, inevitably, be some nations whose national aspirations would go unsatisfied. There would be other nations which would achieve their own states, but with borders that left millions of their people living as ethnic minorities in neighboring countries. Indeed, many of the new states created after the First World War contained significant German minorities within their borders. It was Hitler's efforts to unite these German minorities in a Greater Germany that sparked the Second World War.

In the case of Nazi Germany, nationalism and racism were mixed together in a lethal cocktail. With the Nazis, it is impossible to discern where romantic nationalism ended and racial supremacism began. They saw themselves as both a superior German nation and the vanguard of a supreme Aryan race. The Jews, by contrast, were reviled as the chief impediment to the full flowering of both German national genius and Aryan racial perfection.

The theories of race and nation were originally competing ideas. It did not take long before they were co-opted by evil men and transformed into two complementary rationales for genocide. While these theories may have differed on *how* men are divided, they agreed passionately that men *are* divided and that such divisions are of deep significance. No matter what their original intent, ideas that stress the importance of human divisions over our fundamental unity have opened the door to the worst of atrocities.

The Rise of Communism

Herder was by no means the only student of Kant to break with the master. Hegel's development of Kant's thought, and his frequent criticism of it, made him one of the most influential thinkers of his day. Yet while he criticized Kant, he did so from the position of one who had already embraced Kant's fundamental assumptions. As Bertrand Russell noted, Hegel's system "could never have arisen if Kant's had not existed."[61]

Hegel's interpretation of Kant was the philosophical launching point for Karl Marx. Marx began his intellectual life as part of a group called the "Young Hegelians," who espoused a left-leaning interpretation of their master's work. Marx later broke with the Young Hegelians and struck out on his own together with another young philosopher, Friedrich Engels.

Throughout his philosophical wanderings, Marx always accepted the Enlightenment's key assumptions. He believed passionately that the world operated according to a set of principles which would yield to rational analysis. He believed further that such scientific inquiry could unlock the secrets not only of the physical realm but also of the social realm. And Marx maintained, along with the most optimistic Enlightenment thinkers, that men could apply these insights to accomplish nothing less than the perfection of humanity.

More than most of his contemporaries, Marx embraced and extended the Enlightenment's universalism. Marx rejected nationalism. He believed that national differences were insignificant and would vanish under Communism. As he famously wrote in the *Communist Manifesto,* "The working men have no country." Marx likewise rejected racism. It is little wonder that so many Jews flocked to the ranks of the Communists. Few other political groups were prepared to even admit Jews, let alone recognize them as full equals.

Yet like Herder, Marx did not reject the divisions of humanity in favor of a true universalism. Marx, too, replaced these old divisions with new ones of his own making. For Marx, the divisions that mattered most were not those of race or nation but those of class.

As we have seen, Marx believed that humanity could be divided into two primary classes: the bourgeoisie who owned the factories and the proletariat who worked in them. Marx's class divisions were, from the start, hierarchical and highly charged. He championed the working class against the bourgeoisie, whom he viewed as the most evil of exploiters.

For Marx, the conflict between these two classes was the mechanism by which humanity would be perfected. The workers' inevitable triumph in this struggle was to be the historical pivot that would usher in a golden era free from poverty, injustice, and crime. Thus Marx believed that his great mission was not to avert this impending clash, but to accelerate it. Class conflict was not incidental to Marxism; class conflict was Marxism's beating heart.

The class conflict Marx sought was not merely a war of ideas. Marx's goal—and the goal of the Communist ideology he created—was to "wrest all capital from the bourgeoisie." In order for this to happen, the Communists would need to replace their capitalist-controlled governments with a "dictatorship of the proletariat." Marx did not hide his belief that this cherished end could only be achieved by force. He closed the *Communist Manifesto* with a clear call to arms:

> The Communists disdain to conceal their views and aims. They openly declare that their ends can be attained only by the forcible overthrow of all existing social conditions. Let the ruling class tremble at a Communistic revolution. The proletarians have nothing to lose but their chains. They have a world to win.[82]

〜

THE TWENTIETH CENTURY was, from start to finish, a century punctuated by genocide. The past century was truly without precedent when it comes to both the number of genocides and the vast death toll they left behind. Almost every one of these genocides was motivated by one or more of the modern ideologies of racism, nationalism, and Communism. It is bitterly ironic, yet unavoidably true, that the greatest atrocities in human history were fueled by these competing visions for the perfection of man.

The twentieth century's first genocide was perpetrated by the German army against the Herero and Nama peoples of the German colony of South West Africa. This bloodbath was motivated by a combination of nationalism and racism. The Turkish slaughter of the Armenians was largely a product of nationalism. The Nazi Holocaust was fueled by a toxic mixture of nationalism and racism. Stalin's genocide of the Ukrainian peasantry was driven by a combination of Communist class hatred and nationalism. Mao's genocide of China's peasants was primarily the product of Communist class hatred. Pol Pot's genocide of Cambodia's city dwellers was likewise fueled largely by Communist class hatred. The genocides that closed the century in the former Yugoslavia were driven mostly by Serbian nationalism.

Of all the twentieth century's widely acknowledged genocides, only the 1994 Rwandan genocide was not primarily the product of these modern ideologies. The Hutu ethnic hatred of Tutsis which fueled these massacres resembles, but predates, modern racism and nationalism. Yet even in this case, Western ideology—namely nationalism—played a supporting role. Hutus and Tutsis had lived independently of one another for centuries. Only when German and Belgian imperialists created the modern state of Rwanda were the fates of these two peoples suddenly intertwined. It is questionable whether the Hutus' hatred of the Tutsis would have boiled over into genocide had these rival tribes not been forced to share a country.

Hubris and Humility

If civilization is to be saved from the wreckage threatened by
intelligence not consecrated by love, it must be saved by the
moral code of the meek and lowly Nazarene.

—WILLIAM JENNINGS BRYAN, AMERICAN STATESMAN

P eople of deep Christian faith have emerged as the most
important constituency for human rights in our time.
They have protested totalitarian tyranny in North Korea
and religious persecution in China. They have fought genocide
in Sudan and the spread of AIDS throughout Africa. They have
led the effort to relieve the third world of its crushing debt burden. They have spearheaded a modern abolition movement to
end a resurgent slave trade.

These Christian activists have by no means labored alone.
People from other faiths and from dedicated secular organizations have joined in these efforts. Yet in each of these campaigns,
Christians have formed the vital core. They have provided the
leaders. They have mobilized an army of grassroots activists to
add political muscle to their high-minded rhetoric. They have
pushed otherwise stalled efforts to successful completion.

This modern Christian activism is neither new nor aberrant.
The Christians who today struggle against the oppression and suffering of their fellow human beings are not pioneers blazing a fresh
trail of compassion through a jungle of religious indifference. On

the contrary, these activists are marching down a broad boulevard cleared by the footsteps of Las Casas and Evarts, Wilberforce and Garrison, Clarkson and Weld, Martin Luther King and the SCLC, and the millions of Christians these leaders motivated to join them in action on behalf of the oppressed. Today's Christian activists are answering a call that has always issued loudly from their core texts and key prophets. They are drinking directly from the deep wells that have been the West's primary source of compassion and love.

Yet much of the West remains oblivious to the central humanitarian role that people of faith have played in our civilization. Say the words "evangelical Christian" in the capitals of Europe or the cities of America's coasts, and you are not likely to conjure up the image of a loving human rights activist. For too many people, serious Christians and others of deep religious faith are the source of human suffering, not its antidote.

⌣

YET ACTIVISM so prodigious and results so profound cannot be completely ignored. Some cracks are showing in this monolithic disdain of religious folk.

In 2002, Nicholas Kristof, a columnist for the *New York Times,* had the blinders removed from his eyes. That year he visited the Philippine island of Basilan, home of the violent Abu Sayyaf rebel group. Kristof learned that most humanitarian aid workers had left the island once it became clear that the rebels were targeting them along with the island's natives. The only group still busy providing food and medicine in this war zone was the Christian Children's Fund. "I've lost my cynicism about evangelical groups," Kristof later wrote, "because I've seen them at work abroad."[1]

Kristof is an exceptional man. He has seen the bodies of the murdered and the faces of the enslaved. He is determined to save lives and break chains. People possessed of such passion and urgency lose their patience for prejudice and put away the children's game of partisanship. The truth emerges suddenly, powerfully, as the only thing that matters. Through such a process, Kristof became one of the first and only journalists in America's mainstream media to recognize the key role that evangelical Christians are playing in the modern struggle for human rights.

Since this breakthrough, Kristof has repeatedly returned to the topic of Christian human rights activism. He noted in 2002 that "America's evangelicals have become the newest internationalists."[2] He later characterized this "wave of activity abroad by U.S. evangelicals" as "one of the most important—and welcome—trends in our foreign relations."[3] In 2005, Kristof observed that "the growing engagement of conservative Christians on international issues is welcome because for the first time it has turned the American heartland into a constituency for foreign aid and humanitarian action."[4]

～

NICHOLAS KRISTOF ACKNOWLEDGES that he was skeptical about evangelical Christians at home prior to observing their work abroad. He also recognizes that his cynicism was part of a broader prejudice that is still alive in America. In Kristof's words:

> Liberals believe deeply in tolerance and over the last century
> have led the battles against prejudices of all kinds, but we have
> a blind spot about Christian evangelicals. They constitute one
> of the few minorities that, on the American coasts or univer-
> sity campuses, it remains fashionable to mock.[5]

Elsewhere, Kristof notes more bluntly that "evangelicals are usually regarded by snooty, college-educated bicoastal elitists ... as dangerous Neanderthals."[6]

Kristof is right. The current discourse regarding evangelical Christians in America is poisoned by prejudice. The same bias often extends to orthodox Catholics and Jews and anyone of deep religious faith. It is not hard to find the source of this disdain. Unlike so many other modern hatreds, contempt for

America's evangelicals can be traced to a triggering event and a dominant prophet. The event was the Scopes Trial of 1925. And the prophet was journalist H. L. Mencken.

Hubris

In March 1925, the state of Tennessee passed the Butler Act, which made it unlawful for any state-funded school "to teach any theory that denies the Divine Creation of man as taught in the Bible, and to teach instead that man has descended from a lower order of animals." This law was an obvious effort to stop the teaching of evolution.

The Butler Act provoked an immediate response from the American Civil Liberties Union. The ACLU announced that it wanted to bring a lawsuit to challenge the Butler Act and would defend any teacher prosecuted thereunder. In Dayton, Tennessee, a group of prominent businessmen more interested in publicity for their small town than in the merits of the law resolved to bring a test case. They asked a local football coach and substitute teacher named John Scopes to step forward and force a prosecution. Scopes was not certain that he had ever actually taught evolution. But for the purposes of the legal challenge, he repeatedly claimed to have done so. He even encouraged his students to testify against him.[7]

If Dayton's elders wanted publicity for their hometown, they succeeded beyond their wildest dreams. The ACLU recruited one of America's most famous trial lawyers, Clarence Darrow, to defend Scopes. The prosecution recruited one of the nation's most prominent political leaders, William Jennings Bryan, to make the case against Scopes. In the midst of a July heat wave, these two legal titans clashed in the first American trial to be broadcast live on national radio.

The Scopes trial lasted just eight days. The court quickly rejected the constitutional challenge to the Butler Act. The court likewise blocked the defense's efforts to demonstrate that teaching evolution did not in fact violate the Butler Act's prohibition against denying "the Divine Creation of man as taught in the Bible." The only issue thus left before the trial court was whether Scopes had in fact taught evolution. This was a fact which Scopes readily admitted and which his defense team freely acknowledged. Hoping for an opportunity to address the larger issues on appeal, the defense joined the prosecution in asking the jury to return a guilty verdict. It took the jury only nine minutes to do so.*

Yet while the trial's focus quickly narrowed, the famous lawyers on each side could not resist the opportunity to opine on the broader debate over evolution and its implications that was then embroiling the country. The leading American journalists of the day—so many of whom were literally camped out in Dayton—hung on every word. Our understanding of the Scopes Trial today comes primarily from the way in which the media covered this largely extraneous debate.

Among those journalists sweating in Dayton that July was a reporter for the *Baltimore Sun* named H. L. Mencken. Although Mencken was already one of the most prominent journalists in America, his reports from Dayton would be among his most famous. More than those of any other reporter, Mencken's dispatches would define the Scopes Trial for millions of Americans far away from that small Tennessee town.

Far from approaching the trial with a journalistic detachment, Mencken arrived in Dayton a committed foe of evangelical Christianity in general, and of William Jennings Bryan in particular. For Mencken, the Scopes trial presented a golden opportunity to discredit both. He was determined to prove, in his words, that "evangelical Christianity is nonsense."[8] Conferring with the Scopes defense team before the trial, Mencken urged them to make the case "a headlong assault on Bryan." He

---

*The hopes of Darrow and the ACLU for a Supreme Court challenge were dashed when the Tennessee Supreme Court overturned Scopes's conviction on a technicality and never reached the constitutional issues.

suggested that they put Bryan on the witness stand so that they could "make a monkey of him before the world."[9]

Mencken succeeded in this larger mission to a greater extent than he could possibly have imagined. In his reporting during and shortly after the trial, he permanently blackened Bryan's reputation. At the same time, Mencken launched a stereotype of evangelical Christians that persists to this very day. The picture he painted of America's evangelicals bore little resemblance to reality. Yet this picture still hangs prominently in the mental corridors of millions of Americans.

～

MENCKEN SEEMS TO have had two chief complaints about evangelical Christians.* First, he claimed that they were ignorant. In an article bearing the not-so-subtle title "Evangelical Ignoramuses," Mencken set forth his not-so-subtle theory:

> What one mainly notices about these ambassadors of Christ, observing them in the mass, is their colossal ignorance. They constitute, perhaps, the most ignorant class of teachers ever set up to lead a civilized people; they are even more ignorant than the county superintendent of schools. Learning, indeed, is not esteemed in the evangelical denominations, and any literate plowhand, if the Holy Spirit inflames him, is thought to be fit to preach.[10]

This theme of evangelical ignorance was one to which Mencken repeatedly returned. In another memorable formulation, for example, Mencken wrote of evangelicals: "They are

---

*The Christians who most actively opposed the teaching of evolution are more accurately referred to as "fundamentalists" than "evangelicals." Yet the border between these two categories of Christian is often blurry at best. The fact is that the evangelical community largely merged into the fundamentalist community during this era, only to reemerge as something distinct years later. As Mencken's choice of words makes clear, critics of religion typically lump these two groups together. As a result, both groups suffer to this day from the stigma these critics created.

everywhere that learning is too heavy a burden for mortal minds, even the vague, pathetic learning on tap in the little red schoolhouses."[11]

When it came to evolution, Mencken simply refused to acknowledge that Darwin's theories raised any issues worthy of debate or concern. He therefore concluded that all who disagreed with him on the topic were simply unable to understand it. For Mencken, evangelical opposition to the teaching of evolution was nothing more than a disturbing symptom of the ignorance he had already diagnosed.

Yet Mencken did not limit his critique to the brains of evangelicals. His attack was far more radical; he also questioned their hearts. In Dayton, Mencken invented the idea that evangelical Christians are agents of intolerance. In Mencken's words: "Evangelical Christianity, as everyone knows, is founded upon hate."[12] Elsewhere, Mencken elaborated on this theme:

> In those parts of the Republic where Beelzebub is still as real as Babe Ruth or Dr. Coolidge, and men drink raw fuel oil hot from the still—for example, in the rural sections of the Middle West and everywhere in the South save a few walled towns— the evangelical sects plunge into an abyss of malignant imbecility, and declare a holy war upon every decency that civilized men cherish. First the Anti-Saloon League and now the Ku Klux Klan have converted them into vast machines for pursuing and butchering unbelievers. They have thrown the New Testament overboard, and gone back to the Old and particularly to the bloodiest parts of it. Their one aim seems to be to break heads, to spread terror, to propagate hatred. Everywhere they have set up enmities that will not die out for generations. Neighbors look askance at neighbor, the land is filled with spies, and every man of the slightest intelligence is suspect.[13]

Mencken's reference to the Ku Klux Klan was hardly a one-time rhetorical overreach. Just like the modern critics who equate religious Christians with the Taliban and al Qaeda,

Mencken repeatedly tried to tie them to the leading terrorists of his day.* Throughout his reporting from Dayton, Mencken refers to the local evangelicals as "Ku Klux Protestants," "Ku Klux Klergy," and "Ku Klux theologians."[14] Elsewhere Mencken claimed that "in every country town in America today the chief engine of the Klan is a clerk in holy orders."[15]

For Mencken, the evangelicals' most prominent personality, William Jennings Bryan, was the embodiment of all of their worst traits. "He seemed only a poor clod like those around him," Mencken wrote of Bryan, "deluded by a childish theology, full of an almost pathological hatred of all learning, all human dignity, all beauty, all fine and noble things."[16] Over and over, Mencken narrowed his target from evangelicals in general to their outspoken leader, Bryan. In pursuing his goal of slaying the evangelicals, Mencken's primary strategy was decapitation.

By the time Mencken was done, the transformation was complete. The seed of a powerful stereotype had been planted in the minds of millions of Americans. Despite their passion for opening schools and colleges, evangelicals were now champions of ignorance. Despite their compelling record of humanitarian activism, evangelicals were now apostles of hate. And despite so much current evidence to the contrary, these stereotypes live on in the minds of Mencken's heirs in the media and their readers.

～

MENCKEN DID NOT uncover truth in Dayton; he obscured it. His reporting did not provide insight; it launched stereotype.

---

*It is a sad testament to the lingering influence of Mencken's stereotypes that this footnote is necessary, but it is important to note that evangelical Christians played no such role in the Klan. Dismissing such "Mencken-like assumptions," scholars such as Leonard Moore have demonstrated that the Klan of the 1920s represented "a wide cross section of society" and that "their religious affiliations mirrored the whole of white Protestant society, including those who did not belong to any church." See Leonard J. Moore, *Citizen Klansmen* (Chapel Hill: The University of North Carolina Press, 1991).

Mencken took a nuanced issue and painted it in black and white. In the process, he became the very demagogue he sought to denounce.

The actual William Jennings Bryan bore little resemblance to Mencken's caricature. By the time he arrived in Dayton, Bryan had been a congressman, the Democratic Party's nominee for president on three separate occasions, and President Woodrow Wilson's secretary of state. Bryan was a spellbinding orator and a cautious elder statesman, a devout evangelical Christian and a devoted progressive. Most of the major reforms he championed eventually became the law of the land. More than most historical figures, Bryan defies stereotype.

Like so many evangelical leaders before him, Bryan devoted his career to lifting the downtrodden. For Bryan, those most in need of Christian love and justice were the poor "dirt" farmers of America's heartland and the masses of impoverished workers in the rapidly growing cities. In his analysis of their worsening plight, Bryan identified a clear culprit: the laissez-faire economics of the Gilded Age. He believed that as the titans of industry and finance acquired unprecedented wealth and power, they were using it to exploit the lower classes. Bryan was therefore among the first national leaders to call for a larger federal government with sufficient strength to confront these oligarchs.[17]

Bryan supported labor unions, collective bargaining, and a minimum wage for urban workers. He promoted subsidies and guaranteed minimum prices for farmers. Bryan played a pivotal role in securing passage of the constitutional amendments that gave the vote to women, permitted the imposition of an income tax, and established the direct election of senators. Bryan was not only a progressive, he was in many ways *the* progressive.

When it came to foreign policy, Bryan resisted war to the point of pacifism. He accepted the position of secretary of state in 1913 only after President Wilson agreed to let him continue pursuing his grand project for international peace. Since 1905, Bryan had been promoting a multilateral peace treaty which would require the submission of all international disputes to a permanent tribunal for investigation and resolution. By 1915, Bryan had convinced thirty nations to sign the treaty. The signatories included every major world power with the exception of Germany, Austria-Hungary, and Japan.[18]

Despite the outbreak of World War I in 1915, Bryan continued to promote his treaty scheme. He also worked diligently to keep the United States out of the war. When German U-boats began firing upon American vessels at sea, Bryan called upon America to "exercise Christian forbearance."[19] Yet President Wilson ignored his counsel and responded to these provocations with escalating action and rhetoric. Bryan resigned as secretary of state in the summer of 1915 to protest policies that he believed would inevitably draw America into the conflict. On April 6, 1917, the United States declared war on Germany.

～

SHORTLY AFTER THE turn of the century, William Jennings Bryan declared that while he did not believe in evolution, he had no "quarrel" with those who did.[20] Up until World War I, he largely ignored the topic.

As time passed, however, Bryan began to see mounting evidence that the teaching of evolution had some troubling repercussions. Bryan had devoted his life to lifting society's poor and weak. Yet the rich and powerful were now invoking social Darwinism and "the survival of the fittest" in their fight against progressive reforms. Bryan abhorred war. Yet when he studied the German militarists who helped to spark World War I, he traced their glorification of strength and battle to Darwin by way of Nietzsche. Bryan treasured human life. Yet many of Darwin's leading disciples were applying his ideas to promote the practice of eugenics.[21]

Bryan never expressed much concern about the *science* of evolution. Yet he grew increasingly alarmed by the *philosophy* of social Darwinism, which sought to apply this theory about prehistoric nature to contemporary social problems. Bryan was explicit about the fact that his primary concern about evolution was not that "it is not true." Instead, he stressed, "the principal objection to evolution is that it is highly harmful to those who accept it."[22] In 1916, Bryan warned that:

> we must be careful how we apply this doctrine of the strongest, for I have found ... that the evolutionary theory has been consciously or unconsciously absorbed in a way which has a tendency to paralyze the conscience. Whether men know it or not, they have permitted it to become antagonistic to the principles of Christianity which make the strongest the servants of humanity, not its oppressors.[23]

It was for these reasons that Bryan objected to teaching evolution to children in public schools *as fact*.[24] Bryan never opposed the teaching of evolution as a theory. Bryan also recognized, moreover, that his objections would have to yield when and if "more conclusive proof is produced" in support of Darwin's theories.[25] Bryan never suggested that the Bible or Creationism be taught in the public schools.*

Finally, those who criticize Bryan for supporting a bill as clearly unconstitutional as the Butler Act would benefit from a refresher course in constitutional law. The Butler Act certainly runs afoul of the Establishment Clause of the First Amendment, which prohibits laws "respecting an establishment of religion." Yet it was not until twenty-two years *after* the Scopes Trial that the Supreme Court first ruled that the Establishment Clause applies

---

*Bryan's primary objection to the science of evolution involved Darwin's thesis that natural selection was the mechanism driving evolution. In Bryan's day, the scientific community had not yet formed a consensus in support of natural selection. Bryan accurately assessed the reality, if not the direction, of this debate when he wrote in a 1922 *New York Times* article that "natural selection is being increasingly discredited by scientists." As Nicholas Wade noted in 2009, "Biologists quickly accepted the idea of evolution, but for decades they rejected natural selection." (Nicholas Wade, "Darwin, Ahead of His Time, Is Still Influential," *New York Times*, February 10, 2009)

to laws passed by the states. Up until that point, the Court had maintained that the Establishment Clause applied only to laws passed by "Congress," as its plain language specified. In Bryan's day, therefore, the opponents of the Butler Act were the ones who labored against the prevailing First Amendment jurisprudence.

〜

WITH THE BENEFIT of our extensive hindsight, we can see that Bryan exaggerated the threat. The teaching of evolution does not necessarily lead to the embrace of social Darwinism, the rise of militarism, or the legitimization of eugenics. There is some traction on that slope.

Yet even from our secure perch, we can surely acknowledge that the situation must have looked very different indeed back in 1925. In the 1920s, many of the most prominent proponents of evolution had yet to recognize the moral limits of its application. This was an era when social Darwinism was enjoying increasing legitimacy. Equally influential was German philosopher Friedrich Nietzsche, who rejected Christian love in favor of an ethic which celebrated the strong and anticipated the elimination of the "weak" and the "botched." And eugenics was experiencing a steady rise in popularity. Two years after the Scopes trial, in 1927, the United States Supreme Court upheld Virginia's eugenics statute. It was during the 1920s and early 1930s that twenty-nine states passed statutes authorizing the forced sterilization of those deemed unfit to reproduce.

Further blurring these distinctions was the fact that the leading proponents of evolution were typically the ones stressing the connection between Darwin's theory and its more noxious progeny. While Darwin never used the term "survival of the fittest" and never directly applied his ideas to social policy, some of his most zealous acolytes developed and promoted social Darwinism. It was Darwin's cousin and disciple, Francis Galton, who proposed eugenics as a means to accelerate the genetic benefits of evolution. Darwin's son Leonard later became president of the Eugenics Education Society.

The belief that the theory of evolution justified social Darwinism and eugenics was so widespread at the time that even school textbooks accepted it. In fact, the very textbook that John Scopes had allegedly used to teach his students about evolution also promoted eugenics. In *A Civic Biology,* George W. Hunter wrote the following about people who suffered from deficiencies such as being "feeble-minded," "drunkards," "epileptic," or "sexually immoral":

> If such people were lower animals, we would probably kill them off to prevent them from spreading. Humanity will not allow this, but we do have the remedy of separating the sexes in asylums or other places and in various ways preventing intermarriage and the possibilities of perpetuating such a low and degenerate race. Remedies of this sort have been tried successfully in Europe and are now meeting with success in this country.[26]

A Civic Biology was the era's best-selling biology text. Far from banning it, Tennessee had made Hunter's book the official biology textbook of the state's public schools.*[27] And Hunter was far from the only leading biologist to make this connection between evolution and eugenics.

Bryan was absolutely right to object to the teaching of such repugnant ideas in the public schools. He was wrong only in agreeing with the primary proponents of evolution that these ideas were the inevitable offspring of Darwin's theory.

❧

---

*The fact that the state of Tennessee endorsed a biology text that taught evolution and then passed a law banning the teaching of evolution was one of the great ironies of the controversy surrounding the Butler Act and the Scopes Trial.

FINALLY, BEFORE WE criticize Bryan for his position in 1925, it is important to recognize that in the near term his warnings were not exaggerated, but prescient. Yes, today most proponents of evolution better recognize the ethical boundaries of its application. But as we have seen, neither science nor society immediately appreciated these boundaries, and they did not come to recognize them through the power of reason alone. The West began to respect the safe outer limits of evolutionary thinking only after suffering the tragic repercussions of excess. Bryan may not have foreseen our present calm, but unlike so many of his contemporaries he was able to spot the storms on the horizon.

The Scopes trial ended before Bryan was able to give his closing argument. Yet the text survives, and parts of it sound very much like the warnings that Albert Einstein and others would later issue after unleashing the atomic bomb. "Unless the development of morality catches up with the development of technique," Bryan warned, "humanity is bound to destroy itself."[28] Elsewhere, Bryan struck a more Christian chord when he asserted, "If civilization is to be saved from the wreckage threatened by intelligence not consecrated by love, it must be saved by the moral code of the meek and lowly Nazarene."[29]

It is doubtful that Bryan ever heard of Adolf Hitler. But Bryan could see very clearly that many of his contemporaries were treading a dangerous path that led from Darwinism to social Darwinism to Nietzsche and beyond. The point is not that Darwin and Nietzsche made Hitler inevitable; they did not. Nor is it the point that Hitler correctly interpreted and applied the ideas of these two thinkers; he did not. The point is simply that, right or not, the Nazis and their ideological forebears were blazing this ideological trail. Bryan not only recognized that this effort was underway, but he was able to accurately predict where it would lead.

H. L. Mencken, meanwhile, consistently and cavalierly downplayed the threat Hitler posed. After Hitler rose to power in 1933, Mencken dismissed him as a "clown" and even joked that "a man who wears a Charlie Chaplin moustache can't be altogether bad."[30] Mencken was certainly not the only one to underestimate the Nazi threat in these early years. But as the evidence of Hitler's militarism and anti-Semitism mounted, he found himself increasingly alone. Even a 1938 visit to the heart of Nazi Germany did not rouse Mencken from his relatively benign view of the Nazi regime.[31] About the worst thing Mencken ever said about Hitler was to compare his speeches to those of a Klansman, and to predict that he would eventually fall from power like other populists such as William Jennings Bryan.[32]

When it came to evolution, Bryan certainly grasped the theory. He could see everything Mencken saw. The difference is that Bryan was looking past Mencken, seeing the danger that lay ahead around the bend. When it came to the tragedies that would unfold over the course of the next twenty years, Bryan was far more prescient than Mencken. We should, perhaps, forgive Bryan for not seeing even further into the future, to our present sobriety about the implications of evolution. Exactly how far down the arc of history can we expect a man to see?

The Evangelical Retreat and Return

For America's evangelicals, the Scopes Trial was no mere public relations failure. It was a historic turning point. As historian George Marsden has noted, "It would be difficult to overestimate the impact of 'the Monkey Trial' at Dayton, Tennessee, in transforming fundamentalism."[33] The myths Mencken created certainly changed the way the secular world viewed evangelicals. But they also changed the way evangelicals viewed the secular world.

Ever since the founding of the American Republic, evangelicals had played a prominent role in the public square. Time after time, decade after decade, they took their values out of their churches and sought to influence the culture and the country. From the campaign to end the ethnic cleansing of the Indians, through the abolition movement, and right up to Bryan's fight for a minimum wage, evangelical activism was typically at the cutting edge of American policy.

After the Scopes Trial, this prodigious activism came to an abrupt halt. In the face of massive rejection and widespread derision, evangelicals abandoned the public square. They retreated into their churches and schools and narrowed their focus to questions of personal salvation. Having lost confidence in their ability to change the culture, they grew fearful that the culture would change them. By the close of the 1920s, evangelicals had largely gone underground.

In some respects, the process of turning inward had been underway for some time. In the years leading up to the Scopes Trial, evangelicals had lost a number of doctrinal battles at the denominational and church levels. One of their largest public policy victories, the prohibition of alcoholic beverages, was rapidly unraveling. Yet the fallout from the Scopes trial accelerated this withdrawal and gave it a generational duration.

Magnifying its impact, the Scopes trial left evangelicals without a national leader. William Jennings Bryan died twice in Dayton. Five days after the trial's end, before he had even left town, Bryan died in his sleep during an afternoon nap. Upon hearing the news of Bryan's passing, Mencken gloated, "We killed the son-of-a-bitch!"[34] The three merciless obituaries Mencken wrote, combined with his prior reporting from Dayton, ensured that Bryan's reputation died along with his body.

Bryan was by far the leading evangelical politician of his day. In fact, he may well have been the most influential of the long line of evangelical politicians and activists who had played so central a role in American politics since before the birth of the Republic. Although he never won a presidential election, Bryan did win a series of legislative and policy battles through which he brought his Christian values to bear on public policy. When Bryan died in Dayton, so did the tradition of evangelical political activism that he embodied.

∼

FOR THE NEXT five decades, evangelicals shunned politics. Even in the mid-1960s, the two leaders most commonly associated with the resurgence of evangelical political activism—Jerry Falwell and Pat Robertson—were still deeply committed to eschewing the public square. During the 1960s, Falwell later reflected, he witnessed "millions of people" taking public stands on a host of issues, some of which he favored and many of which he opposed. Yet he steadfastly refused to "carry a sign" or "march for or against any issue." Instead he preached that "the government could be trusted to correct its own ills."[35] The best way for Christians to change society, Falwell argued, was to study the Bible, preach the Gospel, and build Christian churches and schools.[36]

As late as 1965, Jerry Falwell was outspoken in his condemnation of his fellow clergy who engaged in political activism, including the civil rights movement:

> Believing the Bible as I do, I would find it impossible to stop preaching the pure saving gospel of Jesus Christ and begin doing anything else—including the fighting of communism, or participating in civil rights reforms.... Preachers are not called to be politicians but to be soul winners.... Nowhere are we commissioned to reform the externals. The gospel does not clean up the outside but rather regenerates the inside.[37]

Pat Robertson took this view to an extreme. When his father, Virginia senator A. Willis Robertson, was running for reelection in 1966, Pat "yearned" to go to work on his behalf. But he felt that he lacked divine sanction to do so. Robertson believed that God had called him to a ministry that was more important than "the success of any political candidate"—including his own father.[38] Pat Robertson sat out the election. Senator Robertson was defeated in one of the great upsets of the 1966 campaign.

～

BY THE END of the 1970s, Falwell had completely changed his views. He had come to believe that Christians had an obligation to seek to shape the nation's politics and policies. When he founded the Moral Majority in 1979, he officially ended the evangelical retreat from politics.

As evangelicals burst onto the political scene in the early 1980s, most observers believed that they were witnessing an entirely new phenomenon. This was, after all, the first time in their lives that evangelicals were playing so active a political role. But this activism was no innovation; it was a continuation. As evangelical scholar Mark Noll has observed:

> With the New Christian Right, we have returned, mutatis mutandis, to William Jennings Bryan. . . . Injustice to the unborn replaced injustice to debtors, but campaigns for at least some classes of unrepresented oppressed were nonetheless again respected as Christian service. Although the political party of choice for restoring Christian morality was now the GOP, evangelicals beyond doubt had returned to the fray.[29]

The Christian Right was picking up where Bryan had left off. Yet, as Noll notes, the intervening half-century had shuffled the policy agenda. Now, abortion was legal in every state in the union. Prayer was no longer allowed in the public schools. Social norms that had long been taken for granted were being challenged and overturned. Many evangelicals were determined to restore them.

In seeking to reverse these trends, evangelicals were simply resuming their traditional focus on social issues. In addition, they were seeking to reassert the compassion that had defined their activism from the start. Especially when it came to their top priority—abortion—evangelicals believed that they were once again taking a bold stand for society's weakest.

Yet the terms of the abortion debate tended to obscure this underlying continuity. In their past campaigns, evangelicals had confronted slaveholders and robber barons who asserted a set of dubious property rights in the face of glaring oppression and poverty. Now, evangelicals were challenging what a far larger segment of society believed to be among their most fundamental rights. At the same time, the victims at issue—human fetuses—were not as readily apparent to those outside the church. What evangelicals believed to be a brave defense of the weak was perceived by their opponents as a fierce assault on the free.

Not only did the Christian Right pursue a new set of issues, but it often did so with a changed tone. Evangelicals had not chosen to retire from politics; they were hounded out by opponents devoted to their demise. Their return to politics fifty years later was likewise largely a response to external pressures. It was only the conclusion that their most cherished values were under assault that led evangelicals to abandon the safety of their isolation and reenter the public square. Thus when evangelicals returned to politics in the late 1970s, they did so with a literal vengeance. They rose out of a defensive crouch. They had their fists up.

Under these circumstances, the tone some Christian leaders struck was too often angry. The Religious Right began the evangelical march back into politics by stressing themes that at times poorly matched their core values and proud history. Evangelicals had appealed to government to save the Indians and the slaves and the poor. Now government was dismissed as the enemy. Evangelicals had consistently emphasized the compassion driving their efforts. Now they too often pursued their agenda with harsh words manifesting little love. The difference between the new evangelical activism and the old typically had more to do with style and emphasis than with underlying values. But to a public expecting Mencken's caricature, these new activists often appeared to fit the script.

Following Mencken's lead, the media often magnified any missteps these Christian leaders made. While their most unfortunate comments were repeated in an endless loop, their apologies for such comments, along with the rest of their careers, were largely ignored. Few ever learned, for example, that Pat Robertson began his career working with the poor of Bedford-Stuyvesant. Few have reported that the charity Robertson founded, Operation Blessing, has provided more than $1.7 billion in food and humanitarian aid in over 105 countries around the world.[40] Like so many of his colleagues, Robertson has been defined by his most controversial words, not by his daily deeds.

⁓

IT IS GETTING INCREASINGLY difficult to maintain such stereotypes. In recent years, there has been an undeniable shift in the evangelicals' tone. Their initial anger has largely faded. As evangelicals have matured in their renewed activism and gained confidence in their restored power, they have grown less defensive. They are once again stressing the love and compassion at their core.

Not only have evangelical activists softened their tone, but they have broadened their agenda. This is no longer a constituency which focuses solely on the issues of abortion and gay marriage. Evangelical activists are once again speaking up for the widow, the orphan, and the poor. In recent years, they have undertaken historic campaigns to fight modern slavery, end modern genocide, and treat modern disease. These efforts more clearly parallel the historic Christian campaigns to confront these ancient evils. In both tone and agenda, evangelical activists have returned to the status quo ante-Scopes.

As the Christian Right has broadened its focus, it has also ceased to speak for all evangelicals in politics. There is now a robust evangelical left devoted to the issues of poverty and social justice that typically aligns more closely with the Democratic Party than with the Republicans. There is also an emerging evangelical center seeking to transcend partisanship altogether. This new breed of nonpartisan evangelical is exemplified by activists such as Bono who go to great lengths to appeal to the core values shared on both sides of the aisle.

Yet while the Christian activists have been changing, many in the media have not. They still cling bitterly to the stereotype created by Mencken. They still report only those words or actions which confirm, or can be twisted into confirming, their preconceived notions. They still invoke the Crusades, the Inquisition, and the Scopes Trial as all the proof they will ever need that no good can come from religion. When a suicide bomber kills in the name of Islam, their contempt for believing Christians and Jews somehow grows.

Humility

Writing in early 2008, Nicholas Kristof observed:

> In parts of Africa where bandits and warlords shoot or rape anything that moves, you often find that the only groups still operating are Doctors Without Borders and religious aid workers: crazy doctors and crazy Christians.[41]

Kristof is right. But he is underestimating the number of "crazy Christians." His two categories of humanitarian zealot are not mutually exclusive.

Doctors Without Borders is a relief organization dedicated to providing emergency medical care to the victims of war and disaster. The organization was founded by Bernard Kouchner, a French doctor and political activist who became France's foreign minister in 2007. Kouchner came of age as a Communist student activist in the 1960s, and he rose in French politics as a stalwart of the left. He is a purely secular humanist.

Yet as time passed, Kouchner noticed that the people on the front lines with him on his medical missions, the people risking their lives for others, did not much resemble him or his fellow travelers back in the cafés of Paris. Kouchner shared this observation in the course of a 2003 debate with Daniel Cohn-Bendit, another student radical turned left-wing politician. Author Paul Berman relates what transpired:

Kouchner noticed that most people toiling at his side in one dangerous mission after another over the years came from backgrounds of a rather different sort. And what were these very different backgrounds? They were religious.

But, having made this observation, Kouchner had nothing else to say, and neither did Cohn-Bendit—quite as if the two of them, in contemplating the humanitarian enthusiasm of people from religious backgrounds, had tiptoed to the edge of their political understandings, and could only pause and wonder about what might lie beyond. For what exactly is the urge that leads some people, and not others, to devote themselves to the cause of the oppressed in faraway places, and to push aside the many sophisticated arguments that may stand in the way of doing so, and to risk their own necks? What is the inner force, the pressure, that prompts some people to commit themselves to this kind of life? There is a left-wing answer to this question, but there are other answers, too, and Kouchner and Cohn-Bendit, for all their experience and virtues and courage, were not the right men to come up with those answers.[42]

～

THE STAKES ARE too high for ignorance. The challenges are too urgent for prejudice. Lives are on the line. We need to transcend our egos and insecurities to seek an honest answer to this question. What is it, indeed, that leads some people to transcend their selfish genes and, as Berman asks, "devote themselves to the cause of the oppressed in faraway places"? What can motivate a man to, in the words of the Bible, "lay down his life for his friends"? What are the sources of a love so large that it can motivate action on behalf of strangers down the street or across an ocean? This is the question at the heart of this book.

There is no one explanation for altruism. Human behavior is too complex to lend itself to absolute rules. Every activist brings his or her own personal experience to the table. Yet any objective analysis of humanitarian action throughout the recent centuries reveals certain significant patterns.

Very often, people have compassion thrust upon them. When we or a loved one endure an ordeal or a loss, we are suddenly filled with sympathy for those who experience the same particular pain. Our fellow sufferers become, in a sense, part of our ingroup. And out of this identification sometimes comes action.

Kouchner and Cohn-Bendit are perfect examples of this phenomenon. Both men were born shortly before World War II, and both spent their childhoods fleeing from the Nazis with their Jewish parents. Both of them emerged from this experience with a passionately dualistic view of human morality. Each saw the world as sharply divided between those who resisted the Nazis and those who, through their deeds or inaction, collaborated with them. And by their own admission, each continues to divide the world along similar lines down to the present day. They judge character, including their own, on the basis of whether one resists oppression or collaborates with it. Since their youth, both have dedicated themselves to resisting oppression with a passion that made them famous student leaders and then famous politicians.[43]

Yet the struggle for human rights cannot rely solely on victims and their families. If the only abolitionists had been former slaves, abolition would have remained a marginal movement. If the only people seeking to relieve Africa of its debts were the Africans themselves, these loans would never have been forgiven. Such humanitarian campaigns will only succeed if enough people find a way to rise above their selfish genes and feel the pain of others without having to first experience that pain themselves. We need a powerful ethic of compassion that can be more easily taught and more widely disseminated.

In Western civilization, the Judeo-Christian tradition has been the primary source of such transcendent love. The Judeo-Christian idea of the sanctity and equality of all humans has enabled people to recognize the suffering of their fellow man, no matter how different or distant. The Judeo-Christian commandment to love our neighbors as ourselves has, even more importantly, motivated prodigious action to end this suffering. More than any other Western concept or teaching, the Judeo-Christian idea has empowered people to overcome their impoverished genetic morality and act on behalf of their brothers and sisters.

Kouchner and Cohn-Bendit have proven to be exceptional. At one time, they led veritable student armies and electrified massive crowds. But while their ideology could motivate protests and passion from students pursuing their self-interest, it failed to instill in them a bigger love. These two men have remained active their whole lives because they possess a passion forged by personal suffering. Yet most of their followers faded away once the cause shifted from their own needs to those of others. What Kouchner and Cohn-Bendit may well have recognized during their debate was the sterility of their compassion. It has produced no offspring.

Humility for Believers

Given the consistent and inspiring record of humanitarian action detailed in these pages, people of faith have much to be proud of. Yet while pride may be justified, it is not recommended. When you seek to walk in the footsteps of giants, humility is a far more reliable guide. Living up to the legacy of the likes of Las Casas, Wilberforce, and King requires more than a passionate embrace of the Judeo-Christian idea. Rising to such heights also demands the heartbreaking recognition of the fact that no matter how noble this ethic may be, we who seek to implement it remain deeply and unalterably flawed.

The heroes honored in this book were exceptional in the literal sense of that word. Almost all of their contemporaries—including most of their fellow believers—were unable to attain such truly disinterested benevolence. To varying degrees, they remained captives of their selfish genes and evil inclinations.

Religious Christians were the only people who recognized the humanity of the American Indians and fought to stop their genocide and ethnic cleansing. Yet the large majority of European settlers in America proved themselves to be Christian in name only as they watched a people disappear. Almost all of the abolitionists in Britain and America were religious Christians. Yet the majority of their countrymen demonstrated the blind spots of their faith by allowing slavery to thrive for centuries. Many of the righteous gentiles who risked their lives to save Jews from the Holocaust did so out of a deep Christian faith. Yet the majority of Europe's churches were silent throughout this long night of murder.

History teaches that religion enables, but by no means guarantees, heroic benevolence. Those who study the Bible, go to church, and pray to God must have the humility not to confuse such efforts with accomplishments. These activities are indicia of a journey, not heralds of an arrival.

Apathy toward those outside of our ingroup remains the overwhelming rule. And there are dangers greater than inaction. People of faith must also guard against misdirected zeal. Better to shutter our windows against our neighbor's screams than to be the ones wielding the sword against them.

For centuries, Christians preached the dangerous doctrines that the Jews in every generation were responsible for killing Jesus and that God had rejected the Jewish people. Christian Inquisitors condemned heretics to death, and Christian Crusaders killed innocents in the name of their faith. Here in America, millions of Christians twisted the Bible into an apology for slavery. Even today, zeal for God's word sometimes overwhelms compassion for God's creatures.

Even a cursory review of history demonstrates that faith does not always triumph over the evil impulse; sometimes faith is co-opted. In human hands, even the noblest of ideals can be twisted into tools for promoting our worst instincts instead of transcending them. Humility and introspection must be the constant companions of faith.

Secular opponents have often been angry and dishonest in their critique of faith. In their effort to denigrate what they do not possess and rarely understand, they have turned rules into exceptions and exceptions into rules. In the face of such ugly attacks, it is enormously tempting to retreat into defensiveness and self-righteousness. But our faith demands better. We must humbly vindicate our values though our actions. We must love our neighbors. And yes, we must love our enemies.

Humility for Skeptics

The record of the Judeo-Christian idea in motivating people to humanitarian action also holds important lessons for the secular community. While the rejection of religious faith is now commonplace, it is hardly an accomplishment. There is little reason why such skepticism should be the source of the enormous pride it so often generates among so many non-believers.

When it comes to what really matters—action on behalf of our fellow human beings—history should teach humility to the secular. As they have abandoned the core Judeo-Christian morality, secular folk have repeatedly embraced dangerous new ideas which challenge the sanctity and equality of all humans. Acting on these ideas has led to the greatest atrocities in history.

In addition to the problem of secular ideas, there remains a problem of secular action. As Charles Marsh has observed, "It is unlikely that anyone has ever read Friedrich Nietzsche's *Thus Spake Zarathustra* or Jacques Derrida's *Disseminations* and opened a soup kitchen."[44] Secular philosophy has yet to demonstrate an ability to motivate and sustain true disinterested benevolence.

Despite so many angry arguments to the contrary, the absence of faith need not be a barrier to embracing the rich moral insights of the Judeo-Christian idea. Even the most hardened atheist can still engage with the Judeo-Christian tradition, study its foundational documents, and take inspiration from its most noble exemplars. We can recognize that our culture's core morality is built on the foundation of this religious tradition. And in acknowledging the ultimate source of the values most of us still hold dear, we can seek to preserve what is best in our culture rather than hack away at the pillars upon which it stands.

Western civilization has been fed by two mighty sources, one flowing from Athens and the other from Jerusalem. When it comes to Athens, we have been good at recognizing our intellectual debt. We no longer believe that Zeus sits on Mount Olympus and sends thunderbolts crashing down to terrorize the mortals living below. Yet we study the classics written by those who believed in Zeus in recognition of their profound wisdom and ongoing relevance. There is no reason why we shouldn't apply a similar standard to Jerusalem. Even if we don't believe in the God of Abraham, Isaac, and Jacob, there are critical lessons we can and should learn from the books written by those who did.

Nor should our respect be limited to the texts at the heart of the Judeo-Christian tradition. It can and should extend to the people who sincerely strive to live in accordance with the high ideals of these texts. As we've seen, the people most closely connected to the Judeo-Christian tradition—people of religious faith—have consistently been the people who have taken the tradition's moral code most seriously and have acted on this morality most passionately. In so doing, they have injected this morality back into our culture-stream. Books alone cannot keep values alive. Unless we and our neighbors continue to live by them, these values will cease to be the signposts of a living culture and will become merely the artifacts of an ancient one.

When activists like Las Casas and Evarts fought for the humanity of the Indian, they bore witness to their contemporaries of the sanctity of all humans. When abolitionists like Wilberforce and Garrison preached against slavery, they reminded their fellow citizens of the equality of all men. When Martin Luther King spoke about loving our brothers, he made Christian love real for an entire generation. Whether we realize it or not, heroes like these have a profound impact on the broader culture; they turn the Bible's values into our values.

For those who simply cannot bring themselves to study the Bible or respect the faithful, there is one final recourse: Do no harm. Yes, there is much hypocrisy in religion—and elsewhere—that we can rightfully criticize. Yes, the faithful—and all of us—fall short of the ideals we cherish in myriad ways. But when we go beyond such valid critiques and take an axe to the entire moral foundation upon which our culture is built, we court collapse. When we insist that "religion poisons everything," we end up poisoning the very source of the morality upon which our critique is based.

It is tempting indeed to assume that the morality at the heart of the Judeo-Christian tradition is so easy or obvious that we need not protect its sources and preserve its foundations. Yet such a view stands in sharp contrast to overwhelming evidence to the contrary. If the twentieth century proved one thing, it is the rapidity with which a society's morality can shift and plummet. The experiments have already been conducted, and the price has already been paid. We should at least have the decency to learn the lessons.

The challenge of maintaining our morality is one we can ill afford to ignore or oversimplify. Our morality is not perennial. To paraphrase Thomas Jefferson, the tree of virtue must be constantly refreshed. Thankfully, it does not take the blood of martyrs to do so. The love of the faithful and the respect of the secular is enough.

Who Will Lie Across the Tracks?

During World War II, the German industrialist Oskar Schindler saved approximately twelve hundred Jews from the Nazi death camps. Thousands of ordinary Danes participated in a boatlift that ferried Denmark's approximately seven thousand Jews to safety in neutral Sweden. But the most successful effort to save

Jews from Hitler's grasp, in terms of sheer numbers, is far less well known. It was the rescue of the Bulgarian Jewish community.

Toward the end of the war, the Nazis ordered their collaborators in Bulgaria to transport the nation's Jews to the death camps. The Bulgarians obeyed and organized the first trainloads of Jews for deportation. In Plovdiv, Bulgaria's second-largest city, the authorities rounded up hundreds of Jews and held them overnight in a schoolyard near the train station until they received instructions to load the trains.

When Kyril, the metropolitan (bishop) of Plovdiv, heard the news, he sent urgent telegrams to the Bulgarian king and other leaders demanding that they rescind the deportation order. But then Kyril did something even more impressive. He ran down to the train station, where he learned that the Jews were still being held in the schoolyard. The metropolitan warned the police and the rail workers that if a train loaded with Jews tried to leave the city, he would stop it by lying across the railroad tracks.[45]

Metropolitan Kyril proceeded to the school where the Jews were being held. An army officer tried to bar his entrance. "I cannot enter?" the metropolitan asked. "Try to stop me!" He then climbed the fence, entered the school yard, and addressed the Jews who crowded around him. Echoing the stirring biblical words of Ruth, Kyril told the frightened crowd, "Wherever you go, I'll go."[46]

Metropolitan Kyril was not the only Bulgarian hero to emerge at this critical juncture. Metropolitan Stefan of Sofia launched an emergency campaign to stop the deportation, and all of the Bulgarian church's remaining metropolitans gave him their full support. A member of the Bulgarian parliament named Dimitar Peshev was likewise tireless in his efforts to save his country's Jews. Together, these Bulgarians accomplished a rare humanitarian feat. They created political pressure at home sufficient to outweigh Nazi demands from abroad. As a result, not one Jew was deported from Bulgaria proper. The entire Bulgarian Jewish community of fifty thousand survived the war.

◠

UNTIL HIS DEATH in 2008, Tom Lantos was the only Holocaust survivor to serve in the United States Congress. Lantos was one of the many congressmen who worked closely with Irish rock star Bono in the effort to combat the African AIDS epidemic. As the two were talking one day, Lantos shared with Bono his memories of the day the Nazis forced him and his siblings onto the train that would take them from their homes in Budapest to the death camps. What stuck in Lantos's mind was not the cruelty of the soldiers, but the apathy of his neighbors. He was haunted by the fact that the citizens of Budapest crowded around the trains not to stop them, but simply to watch. "Didn't anyone ask where those children are going?"[47] Lantos asked Bono so many years later.

Lantos's question provided Bono with the central metaphor in his campaign to save the thousands of Africans who die daily from disease and poverty. He warns audience after audience that if they do not do something to stop this massive death toll, "we will be that generation that watched our African brothers and sisters being put on the trains."[48] Bono has embraced one clear and simple mission: "I want to find people who will lie across the tracks."[49]

This is the ultimate question and the only test that matters. Where do we find people who will lie across the tracks? What motivated Metropolitan Kyril to threaten this very action to prevent his city's Jews from being deported? What permitted the citizens of Budapest to stand by and watch a train filled with Jewish children slowly disappear into the distance? For the large majority of us who do nothing, why is it that we cannot hear the cries of those who suffer in Africa or even down the street?

When Bono needed people to lie across the tracks, he embarked on a tour of the churches of America's heartland. In so doing, he was making a most pragmatic decision. Time after time throughout Western history, the people most willing to take selfless action on behalf of their fellow man have come out of churches and synagogues. If we are people of faith, then we should pray that our faith will lead us to follow their example. If we lack faith, or struggle with it, then we should at least have the humility and the humanity to acknowledge the limited value of our doubt to a hurting world. We must nurture the love in our culture no matter what its source. And we must do so quickly. The next train is already leaving the station.

Notes

Introduction ～ The Sanctity of Life and Its Discontents

[1] Peter Singer, *Practical Ethics* (New York: Cambridge University Press, 1993), 172.

[2] Tacitus *Histories* 5.5.

[3] Rodney Stark, *The Rise of Christianity* (San Francisco: Harper San Francisco, 1997), 118.

[4] Ibid., 97–98.

[5] Sam Harris, *Letter to a Christian Nation* (New York: Knopf, 2006), 18–19.

[6] *Buck v. Bell*, 274 U.S. 200 (1927).

[7] Edwin Black, *War Against the Weak* (New York: Thunder's Mouth Press, 2004), 108–122.

[8] Cited in part in Black, *War Against the Weak*, 120 and in part in Albert Alschuler, *Law Without Morals* (Chicago: The University of Chicago Press, 2000), 24.

[9] Cited in Alschuler, *Law Without Morals*, 26.

[10] Ibid., 27.

[11] Ibid.

[12] Black, *War Against the Weak*, 122–123.

[13] Cited in Charlotte Hunt-Grubbe, "The Elementary DNA of Dr. Watson," *Sunday Times*, October 14, 2007.

[14] Ibid.

[15] Black, *War Against the Weak*, 52.

[16] Paul Lombardo, "Eugenics Sterilization Laws," hosted in the Image Archive on the American Eugenics Movement of the Dolan DNA Learning Center of the Cold Springs Harbor Laboratory (www.eugenicsarchive.org).

[17] Black, *War Against the Weak*, 185–205; John Higham, *Strangers in the Land* (New Brunswick, NJ: Rutgers University Press, 2007), 300–330.

[18] Peter Singer, *Practical Ethics* (New York: Cambridge University Press, 1993), 169–170.

[19] Ibid., 170.

[20] Ibid., 172.

[21] Ibid., 172–173.

[22] Ibid., 181–191.

[23] Ibid., 173.

[24] Paul Zielbauer, "Princeton Bioethics Professor Debates Views on Disability and Euthanasia," *New York Times,* October 13, 1999.

[25] Ibid.

[26] Amartya Sen, "More Than 100 Million Women Are Missing," *New York Review of Books,* December 20, 1990.

[27] Amartya Sen, "Missing Women—Revisited," *British Medical Journal,* December 6, 2003, Vol. 327.

[28] Mahbub ul Haq Human Development Center, *Human Development in South Asia 2000: The Gender Question* (Oxford: Oxford University Press, 2000), 6.

[29] Gautam N. Allahbadia, "The 50 Million Missing Women," *Journal of Assisted Reproduction and Genetics,* September 2002, Vol. 19, No. 9.

[30] United Nations Population Fund, "Gender-Based Violence: A Price Too High," *State of World Population 2005,* www.unfpa.org.

[31] Shuzhuo Li, "Imbalanced Sex Ratio at Birth and Comprehensive Intervention in China," presented at the Fourth Asia Pacific Conference on Reproductive and Sexual Heath Rights held in Hyderabad, India in October 2007.

[32] Credit for coining this term is typically given to Mary Anne Warren, author of the 1985 book *Gendercide: The Implications of Sex Selection.*

[33] Cited in Eric Baculinao, "China Begins to Face Sex-Ratio Imbalance," MSNBC.com, September 14, 2004.

[34] Howard French, "As Girls 'Vanish,' Chinese City Battles Tide of Abortions," *New York Times,* February 17, 2005.

Chapter One ～ Our Morality: Selfish Genes and Cultural Clout

1 Richard Dawkins, *The Selfish Gene* (New York: Oxford University Press, 2006), 3.

2 Hannah Arendt, *Eichmann in Jerusalem* [1963] (reprint, New York: Penguin Books, 2006), 252.

3 Ibid., 135–136.

4 Ibid., 136.

5 Ibid., 33.

6 Ibid., 114.

7 Ibid., 116.

8 Charles Darwin, *The Descent of Man* [1879] (reprint, New York: Penguin Books, 2004), 148.

9 Richard Weikart, *From Darwin to Hitler* (New York: Palgrave MacMillan, 2004), 37–40.

10 Steven Pinker, "The Moral Instinct," *New York Times,* January 13, 2008.

11 Ibid.

12 Cited in Steven Pinker, *The Blank Slate* (New York: Penguin Books, 2002), 56.

13 Dawkins, *The Selfish Gene,* 2.

14 Richard Dawkins, *The God Delusion* (New York: Houghton Mifflin, 2006), 217.

15 Edward O. Wilson, *On Human Nature* (Cambridge, MA: Harvard University Press, 2004), 163.

16 Darwin, *The Descent of Man,* 141.

17 Dawkins, *The Selfish Gene,* 2.

18 Ibid., 200–201.

19 Ibid., 3.

20 Ibid.

21 Wilson, *On Human Nature,* 153.

22 Marc Hauser, *Moral Minds* (New York: Harper Collins, 2006), 44.

23 Ibid., 420.

[24] Cited in Derek Hughes, *Culture and Sacrifice* (Cambridge: Cambridge University Press, 2007), 53–54.

[25] Wilson, *On Human Nature,* 94.

[26] Darwin, *Descent of Man,* 125.

[27] In writing this section, I have benefitted significantly from the summary of the relevant literature provided by Steven Pinker in his book *The Blank Slate.*

[28] Cited in Pinker, *The Blank Slate,* 5.

[29] Cited in Robert Wright, *Moral Animals* (New York: Vintage, 1995), 5.

[30] Cited in Pinker, *The Blank Slate,* 19.

[31] Information about the history of these SS photos and their content comes from Neil Lewis, "In the Shadow of Horror, SS Guardians Frolic," *New York Times,* September 19, 2007, as well as from an online exhibit on the United States Holocaust Museum website entitled "Auschwitz through the lens of the SS: Photos of Nazi leadership at the camp." This exhibit included a display of the photos (www.ushmm.org).

[32] Darwin, *The Descent of Man,* 149.

[33] Ibid., 150.

Chapter Two ⟿ The Judeo-Christian Idea: Transcending Our Selfish Genes

[1] Charles Finney, "Refuges of Lies," 1850 (www.charlesgfinney.com).

[2] Abraham J. Heschel, *The Prophets* [1962] (reprint, New York: Harper Perennial, 2001), xxv.

[3] Cited in Edward Kaplan, *Spiritual Radical* (New Haven, CT: Yale University Press, 2007), 225.

[4] Leviticus 19:17–18.

[5] Leviticus 19:33–34.

[6] Exodus 23:4.

[7] Babylonian Talmud, Tractate Shabbat, 31a., cited in Yitzhak Buxbaum, *The Life and Teachings of Hillel* (Lanham, MD: Rowman & Littlefield, 2004), 95.

8 Sifra on Leviticus 19:18, cited in Brad Young, *Meet The Rabbis* (Peabody, MA: Hendrickson Publishers, 2007), 76.

9 Avot d'Rabbi Natan, verse B, chapter 26, cited in Buxbaum, *The Life and Teachings of Hillel*, 100–101.

10 Deuteronomy 6:5.

11 Deuteronomy 6:6–9.

12 Genesis 1:26–27.

13 Genesis 1:27.

14 Amos 5:21–24.

15 Paul Johnson, *Cities of God* (New York: Harper One, 2007), 6 and Paul Johnson, *A History of the Jews* (New York: Harper Perennial, 1988), 112.

16 Johnson, *A History of the Jews*, 132.

17 Moses Maimonides, *Mishneh Torah*, Hilchot Melachim, ch. 11, h. 3.

18 Irving Greenberg, *For the Sake of Heaven and Earth* (Philadelphia: The Jewish Publication Society, 2004), 97.

19 Matthew 22:34–40.

20 Matthew 7:12.

21 1 John 4:16.

22 1 John 4:20.

23 1 Corinthians 13:1–3.

24 1 Corinthians 13:13.

25 Matthew 25:31–40.

26 James 2:14–17.

27 John 3:16.

28 Max Weber, *The Protestant Ethic and the "Spirit" of Capitalism* [1905] (reprint, New York: Penguin Books, 2002), 78–79.

29 This section on the social activism of Wesley and the Oxford Holy Club is based upon Kenneth J. Collins, *The Theology of John Wesley*, (Nashville, TN: Abingdon Press, 2007), 267–268; Manfred Marquardt, *John Wesley's Social Ethics* (Nashville, TN: Abingdon Press, 1992), 23–30, 77–86; and *John Wesley the Methodist* (New York: The Methodist Book Concern, 1903) at the Wesley Center Online (http://wesley.nnu.edu), Chapter V: The Holy Club.

[30] Cited in Marquardt, *John Wesley's Social Ethics*, 32.

[31] Cited in Collins, *The Theology of John Wesley*, 6.

[32] Ibid., 20.

[33] Ibid., 227.

[34] Ibid., 253.

[35] Cited in John Bartlett, ed., *Bartlett's Familiar Quotations* (Boston: Little, Brown and Company, 1980), 346.

[36] Cited in Marquardt, *John Wesley's Social Ethics*, 100.

[37] Jonathan Edwards, "Sinners in the Hands of an Angry God" [1741] in John E. Smith, Harry S. Stout, and Kenneth P. Minkema, eds., *A Jonathan Edwards Reader* (New Haven, CT: Yale Nota Bene, 2003), 97.

[38] Jonathan Edwards, *The Nature of True Virtue* (1765) in Smith, Stout and Minkema, eds., *A Jonathan Edwards Reader*, 245.

[39] Ibid., 254–255.

[40] Samuel Hopkins, *Inquiry into the Nature of True Holiness* [1773], reprinted by Kessinger Publishing (www.kessinger. net), 8.

[41] Ibid., 11.

[42] Ibid, 28–29.

[43] Cited in Keith Hardman, *Charles Grandison Finney 1792–1875* (Grand Rapids, Michigan: Baker Books, 1987), 332.

[44] Charles Finney, "Refuges of Lies," 1850 (www.charlesgfinney. com).

[45] Cited in Mark Noll, *America's God* (New York: Oxford University Press, 2002), 307–308.

[46] Hardman, *Charles Grandison Finney 1792–1875*, 203–205 and Michael P. Young, *Bearing Witness against Sin* (Chicago: University of Chicago Press, 2006), 115–117.

[47] Pope Benedict XVI, *God Is Love* (San Francisco: Ignatius Press, 2006), 7.

[48] Ibid., 8.

[49] Ibid., 41.

[50] Ibid., 51.

⁵¹ Ibid., 55.

⁵² Ibid., 93.

Chapter Three ∽ **The Judeo-Christian Idea Against Genocide**

¹ Bartolome de Las Casas, *In Defense of the Indians* [c. 1550] (reprint, DeKalb: Northern Illinois University Press, 1992), 40.

² David E. Stannard, *American Holocaust* (New York: Oxford University Press, 1992), 10–11. I have taken most of my pre-Columbian population statistics from Stannard's book. Stannard convincingly documents the numbers he uses both in the pages cited in these notes, as well as in his appendix "On Pre-Columbian Settlement and Population' on pages 261–268.

³ Ibid., 267.

⁴ Ibid., 33.

⁵ Tzvetan Todorov, *The Conquest of America* (Norman: University of Oklahoma Press, 1999), 133.

⁶ Stannard, *American Holocaust,* 151.

⁷ Ibid., 85–87.

⁸ Ibid., 74–75.

⁹ Bartolome de Las Casas, *A Short Account of the Destruction of the Indies* [1542] (reprint, London: Penguin Books, 2004), 27–28.

¹⁰ Cited in Stannard, *American Holocaust,* 202.

¹¹ Las Casas, *A Short Account,* 13.

¹² Cited in Lewis Hanke, *The Spanish Struggle for Justice in the Conquest of America* (Dallas: Southern Methodist University Press, 2002), 17.

¹³ Lewis Hanke, *Aristotle and the American Indians* (Chicago: Henry Regnery Company, 1959), 15.

¹⁴ Ibid., 18 and Francis Patrick Sullivan, *Indian Freedom: The Cause of Bartolome de Las Casas* (Kansas City, MO: Sheed & Ward, 1995), 142–145.

[15] Hanke, *The Spanish Struggle for Justice,* 23–25 and Lewis Hanke, *All Mankind Is One* (DeKalb: Northern Illinois University Press, 1994), 8–9.

[16] Cited in Hanke, *All Mankind Is One,* 8–9.

[17] Ibid., 17–19.

[18] Ibid., 20.

[19] Ibid.

[20] Ibid., 21.

[21] Ibid.

[22] Rodney Stark, *For the Glory of God* (Princeton, NJ: Princeton University Press, 2003), 332.

[23] Sullivan, *Indian Freedom,* 2.

[24] Ibid., 152.

[25] Ecclesiasticus 34:21–22.

[26] Sullivan, *Indian Freedom,* 152–156.

[27] Anthony Pagden, introduction to Las Casas, *A Short Account,* xxvii and Hanke, *The Spanish Struggle for Justice,* 91–92.

[28] Hanke, *All Mankind Is One,* 67.

[29] Cited in Todorov, *The Conquest of America,* 153.

[30] Cited in Hanke, *The Spanish Struggle for Justice,* 122.

[31] Hanke, *All Mankind Is One,* 37.

[32] Las Casas, *In Defense of the Indians,* 39.

[33] Ibid.

[34] Ibid., 11.

[35] Ibid., 39–40.

[36] Ibid., 40.

[37] Ibid., 18.

[38] Cited in Hanke, *All Mankind Is One,* 66–67.

[39] Cited in Althea Bass, *Cherokee Messenger* (Norman: University of Oklahoma Press, 1996), 38.

[40] Cited in Theda Perdue and Michael Green, *The Cherokee Nation and the Trail of Tears* (New York: Viking, 2007), 47.

[41] Stannard, *American Genocide,* 120.

[42] Ibid.

[43] Ibid., 240.

44 Ibid.

45 Ibid., 121–122.

46 Ibid., 245.

47 Ibid.

48 Ibid., 126.

49 Perdue and Green, *The Cherokee Nation and the Trail of Tears,* 48–49.

50 Cited in John Andrew III, *From Revivals to Removal* (Athens: University of Georgia Press, 1992), 14.

51 The details of Evarts's lobbying campaign come from Andrew, *From Revivals to Removal,* 169–228 and from Perdue and Green, *The Cherokee Nation and the Trail of Tears,* 61–65.

52 Andrew, *From Revivals to Removal,* 185.

53 Talbot W. Chambers, *Memoir of the Life and Character of the Late Hon. Theo. Frelinghuysen* (New York: Harper & Brothers, 1863), reprinted by the University of Michigan as part of The Michigan Historical Reprint Series, 213.

54 Cited in Robert Remini, *The Life of Andrew Jackson* (New York: Harper Perennial, 1990), 213.

55 Transcript of Senator Frelinghuysen's April 6, 1830, floor speech (Washington, DC: National Journal, 1830), reprinted by Kessinger Publishing (www.kessinger.net), 9.

56 Ibid., 7.

57 Ibid., 28.

58 Cited in Remini, *The Life of Andrew Jackson,* 214.

59 *The Cherokee Nation v. The State of Georgia,* 30 U.S. (5 Peters) 1 (1831).

60 Robert Remini, *Andrew Jackson and His Indian Wars* (New York: Penguin Books, 2002), 257.

61 *Samuel A. Worcester v. The State of Georgia,* 31 U.S. (6 Peters) 515 (1832).

62 Cited in Remini, *The Life of Andrew Jackson,* 216.

63 Perdue and Green, *The Cherokee Nation and the Trail of Tears,* 123.

64 Ibid., 123–126; Remini, *Andrew Jackson and his Indian Wars,* 269; and Stannard, *American Holocaust,* 123.

[65] Details about the Trail of Tears come from Perdue and Green, *The Cherokee Nation and the Trail of Tears*, 116–140; Remini, *Andrew Jackson and his Indian Wars*, 269–270; and Stannard, *American Holocaust*, 121–125.

[66] Remini, *The Life of Andrew Jackson*, 218 and Perdue and Green, *The Cherokee Nation and the Trail of Tears*, 139.

[67] Stannard, *American Holocaust*, 124; and Remini, *Andrew Jackson and his Indian Wars*, 269.

[68] Remini, *Andrew Jackson and his Indian Wars*, 269.

[69] Perdue and Green, *The Cherokee Nation and the Trail of Tears*, xv.

[70] Remini, *The Life of Andrew Jackson*, 218.

[71] Ibid., 117.

[72] Cited in Andrew, *From Revivals to Removal*, 222.

[73] Ibid., 217.

[74] Ibid., 225.

[75] Ibid., 202.

[76] Ibid.

[77] Chambers, *Memoir of the Life of Theo. Frelinghuysen*, 70–71.

Chapter Four ～ The Judeo-Christian Idea Against Slavery

[1] Thomas Clarkson, *The History of the Rise, Progress and Accomplishment of the Abolition of the African Slave Trade by the British Parliament* [1839], reprinted by Kessinger Publishing (www.kessinger.net), 31.

[2] Stark, *For the Glory of God*, 307–308.

[3] David Brion Davis, *Slavery and Human Progress* (New York: Oxford University Press, 1984), 51.

[4] Davis, *Slavery and Human Progress*, 74 and Adam Hochschild, *Bury the Chains* (New York: Mariner Books, 2005), 300.

[5] Hochschild, *Bury the Chains*, 54.

[6] Cited in Garth Lean, *God's Politician* (Colorado Springs, CO: Helmers & Howard, 1987), 50.

[7] Cited in Hochschild, *Bury the Chains*, 89.

[8] Ibid., 95.

[9] Ibid., 4.

10 Cited in Eric Metaxas, *Amazing Grace* (San Francisco: Harper San Francisco, 2007), 68.

11 Hochschild, *Bury the Chains,* 123.

12 Cited in Seymour Drescher, ed., *Tocqueville and Beaumont on Social Reform* (New York: Harper & Row, 1968), 138.

13 Hochschild, *Bury the Chains,* 2.

14 Stark, *For the Glory of God,* 352.

15 Cited in Metaxas, *Amazing Grace,* 136.

16 Ibid., 232.

17 Thomas Clarkson, *An Essay on the Slavery and Commerce of the Human Species, Particularly the African* [1786] (reprint, Charleston, SC: Biblio Bazaar, 2006), 159.

18 Ibid., 158.

19 Ibid., 159.

20 Ibid., 161.

21 Metaxas, *Amazing Grace,* 86.

22 Ibid., 156.

23 Ibid., 155–156.

24 Cited in Lean, *God's Politician,* 58.

25 Henry Meyer, *All on Fire* (New York: St. Martin's Griffin, 2000), 125.

26 Details of the encounter between Garrison and Wilberforce come from Meyer, *All on Fire,* 157–159.

27 Robert Abzug, *Passionate Liberator* (New York: Oxford University Press, 1980), 90–91.

28 Ibid., 116.

29 Gilbert Hobbs Barnes, *The Anti-Slavery Impulse* (New York: Harbinger Books, 1964), 68.

30 Ibid., 77.

31 Ibid., 73.

32 Joan Hedrick, *Harriet Beecher Stowe* (New York: Oxford University Press, 1994), vii.

33 Ibid., 230.

34 This point is made quite convincingly in Barnes, *The Anti-Slavery Impulse,* 107.

35 Ibid., 104–105.

36 Barnes, *The Anti-Slavery Impulse,* 98.

37 Mayer, *All on Fire,* 48.

38 Cited in Robert Abzug, *Cosmos Crumbling* (New York: Oxford University Press, 1994), 45.

39 Ibid., 151.

40 Cited in William Cain, ed., *William Lloyd Garrison and the Fight against Slavery* (Boston: Bedford Books, 1995), 92.

41 Mayer, *All on Fire,* 224.

42 Ibid.

43 Cited in Cain, *William Lloyd Garrison and the Fight against Slavery,* 54.

44 Abzug, *Passionate Liberator,* 47.

45 Ibid., 48.

46 Cited in Hardman, *Charles Grandison Finney,* 88.

47 Ibid.

48 Ibid.

49 Cited in Abzug, *Cosmos Crumbling,* 157.

50 Abzug, *Passionate Liberator,* 145.

51 Gabe Levenson, "Where the Twain Shall Meet," *New York Jewish Week,* January 19, 2007.

52 Cited in Charles Edward Stowe, *Life of Harriet Beecher Stowe* [1889] (reprint, Charleston, SC: BiblioBazaar, 2006), 278.

53 Cain, *William Lloyd Garrison and the Fight against Slavery,* 43.

54 Mayer, *All on Fire,* 203–206.

55 Ibid., 246.

56 Ibid., 199.

57 Barnes, *The Anti-Slavery Impulse,* 86.

58 Ibid.

59 Ibid., 59

60 David Herbert Donald, *Lincoln* (New York: Simon & Schuster, 1995), 165.

Chapter Five ～ Falling Backwards: The Abandonment of the Judeo-Christian Idea and the Return of Genocide and Slavery

1. Aleksandr Solzhenitsyn, Templeton Lecture, May 10, 1983, in Edward Ericson and Daniel Mahoney, eds., *The Solzhenitsyn Reader* (Wilmington, DE: ISI Books, 2006), 577.

2. Robert Conquest, *The Harvest of Sorrow* (New York: Oxford University Press, 1986), 256.

3. Cited in Richard Weikart, *From Darwin to Hitler* (New York: Palgrave MacMillan, 2004), 76.

4. Adolf Hitler, *Mein Kampf* [1925] (reprint, New York: Mariner Books, 1999), 307.

5. Hugh Trevor-Roper, ed., *Hitler's Table Talk 1941–1944* (New York: Enigma Books, 2000), 77. Please see the extended note on the debate over the authenticity of *Hitler's Table Talk* at the end of the endnotes section.

6. Richard Steigmann-Gall, *The Holy Reich* (New York: Cambridge University Press, 2004), 252.

7. *Hitler's Table Talk*, 7.

8. Ibid., 39.

9. Ibid., 124.

10. Hitler, *Mein Kampf*, 289.

11. Ibid., 290.

12. Ibid., 255.

13. Ibid., 404.

14. Ibid., 383.

15. Ibid., 383.

16. Ibid., 296.

17. *Hitler's Table Talk*, 142.

18. Ibid., 336.

19. Hitler, *Mein Kampf*, 383.

20. Weikart, *From Darwin to Hitler*, 216.

21. Ibid., 132.

22. Cited in Weikart, *From Darwin to Hitler*, 215.

23. *Hitler's Table Talk*, 51.

24. Hitler, *Mein Kampf*, 289.

25 Ibid.

26 Ibid., 287.

27 Ibid.

28 United States Holocaust Memorial Museum, "Forced Labor in Depth," *Holocaust Encyclopedia,* and United States Holocaust Memorial Museum, "Polish Victims," *Holocaust Encyclopedia,* both at www.ushmm.org.

29 United States Holocaust Museum, "Forced Labor in Depth."

30 Ibid.

31 United States Holocaust Museum, "Polish Victims."

32 United States Holocaust Memorial Museum, "The Holocaust," *Holocaust Encyclopedia,* at www.ushmm.org.

33 Ibid.

34 Weikart, *From Darwin to Hitler,* 225.

35 United States Holocaust Memorial Museum, "Euthanasia Program," *Holocaust Encyclopedia,* at www.ushmm.org.

36 Letter from the International Workingmen's Association to Abraham Lincoln, presented to U.S. Ambassador Charles Francis Adams on January 25, 1865, posted on the *Marx & Engels Internet Archive* (www.marxists.org).

37 Ibid.

38 John Spargo, "Today Is 100th Anniversary of Marx's Birth," *New York Times,* May 5, 1918.

39 Karl Marx, *Communist Manifesto* [1848], reprinted in David McLellan, ed., *Karl Marx: Selected Writings* (New York: Oxford University Press, 2000), 271.

40 Karl Marx, "Towards a Critique of Hegel's *Philosophy of Right,*" [1844], reprinted in McLellan, *Karl Marx: Selected Writings,* 72.

41 Ibid.

42 Karl Marx, "On the Jewish Question," [1843] reprinted in McLellan, *Karl Marx: Selected Writings,* 67.

43 Ibid., 69.

44 Ibid.

45 Vladimir Lenin, "Socialism and Religion," December 3, 1905, reprinted in *Lenin on Religion* (Moscow: Progress Publishers, 1981), 7–8.

46 Ibid., 8.

47 Marx, *Communist Manifesto,* in McLellan, *Karl Marx: Selected Writings,* 246.

48 Cited in George Brenkert, *Marx's Ethics of Freedom* (Boston: Routledge & Kegan Paul, 1983), 121.

49 Marx, *Communist Manifesto,* in McLellan, *Karl Marx: Selected Writings,* 271.

50 Brenkert, *Marx's Ethics of Freedom,* 166.

51 Letter from Karl Marx to Ferdinand Lassalle, January 16, 1862, in McLellan, *Karl Marx: Selected Writings,* 565.

52 Cited in Brenkert, *Marx's Ethics of Freedom,* 169–170.

53 Vladimir Lenin, speech delivered at the Third All-Russia Congress of the Russian Young Communist League, October 2, 1920, in *Lenin on Religion,* 60.

54 Ibid., 58.

55 Anne Applebaum, *Gulag* (New York: Anchor Books, 2004), xviii.

56 Ibid., xvi.

57 Ibid., xxxviii.

58 Ibid., xvi.

59 Ibid., xvii.

60 Ibid.

61 Ibid., xxix.

62 Cited in Conquest, *Harvest of Sorrow,* 115 and Robert Gellately, *Lenin, Stalin and Hitler* (New York: Knopf, 2007), 169.

63 Gellately, *Lenin, Stalin and Hitler,* 170.

64 Conquest, *Harvest of Sorrow,* 123.

65 Ibid., 121.

66 Ibid., 127, 142, 306.

67 Robert Conquest, *The Great Terror: A Reassessment* (New York: Oxford University Press, 1990), 18.

68 Ibid., 19 and Conquest, *Harvest of Sorrow,* 182.

69 Conquest, *Harvest of Sorrow,* 225.

70 Ibid., 327–328.

71 Ibid., 249.

72 Ibid., 301, 306. Please see the extended note on the debate over, and causes of, the Ukranian famine at the end of the endnotes section.

73 Ibid., 241.

74 Ibid., 243.

75 Ibid., 306.

76 Ibid., 323–326.

77 Ibid., 3.

78 Ibid., 129.

79 Ibid., 233.

80 Ibid., 129.

81 Sullivan, *Indian Freedom, The Cause of Bartolome de Las Casas,* 151.

82 Conquest, *Harvest of Sorrow,* 245.

Chapter Six ~ The Rising: The Judeo-Christian Idea in the Post-War World

1 Martin Luther King, Jr., speech at the Holt Street Baptist Church (December 1956), cited in Charles Marsh, *The Beloved Community* (New York: Basic Books, 2005), 1.

2 Clayborne Carson, ed., *The Autobiography of Martin Luther King, Jr.* (New York: Warner Books, 1998), 60.

3 Ibid., 76.

4 Ibid., 77.

5 Ibid., 77–78.

6 Ibid., 79.

7 Ibid., 80.

8 Ibid., 38.

9 Carson, *The Autobiography of Martin Luther King, Jr.,* 103.

10 Ibid.

11 Hitchens, *God Is Not Great,* 176.

12 David J. Garrow, *Bearing the Cross* (New York: Perennial Classics, 2004), 86, 91.

13 Mark Noll, *God and Race in American Politics* (Princeton, NJ: Princeton University Press, 2008), 119.

14 Cited in David Chappell, *A Stone of Hope* (Chapel Hill: The University of North Carolina Press, 2004), 88.

15 Ibid., 62–63.

16 Marsh, *The Beloved Community*, 88.

17 Ibid., 3.

18 Ibid., 88.

19 Ibid., 3.

20 Cited in Chappell, *Stone of Hope*, 76.

21 Cited in Marsh, *The Beloved Community*, 91.

22 Dawkins, *The God Delusion*, 271.

23 Garrow, *Bearing The Cross*, 68.

24 Carson, *The Autobiography of Martin Luther King, Jr.*, 67.

25 Ibid.

26 Mohandas K. Gandhi, *An Autobiography* [1957] (reprint, Boston: Beacon Press, 1993), 137–138.

27 Ibid., 90.

28 Ibid., 160.

29 Leo Tolstoy, *The Kingdom of God Is Within You* [1893], reprinted by Wildside Press (www.wildside.com, 2006), 19.

30 Charles Marsh, *God's Long Summer* (Princeton, NJ: Princeton University Press, 1997), 17. The story of Fannie Lou Hamer's life and faith is taken from the first chapter of Marsh's excellent book.

31 Ibid., 18.

32 Ibid., 22.

33 This summary of Merton's comments is taken verbatim from Marsh, *The Beloved Community*, 2. I have not used quotation marks so as not to give the impression that I am directly quoting Merton.

34 See Chappell, *A Stone of Hope*, 112–113.

35 Ibid., 112.

36 Ibid., 5.

37 Ibid., 140.
38 Ibid., 144.
39 Ibid., 121.
40 Marsh, *God's Long Summer*, 25.
41 Martin Luther King, Jr., "Letter from Birmingham City Jail" [1963], in James M. Washington, *A Testament of Hope* (New York: Harper San Francisco, 1986), 299.
42 James Reston, "The First Significant Test of the Freedom March," *New York Times*, August 29, 1963.
43 Ibid.
44 James F. Findlay, Jr., *Church People in the Struggle* (New York: Oxford University Press, 1993), 50; Michael B. Friedland, *Lift Up Your Voice Like a Trumpet* (Chapel Hill: The University of North Carolina Press, 1998), 88; Robert W. Spike, *The Freedom Revolution and the Churches* (New York: Association Press, 1965), 106.
45 Ibid., 55–36; Friedland, *Lift Up Your Voice Like a Trumpet*, 100; John G. Stewart, "The Civil Rights Act of 1964: Tactics II," in Robert D. Lovey, ed., *The Civil Rights Act of 1964* (Albany: State University of New York Press, 1997), 286.
46 Friedland, *Lift Up Your Voice Like a Trumpet*, 100.
47 Findlay, *Church People in the Struggle*, 55.
48 Findlay, *Church People in the Struggle*, 51; Friedland, *Lift Up Your Voice Like a Trumpet*, 91; and Stewart, "The Civil Rights Act of 1964: Tactics II," in Lovey, ed. *The Civil Rights Act of 1964*, 285–286.
49 Friedland, 91.
50 Hubert H. Humphrey, "Memorandum on Senate Consideration of the Civil Rights Act of 1964," in Lovey, ed., *The Civil Rights Act of 1964*, 89.
51 Cited in Spike, *The Freedom Revolution and the Churches*, 108.
52 Friedland, *Lift Up Your Voice Like a Trumpet*, 101.
53 Cited in Steve Stockman, *Walk On* (Orlando, FL: Relevant Books, 2005), 10.

54 Ibid., 23–31; Michka Assayas, *Bono in Conversation with Michka Assayas* (New York: Riverhead Books, 2005), 122, 146–147; and James Traub, "The Statesman," *New York Times,* September 18, 2005.

55 Stockman, *Walk On,* 53–54.

56 Cited in Christian Scharen, *One Step Closer* (Grand Rapids, MI: Brazos Press, 2006), 25.

57 Martin Dent and Bill Peters, *The Crisis of Poverty and Debt in the Third World,* cited in Yale School of Management Case Study, *Faith and Globalization,* "Jubilee 2000" (cases.som.yale.edu).

58 Martin Dent, "Jubilee 2000," interview on *The Religion Report* on Radio National (Australian Broadcasting Company), April 14, 1999 (transcript at www.abc.ret.au).

59 Leviticus 25:8–54.

60 Martin Wroe, "An Irresistible Force," *Sojourners Magazine,* May-June 2000, Vol. 29, No. 3.

61 Marlene Barrett, ed., "The World Will Never Be the Same Again," Report of the Jubilee 2000 Coalition, December 2000, 8.

62 Noreena Hertz, *The Debt Threat* (New York: Collins, 2004), 4.

63 Wroe, "An Irresistible Force," *Sojourners.*

64 Ibid.

65 Dent and Peters, *The Crisis of Poverty and Debt in the Third World,* cited in Yale School of Management Case Study, *Faith and Globalization,* "Jubilee 2000."

66 Michael Hirsh and Weston Kosova, "Can Bono Save the Third World?" *Newsweek,* January 24, 2000.

67 Traub, "The Statesman."

68 Susan Baer, "U2's Bono in Washington," *Washingtonian Magazine,* March 2006.

69 Traub, "The Statesman."

70 Traub, "The Statesman."

71 Ibid.

72 Sebastian Mallaby, "Why So Stingy on Foreign Aid?" *Washington Post,* June 27, 2000.

73 Hertz, *The Debt Threat,* 14.

74 Traub, "The Statesman."

75 Assayas, *Bono in Conversation,* 87. Bono attributes this story to Harry Belafonte, an actor who participated in the civil rights movement alongside King.

76 Jim Wilson, "Bono: Appeal to America's Greatness in Aid to Africa" (interview with Bono), *USA Today,* September 15, 2003.

77 Jonathan Peterson, "The Rock Star, the Pope and the World's Poor," *Los Angeles Times,* January 7, 2001.

78 Hertz, *The Debt Threat,* 16–17.

79 Allen D. Hertzke, *Freeing God's Children* (Lanham, MD: Rowman and Littlefield Publishers, 2004), 343.

80 Peterson, "The Rock Star, the Pope and the World's Poor."

81 Cited in Joshua William Busby, "Bono Made Jesse Helms Cry: Jubilee 2000, Debt Relief, and Moral Action in International Politics," *International Studies Quarterly* (2007) 51, 247–275.

82 Cathleen Falsani, "Bono's American Prayer," *Christianity Today,* March 2003.

83 Traub, "The Statesman."

84 Baer, "U2's Bono in Washington."

85 Cathleen Falsani, "Bono Credits Church for Leading AIDS Fight," *Chicago Sun-Times,* December 5, 2003.

86 Andy Argyrakis, "Bono: Ensuring America Keeps Its Promise," *Christianity Today,* July 7, 2003.

87 Assayas, *Bono in Conversation,* 80.

88 Ibid., 207.

89 Ibid., 80.

90 Ibid., 81.

91 Ibid.

92 Anthony DeCurtis, "Bono: The Beliefnet Interview," *Beliefnet* (www.beliefnet.com), February 2001.

93 Falsani, "Bono's American Prayer."

94 Ibid.

95 Argyrakis, "Bono: Ensuring America Keeps its Promise."

96 Stockman, *Walk On,* 239.

97 Kevin Bales, *Disposable People* (Berkeley: University of California Press, 2000), 8–9. Bales's definition of slavery is a reasonable one. He includes as slaves only those who are forced to work without pay under the threat of violence.

98 Ibid., 9.

99 David Batstone, *Not for Sale* (New York: Harper One, 2007), 9.

100 Hertzke, *Freeing God's Children,* 146.

101 Cited in Hertzke, *Freeing God's Children,* 137.

102 Sam Brownback, *From Power to Purpose* (Nashville, TN: Thomas Nelson, 2007), 65–66.

103 Ibid.

104 Michael Cromartie, "The Jew Who Is Saving Christians," *Christianity Today,* March 1, 1999.

105 Ibid.

Chapter Seven ～ Myths about Biblical Immorality

1 Paul Johnson, *A History of Christianity* (New York: Simon & Schuster, 1976), 437.

2 Thomas Paine, *The Age of Reason* [1794] (reprint, New York: Citadel Press, 1974), 60.

3 Harris, *Letter to a Christian Nation,* 8.

4 Dawkins, *The God Delusion,* 237.

5 Hitchens, *God Is Not Great,* 102.

6 Exodus 17:14.

7 Deut 25:19.

8 1 Samuel 15.

9 Deut 20:16–17.

10 Babylonian Talmud, Tractate Sanhedrin, 96b.

11 Genesis 36:12, 22, and 29.

12 Babylonian Talmud, Tractate Sanhedrin, 99b.

13 Avi Sagi, "The punishment of Amalek in Jewish tradition: coping with the moral problem," *Harvard Theological*

Review, Vol. 87, No. 3 (July 1, 1994) and Elliott Horowitz, *Reckless Rites* (Princeton, NJ: Princeton University Press, 2006), 134–137.

14 Aron Moss, "Wipe out Amalek, Today?" under *Mitzvot and Jewish Customs* at www.chabad.org.

15 Cited in Horowitz, *Reckless Rites,* 135.

16 Ibid.

17 Stanley N. Gundry, ed., *Show Them No Mercy* (Grand Rapids, MI: Zondervan, 2003).

18 Ibid., 93.

19 Leviticus 25:44–46.

20 Ephesians 6:5–9.

21 1 Peter 2:18.

22 Saint Augustine, *City of God* [c. 1410] (reprint, New York: The Modern Library, 1993), 693–694.

23 Cited in Mark Noll, *The Civil War as a Theological Crisis* (Chapel Hill: The University of North Carolina Press, 2006), 120.

24 Ibid., 56.

25 Exodus 21:16.

26 Deuteronomy 23:15.

27 Exodus 21:26–27.

28 Exodus 21:20. While the exact punishment is not entirely clear, it is widely believed to have been death.

29 Exodus 21:2. The only way Hebrew servants were permitted to serve beyond this term was if they asked to do so and participated in a formal public ritual extending their service (Exodus 21:6).

30 Leviticus 25:43, 46.

31 Deuteronomy 15:13–14.

32 Babylonian Talmud, Tractate Kiddushin, 20a.

33 Moses Maimonides, *Mishneh Torah,* Avadim, 9:8.

34 Ephesians 6:9.

35 Colossians 4:1.

36 Galatians 3:28.

37 Philemon 16.

38 Noll, *America's God*, 391.

39 Clarkson, *An Essay on the Slavery and Commerce of the Human Species*, 158–159.

40 Thomas Clarkson, "A Letter to the Clergy of Various Denominations, in the Slave States of America," January 27, 1841, reprinted by the Cornell University Library, 31.

41 Ibid., 32.

42 Parker Pillsbury, *Guilty or not Guilty?* (Leeds, England: Edward Baines & Sons, 1855), reprinted by the Cornell University Library, 15–16.

43 Ibid., 16.

44 Theodore Weld, *The Bible Against Slavery* (Pittsburgh, PA: United Presbyterian Board of Publication, 1864), reprinted by the Cornell University Library, 21.

45 Ibid.

46 Cited in Noll, *The Civil War as a Theological Crisis*, 134–135.

47 Moses Maimonides, *The Guide for the Perplexed* [c. 1190], (BN Publishing, www.bnpublishing.com, 2006), 323.

48 Cited in Stark, *For the Glory of God*, 175.

49 Ibid.

50 Clarkson, *An Essay on the Slavery and Commerce of the Human Species*, 159.

51 Cited in Noll, *The Civil War as a Theological Crisis*, 37.

52 Ibid., 42.

53 Cited in Noll, *The Civil War as a Theological Crisis*, 121.

54 Noll, *America's God*, 400.

55 Noll, *The Civil War as a Theological Crisis*, 7.

56 Ibid.

Chapter Eight ⁓ Myths about Judeo-Christian Atrocities

1 Cited in Rabbi Ephraim of Bonn, *The Book of Remembrance*, reprinted in Shlomo Eidelberg, ed., *The Jews and the Crusaders* (Hoboken, NJ: KTAV Publishing House, 1996), 122.

2 Cited in Henry Kamen, *The Spanish Inquisition* (New Haven, CT: Yale University Press, 1998), 49.

[3] Paine, *The Age of Reason*, 182.

[4] Sam Harris, *The End of Faith* (New York: W. W. Norton & Company, 2005), 12.

[5] Dawkins, *The God Delusion*, 303.

[6] Hitchens, *God Is Not Great*, 13.

[7] Bernard Lewis, *What Went Wrong?* (New York: Oxford University Press, 2002), 4.

[8] Thomas Madden, *The New Concise History of the Crusades* (Lanham, MD: Rowman & Littlefield Publishers, 2006), x.

[9] Bernard Lewis, *The Crisis of Islam* (New York: Random House, 2004), 51.

[10] The details of these attacks on the Rhine Valley's Jewish communities are taken from Robert Chazan, *In the Year 1096* (Philadelphia, PA: The Jewish Publication Society, 1996), 29–43 and Eidelberg, *The Jews and the Crusaders*, 3–7.

[11] The details of the efforts by the local churchmen to save their Jewish communities are taken from Chazan, *In the Year 1096*, 29–43, and Eidelberg, *The Jews and the Crusaders*, 3–7.

[12] Rabbi David Dalin, *The Myth of Hitler's Pope* (Washington, DC: Regnery Publishing, 2005), 20.

[13] Cited in Rabbi Ephraim, *The Book of Remembrance*, reprinted in Eidelberg, *The Jews and the Crusaders*, 122.

[14] Kamen, *The Spanish Inquisition*, 59.

[15] Ibid., 60.

[16] Ibid., 288.

[17] Edward Peters, *Inquisition* (Berkeley: University of California Press, 1989), 81–82 and B. Netanyahu, *The Origins of the Spanish Inquisition* (New York: Random House, 1995), 127–128.

[18] Netanyahu, *The Origins of the Spanish Inquisition*, 325.

[19] Ibid., 381–382.

[20] Ibid., 338.

[21] Kamen, *The Spanish Inquisition*, 34.

[22] Netanyahu, *The Origins of the Spanish Inquisition*, 1047.

[23] Ibid., 1031.

[24] Kamen, *The Spanish Inquisition*, 168.

[25] Netanyahu, *Origins of the Spanish Inquisition,* 1008.

[26] Ibid., 1055.

[27] Ibid., 1064.

[28] Ibid., xix.

[29] Ibid., xvii.

[30] Kamen, *The Spanish Inquisition,* 63.

[31] Netanyahu, *The Origins of the Spanish Inquisition,* 990–991.

[32] Peters, *Inquisition,* 84.

[33] Kamen, *The Spanish Inquisition,* 48.

[34] Ibid., 71.

[35] Ibid.

[36] Netanyahu, *The Origins of the Spanish Inquisition,* 1063.

[37] Kamen, *The Spanish Inquisition,* 78.

[38] Chazan, *In the Year 1096,* 139–140.

[39] James Carroll, *Constantine's Sword* (Boston: Mariner Books, 2001), 219.

[40] Horowitz, *Reckless Rites,* 228–247.

[41] Ibid., 11.

[42] Ibid., 160–177.

Chapter Nine ～ The Myth of Enlightenment Perfection

[1] Max Horkheimer and Theodor Adorno, *Dialectic of Enlightenment* [1947] (reprint, Stanford, CA: Stanford University Press, 2002), 1.

[2] Letter from Thomas Jefferson to the Count de Buffon, October 1, 1787, in *Thomas Jefferson: Writings* (New York: The Library of America, 1984), 909.

[3] Ibid., 909–910.

[4] Ibid., 910.

[5] Cited in I. Bernard Cohen, *Science and the Founding Fathers* (New York: W. W. Norton & Company, 1997), 77.

[6] Ibid.

[7] Cited in Thomas Jefferson, *Notes on the State of Virginia* [1787], reprinted in *Thomas Jefferson: Writings,* 190.

[8] Ibid., 184.

9 Ibid., 187.

10 Ibid., 188.

11 Ibid., 190.

12 Paine, *The Age of Reason*, 49.

13 Jefferson, *Notes on the State of Virginia*, reprinted in *Thomas Jefferson, Writings*, 266.

14 Ibid.

15 Ibid., 265.

16 Ibid., 270.

17 Cited in Garrett Ward Sheldon, *The Political Philosophy of Thomas Jefferson* (Baltimore, MD: Johns Hopkins University Press, 1991), 139.

18 Orlando Patterson, *Slavery and Social Death* (Cambridge, MA: Harvard University Press, 1982), vii.

19 Stark, *For the Glory of God*, 297–299.

20 David Brion Davis, *The Problem of Slavery in Western Culture* (New York: Oxford University Press, 1966), 66.

21 Aristotle, *Politics*, excerpt reprinted in Stanley Engerman, Seymour Drescher, and Robert Paquette, eds., *Slavery* (New York: Oxford University Press, 2001), 10.

22 Ibid., 11.

23 Ibid.

24 Aristotle, *Nicomachean Ethics*, excerpt reprinted in Engerman, Drescher, and Paquette, *Slavery*, 15.

25 David Brion Davis, *The Problem of Slavery in the Age of Revolution* (New York: Oxford University Press, 1999), 45.

26 Thomas Hobbes, *Leviathan* [1651] (reprint, New York: Penguin Books, 1985), 186; Thomas Hobbes, *On the Citizen* [1647] (reprint, Cambridge: Cambridge University Press, 1998), 12.

27 Hobbes, *On the Citizen*, 105.

28 Ibid., 102–103.

29 Ibid., 104.

30 Ibid., 105.

31 Sheldon, *The Political Philosophy of Thomas Jefferson*, 41.

32 John Locke, *Second Treatise of Government* [1690] (reprint, Indianapolis, IN: Hackett Publishing Company, 1980), 17.

33 Davis, *The Problem of Slavery in Western Culture,* 183–185.

34 Ibid., 118.

35 Montesquieu, *The Spirit of the Laws* [1748] (reprint, New York: Cambridge University Press, 1989), 247.

36 Ibid., 251.

37 Ibid., 252.

38 Ibid., 254, 259, and 261.

39 Voltaire, "Essay on the Manners and Spirit of Nations," in Ben Ray Redman, ed., *The Portable Voltaire* (New York: Penguin Books, 1977), 551.

40 Jean-Jacques Rousseau, *The Social Contract* [1762], reprinted by BN Publishing (www.bnpublishing.com, 2007), 16.

41 Cited in Jack Fruchtman, Jr., *Atlantic Cousins* (New York: Thunder's Mouth Press, 2005), 244.

42 Cited in Lewis Sala-Molins, *Dark Side of the Light* (Minneapolis: University of Minnesota Press, 2006), 13.

43 Ibid., 14.

44 Ibid., 18.

45 Ibid., 42.

46 Jefferson, *Notes on the State of Virginia,* reprinted in *Thomas Jefferson, Writings,* 264 and Thomas Jefferson, *Autobiography* [1821], reprinted in *Thomas Jefferson, Writings,* 44.

47 Sheldon, *The Political Philosophy of Thomas Jefferson,* 133–134.

48 Jefferson, *Autobiography,* reprinted in *Thomas Jefferson, Writings,* 44.

49 Jefferson, *Notes on the State of Virginia,* reprinted in *Thomas Jefferson, Writings,* 270.

50 Jefferson, *Autobiography,* reprinted in *Thomas Jefferson, Writings,* 44.

51 Thomas Jefferson, "Answers and Observations for Demeunier's Article on the United States in the Encyclopédie Méthodique, 1786," reprinted in *Thomas Jefferson, Writings,* 592.

52 Thomas Jefferson, letter to James Heaton, May 20, 1826, in *Thomas Jefferson, Writings,* 1516.

53 Jefferson, "Answers and Observations for Demeunier's Article," reprinted in *Thomas Jefferson, Writings,* 592.

54 Cited in Ben Kiernan, *Blood and Soil* (New Haven, CT: Yale University Press, 2007), 49.

55 Ibid., 51.

56 Ibid., 68.

57 Bruce Baum, *The Rise and Fall of the Caucasian Race* (New York: New York University Press, 2006), 65–66.

58 Ibid., 69.

59 Ibid., 76.

60 Ibid., 66.

61 Georges-Louis Leclerc, Count de Buffon, *A Natural History, General and Particular* [1748–1804], excerpt reprinted in Emmanuel Chukwudi Eze, ed., *Race and the Enlightenment* (Malden, MA: Blackwell Publishing, 1997), 26.

62 Johann Friedrich Blumenbach, *On the Natural Varieties of Mankind* [1776], excerpt reprinted in Eze, *Race and the Enlightenment,* 84, 86.

63 Cited in Robert Bernasconi, "Who Invented the Concept of Race?" in Robert Bernasconi, ed., *Race* (Malden, MA: Blackwell Publishers, 2001), 25.

64 Ibid., 20.

65 Cited in Baum, *The Rise and Fall of the Caucasian Race,* 63.

66 Bernasconi, "Who Invented the Concept of Race?" in Bernasconi, *Race,* 21.

67 Voltaire, *The Philosophy of History* [1765], excerpt reprinted in Robert Bernasconi and Tommy Lott, eds., *The Idea of Race* (Indianapolis, IN: Hackett Publishing Company, 2000), 5–6.

68 Immanuel Kant, "On the Different Races of Man" [1775], excerpt reprinted in Eze, *Race and the Enlightenment,* 41.

69 Immanuel Kant, *Physical Geography* [1804], excerpt reprinted in Eze, *Race and the Enlightenment,* 63.

70 Ibid., 64.

71 Immanuel Kant, *Observations on the Feeling of the Beautiful and the Sublime* [1764], excerpt reprinted in Eze, *Race and the Enlightenment,* 55.

72 Ibid., 57.

73 David Hume, *Essays, Moral and Political* [1742], excerpt reprinted in Isaac Kramnick, *The Portable Enlightenment Reader* (New York: Penguin Books, 1995), 629.

74 Ibid.

75 Dennis Diderot, "Encyclopédie," entry from the *Encyclopédie* [1751–1772], reprinted in Kramnick, *The Portable Enlightenment Reader,* 18.

76 M. le Romain, "Negre," entry from the *Encyclopédie,* reprinted in Eze, *Race and the Enlightenment,* 91.

77 "Negro," entry from the *Encyclopedia Britannica,* First American Edition [1798], excerpt reprinted in Eze, *Race and the Enlightenment,* 94.

78 Johann Gottfried von Herder, *Ideas on the Philosophy of the History of Humankind* [1784], excerpt reprinted in Bernasconi and Lott, *The Idea of Race,* 26.

79 Ibid.

80 Noel Malcolm, *Bosnia: A Short History* (New York: New York University Press, 1994), 153.

81 Bertrand Russell, *The History of Western Philosophy* (New York: Touchstone Books, 1945), 730.

82 Marx, *Communist Manifesto,* reprinted in McLellan, *Karl Marx: Selected Writings,* 271.

Conclusion 〜 Hubris and Humility

1 Nicholas Kristof, "Following God Abroad," *New York Times,* May 21, 2002.

2 Ibid.

3 Nicholas Kristof, "God on Their Side," *New York Times,* September 27, 2003.

4 Nicholas Kristof, "Bleeding Hearts of the World, Unite!" *New York Times,* November 6, 2005.

5 Nicholas Kristof, "Evangelicals a Liberal Can Love," *New York Times,* February 3, 2008.

6 Kristof, "Following God Abroad."

7 Edward J. Larson, *Summer for the Gods* (New York: Basic Books, 1997), 89–91 and 108; Marvin Olasky and John Perry, *Monkey Business* (Nashville, TN: Broadman & Holman Publishers, 2005), 14–16, 88, and 251 (Appendix A: transcript of "Scopes 75th Anniversary Broadcast," *Science Friday* with host Ira Flatow, July 21, 2000, National Public Radio).

8 H. L. Mencken, "The Tennessee Circus," *Baltimore Evening Sun,* June 15, 1925, reprinted in *A Religious Orgy in Tennessee* (Hoboken, NJ: Melville House Publishing), 4.

9 Cited in Marion Elizabeth Rodgers, *Mencken: The American Iconoclast* (New York: Oxford University Press, 2005), 272.

10 H. L. Mencken, "Evangelical Ignoramuses," *American Mercury,* November 1925, reprinted in S. T. Joshi, ed., *H. L. Mencken on Religion* (Amherst, NY: Prometheus Books, 2002), 125.

11 H. L. Mencken, "To Expose a Fool," *American Mercury,* October 1925, reprinted in *A Religious Orgy in Tennessee,* 134.

12 H. L. Mencken, "Bryan," *Baltimore Evening Sun,* July 27, 1925, reprinted in *A Religious Orgy in Tennessee,* 105.

13 H. L. Mencken, "The Decline of Protestantism," *American Mercury,* March 1925, reprinted in Joshi, ed., *H. L. Mencken on Religion,* 105.

14 See, for example, Mencken's "The Tennessee Circus," reprinted in *A Religious Orgy in Tennessee,* 3–9.

15 Mencken, "Evangelical Ignoramuses," reprinted in Joshi, *H. L. Mencken on Religion,* 125.

16 Mencken, "Bryan," reprinted in *A Religious Orgy in Tennessee,* 109.

17 Michael Kazin, *A Godly Hero* (New York: Anchor Books, 2006), xviii.

18 Lawrence W. Levine, *Defender of the Faith: William Jennings Bryan* (Cambridge, MA: Harvard University Press, 1987), 6–7.

19 Cited in Larson, *Summer for the Gods,* 38.

[20] Levine, *Defender of the Faith,* 261.

[21] See Larson, *Summer for the Gods,* 26–28; Levine, *Defender of the Faith,* 261–270; and Jeffrey P. Moran, *The Scopes Trial: A Brief History with Documents* (Boston: Bedford/St. Martin's, 2002), 15–18.

[22] Levine, *Defender of the Faith,* 281.

[23] Ibid., 262.

[24] Larson, *Summer for the Gods,* 45, 47.

[25] William Jennings Bryan, "The Prince of Peace," cited in Olasky and Perry, *Monkey Business,* 22.

[26] George W. Hunter, *A Civic Biology* [1914], excerpt reprinted in Moran, *The Scopes Trial: A Brief History with Documents,* 188.

[27] Moran, *The Scopes Trial,* 25.

[28] William Jennings Bryan, *Text of Proposed Address in Scopes Case,* reprinted in Olasky and Perry, *Monkey Business,* 324.

[29] Ibid., 325.

[30] Cited in Rodgers, *Mencken: The American Iconoclast,* 393.

[31] Ibid., 448–455.

[32] Ibid., 396–397.

[33] George M. Marsden, *Fundamentalism and American Culture* (New York: Oxford University Press, 1980), 184.

[34] Rodgers, *Mencken: The American Iconoclast,* 292.

[35] Jerry Falwell, *Strength for the Journey* (New York: Simon and Schuster, 1987), 337–338.

[36] Ibid., 338.

[37] Cited in Ronald J. Sider, *The Scandal of Evangelical Politics* (Grand Rapids, MI: Baker Books, 2008), 15.

[38] Pat Robertson, *Shout it From the Housetops.* (South Plain-field, NJ: Bridge Publishing, 1972), 272.

[39] Mark A. Noll, *The Scandal of the Evangelical Mind* (Grand Rapids, MI: Eerdmans Publishing, 1994), 171.

[40] "About Operation Blessing," www.ob.org.

[41] Kristof, "Evangelicals a Liberal Can Love."

[42] Paul Berman, *Power and the Idealists* (New York: W. W. Norton & Company, 2005), 245–246.

[43] Ibid., 202–204.

[44] Marsh, *The Beloved Community,* 5–6.

[45] Michael Bar-Zohar, *Beyond Hitler's Grasp—The Heroic Rescue of Bulgaria's Jews* (Avon, MA: Adams Media, 1998), 126.

[46] Ibid., 126.

[47] Cited in Assayas, *Bono in Conversation with Michka Assayas,* 96.

[48] Falsani, "Bono's American Prayer."

[49] Assayas, *Bono in Conversation with Michka Assayas,* 96.

Note regarding the source *Hitler's Table Talk*

Almost of all the Hitler quotations I cite in Chapter Five come from two sources. The first is Hitler's own book, *Mein Kampf.* The second source is a book called *Hitler's Table Talk.* Since some questions have been raised about the accuracy of this second source, I have decided to summarize them here for the benefit of the interested reader.

Most of the facts concerning *Hitler's Table Talk* are not in dispute. Hitler's private secretary, Martin Bormann, claimed to be deeply impressed with the observations his boss would share with guests over meals and decided to preserve them for posterity. Bormann instructed two Nazi officials, first Heinrich Heim and then Henry Picker, to write down Hitler's most important mealtime pronouncements. The large majority of these notes were made during the period from July 1941 to September 1942.

Bormann later compiled and edited the notes from these two scribes and made two copies of the resulting volume. One of these copies was destroyed in a fire toward the end of World War II. But a second copy that Bormann had entrusted to his wife survived the war. A Swiss financier and Nazi sympathizer named Francois Genoud purchased this copy and published a French translation of it in 1952. In 1953, a leading English historian of Nazi Germany named Hugh Trevor-Roper published an English-language version of this document under the title *Hitler's Table Talk.* It is this version that I have used.

Hitler's Table Talk is widely accepted as an authoritative source which makes an important contribution to our understanding of Hitler's philosophy and psychology. Hugh Trevor-Roper continued to view this book as an important historical document until his death in 2003.

In his widely respected 1998 biography of Hitler, Ian Kershaw seems to have relied primarily upon the original German transcripts of Hitler's dinner conversations. Yet he repeatedly cites *Hitler's Table Talk* as well—one assumes for the benefit of those who don't speak German—albeit with complaints about the quality of the translation. (Ian Kershaw, *Hitler 1889–1936: Hubris*, New York: W. W. Norton & Co., 1998, p. 779)

In 2003, historian Richard Steigmann-Gall wrote that *Hitler's Table Talk* "is widely regarded as the source of Hitler's true wartime feelings about Christianity." While he noted the controversy that has emerged about its accuracy (discussed below), he concluded that he would "examine *Hitler's Table Talk* due to the importance attached to it by that school which argues that Hitler's 'true feelings' about Christianity are to be found here." (Richard Steigmann-Gall, *The Holy Reich*, New York: Cambridge University Press, 2003, p. 253)

In recent years, some questions have been raised regarding the accuracy of the English translation of *Hitler's Table Talk*. The person at the forefront of this criticism is a historian named Richard Carrier. In an article in *German Studies Review* 26/3 (2003), Carrier claims that Trevor-Roper's English edition of *Hitler's Table Talk* was translated from Genoud's French version rather than from the German original. Carrier further argues that the French translation added an anti-Christian emphasis to the text that does not accurately reflect the German original. Carrier is thus claiming that some of the sections of *Hitler's Table Talk* most relevant to my thesis may not accurately reflect Hitler's views.

I am in no position to judge Mr. Genoud's translation or Mr. Carrier's scholarship. Given the ongoing consensus regarding the validity and value of *Hitler's Table Talk*, I have decided to use it as a source. But given the concerns that Mr. Carrier has raised, I have placed three conditions on this use. First and foremost, I chose to note Carrier's concerns here. Next, I decided not to cite some of the best known and most vehement anti-Christian quotations from *Hitler's Table Talk*—including one in which Hitler happily prophesies the end of the "disease of Christianity"—since these are among the four quotations that Carrier specifically calls into question in his article. Finally, I have confined my use of this source to corroborating and supplementing ideas which are established in their first instance by more direct sources, such as Hitler's *Mein Kampf*. I believe that going further than this and rejecting *Hitler's Table Talk* altogether would be more than the record currently warrants.

Note regarding the Ukrainian famine

In writing the section on the Ukrainian famine in Chapter Five, I have relied primarily on the work of historian Robert Conquest. Conquest is a senior research fellow at Stanford University's Hoover Institution. He is a former Communist who has long been one of the foremost academic critics of the Soviet Union. In particular, Conquest was among the first to document the Stalin regime's mass crimes in his books *The Great Terror* (1968) and *The Harvest of Sorrow* (1986).

Both of Conquest's books have stirred controversy in the academic community and beyond. From the start there have been those who argued that Conquest was exaggerating the scope of Stalin's atrocities to further an anti-Soviet political agenda. Some critics claimed that his victim counts were too high, while others acknowledged the accuracy of his numbers but took issue with the conclusions he drew from them.

In the years that have passed since the publication of his books, the academic consensus has moved in Conquest's direction. New information made available after the fall of the Soviet

Union has helped to confirm the accuracy of his research. Especially when it comes to the depth of Stalin's depravity and atrocity, Conquest's position has largely been vindicated.

At one time, the Soviet Union and its apologists denied that there had even been a famine in the Ukrainian countryside during the winter of 1932–33. When its existence could no longer be denied, the Soviet authorities acknowledged the famine but blamed it entirely on natural causes such as drought. Since then, enough facts have emerged to disprove this claim as well.

Today there is widespread agreement that the famine was primarily caused by a combination of Stalin's policy of collectivization, which reduced the 1932 grain harvest, and the confiscation of this harvest by the Soviet regime. In other words, there is a consensus that a disaster on this scale would never have taken place had Stalin not intervened so forcefully in the countryside.

While a new consensus has emerged, however, the debate continues. Today, the debate is focused not on *whether* Stalin's policies starved millions of people to death, but on whether Stalin *intended* to starve millions to death.

As discussed in Chapter Five, Robert Conquest provides convincing evidence that Stalin not only caused the famine but did so intentionally. At the very least, Conquest argues, Stalin was aware that his policies were causing mass starvation and could have reversed them, but he chose not to do so. As Conquest notes, Stalin even continued to *export* grain despite the fact that millions of his citizens were starving.

A professor at West Virginia University named Mark Tauger has taken the lead in arguing that the famine was unintentional. According to Mr. Tauger, the prime cause of the famine was the fact that the 1932 harvest was much smaller than had been expected. Tauger argues that Stalin would have liked to have fed everyone but simply did not have enough food to do so. Thus starvation was inevitable and difficult choices needed to be made.

Yet Tauger's analysis by no means exonerates Stalin. Tauger identifies Stalin's disastrous collectivization policy as the main reason why the 1932 harvest was so poor. And Tauger acknowledges that Stalin's rigid preference for the urban workers was the only reason why the peasants were stripped of almost all of the food they did manage to grow. In Tauger's words:

> Although the low 1932 harvest may have been a mitigating circumstance, the regime was still responsible for the deprivation and suffering of the Soviet population in the early 1930's. The data presented here provide a more precise measure of the consequences of collectivization and forced industrialization than has previously been available; if anything, these data show that the effects of those policies were worse than had been assumed. They also, however, indicate that the famine was real, the result of a failure of economic policy, of the "revolution from above," rather than of a "successful" nationality policy against Ukrainians or other ethnic groups. (Mark B. Tauger, "The 1932 Harvest and the Famine of 1933," Slavic Review, Volume 50, Issue 1, Spring 1991, 70–89)

Tauger also recognizes that the grain Stalin continued to export throughout this period could have fed millions and alleviated the famine.

When this evidence is taken together, I believe it is both fair and accurate to conclude that Stalin and his regime were guilty of the genocide of the Ukrainian peasants by starvation. Scholars may continue to debate whether Stalin's goal was to starve these people as a nationality or as a class, or whether he would have starved them at all had there been enough food left over after feeding the people he preferred. But the fact that Stalin starved millions of peasants to death, and did so knowingly, is largely beyond dispute. It is a long-settled principle of criminal law that this level of intentionality—knowing that one's actions will cause someone's death but nevertheless continuing them—is more than sufficient to establish guilt for the crime of murder.

Index